Researching
CRIME &
CRIMINAL
JUSTICE

Crime, Order and Social Control Course Team

The Open University

Sally Baker	*Subject Librarian, Education and Social Sciences*
David Calderwood	*Project Control*
Hilary Canneaux	*Course Manager*
John Clarke	*Professor of Social Policy*
Jonathan Davies	*Graphic Design Co-ordinator*
Margaret Dickens	*Print Buying Co-ordinator*
Nigel Draper	*Editor, Social Sciences*
Clive Emsley	*Professor of History, Arts*
Janis Gilbert	*Graphic Artist*
Peggotty Graham	*Staff Tutor, Social Sciences*
Fiona Harris	*Editor, Social Sciences*
Celia Hart	*Picture Researcher*
Frank Heathcote	*Staff Tutor, Social Sciences*
Pauline Hetherington	*Discipline Secretary*
Gordon Hughes	*Lecturer in Social Policy*
Jonathan Hunt	*Book Trade Department*
Sue Lacey	*Secretary*
Mary Langan	*Lecturer in Social Policy*
Patti Langton	*Producer, BBC/OUPC*
Eugene McLaughlin	*Senior Lecturer in Criminology and Social Policy*
John Muncie	*Senior Lecturer in Criminology and Social Policy (Course Team Chair)*
Lesley Passey	*Graphic Designer*
Doreen Pendlebury	*Course Secretary*
Roger Sapsford	*Reader in Psychology, University of Teesside*
Esther Saraga	*Staff Tutor, Social Sciences*
Richard Skellington	*Project Officer, Social Sciences*
Gill Smith	*Editor, Social Sciences*
Paul Smith	*Social Sciences Liaison Librarian*
Alison Tucker	*Producer, BBC/OUPC*
Liz Yeomans	*Freelance Graphic Designer*

Consultant Authors

Seán Damer	*Honorary Research Fellow, University of Glasgow*
Loraine Gelsthorpe	*Lecturer in Criminology, University of Cambridge*
Paul Gordon	*Academic Consultant, London*
Victor Jupp	*Head of Sociology, University of Northumbria*
Jim Sharpe	*Senior Lecturer in History, University of York*
Richard Sparks	*Professor of Criminology, University of Keele*
Sandra Walklate	*Professor of Sociology, Manchester Metropolitan University*

External Consultants

Pat Carlen	*Professor of Criminology, University of Bath (Course Assessor)*
Tony Jefferson	*Professor of Criminology, University of Keele (Course Assessor)*
Victor Jupp	*Head of Sociology, University of Northumbria (Book Assessor)*
Ken Pease	*Professor of Criminology, University of Huddersfield (Examiner)*
Sandra Walklate	*Professor of Sociology, Manchester Metropolitan University (Examiner)*

Tutor Panel

Tom Burden	*Policy Research Unit, Leeds Metropolitan University*
Hilary Hiram	*School of Law, University of Glasgow*
Marilyn Woolfson	*Open University Tutor and Tutor Counsellor, London*

Researching
CRIME &
CRIMINAL
JUSTICE

Edited by

Roger Sapsford

The Open
University

This book is one component of The Open University course D315 *Crime, Order and Social Control.*
Three further volumes in the series are published in association with Sage Publications Ltd. These are:

The Problem of Crime
edited by John Muncie and Eugene McLaughlin

Controlling Crime
edited by Eugene McLaughlin and John Muncie

Criminological Perspectives: A Reader
edited by John Muncie, Eugene McLaughlin and Mary Langan

Details of this and other Open University courses can be obtained from the Course Reservations Centre,
PO Box 724, The Open University, Milton Keynes MK7 6ZS, United Kingdom: tel. +44 (0)1908 653231,
email ces-gen@open.ac.uk

Alternatively, you may visit the Open University website at http://www.open.ac.uk
where you can learn more about the wide range of courses and packs offered at all levels by
The Open University.

For availability of other course components, including video- and audio-cassette materials, contact
Open University Worldwide Ltd, The Berrill Building, Walton Hall, Milton Keynes MK7 6AA,
United Kingdom: tel. +44 (0)1908 858785; fax +44 (0)1908 858787; e-mail ouwenq@open.ac.uk;
website http://www.ouw.co.uk

The Open University, Walton Hall, Milton Keynes MK7 6AA

© The Open University 1996

First published in 1996

Reprinted in 1998, 2000

The opinions expressed are not necessarily those of the Course Team or of The Open University.

ISBN 0 7492 7716-5 (pbk)

Edited, designed and typeset by The Open University

Printed by The Bath Press, Glasgow

1.3

Contents

Introduction

Researching Crime and Criminal Justice is the final book in The Open University course D315 *Crime, Order and Social Control*. Unlike Books 1 and 2 and the Reader, this volume deals not with criminological theories, but with what *underlies* them – criminological research – and with the relationship of research to theory, policy and practice. Whereas Book 1 – *The Problem of Crime* – focused on the shifting ways in which crime is defined, and Book 2 – *Controlling Crime* – examined the changing and expanding parameters of criminal justice, the aim of Book 3 is to encourage a critical reflection on the nature of criminology itself by raising issues about how research is formulated and carried out and to outline the arguments which lie behind and give support to research procedures.

Like Books 1 and 2, however, and in keeping with The Open University's proven and particular style of distance teaching, this volume is also designed to be part of an interactive form of study. The chapters should be read sequentially, as each builds on those that have gone before, and each concludes with suggestions for further reading. In addition, built into the main structure of the text are exercises in which readers are encouraged to take an active part whilst working through the text, in order to test understanding and encourage critical thinking. Where appropriate, these exercises are followed by comments which provide feedback and an opportunity for readers to check their own responses.

While the book is self-contained, there are also a number of references back and forward to other materials, including chapters in the other volumes, in the course. These cross-references are printed in bold type. A further feature of this volume is that the majority of chapters include appendices which are integral to the exercises and to the discussion as it develops and are designed as an aid in the application of central ideas and concepts to contemporary research into crime and criminal justice. The aim of all these features is to help readers more readily to understand and examine critically the principal arguments not only of each chapter, but of both the book and the course as a whole.

After reading Book 3 and working through the exercises, readers should be in a better position to write informed critiques of research reports and to begin to plan research of their own.

The first chapter, 'Contours of criminology', looks at the institutional bases of criminological research and theory and at recent developments in the ways we have available for thinking about crime and public order. It does not prescribe ways of thinking, but instead opens up the debates in order that readers may participate in them and explore different ways of thinking for themselves.

Chapter 2, 'The politics of criminological research', brings to our attention the political factors which necessarily underpin every stage of the research process in criminology – the relationships of criminological research to the state, the uses made of informants and research opportunities and the relationship of research to social policy and social control. Chapters 1 and 2 remind us that criminology is not just, or even mainly, part of an academic discipline, but something politically and morally engaged in the real social world. The phenomena which it seeks to explain or understand often constitute a real world of pain, suffering and constraint. Its subject matter lies, on the one hand, with the question of how we are to be protected from such suffering; on the other hand, it is concerned with the degree to which the state can and does order our lives.

Chapters 3, 4 and 5 deal more directly with how we can form judgements about criminological (and other) research evidence. In other words, they offer an introductory training in research methods. 'Doing' research is not a mysterious and technical process – most of what researchers do applies ordinary logic and common sense to the business of collecting evidence – but there *are* technical questions, and these three chapters introduce those we really need to know about in order to make critical sense of published research. The aim is not to overload or bore readers with technicalities, but to help them to develop tools for assessing the worth of research evidence and to think about how they would carry out research of their own.

It is usual to distinguish three broad 'styles' of research, and these chapters use this distinction as a structuring principle. Chapter 3, 'Reading quantitative research', is about 'quantitative' approaches to providing evidence to support an author's conclusion. Chapter 4, 'Reading qualitative research', considers 'qualitative' and 'critical' approaches to the same task. (The distinction is used for the purpose of laying out material for ease of reading, but, as we shall see, it is not necessarily to be taken too seriously.)

'Quantitative' or 'scientific' research aims to mimic the physical sciences as closely as the different subject matter will allow: to describe the world in a precise, replicable and unbiased way and to test and develop generalizations about the human social condition which are like 'the laws of science'. 'Qualitative' or 'appreciative' research is less concerned with laws and more with understanding the *meaning* of what is going on from the point of view of participants. 'Critical analysis' is another qualitative research tradition, but this is less concerned with the beliefs and attitudes held by participants and more with the meaning systems which *underlie* what they say and which are embedded in the texts they produce. That is, critical analysis is concerned with the ideologies, discourses and models of the person and of social relations which are presupposed in their way of thinking (and with the clashes between ideologies – both between speakers and within texts – produced by a single person or by an institution). Each approach has its strengths – each can deliver something which is beyond the power of the others – but each pays for strength with corresponding weaknesses. These strengths and weaknesses will be pointed out when the approach is discussed, so it is important to be able to recognize the 'style' of a piece of research in order to assess it.

Chapter 5, 'Theory, argument and evidence', looks at what the evidence is used *for* and offers guidelines for assessing research *arguments* as well as research *evidence*. In addition to revising questions of logic and plausibility, the chapter is concerned with the relationship of research evidence to criminological and social theory on the one hand, and to policy and practice on the other. It discusses the ethics of research and the place of research practices, research results and criminological theories in the spectrum of political thought and action. It also considers how one can begin to think about planning research of one's own and the issues which have to be taken into consideration if the results are to be useful.

The production of this volume – and the course as a whole – has been made possible not simply through the work of its editors and chapter authors but through the collective endeavours of an entire Open University Course Team. Each chapter has gone through three drafts whereby content and teaching strategy have been modified and refined. In this respect, we are indebted to our consultants, tutor-testers and assessors who have given invaluable advice; a course manager who, against all odds, has ensured that all our efforts have been co-ordinated and that deadlines have been met; a course secretary who has suffered more than most from being asked to do the impossible; and a supportive team of production editors, designers, graphic artist and media librarian who have made sure the final product looks as good as it does.

Roger Sapsford
April 1996

Chapter 1
Contours of Criminology

by Victor Jupp

Contents

1   Introduction

*T*his chapter is concerned with mapping some of the contours of criminology in the UK. This will be done by providing an overview of the study of crime, criminals, criminality and criminal justice from the late nineteenth century up to the mid 1990s. The analysis is founded on the premise that there is no single conception of crime. Nor is there universal agreement on what are or should be the central problems of criminology, its key theoretical underpinnings or the primary means of carrying out criminological research. There are differing histories of criminology and even debate as to whether there can be such a thing as 'criminology' in the first place.

By the mid 1990s criminology appeared to be characterized by fragmentation and diversity in terms of what is seen as problematic – the ways in which such problems are addressed theoretically and methodologically – and in the range of strategies and policies for crime control which are put forward. Such fragmentation and diversity have evolved as the outcome both of internal developments within criminology in the UK and of external changes in wider social and political contexts, especially those relating to law and order, and how these have impacted on the study of crime and criminal justice.

In addressing the development of criminology and the central themes of fragmentation and diversity, the chapter has a number of aims: first, to examine different 'ways of thinking' about the problem of crime, crime causation, criminalization and crime control; second, to examine shifts over time in criminological 'ways of thinking'; third, to relate such 'ways of thinking' to the social organization of criminology and the key institutional bases of criminological practice, policy, theorizing and research; and, finally, to suggest a reflexive strategy for examining contours in criminology.

2   Deconstructing criminology

A reflexive strategy starts from a position of looking at 'criminology-as-a-form-of-knowledge'. It then seeks to take apart or *deconstruct* that knowledge in terms of its key elements and the relations between them. Three key elements have already been addressed in this course: first, the central *problems* of criminology (as discussed in **Book 1, Chapter 1**); second, the *theoretical approaches* used to address these problems (see, especially, **Reader Guide 1**); and, third, the range of *strategies of crime control* – indicated in part by theoretical approaches – to deal with that which is seen as problematic (see, especially, **Reader Guide 2**). To this we can add a fourth element, which is the focus of this book – the kinds of *research* which are carried out.

Deconstructing knowledge in terms of problem–theory–method–strategy uncovers the distinctiveness of criminology at any given point in time. But the process of deconstruction goes further in terms of seeking to relate those key elements, and relations between them, to underpinning institutional and social contexts. In this way the strategy of deconstruction does not simply involve taking apart knowledge, but also involves identifying the *location of its production*. In turn this allows us to examine the range and the respective credibilities of different forms of criminological knowledge and how these vary over time. This is what is meant by exploring the contours of criminology.

2.1 Analysing discourses

The process of deconstruction will enlist some of the core ideas of discourse analysis, and especially questions which form part of a research agenda (or *aide-mémoire* for analysis) which emanate from these core ideas. Discourse analysis represents an important development in the critical tradition (as discussed in Chapter 4, especially section 4 on analysing sub-texts) and is closely associated with the French social theorist Michel Foucault, although it is not restricted to him. Its central tenets are as follows:

- First, a fundamental feature of discourse is that it is social – that is, words and their meanings depend on where they are used, by whom and to whom. Therefore, words and their meanings can differ according to the social relations and the institutional settings within which they are produced, reproduced and sometimes reshaped. The implication of this is that there is no such thing as a fundamental and universal discourse which is shared by all. In this way, if we treat criminology as discourse it follows that there is no such thing as a fundamental and universal knowledge called 'criminology', but several criminologies (as in **Reader Guide 1**).

- Second, the assumption is not solely that discourses can differ, but also that, typically, a discourse does not exist in isolation but in relation to others.

- Third, discourses can be, and frequently are, in conflict with one another in the ways in which they promulgate certain concepts, explanations and solutions, and seek to marginalize others.

- Fourth, one can move beyond the notions of relational and conflicting discourses to think in terms of hierarchies of discourses within which one person's or one group's discourse – its definitions, explanations and solutions – carry great weight compared with others and therefore have credibility as 'knowledge' or as what is seen as 'right' and 'correct'.

- Fifth, the concept of power is vital to discourse analysis via the theoretical connection between the production and legitimation of discourses and the exercise of power. The two are very closely interwoven and in some theoretical formulations are viewed as one and the same.

- Finally, some theorists see the production of all knowledge as lying with the state, whereas others view the production of discourses as more dispersed across society. For Foucault there is not just one focus of knowledge and power – that is, the state – but several semi-autonomous pockets of production where the state has little influence. This encourages us to look for the production of criminological knowledge in a range of institutional settings (for example, universities, pressure groups, the professions) and not just in and by the state.

ACTIVITY 1.1

Extract 1.1 is a research agenda of questions adapted from a suggestion by Jupp and Norris (1993), based on a distillation of core ideas from discourse analysis. You should read the items in this agenda with care and consider how they can help us explore forms of criminological knowledge.

Extract 1.1 Jupp and Norris: 'Agenda for examining discourse'

1   What public and/or institutional discourses are important in terms of knowledge of what is 'right' and what is 'wrong'?

2   In what kind of documents and texts do such discourses appear?

3   Who writes or speaks these discourses, whom do they represent or purport to represent, and who is their intended audience?

4   What does a critical reading of the discourse uncover in terms of:
     (a) what is defined as 'right' and 'wrong' and therefore what is seen as problematic;
     (b) what explanation is offered for what is seen as problematic;
     (c) what, therefore, is seen as the solution?

5   What *alternative* discourses exist and what does a critical reading of these tell us?

6   What is the relationship between discourses? Where does each lie on the hierarchy of credibility? How does such positioning relate to the exercise of power?

7   Is there evidence of negotiation with, or resistance to, dominant discourses?

8   How do discourses relate to institutional bases? Are they refracted through one source – the state – or are they more dispersed throughout society?

(adapted from Jupp and Norris, 1993, p.50)

COMMENT

This agenda can be adapted to explore – or *deconstruct* – forms of criminological knowledge by posing the following questions:

Agenda item 1: What criminological discourses exist – for example, about the causes of individual criminality or about the state as perpetrator of crime?

Agenda item 2: Where can they be found – for example, in reports of Royal Commissions on criminal justice, Home Office Research Bulletins, or in academic journals?

Agenda item 3: Who 'speaks' them, who do they represent, and to whom are they directed – for example, the state, criminal justice agencies, pressure groups or academics representing a 'master science'?

Agenda item 4: What do they say in terms of what is viewed as *problematic* – say, individual delinquency or public protest; what is seen as the *explanation* – say, personality as opposed to social disorganization; and what is posited as the *solution* – say, individual treatment or community development?

Agenda item 5: What alternative discourses exist and what do they define as problematic, and provide as the explanation and solution?

Agenda item 6: Where do different forms of knowledge lie on the hierarchy of credibility?

Agenda item 7: How do alternative criminologies-as-knowledge relate to one another in terms of struggle, conflict, negotiation or accommodation? How and why do forms of knowledge emerge to address other forms of knowledge?

Agenda item 8: How do forms of criminological knowledge relate to institutional bases – say, the Home Office, universities or pressure groups? What is the location of the production of knowledge? For example, **Garland (1988)** charts the way in which early British criminology was firmly anchored to institutions of criminal justice, especially penal institutions and the courts. The issue of the institutional bases of the production and, indeed, the dissemination of knowledge raises questions about the interconnections between 'criminology-as-knowledge' and power and politics.

With regard to how research is carried out, an important question concerns the *role* of research in the production of knowledge. One way of examining this is by looking at the ways in which different types of research design (discussed more fully in Chapters 3 and 4) – for example, surveys, experiments, observation – address and relate to particular kinds of criminological theories. There are no necessary connections between types of problem, types of theory and types of research, but there are mutual attractions. For example, criminologies which address questions about predeterminants of criminality are often founded on individualist–positivistic theoretical approaches which search for causes. Also, they are typically associated with research, often survey-based, which seeks quantitative evidence of correlations on which to base causal inferences. Looking at constellations of connections between types of problem, theory and method helps us identify forms of criminolgy-as-knowledge (and the crime control strategies implicit in them).

We can now start our reflexive analysis by putting flesh on some of the itemized questions – especially question 4 – listed as part of the research agenda outlined above. This involves outlining the kinds of concerns which criminologists have addressed and, more briefly, the range of explanatory frameworks and research strategies they have employed in relation to these.

2.2 Criminological problems

One of the first, and perhaps most obvious, problems to engage criminologists is the question: *Why do individuals commit crimes?* Several broad theoretical strands have been concerned with this question (see **Reader Guide 1**). These include, for example, theories which are concerned with biological differences between individuals and the way in which human behaviour, in this case criminal behaviour, is genetically determined. The work of Lombroso (1876), which was influential in the nineteenth-century European movement, was typical of this strand, although as we shall see later it was considered to be of little significance in British criminological circles. The medico-psychoanalytical theories of those who worked closely with the courts and the penal institutions were much more prominent in the hierarchies of credibility in the early part of the twentieth century. Although the theories of Lombroso and those of the British medico-psychoanalytical practitioners come from different disciplinary bases and differ from each other in significant ways, what is of interest to each is a focus on the individual as the primary unit of analysis and the conceptualization of the central problem of criminology as being about why individuals commit crimes.

By way of contrast, one of the main contributions of the sociological tradition has been to pose the question: *What are the social and cultural preconditions of crime?* The French sociologist Emile Durkheim, also much more influential in Europe than in the UK at the turn of the century, was central to the development of theories organized around the concept of 'anomie', especially in relation to suicide (Durkheim, 1952). To varying degrees his work influenced subsequent writers such as Robert Merton (1957) who placed strain theory on the criminological map, and other theorists and researchers in the USA, and later in the UK, who sought to explore the development and maintenance of sub-cultures of crime. Collectively, what such work contributed was a focus on questions concerning the social and cultural, as opposed to the individual, bases of crime (see **Reader Guide 1, section 4**).

A third, and enduring, research problem confronting criminology relates to the question: *How much crime is there?* The Durkheimian tradition and its concern with the social bases of crime was closely tied to the use of official statistics to measure the extent of crime and other deviant acts. Durkheim's classic work on suicide is grounded in such statistics and Merton's work on anomie and crime starts from the assumption that official statistics provide the best, albeit imperfect, indices of society's crime level. Since that time there have been major theoretical and methodological disputes as to whether official statistics can legitimately be used to measure the objective 'facts' of crime. There have also been the development and refinement of particular tools of data collection, such as victim surveys, which aim to obtain some estimate of the disparity between officially recorded crime and the true extent of victimization (see **Book 1, Chapter 1**). Contributions of early writers such as Durkheim and Merton, and subsequent debates about the use of official statistics and the development of victim surveys, all focus on the basic criminological question of: How much crime is there?

In turn, this relates to the question: *Who are the victims?* The 1980s and 1990s witnessed an upsurge of interest in victimization. This emanated, first, from a belief that there was a gap between the amount of reported crime and the true amount of victimization; and, second, from the belief that this gap varied according to different groups in society. For example, it came to be recognized that the true extent of sexual crimes against women, particularly in the home, was reflected to a much lesser degree in official statistics than crimes such as car thefts or house burglaries, where reporting to the police was a condition of an insurance claim. This concern with victimization came from a number of angles – for example, from what later in the chapter will be described as Home Office administrative criminology, in the form of the British Crime Surveys; from left realism, in the form of local victimization surveys; and from feminist criminology, in the form of studies of women as victims of crime (see **Book 1, Chapter 5**). In their differing ways these strands are concerned with examining the true extent of victimization and its social and ecological distribution. The focus on victimization and the representation of crime and portrayal of victims in the press has stimulated a debate about the connections between crime and the fear of crime. For example, the 1982 British Crime Survey (Hough and Mayhew, 1983) produced findings which indicated that, although the fear of crime in the population as a whole (or sub-sections of it) was great, such fear was out of all proportion to the likelihood of actual victimization. These findings and claims have been challenged by others, particularly researchers from the left-realist position. Such disputes and debates have focused considerable academic and political concern on the problem of *the reality of crime and the fear of crime and their connection* (see **Book 1, Chapters 1 and 4**).

In the preceding discussion, criminology has been portrayed as problematizing crime, criminals and victims as central concerns. At first sight, that would seem quite sensible. However, one of the noticeable features of the development of criminology is the way in which what might appear to be the immediate problems worthy of consideration have taken on a wider focus to embrace, for example, *the criminal justice system* and *the location of crime and criminal justice in unequal power relations in society* and the ways in which these evolve and are sustained. In differing ways criminology has stretched its horizons beyond the narrower focus to encompass and embrace an interest in the criminal justice system as a whole. This includes concerns with: the institutions of criminal justice, such as the police, courts, prisons, their internal functioning and their relations with one another; the policies and practices of personnel such as police officers, judges and magistrates who work within such institutions; and the social processes of justice as a whole. This widening interest can be illustrated by a number of diverse strands within criminology – for example, so-called administrative criminology and the work of the Home Office Research and Planning Unit in evaluating policy initiatives; labelling theory and its particular interest in processes of criminalization; feminist criminology and its interest in the treatment of women within the criminal justice system; and what **Ericson and Carriere (1994)** describe as the 'liberal' approach with its concern with due process of law and efficiency and humaneness in its administration.

The institutions of criminal justice and their personnel do not operate in a vacuum. They are a fundamental part of society, its structure and the way in which social order is maintained and social control exercised. Therefore to separate crime and systems of criminal justice from the wider social structure and the interests and conflicts which are part of it would involve missing crucial dimensions of the generation of crime and criminalization and the exercise of crime control. This is illustrated in the contribution of the radical tradition in criminology which gained impetus in the mid 1970s through the publication of *The New Criminology* (**Taylor *et al.*, 1973**) which argued for a reformulation of the central issues of criminology in terms of social structure and its historical development, with particular reference to economic and class relations. In general terms, this tradition seeks to explain crime, not in causal terms, but in terms of unequal power relations in society; it seeks to understand the functioning of the criminal justice system in terms of the role of the state in maintaining social order and also in terms of the relationship of the state to economic and class interests. More fundamentally, it seeks to address questions about the definition and the nature of crime and about what, at any given time, is treated as criminal and why. More recently, strands of feminism have sought to locate issues in crime and criminal justice, not within what might seem a relatively narrow domain of criminology nor exclusively within economic and class relations, but within questions about inequalities and power relations with regard to patriarchy (see **Reader Guide 1, section 5.3**). This expansion and diversity of 'criminological concerns' is represented in Figure 1.1.

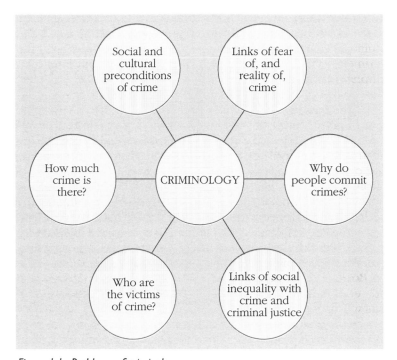

Figure 1.1 Problems of criminology

2.3 Criminological theorizing

There are four points concerning criminological theorizing to be emphasized from the outset. The first of these is that crime and criminal justice are not unitary concepts but are capable of being addressed in differing ways – different questions can be asked of them. This was the main theme of the previous section. One of the key features of theory is to open up the range of such questions. This is one important reason for the plurality and diversity of criminological theorizing being reflected in the diversity and plurality of that which is seen as problematic. The second point is that theories differ with regard to their implicit and explicit features and characteristics. It is these differing features which result in the differing aspects of crime and criminal justice being problematized. For example, theories grounded in biology and psychology and with the individual as the primary unit of analysis tend to problematize the question: *Why do individuals commit crimes?* In contrast, sociological theories which focus on social disorganization tend to problematize the question: *What are the social and cultural bases of crime?* The third point is that the distinctions between theories are not clear-cut dichotomies but matters of emphasis. Nevertheless, such dichotomies are useful for charting types of criminology-as-knowledge (indeed, this was the approach taken in **Reader Guide 1**). Finally, the inversion of key features of theories, or alterations in the degrees of emphasis given to them, often give rise to new and significant reformulations in criminological theorizing (a point which will be illustrated in the remainder of this chapter).

Some of the key features which distinguish criminological theorizing can be itemized. As we saw in **Reader Guide 1**, one key distinction is between those forms of theorizing, whether sociological or psychological, which emphasize determinism and causality and those which give an element of voluntarism and rationality to human actions. For example, mainstream criminology of the 1960s was typically positivist in its search for the causes of crime, whereas administrative criminology, which is said to supersede it, emphasizes crime as the outcome of voluntary rational choices by individuals. Second, a contrast can be made between those theories which make the individual the basic unit of analysis (for example, biological/genetic/psychological theories) and those which emphasize the importance of social categories or social groupings (for example, social disorganization theories). Third, there is the classic distinction between theories founded on a consensus model of society, in which crime is viewed as a deviation from universally agreed norms and values, and those theories founded on a conflict model of society, in which crime and criminalization are viewed as the outcome of inequality and social conflict. Fourth, analyses may be formulated in terms of what at any given point in time is considered to be the root or cause of the problem in question. Such analyses are essentially ahistorical. Other analyses place weight on historical patterns and transitions (as in **Book 1, Chapter 3**). In this latter formulation contemporary 'problems' and 'explanations' are seen as part of those patterns and transitions and as worthy of investigation in their own right.

Next, some theoretical positions may be regarded as being 'top down'. They tend to treat the existing order as given and regard criminals as people who deviate from that social order and who are therefore pathologized. Such positions are typically located in official government or quasi-governmental agencies where work often has implications in terms of policies which emphasize, amongst other things, social control and correctionalism. Other theoretical positions may be regarded as being 'bottom up' in so far as they see crime as not purely the domain of a pathological class of individuals who tend to be located at the lower reaches of society. Instead, those who adopt this position have a much wider vista of what is meant by crime and who are the criminals, and tend to view their criminological work as a form of political praxis. This distinction between top-down and bottom-up is also sometimes the distinction between, on the one hand, 'official' criminology associated with state criminal justice institutions and, on the other, radical criminologies.

Finally, a distinction can be made between those theoretical viewpoints within the narrow bounds of what traditionally has been viewed as criminology (mainly seeking explanations of crime, examining the social and ecological distribution of crime and seeking to improve what is defined in that viewpoint as the effectiveness of the criminal justice system) and theoretical positions which locate criminological concerns in wider economic and social relations. Some elements of critical criminology, for example, focus on crime and criminal justice not in their own right but as mechanisms of state control and the exercise of power in society. Also, some recent forms of feminist thinking argue against feminism operating within criminology on the grounds that criminology is too concerned with the concept of crime *per se* and thereby is too constraining (see, for example, **Smart, 1990**). Instead, it is argued, for example, that acts such as rape or sexual abuse should be located in the wider domains of sexuality and patriarchal relations. The argument is for a separation of feminism from criminology. The problems, explanations and solutions are considered to be outwith or *beyond* a narrow conceptualization of criminology. The distinction being made here is between theorizing which is 'within criminology' and theorizing which is 'beyond criminology'. This will be discussed further in section 5.

2.4   Methods of criminological research

The discussion so far has emphasized plurality in terms of the ways in which criminological problems are conceptualized and also in terms of the kinds of theoretical positions which are brought to bear on such problems. The close relationship between theory and such conceptualization has also been highlighted. This section looks briefly at the diversity and fragmentation of criminology in terms of the type of research which is conducted and how such types of research typically connect with the kinds of problem at the heart of any analysis and also with the theoretical ideas which are being employed. Having regard for the dangers of undue compartmentalization, it is nevertheless possible to distinguish three broad traditions in social research in general and in criminology in particular. These are the quantitative, the qualitative and the critical traditions (for a discussion of the dangers of too sharp a distinction between quantitative and qualitative research see Bryman, 1988).

The *quantitative tradition* has its roots in early attempts to measure the extent of crime using official or quasi-official statistics (see, for example, **Quetelet, 1842**). Despite continual debates about the validity of such statistics, the quantitative tradition remains strong to this day, especially within the more mainstream positivist and administrative criminologies. For example, quantification is used to measure the extent of crime and victimization, and to collect statistical evidence as to the effectiveness, or otherwise, of crime control strategies. It is also typically associated with research which seeks to explain crime in causal terms – for example, in seeking to relate changes in the crime rate to changes in other features of society such as levels of unemployment, consumption (see, for example, **Field, 1990**) and relative deprivation (see, for example, **Lea and Young, 1984**). Such analysis often springs from the search for statistical correlations on which to erect inferences as to causes (see, for example, the article from *The Guardian*, 15 February 1995, reproduced opposite). Methods of research associated with the quantitative tradition include surveys, field and quasi-experiments and the secondary analysis of official statistics.

The *qualitative tradition* is typically associated with ethnography, in other words the description ('graphy') of cultures ('ethno'). It is a methodological approach which seeks to capture the ways in which individuals, and categories of individuals, make sense of the world and how subsequent actions are grounded in such interpretations. Thus it has a commitment to explanation-by-understanding rather than explanation in causal terms and also to the viewpoint that the world is socially constructed. Ethnography was an important part of the methodological approach of the Chicago School of Sociology in describing the cultural aspects of crime in the

Higher levels of employment 'best way to fight poverty'

Study links crime with the dole queue

Keith Harper
Labour Editor

MINISTERIAL denials of any link between crime and the length of the dole queue are challenged in a report today which argues that the evidence connecting crime and joblessness is much stronger than supposed.

The report questions the findings of Home Office research and contends that government studies have not taken adequate account of the fact that unemployment is a 'lagging indicator' of conditions in the economy.

It also suggests that Home Office studies have not been adjusted properly for inadequacies in the official jobless statistics.

The report from the Employment Policy Institute has been written by John Wells, of Cambridge University, who says: 'If we are going to be tough on crime and tough on the causes of crime, then we should come down hard on two of the very well documented causes, unemployment and poverty.'

The EPI, a policy think tank, says crime can be linked to the state of the labour market. Dr Wells says unemployment does not justify crime. It would be wrong to imply that all unemployed people resort to crime, but he points out that the growing sense of illegitimacy of a social order that countenances mass unemployment along with increasing income inequality, can eradicate the normal moral constraints on crime.

Dr Wells says ministers, using Home Office research,

deny any link between crime and unemployment. They attribute the cyclical nature of property crime, for instance, to changes in consumption as the economy expands and contracts, not the length of the dole queue. But Dr Wells challenges the official view and argues instead that there is considerable statistical evidence to support a link.

He says not all crime is reported, and the police do not record every crime that is.

The report says Britain's departure from full employment and the emergence of mass unemployment from the mid 1970s has coincided with a strong trend in recorded crime.

It says the Government has strongly resisted the idea of any causal relationship between crime and unemployment, even during the inner city riots and disorder which accompanied 'spiralling unemployment' during the recession of the 1980s and 1990s.

'This is, perhaps, because having consciously used unemployment as a policy instrument to counter inflation, the

Government wishes to absolve itself of any responsibility for any collateral damage in the form of increased criminality.'

It says 'mass unemployment and the growth of single parenthood' have resulted in poverty on a scale without precedent since the second world war, with one in four children currently from families receiving income support.

The message is that a society 'with such large numbers of children in poverty runs the risk of massive criminal delinquency'. Dr Wells argues that a return to higher levels of employment represents the best way of addressing such poverty.

The Home Office said no significant correlation had been identified between unemployment and recorded crime. The rate of increase in recorded property crime was decreasing in early 1991 even when unemployment was still rising, so it was difficult to come to a general view.

(*The Guardian*, 15 February 1995)

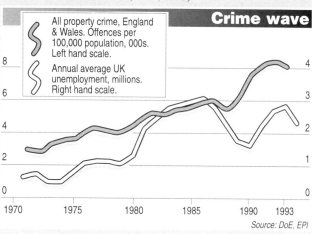

Crime wave

All property crime, England & Wales. Offences per 100,000 population, 000s. Left hand scale.

Annual average UK unemployment, millions. Right hand scale.

Source: DoE, EPI

15

city in the 1930s (see, for example, Shaw's *The Jack Roller*, 1930) and also in labelling and interactionist approaches which emerged in the late 1960s and which gave emphasis to social meanings, stereotyping and their role in labelling processes (see, for example, Young's *The Drugtakers*, 1971). Strategies of data collection and analysis typically associated with the qualitative tradition include various forms of observation, the collection of life histories and the analysis of documents.

The *critical tradition* seems less overtly empirical in the sense that there does not appear to be a fixed set of protocols to be followed in the collection of evidence and the reaching of conclusions (which does not, however, mean that it is unsystematic). Nevertheless, a wide range of strategies has been used to uncover and unearth those features which are seen as central to critical theorizing, such as the distribution and the exercise of power, the preponderance of inequalities in society and injustices in the operation of the criminal justice system (see, for example, Harvey, 1990). One example of such a strategy is the critical analysis of text and the examination of discourses in relation to the treatment of women offenders in the criminal justice system (see, for example, Worrall's *Offending Women*, 1990). As indicated earlier, a central theme of this chapter involves treating forms of criminological knowledge as discourses. In turn, this requires being reflexive and critical in relation to such forms of knowledge and not accepting any one of these as the 'truth' about crime and criminals.

2.5 Criminology on the 'inside' and the 'outside'

A further key feature of this chapter is the search for the institutional bases of the production of criminology-as-knowledge. One core theme to emerge is that the production of criminological knowledge has been closely linked to the institutions of criminal justice, the concerns of such institutions and the development of policies and practices in relation to such concerns. For our purposes we can characterize this as 'production of knowledge on the inside'. Here research is closely tied to the central concerns of these institutions and their efficient functioning and it has an implicit acceptance of these concerns rather than starting from a position of being critical of them. Such production involves, for example, research carried out by, or on behalf of, institutions such as the Home Office, the police and the Crown Prosecution Service. Also, it may be carried out for such institutions by academics working in universities and elsewhere or by social and market research agencies. Where such work is carried out independently by academics and others it is nevertheless characterized by a focus on the efficient functioning of the criminal justice system. Research is typified by methodological approaches, usually quantitative, which are viewed as appropriate to the evaluation of policies or to the surveying of populations which are part of, or likely to become part of, the criminal justice system.

This 'insider' characterization can be distinguished from other kinds of criminological work which is here referred to as the 'production of knowledge on the outside'. Typically, this is work carried out in universities and other academic institutions, by criminal justice pressure groups, and elsewhere. It is less likely to be closely tied to the introduction, evaluation and management of institutional policies; rather, it is more likely to start from a critical stance in relation to such institutions and to address different sorts of questions from those asked on the 'inside' – for example, questions about crimes of the powerful or of the state. It may also carry with it an agenda framed by alternative, possibly radical, theoretical paradigms; and it will probably be characterized by a variety of methodological approaches other than the strict protocols of quantitative research. There have been examples of the denigration by official bodies of critical academic research on the grounds of such research making use of qualitative and critical research methods rather than conventional, quantitative methods.

ACTIVITY 1.2

You should now read the extract by Victor Jupp, 'Gaining access: research in prisons' which can be found as Appendix 1.1 to this chapter. As you study this extract, pay particular attention to the following questions:

1   What were the main features of the way in which Cohen and Taylor carried out their research?
2   On what grounds was this viewed as not 'properly conducted research' and by whom?

To sum up, section 2 has indicated a strategy of analysis which involves treating forms of knowledge as discourses. It has also suggested questions which can be used to deconstruct such knowledge – for example, questions about what is seen as *problematic*; what kinds of *theoretical explanations* are preferred and what are their features; what kinds of *research* are carried out; and what kinds of *policies* and *strategies* are suggested. In addition, questions about the *institutional* and *social contexts* are vital to understanding the production of forms of knowledge, relationships between them and their respective positions in the 'hierarchy of credibility' (Becker, 1967). This strategy of analysis can be used to examine forms of criminological knowledge and their production during the twentieth century.

3   Early British criminology

A typical history of criminology pays due attention to the theoretical ideas and methodological practices of the nineteenth-century Italian criminal anthropologist Cesare Lombroso, especially his theoretical position regarding the connections between physiological make-up and criminality (see, for example, **Lombroso and Ferrero, 1895**). In addition, any self-respecting history typically deals with the influence of the French sociologist Emile Durkheim and with the way in which he distances himself from both physiological and psychological explanations by emphasizing the social bases of crime and deviance (see, for example, **Durkheim, 1964**). Both were positivists, although they differed in their specification as to the underlying causes of crime. In their differing ways they influenced, and indeed characterized, continental European thinking about crime and criminality towards the end of the nineteenth century and at the beginning of the twentieth century. This was much less the case in Britain. Lombroso's and Durkheim's ideas held very little sway and, indeed, according to Garland, criminology as a professional academic discipline did not really exist in Britain prior to 1935 (**Garland, 1988**). The central theme of Garland's essay on British criminology before 1935 is apposite in terms of an examination of the production of knowledge and of the institutional bases of criminology in so far as he argues that the development of the discipline 'can best be understood by concentrating less on the spread of ideas from abroad and more upon the ways in which penal and social institutions acted as a practical surface of emergence for this kind of knowledge' (Garland, 1988, p.1).

ACTIVITY 1.3

You should now read the extract from David Garland's 'British criminology before 1935', which is reproduced as Reader article 8. As you do so, keep the following question in mind:

What features best characterize early (pre-1935) criminology in Britain?

In addressing this question refer back to the 'Agenda for examining discourse' in section 2.1, especially questions relating to who and what was seen as problematic; the theoretical frameworks that were used; the kind of research, if any, that was carried out; and what were the key institutional bases.

3.1 A practical and institutionally based endeavour

Criminal anthropology underpinned by the work of Lombroso, and with its concern for 'criminal types', had an important impact in Europe, but was only of limited significance in Britain. The basic tenets of criminal anthropology were propounded in this country by Havelock Ellis (for example, in *The Criminal,* 1890), although these did not find favour amongst the influential practitioners working in courts and in the penal institutions at that time. These practitioners, especially those working in prisons, were much more concerned with the practical aspects of assessment, classification and containment of individuals. A number of strands can be identified in this endeavour. Their work was based upon psychiatric and medical theoretical frameworks. These were positivist, not in the sense of searching for causes – as with Lombroso – but in the broader sense of being concerned with the objective aspects of society and, more especially, of individual behaviour as opposed to an epistemology grounded in social meanings and social constructions. Their theoretical position had no notion of a separate category of individuals who could be identified as criminal and as having causative predeterminants of criminality, say, in their physiological make-up. As Garland points out:

> Unlike anthropology, psychiatry was not concerned to isolate discrete types of human individuals and classify them by means of racial and constitutional differences. Instead, it was a therapeutically oriented discipline based upon a classification system of psychiatric disorders which, like the disease model of nineteenth century medicine, discussed the condition separately from the individual in whom it might be manifested. Within the classification system of morbid psychology there were a variety of conditions which criminals were typically said to exhibit – insanity, moral insanity, degeneracy, feeble-mindedness, etc. But generally speaking, *the* criminal was not conceived as *a* psychological type. Instead the spectrum of psychiatric conditions might be usefully applied to a part of the criminal population: there was no separate criminal psychology or psychiatry, based upon ontological difference.

> (Garland, 1988, in the Reader, p.57)

A further distinctive feature of the work of the influential practitioners was that, in contrast with the European tradition, as influenced by Lombroso and others, their work was distinctively applied and practical:

> Theorizing about the conditions of individuals was not done in the abstract, but instead was linked to professional tasks such as the giving of psychiatric evidence before a court of law, or the decisions as to classification, diagnosis and regimen which prison medical officers made on a daily basis. This practical experience was crucial in shaping the psychiatric approach to criminological issues because it ensured that psychiatrists and prison medics were well acquainted with the day to day realities of criminal justice and with the need to bring psychiatric propositions into line with the demands of courts and prison authorities.

> (Garland, 1988, in the Reader, p.57)

A final and important point to note is that, in the main, the institutional base of this work was the penal establishment and its concerns. As Garland notes:

> The British tradition of scientific thinking about criminals was thus, from an early age, situated within an institutional framework which had the support of the prison establishment and the prestige of medicine behind it. Partly in consequence, it was generally modest in its claims, and very respectful of the requirements of institutional regimes and legal principles.

> (Garland, 1988, in the Reader, p.57)

There was, especially towards the end of the period up to 1935, some university teaching in criminology. However, this was predominantly located in medical schools, had a medico-psychiatric flavour, and was concerned with the medical examination and assessment of offenders. There was no distinctive criminological teaching or sociological analysis of crime influenced, for instance, by the writings of European theorists such as Emile Durkheim or by sociological and criminological developments in the USA (for example, the Chicago School of Sociology). In addition, as Garland notes, most of the scientific works in Britain before the 1930s were written by those with medical and psychiatric training and working in the Prison Service, and they were to be found in medical and psychiatric journals. Such journals had regular sections devoted to criminological matters.

Outside of this main sweep stood the work of Goring which was characterized by the study of large populations – in this case, offenders (Goring, 1913). His work was not of criminal types in the Lombrosian sense of the term since he saw crime on a continuum with normality. Nevertheless, he did share some similarities with the Italian criminologist in so far as he indicated that there were certain inherited characteristics, especially low intelligence and poor physique, which underpinned criminality. His conclusions had little impact, especially on the influential medical and psychiatric practitioners, on two counts: first, the conclusions were not viewed as sufficiently useful in terms of treating individuals; and, second, as already indicated, there was an aversion to Lombrosian ideas about 'criminal types', and Goring's views on inherited characteristics were considered to have similarities to these. However, his work did subsequently become important in terms of its methodology. It was a study of large populations and predominantly statistical in its measurement of patterns within the population. In this respect it foreshadowed some of the large-scale statistical work, typically survey based, which was to be done by the Home Office in later decades as part of the tradition which became known as 'official' and 'mainstream' criminology (this is discussed further in section 3.4).

To sum up this period, then, criminology in Britain towards the end of the nineteenth century and into the early twentieth century can be characterized as being without a general theory of crime, but as being linked theoretically to medicine and psychiatry. It was relatively untouched by the ideas which predominated in Europe, especially those ideas relating to criminal types or to the sociological factors underpinning crime rates in society. It was clinically based, it focused on the individual, and it was linked to practice. Further, it was grounded in the concerns of the institutions of criminal justice, especially courts and prisons, in dealing with such individuals. It was founded upon a form of enquiry which drew upon the methods of psychiatry and medicine and was based on the individual as the unit of analysis. Being grounded in the concerns of the institutions of criminal justice it was uncritical of these. It was very much a criminology-on-the-inside.

The medical and psychiatric tradition maintained its predominant position in the scientific study of crime and its practical applications until after the Second World War. It was after the war that Barbara Wootton published *Social Science and Social Pathology* (Wootton, 1959) which introduced a new way of looking at the issues of social problems and of crime in particular. Whilst using the word 'pathology' in its title, the book linked it to the 'social' rather than the psychiatric and the individual. In doing so it sought to review critically the contributions of psychiatry to the analysis and amelioration of social problems and urged an emphasis upon social factors underpinning social pathologies. This was a shifting of emphasis rather than a termination of psychiatric work. For example, the contribution of psychiatry to the understanding and explanation of criminal behaviour continues into the 1990s, especially in the writings of Sir Michael Rutter, head of the Department of Child and Adolescent Psychiatry at the London Institute of Psychiatry. On the basis of research findings it has been suggested that psychosocial disorders, including criminal behaviour, in young people are related to economic boom, a more consumerist society and greater individualism (Rutter and Smith, 1995). In addition, using a different theoretical framework, there are occasional resurgences in interest in the potential genetic bases of crime (see the article from *The Guardian*, 14 February 1995, reproduced opposite).

3.2 Pressure group criminology

Subsequent developments in British criminology have been charted in a variety of writings. For example, Morris (1988), following in the footsteps of Garland, takes up the period between 1935 and 1948. As we noted in the previous section, there was the continued development of the psychiatric/therapeutic tradition alongside an increasing interest in the social bases of crime. The period between the two world wars was one of little public debate about crime. However, there was debate in a relatively small but influential section of society on matters concerning the reform of prison conditions and also the abolition of capital punishment. Such debate found its base in pressure groups concerned with such issues. In the main, these pressure groups comprised middle-class intellectuals who were 'well connected', especially in relation to the Prison Commissioners and also Whitehall civil servants. Such pressure groups included the John Howard

Genes' link to crime may be cited in court

Sarah Boseley

SCIENTISTS have identified genes that, under certain circumstances, may predispose people to violent, aggressive, criminal behaviour, though there is no such thing as a specific 'crime gene', a conference was told yesterday.

In a matter of months, or at most a few years, genetic evidence may come to be accepted in courts in the United States in pleas of mitigation, according to Dr Deborah Denno, of the Law School at Fordham University, New York.

Speaking at the Ciba Foundation conference in London, attended by scientists from around the world working in the field of genetics, Dr Denno said: 'I don't think we know enough about genetic evidence to allow it to be a mitigating factor in court, but it is inconsistent not to allow that, but to allow in a lot of other biological evidence about which we also don't know much.'

Evidence concerning premenstrual tension, hyperactivity, attention deficit disorder and urban survival syndrome were all admissible, she said. She could foresee a genetic abnormality being viewed in much the same light.

But, pinpointing the concerns that arise in any discussions of genetics, Dr Denno pointed out that moral and ethical concerns might lead to problems with genetic evidence.

They included historical associations with past abuses by the Nazis during the Holocaust and the potential chilling of our notions of free will. There was the danger that those with relevant identified genes – maybe children – would be stigmatised and there was the risk that society would blame crime on genes and absolve itself of all responsibility for poverty and deprivation.

Within months, the Georgia Supreme Court will rule on the appeal to introduce genetic evidence brought by lawyers for Stephen Mobley. Mobley, now on death row, raided a pizza parlour cash register in 1991 before shooting the manager twice in the back of the neck.

Mobley's father, a self-made multi-millionaire, sent him to many institutions as he grew up, but they were unable to check his violent behaviour. The genetic evidence lawyers wish to present in court relates to violence, aggression and behavioural disorder in uncles, aunts and cousins.

'If genetic evidence is not admitted in the Mobley case in the next month or two, then maybe it will be within five years at a guess,' said Dr Denno.

Professor Sir Michael Rutter, of the Institute of Psychiatry, stressed that genetics could not even attempt to answer questions about the rise in crime over the last 50 years or national differences.

'Even the strongest risk factors only increase the chance of a behaviour occurring, they do not determine it directly. There can be no such thing as a gene for crime,' he said.

'That is not how genes operate. Rather, they affect (along with other factors) how people behave and how they respond to stress.'

Genetics were useful for the light they cast on environmental influences, he said. Dr Greg Carey, of the Institute of Behavioural Genetics at Colorado University, urged that the 'nature versus nurture' argument should be dismissed. 'The participants in this conference view nature and nurture as complementary components of development, not as mutually exclusive adversaries.'

(*The Guardian*, 14 February 1995)

Association and the Penal Reform League, now known as the Howard League for Penal Reform. Morris describes the situation as follows:

> The subtle interaction between those in public office, and here one must include senior civil servants as well as Prison Commissioners, and the penal reformers in this period is difficult to capture. The world of interacting pressure groups and power elites in British society was throughout the period comparatively small and remained so probably until as late as the end of the 1960s. It was, by and large, a leisured world in which the realities of the need to be earning a living did not always obtrude so uncomfortably as they do today; private means had not yet been supplanted by the elusive grant.

(Morris, 1988, p.25)

In terms of the questions posed by the agenda listed in section 2.1, the features of pressure group criminology were as follows:

- It was atheoretical and predominantly non-empirical.

- What were viewed as problematic were prison conditions and capital punishment.

- The activities of the groups were geared to the reform of policies and practices in relation to these.

- The institutional base for their activities was the well-connected middle-class intellectual élite of London which was a part of the 'inside' world of influential policy-makers and politicians.

The groups were critical of some official policies and practices but stopped at that; they were not critical of the system as a whole and, in this respect, pressure group criminology of the time was still very much a 'criminology-of-the-inside'. The pressure groups of the period laid down the foundations for an involvement in criminology and criminal justice policy which continues today in the form of groups such as the Howard League, the Prison Reform Trust, the National Association for the Care and Resettlement of Offenders (NACRO) and others which are actively involved in seeking to challenge and to reform policy and which, in doing so, engage in empirical enquiry to further their arguments and their case.

Some contemporary groups – for example, Radical Alternatives to Prison (RAP), Inquest (which is concerned with deaths in custody) and the National Prisoners Movement, previously known as PROP – have close ties with academics who represent a radical strand in criminology termed 'critical interventionist' (see, for example, Sim *et al.*, 1987; **Scraton and Chadwick, 1991**) and would see themselves as operating both on the 'outside' and from 'below' in terms of seeking to challenge state repression and injustices in the criminal justice system. Other pressure groups, not necessarily engaging in empirical enquiry or publication, are concerned with war crimes and violations of human rights (for example, Amnesty International), law reform (for example, Justice) and women in the criminal justice system (for example, Justice for Women).

3.3 Criminology in universities

The period just before the Second World War was also important in the development of criminology in the university sector and was influenced by the arrival in this country of three individuals who were fleeing Nazism and the impending dangers in Western Europe. In 1935 Hermann Mannheim came to the UK and a year later began teaching at the London School of Economics where he remained until 1955. During that time he influenced, through his teachings, the next generation of criminologists. The second influential figure was Max Grunhut who, on arriving in this country, took up a position at All Souls, at the University of Oxford. A third figure, Leon Radzinowicz, a Polish émigré, introduced criminology at the University of Cambridge in 1939. Although, as noted earlier, there was some teaching in university medical schools, criminology and criminological research and teaching put down roots in higher education in the triangle of the three influential universities just mentioned – London, Oxford and Cambridge – as a result of the endeavours of these three individuals.

The work at that time can best be described as neo-positivist – that is, not the hard deterministic positivism of nineteenth-century Lombroso but the softer positivism organized around the formulation and examination of hypotheses about the causes and treatment of crime. The discipline base of the three criminologists was law, although Mannheim was influenced subsequently by psychiatry and sociology. As Martin (1988) indicates, there were two major intellectual concerns of criminology at that time and up until the end of the 1940s. The first of these was the issue of capital punishment and, indeed, Radzinowicz was one of the members of the Royal Commission on capital punishment which carried out its work from 1949 to 1953. The other major concern was with juvenile delinquency and its treatment especially by psychoanalytical methods:

> It is very hard today to comprehend how predominant this approach was for at least a decade. Psychoanalytic principles were at the heart of the training of social workers and probation officers despite the fact that the method of treatment could only be applied to a handful of individuals, while in any case its efficacy was unproven. Not for the first time treatment was dominated by what powerful clinicians wanted to do. Criminologists who entered the field at this time had, therefore, to struggle to get some sort of balance to the subject so that it actually looked at the crimes committed by ordinary criminals.

> (Martin, 1988, p.39)

The issue of deviance and the boundaries between normality and deviance and between deviance and crime were not viewed as important and did not become so until the development of interactionist and labelling approaches in the late 1960s. During the 1960s British universities went through a major expansion which coincided with the growth of sociology teaching and research and the influence of sociology in the study of crime, especially via what became known as the sociology of deviance. Typically, courses were entitled 'sociology of deviance' rather than criminology and were part of sociology undergraduate and postgraduate programmes. Such courses involved a movement away from theoretical approaches founded on psychiatry and sociological positivism and towards interactionism and labelling (concerned with the social construction of crime) and critical criminology (concerned with connections between crime, law, class and the state). In the 1980s and 1990s undergraduate and postgraduate programmes entitled criminology, criminal justice studies, socio-legal studies and police studies emerged, usually linked to sociology teaching but sometimes in departments of law and of management. In addition, many universities have centres specializing in research on crime and criminal justice.

The Principles of Criminology.

1st Lecture. Dr H. Mannheim Oct 6th 1945.

The study of Criminology is the study of three sets of people.

1.) Those who have been in trouble - brought before Courts convicted. 7000 [8000 in peacetime. More in wartime.

   a) Major crimes - stealing etc.,
   b) Minor crimes - traffic offences et

2.) Those who have committed offences and not been brought to Court. Not found outs or not summonsed.

3.) Those who have not committed any crime that show may in the future.

The study is concerned with the three group as much as the first & second because of the Prevention of Crime.

Social workers should study crime
:: it presents one of the fields approaches to the study of society.
To understand why people commit crime - its understand the picture.

2) How its treat Crime & delinquency.
3) Causes of crime & delinquency
4) Types of people who commit crime
Treatment of crime has to be dealt with historically

Student notes taken from a lecture given by Hermann Mannheim in 1945

3.4 Home Office criminology

The 1950s were important, not only for the further development of criminology in the UK, but also for the way in which it became institutionalized in the Home Office and in the Institute of Criminology at Cambridge University, which was funded by the Home Office. One research study remains a landmark of this period. In 1951 the Home Office commissioned the Government Social Survey, and principally Leslie Wilkins, to assist Hermann Mannheim in carrying out a study which was to evaluate the supposed effects of Borstal training on young offenders. In this context the study is important not for its findings but because it signalled the beginning of Home Office sponsorship for research, Home Office publication of research – the study's findings were published as the first report in *Studies in the Causes of Delinquency and the Treatment of Offenders (SCDTO)*, now known as the *Home Office Research Studies (HORS)* – and because it laid down the methodological foundations for the use of evaluation studies in criminology; Table 1.1 gives a flavour of the research agendas that were dominant between 1955 and 1969. These are studies which are mainly designed to evaluate the efficacy of policies relating to criminal justice (see Chapter 3 for more detail on evaluation studies). There are many examples of such research. One study in the 1980s, which came to be a *cause célèbre* as a result of it becoming involved in party political debate regarding the care–control issue, is the tougher regimes project, sometimes known as the 'short, sharp shock experiment'. In the study two groups of young offenders were assigned to different forms of punishment, one of which was 'tough' (the experimental group), the other of which was not (the control group). The aim of the 'experiment', or evaluation study, was to assess, statistically, whether those receiving the tough regime were less likely to reoffend (Home Office, 1984). This kind of methodology, which emphasizes the evaluation of policies on a before–after basis, is viewed as especially appropriate to assessing the efficacy of crime control strategies – for example, situational crime prevention (see **Clarke, 1980**). It is an important part of administrative criminology, which became the central feature of the Home Office's research strategy in the 1980s and 1990s (this is discussed further in section 4.2).

3.4.1 Institute of Criminology, Cambridge

The Mannheim and Wilkins study (1955; see Table 1.1) laid the foundations for two significant developments in the 1950s in terms of the institutional bases of criminological research. One development was the funding by the Home Office of an Institute of Criminology to be located at Cambridge University under the auspices of Leon Radzinowicz. The Institute had a number of aims which included: conducting research; providing a specialist criminological library; undertaking teaching at postgraduate level and of professionals within the criminal justice system; and providing advice and expert guidance to the government. The Institute continues to be an important centre for carrying out predominantly positivist, quantitative, survey-based research (the earlier, albeit indirect, influence of Goring's large-scale, survey-based statistical research has already been noted in section 3.1: Goring, 1913). A classic example of this is the longitudinal, survey-based Cambridge Study in Delinquent Development directed by West and Farrington (Farrington and West, 1990) (Chapter 3 will examine survey design

Table 1.1 *Studies in the Causes of Delinquency and the Treatment of Offenders (SCDTO)*: titles published for the Home Office, 1955–69

1   Prediction methods in relation to Borstal training. Hermann Mannheim and Leslie T. Wilkins. 1955. viii + 276pp. (11 340051 9).

2   Time spent awaiting trial. Evelyn Gibson. 1960. v + 45pp. (34–368–2).

3   Delinquent generations. Leslie T. Wilkins. 1960. iv + 20pp. (11 340053 5).

4   Murder. Evelyn Gibson and S. Klein. 1961. iv + 44pp. (11 340054 3).

5   Persistent criminals. A study of all offenders liable to preventive detention in 1956. W.H. Hammond and Edna Chayen. 1963. ix + 237pp. (34–368–5).

6   Some statistical and other numerical techniques for classifying individuals. P. McNaughton-Smith. 1965. v + 33pp. (34–368–6).

7   Probation research: a preliminary report. Part I. General outline of research. Part II. Study of Middlesex probation area (SOMPA). Steven Folkard, Kate Lyon, Margaret M. Carver and Erica O'Leary. 1966. vi + 58pp. (11 340374 7).

8   Probation research: national study of probation. Trends and regional comparisons in probation (England and Wales). Hugh Barr and Erica O'Leary. 1966. vii + 51pp. (34–368–8).

9   Probation research. A survey of group work in the probation service. Hugh Barr. 1966. vii + 94pp. (34–368–9).

10   Types of delinquency and home background. A validation study of Hewitt and Jenkins' hypothesis. Elizabeth Field. 1967. vi + 21pp. (34–368–10).

11   Studies of female offenders. No. 1 – Girls of 16–20 years sentenced to Borstal or detention centre training in 1963. No. 2 – Women offenders in the Metropolitan Police District in March and April 1957. No. 3 – A description of women in prison on January 1, 1965. Nancy Goodman and Jean Price. 1967. v + 78pp. (34–368–11).

12   The use of the Jesness Inventory on a sample of British probationers. Martin Davies. 1967. iv + 20pp. (34–368–12).

13   The Jesness Inventory: application to approved school boys. Joy Mott. 1969. iv + 27pp. (11 340063 2).

Source: Mair and Nee, 1990, p.72

in more detail). The aims and broad strategies of the Cambridge study were very much influenced by the Gluecks in the USA, who had indicated the importance and influence of early family socialization and family circumstances on who did, and who did not, become officially defined as delinquent (Glueck and Glueck, 1950). The Gluecks' research involved collecting data about family background retrospectively. However, the Cambridge researchers decided to carry out a prospective longitudinal study in order to follow a sample of individuals throughout their early lives and collect findings at different points in time. In 1961 a sample of 411 working-class boys, aged about 8 years old, was selected from the registers of six state primary schools in an area of London. The sample members were contacted at frequent intervals up to the age of 21, and at the ages of 23 and 24 sub-sections of the sample were purposively selected. These included persistent recidivists, former recidivists who had not been convicted of an offence for five years, and, for the purposes of comparison, a random selection of non-delinquents. Finally, the sample members were contacted when they were 32 years old to examine which of them had continued a 'life of crime' into adulthood, and why. This occurred in 1986. A central aspect of the findings is that a number of clusters of factors were identified as having a statistical relationship to subsequent officially defined and also self-reported delinquency. These included coming from a family with low income, coming from a large family and having parents considered by social workers to have performed their child-raising practices unsatisfactorily (for a brief summary of the research findings see Farrington, 1989). The research, in bringing together explanatory factors from different disciplines, was both interdisciplinary and multivariate. Also, it was heavily empirical and without a strong theoretical influence, using instead 'what worked'. As the research director wrote, it 'began as a basic, fact-finding venture without strong theoretical preconceptions and without much clear notion of where it might lead' (West, 1982, p.4). In all of these senses it typified what Cohen (1981) has described as the dominant approach of that time: 'mainstream', 'official' criminology.

3.4.2 Home Office Research Unit

A further related development was the formation of the Home Office Research Unit in 1956. The Research Unit became a major locus of criminological research in its own right, employing at varying times up to 50 members of staff carrying out research within the Home Office. In addition, the Unit became a major dispenser of research grants to academics and others and a disseminator of criminological findings via the *Home Office Research Series* and the *Home Office Research Bulletins*. In theoretical and methodological terms it was, along with the Cambridge Institute, the centre of mainstream official criminology. (In 1981 the Research Unit underwent reorganization and a new Home Office Research and Planning Unit (HORPU) was inaugurated, which roughly corresponded to the development of what is labelled 'administrative criminology' which will be looked at further in section 4.)

Cohen (1981) identified four main features which, up until the late 1960s and early 1970s, were central to mainstream criminology:

1 *Pragmatism:* by which is meant an overall distrust of broad theory in explaining and tackling crime and a viewpoint that one can take elements from different theories and put them together in a way which may be seen as best suited to explaining and dealing with particular problems. Pragmatism was represented earlier by the rejection of the major theoretical schools or traditions which existed in Europe from the mid to late nineteenth century. In addition, this pragmatism was highly *empiricist*. Cohen summarizes it as follows: 'Find out the facts, then let the well meaning chaps (for example in the Home Office) make obvious inferences and do the rest' (Cohen, 1981, p.223).

2   In line with pragmatism, mainstream criminology was also typified by an *interdisciplinary conception* – that is, taking 'what works' from different disciplines. Cohen cites the interdisciplinary articles which typified the early years of the *British Journal of Criminology* (which started as the *British Journal of Delinquency* in 1950) and the background of members of the British Society of Criminology (which emerged from the Institute for the Study and Treatment of Delinquents in the late 1950s) which showed a broad interdisciplinary spread but with a heavy bias towards the clinical. There was a sparsity of members with a sociological background. In addition, this interdisciplinarity was grounded largely in British work. It was parochial in terms of ignoring theoretical ideas from Europe and more especially from the USA, where interesting and novel work was taking place (compare, for example, the contents of *The British Journal of Delinquency* from 1950 and *The British Journal of Criminology* from 1995, reproduced opposite).

3   According to Cohen, mainstream criminology was characterized by *correctionalism*. Within this there was an interest in making the correctional system more efficient and at the same time a humanitarian interest in reforming the system. However, commitment within mainstream criminology to correctionalism did not involve any challenging of the official system's aims and views as to what should be researched, how and with what effect. At the time American sociologists, and especially Howard Becker (1967), were asking questions which sought to challenge the system and which posed the fundamental questions for academics of: Whose side are we on? and: Whose side should we be on? Such questions were becoming fundamental in social science, and in the sociology of deviance in particular: 'But within the institutions of British criminology and the official or quasi-official grant giving bodies on which individual researchers were dependent, the questions were simply not on the agenda' (Cohen, 1981, p.229).

4   Perhaps above all, mainstream criminology was characterized by *positivism*. This involved a commitment to determinism and to the search for causes of crime; a commitment to empirical, quantitative and statistically based work as a means of seeking evidence; an implicit belief in the objective aspects of crime and criminality; and the denial of social meanings and of the attempts to understand and 'appreciate' the social world of deviance which were finding prominence in American sociology of the time. These commitments were reflected in the large-scale longitudinal study carried out by the Institute of Criminology at Cambridge (and funded by the Home Office) described in section 3.4.1 above.

4   The aetiological crisis

It was especially the positivist features of mainstream criminology which came under challenge towards the end of the 1960s. This is what **Young (1986)** has described as the aetiological crisis of mainstream criminology. He argued that a number of subsequent strands emerged within the study of crime and deviance, including one with which he is closely associated, left realism. In his article 'The failure of criminology: the need for a radical realism' he provided a portrayal, from a left-realist position, of forms of criminological knowledge, their development and relations between them.

Selected contents from The British Journal of Delinquency, 1950 *and* The British Journal of Criminology, 1995, *compared*

Formerly THE BRITISH JOURNAL OF DELINQUENCY — Volumes 1–10: 1960–1960

The

British Journal of Criminology

Delinquency and Deviant Social Behaviour

Volume 35 No. 1 Winter 1995

Contents

Articles

THE BRITISH JOURNAL OF DELINQUENCY

The Official Organ of the Institute for the Study and Treatment of Delinquency

CONTENTS OF VOLUME I

ORIGINAL PAPERS AND NOTES

The titles of Original Papers are printed in Roman Type; those of Notes in italics.

ACTIVITY 1.4

Read the extract from Jock Young's article 'The failure of criminology: the need for a radical realism', which is reproduced as Reader article 40. This provides a *left-realist* history of British criminology in the 1980s and 1990s. While reading this article consider the following questions:

1 How cogent is Young's argument concerning the aetiological crisis and, by way of response, the development of an administrative criminology?

2 What do you think are the strengths, if any, of his viewpoint that an idealistic position has failed criminology (as well as victims and would-be victims)?

3 What value do you give to his argument that a left-realist position is both radical and also fills a void between, on the one hand, administrative criminology and, on the other, left idealism?

The aetiological crisis is closely linked to the positivist features of mainstream criminology as outlined in the preceding section and especially to the search for causes of crime. This crisis was identified by Young as a key motor of change within criminology at that time and was brought about by a combination of factors within what, in another article, Young (1988) described as changes in both the interior history of criminology and changes in external social, political and cultural conditions. For example, the importing of labelling theory from the USA, with its scepticism about the value of explanations set in causal terms, began to sway some academics against the kind of positivist research conducted within mainstream criminology. What is more, policy-makers and politicians were also beginning to question research which did not really seem to find causal factors of any significance, statistically, socially or politically. This was all against a wider external social and political background of wholesale improvements in social conditions after the Second World War. Yet, at the same time, the crime rate continued to increase – indeed, it was growing within a welfare state which had resulted in an amelioration of the social factors which positivist criminology had indicated were the very root causes of crime. How could this be the case, it was asked? As Young argued: 'All the factors which should have led to a drop in delinquency if mainstream criminology were even half correct were being ameliorated and yet precisely the opposite effect was occurring' (Young, 1986, p.6).

This wholesale concern with the inability to find significant and meaningful causes and determinants of crime – the aetiological crisis – was mirrored by the inability of interventionist and rehabilitative establishment penology to control crime. Young tried to make sense of such 'failure' by charting the development of three alternative positions, each with their own theoretical and methodological underpinnings and institutional bases. These were, first, the development of radical criminology (emanating from interactionist and labelling approaches), which subsequently developed into what Young termed 'left idealism'; second, the development of administrative criminology; and, third, the development of left realism. We will look at each of these in turn in the following three sub-sections.

4.I   Radical criminology

The early formulations of what Young terms 'idealism' were influenced by a number of theoretical strands which came from the USA, especially those emanating from interactionism and labelling theory. As indicated in section 3.3, these theories found a ready home in the expanding university sociology departments of the late 1960s and early 1970s, and also in the National Deviancy Symposium, to become the National Deviancy Conference (NDC), which first met in York in the early 1970s. The interactionist and labelling (and subsequently social reaction) approaches had slightly different emphases, but shared a rejection of notions of causality and also of the notion of a class or category of individuals whose biological, physiological or psychological backgrounds predetermined that they would subsequently become criminals (see **Reader Guide 1**). Theirs was an avowedly sociological approach to crime and deviance rather than the pragmatic and interdisciplinary approach of mainstream criminology. Research agendas were concerned with the social construction of crime, the processes of stereotyping and labelling, the implications of control agencies for the creation of deviance, a debunking of official statistics as 'true' measures of crime in society and a strong interest in the appreciative aspects of deviance (see, for example, **Becker, 1963**).

These issues were addressed by methodological strategies which were ethnographic in nature (see Chapter 4 for further discussion of qualitative ethnographic methods). Ethnographic methods have a commitment to capturing social meanings and stereotypes, to the examination of how these are expressed in social interactions between individuals and to the study of such interactions in natural surroundings. A key method of collecting data within the ethnographic tradition is participant observation. Interactions between law-enforcement officers and would-be deviants could be observed. In addition, there were a number of ethnographies of deviant sub-cultures such as Young's study of drug takers (Young, 1971). In a commentary on the period, Cohen summarizes the attraction of participant observation as follows:

> Some of the original, and even more of the later members of the New Deviancy Conference, were on the fringes of what Jock Young nicely called the 'middle underground'. Involved as participants, we couldn't resist the lure to be also observers – and make a decent living from it! The romantic, voyeur-like appeal of the subject matter was thus important; one doubts whether a similar group could have sprung up around, say, industrial sociology, educational sociology or community studies.

(Cohen, 1981, p.234)

These interactionist and labelling approaches soon became closely intertwined with the emergence of a criminology with a more critical cutting edge in which the concern with the labelling by law-enforcement agents of acts as deviant was not *in itself* considered sufficient. It was felt necessary to examine how such processes were imbued with power and also the sources and consequences of such power. This led, especially via the publication of *The New Criminology* (**Taylor et al., 1973**), to the development of a so-called fully social theory of crime which sought to locate the processes of labelling and social reactions within wider economic and social relations, especially class relations. It is this critical criminology which Young, himself, subsequently caricatured as 'left idealism'.

The early interactionist and subsequent critical traditions had a strong institutional base within the growing social science departments in universities, the then polytechnics and other institutions of higher education and had a profound influence on academic thinking, especially regarding the processes of criminalization and the role of the state in these processes. So-called 'left idealism' also had an influence within the Labour Party via the New Left. However, it did not have any significant effect on the power house of criminological research within the Home Office and its associated institutions. As Cohen, in reference to the Home Office Research Unit, wrote in 1981: 'At the centre of the criminological enterprise it is business as usual' (Cohen, 1981, p.237). And as Young, writing in 1988, commented: 'what radical criminology did not do to any significant degree is challenge the criminological establishment. For the policy centres in British society were, and remain, remarkably unaffected, both in the Home Office itself and the university institutions it helps to finance' (Young, 1988, p.170).

4.2 Administrative criminology

In 1981 research in the Home Office was reorganized and reformulated under a new Home Office Research and Planning Unit (HORPU) instead of the Home Office Research Unit (HORU). The insertion of the word 'planning' in the title, especially in relation to policy, was significant. The Home Secretary announced that the new Unit would continue to be multi-disciplinary, that it would continue with publication of research studies, and also that it would carry out in-house research and continue funding for extra-mural research. But:

> the work of the Unit will however be more closely associated with the formulation and monitoring of policy. This will be achieved partly by grouping it with the criminal departments and partly by outposting some of its staff to other departments of the Home Office; in the first instance the prison department, the police department, and the community programmes and equal opportunities department.

> (quoted in Croft, 1982, p.4)

In relation to both internal research and external funding there was, and continues to be, emphasis on the 'customer–contract' principle – that is, research must be of use to, and have direct application to, a customer within some area of the criminal justice system, especially in relation to planning and policy.

These new organizational arrangements were in line with a subtle shift of research focus and research strategies within the Home Office towards what Young terms 'administrative criminology'. We have already noted how the mainstream official criminology faced the so-called aetiological crisis towards the end of the 1960s. Within such criminology, and facing such crisis, the mainstream was not replaced by the critical or the radical. Instead, mainstream criminology underwent a quiet but significant change from within, especially in relation to its positivist base. This change is characterized by Young and others as the development of administrative criminology. There are several strands to this but the basic tenets are as follows.

First, there is a lack of concern with the causes of crime. This is not a rejection of the concept of causality but a recognition that any single cause is statistically insignificant, relatively unimportant and politically impossible to tackle. Many of the pieces of research carried out under the umbrella of mainstream criminology found multiple causes, each of which was relatively insignificant in its own right and which also interacted with another. Such studies produced a rather complex agenda for action. In the face of this, the search for causes within administrative criminology adopted a very low profile. A second tenet is the belief in free will in relation to criminal actions. This fits with the downplaying of causality and determinism. Underpinning administrative criminology is the notion that individuals have rational choices as to whether or not to carry out criminal acts (see, for example, Cornish and Clarke, 1986). In this respect there are similarities with some of the tenets of conservative realism (see **Reader Guide 1, section 6.1.1**). This links to a third and perhaps the most important characterizing feature of administrative criminology: namely, the emphasis on policies to prevent and deter crime. Such strategies and policies, it is felt, play an important part in swaying the rational decision-maker away from criminal actions. In this way, administrative criminology is situational rather than dispositional (that is, altering the *situations* in which crime might be committed rather than treating individual *dispositions* to crime).

To sum up, then, the administrative criminology position is that, if the causes of crime cannot be identified with sufficient certainty, then there is little value in seeking to deal with rising crime rates by tackling such causes. Indeed, it is probably the case that criminal actions are the outcome of free rational thinking. Therefore, the emphasis should be on strategies and policies to prevent and deter crime. This is the main response of administrative criminology to the aetiological crisis which faced mainstream criminology in the 1960s.

The tenets of administrative criminology are very close to those associated with the work of James Q. Wilson in the USA (see, for example, **Wilson, 1983**). In this country it is firmly rooted in the work of the former HORU and now the HORPU, and also in the work of R.V.G. Clarke, one of its leading researchers of the 1980s (who subsequently left to teach in the USA) (see, for example, **Clarke, 1980; Book 2, Chapter 7; Reader Guide 2, section 9**). There are implications in terms of the development of policies and strategies to reduce and control the possibilities of individuals committing crime. Such policies and strategies include Neighbourhood Watch schemes, closed-circuit television (CCTV), architectural design and greater household security. The rationale for such strategies is to influence decision-making by modifying the environment to deter criminal acts and also to increase the risks of detection should such deterrence not work.

As the examples below reveal, an administrative research agenda is typically organized around the examination of such issues as situational factors, evaluation of situational crime prevention strategies, and analysis of the way in which victimization varies according to particular kinds of individuals and particular kinds of situations and contexts.

Examining situational decision-making

An example of this is Bennett and Wright's *Burglars on Burglary* (1984) carried out at the Cambridge Institute of Criminology, sponsored by the Home Office and supervised by Ron Clarke. The researchers were concerned with uncovering burglars' perceptions and definitions of their own and others' actions, particularly with reference to whether or not to commit a burglary. Data were collected from 128 convicted burglars and the interviews were tape-recorded and transcribed verbatim to uncover the burglars' ways of describing and explaining their behaviour (for a discussion of the use of detailed interviews see Chapter 4). The researchers found that definitions and perceptions which determined decisions as to whether or not to commit a burglary were not necessarily the same as the assumptions built into crime prevention programmes and practices about such decision-making. In this way the research contributed to understanding of the definitional and perceptual referrants of decision-making and criminal actions and also has implications, and indeed recommendations, for crime prevention policy.

Evaluating situational crime prevention strategies

Situational crime prevention strategies are evaluated by reforms-as-experiments (Campbell, 1969), sometimes known as evaluation research (Bulmer, 1986). A summary of the discussion of some of the main experiments initiated under the Home Office's research programme can be found in Clarke and Cornish's *Crime Control in Britain* (1983). Basically the research strategy is as follows: two groups of individuals or two contexts are matched to make them as similar as possible. One of them is subjected to the introduction of a crime prevention policy – for example, Neighbourhood Watch or tighter security on houses – after which the two groups or contexts are measured in terms of the extent of victimization. Some conclusion about the efficacy of the introduction of the specific crime prevention policy can be reached by comparing these two groups on a before and after basis.

Counting victimization

With regard to victimization, its extent and its distribution, the flagship within the Home Office is the British Crime Survey which began in 1982. The British Crime Survey is an example of a trend design which samples the extent of victimization at different points in time. At each point in time, sample members are asked whether in recent months they have been a victim of a crime; if so, they are asked to specify the type of crime and to indicate whether the crime was reported to the police. Questions on other topics are added from time to time. The extent of crime is traditionally measured using officially recorded statistics. The value of the British Crime Survey *vis-à-vis* official crime statistics is that it permits some conclusions to be reached about the amount of unreported victimization. Detailed analysis of the data allows inferences to be made about the types of individuals who are likely to become victims and the situations and contexts within which such victimization occurs, thereby providing a basis for recommending or considering differing crime prevention strategies (further detail on reforms-as-experiments and on surveys can be found in Chapter 3).

The institutional base of such research and of administrative criminology in general is the Home Office and also other official and quasi-official agencies (the police and agencies such as Crime Concern, for example) who have a central interest in implementing crime reduction and crime control strategies. Within this broad umbrella the primary interest is in how to devise practical and pragmatic strategies of crime prevention which will make the criminal justice system more efficient and effective in terms of reducing victimization and increasing clear-up rates. This is in contrast to pre-1935 criminology which was also organized around institutions of criminal justice – courts and prisons – but with different kinds of concerns: for example, a focus on classification of offenders rather than on crime prevention.

As indicated earlier, the HORPU carries out its own in-house research as well as funding academics to contribute to the research strategy and research output. A more recent development has been the use of social and market research companies to carry out research to the specification of the Unit. In effect, the contribution of such companies is limited to data collection and analysis. Also, in 1995 plans were announced for the partial disbandment of the Unit and the hiving off, by tender, of research projects to outside bodies such as market research companies and universities (see the article from *Independent on Sunday*, 8 January 1995, reproduced below).

Crime study unit faces sell-off

THE Home Office Research and Planning Unit, one of the most respected centres of academic crime studies in Europe, is being lined up for privatisation, *writes Nick Cohen*.

A government-commissioned study on the possibility of contracting out the work of the 35 researchers – who, in the past, have attempted to ensure that government crime policy had a rational base – has concluded that the private sector could take over the unit's functions.

Management consultants KPMG have identified the opinion poll companies MORI and Harris, Southampton and Cambridge Universities and Social and Community Planning Research, which produces the annual British Social Attitudes Survey, as potential bidders.

Home Office union leaders alleged that the research unit was being punished for coming up with evidence that ministers did not want to hear.

In the Eighties, the unit was at the centre of Douglas Hurd's and Kenneth Baker's attempts to reduce the prison population and find ways of managing offenders in the community.

But since the arrival of Michael Howard its findings have been less in tune with ministerial thinking. Recent research showed a link between unemployment and crime. After Mr Howard made great play of the menace of criminals committing offences while on bail, the unit showed that 'bail banditry' had not got noticeably worse in the past 10 years.

David Faulkner, a former senior Home Office adviser on crime, who is now at Oxford University, said: 'I'm afraid politicians are less interested in findings which do not conform with their dogmatic views.'

By suggesting that commercial organisations could take over the unit's work, the Home Office is taking privatisation to the heart of policy formulation.

(*Independent on Sunday*, 8 January 1995)

4.3 Left realism

According to **Young (1986)**, left realism emerged out of, and still remains part of, a radical tradition. His argument is that the failure of radical criminology (in which he was himself a leading 'player') is a result of a complete side-stepping of the aetiology of crime in its desire to adopt solutions, which, he suggests, can only be described as 'idealistic'. Such 'idealism' is characterized by an over-willingness to reject *all* of the features of mainstream criminology. He refers to this as the problem of 'critique by inversion' – that is, the inversion without discrimination of all of the features of mainstream criminology. The consequences are described by Young as:

> One, the loss of middle and ground level analyses of crime which structural functionalist and interactionist sources could have provided; two, a regression in terms of many of the debates of the sixties; three, a loss of ethnographic and qualitative methods of research; and four, because of the hiatus in terms of the discussion of the aetiology of crime, an easy acceptance of the very economistic New Left ideas on the subject.

(Young, 1986, p.14)

Radical criminology is also portrayed as being 'idealistic' in other ways, for example, in its representation of working-class crime as a creative response to oppression, a response which ignores working-class crime directed *at* working-class people. Further, Young argues, some versions of radical criminology do not even see the study of crime as central and thereby bypass its reality for a substantial section of the population. Third, idealism has a tendency to reductionism whereby every problem such as crime is reduced to explanation in terms of capitalism or the acts of the agents of capitalism. It is argued that in doing this it ignores some of the values of sociological positivist thinking.

The crux of the realist argument, as espoused by Young, is that, following the aetiological crisis of mainstream criminology, a major void existed between, on the one hand, administrative criminology as located in the Home Office and as adopted in right-wing politics, and, on the other hand, radical criminology as espoused by academics working in universities and by left-wing politicians. The essence of this void was the need to face up to the reality of crime and to recognize the extent of victimization in society. Left realism stands for being realistic about the extent of victimization and its distribution, but arguing at the same time for an 'accurate victimology' which would be underpinned by carrying out victim surveys. A typical example of this is the Islington Crime Survey (Jones *et al.*, 1986) and the Merseyside Crime Survey (Kinsey, 1985). Both are more geographically focused than the British Crime Survey but report similar findings with regard to the extent of victimization and fear of crime. However, greater emphasis is placed upon victimization among vulnerable groups in society, particularly women and those from minority ethnic backgrounds. What is more, it is argued that fear of crime within these groups is realistic and therefore needs to be addressed, especially by police who should address these realities and fears by prioritizing their policies accordingly. Effective crime control policies, it is argued, should be conceptualized as a social right for all sections of the community, be part of a comprehensive political programme, multi-pronged and operate primarily at the local level; further, there should be local authority involvement, the mobilization of informal social controls and the democratization and accountability of crime control.

The main platform for realist thinking, research and policy lies with academics such as Jock Young, based at Middlesex University. However, realism does not just have a university and an academic base; it has sought to collaborate with local authorities (especially those that are Labour-controlled) in carrying out victim-orientated research and in the development of crime control strategies. This has introduced a further institutional base to criminological research. Politically, left realism was influential in Labour Party strategy and policy in the late 1980s and early 1990s and typified Labour Party politics at that time. For Young, left realism remains part of a radical tradition but is an approach which has sought to address some of what are viewed as the failures of 'idealist' approaches within that tradition. However, for others it is seen as being very much a criminology of the 'inside', one that is grounded in the concerns of the criminal justice system and its functioning and one that is not sufficiently critical of the system in an 'outsider' role (Cohen, 1988).

ACTIVITY 1.5

By way of review, you should address each of the positions discussed in the preceding sections and portrayed in Figure 1.2 overleaf. You should do this by taking apart each form of criminological knowledge by engaging in reflexive analysis using the research agenda questions posed in section 2.1. In particular, reflect on the central features of each form of knowledge in terms of:

1   what is seen as *problematic* (see section 2.2);
2   what types of *theory* predominate (see section 2.3);
3   what kind of *research* is used (see section 2.4);
4   what are the *institutional bases* of the production of each form of knowledge (see sections 3 and 4);
5   how can each be characterized in terms of 'criminology-on-the-inside' or 'criminology-on-the-outside' (see section 2.5)?

Provide a characterization of each form of criminology-as-knowledge in terms of these five features.

5   Beyond criminology

A reflexive analysis will identify important differences in forms of knowledge, in terms of institutional bases and also in terms of whether each can be characterized as being 'on the inside' or 'on the outside'. Despite these differences, all the forms of knowledge in Figure 1.2 engage the central concerns *within* contemporary criminology in terms of criminological problems, criminological theories and criminological styles of research. For some, the ways in which these are put together represent inappropriate, 'modernist' forms of knowledge. As a result, some developments in the 1990s have emphasized the importance of 'ways of thinking' which are not within these confines.

Figure 1.2 Components of the criminological traditions

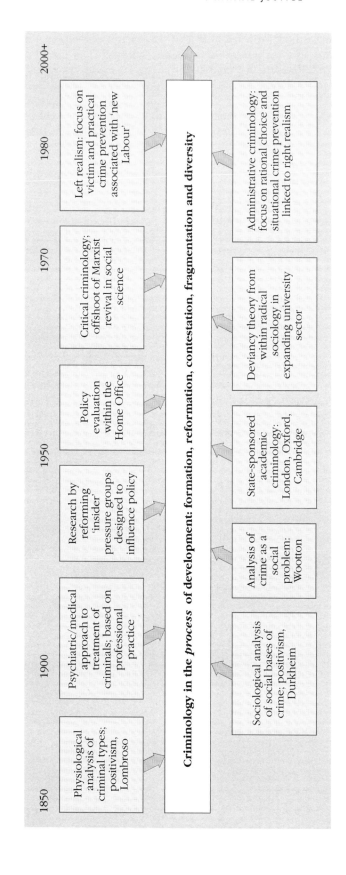

ACTIVITY 1.6

Now read Carol Smart, 'Feminist approaches to criminology or postmodern woman meets atavistic man' (Reader article 41). As you do so, address the following questions:

1 What is meant by modernist ways of thinking and how do these relate to forms of knowledge outlined in preceding sections, including left realism?
2 What feminist contributions to criminology are identified?
3 What is meant by postmodernist ways of thinking and how do these relate to feminist contributions to criminology?

Smart portrays the traditional and mainstream – 'insider' – criminologies as typical of modernist ways of thinking which, it is argued, must be recognized as having failed social science. However, in contrast to Young, and by way of a critique of left realism, she also portrays radical – 'outsider' – criminology as wedded to the modernist enterprise. Her argument is for *postmodernist* forms of thinking which have their foundation outside the social sciences. Some forms of feminism have been generated *within* the confines of criminology, addressing and responding to criminological problems, criminological theorizing and forms of criminological research (see, for example, **Klein, 1973**). However, feminist postmodernism 'starts from a different place and proceeds in other directions' (Smart, 1990, in the Reader, p.462). The promise of feminist postmodernism is such that the traditional question of: What has criminology to offer feminism? should be recast as: What has feminism to offer criminology?' In terms of its conceptualization of problems, its theorizing and its research, postmodernism represents a way of thinking outside and *beyond* criminology (see **Reader Guide 1, section 7.1**).

6 A fragmented criminology?

ACTIVITY 1.7

Read Richard Ericson and Kevin Carriere, 'The fragmentation of criminology' (Reader article 46). In doing so, pay particular attention to the following questions:

1 What are the responses to the fragmented character of modern criminology?
2 What, if anything, is the value of a fragmented criminology?

The picture painted by Ericson and Carriere is of a criminological enterprise which is fragmented and fractured and within which opposing theoretical–methodological–strategy positions 'scorn' one another. Ericson and Carriere deal with most of the criminological stances outlined in the preceding discussion, although they classify, organize and label them in a slightly different way. They argue that criminologists respond to fragmentation by coalescing around one of the three main 'essentialist' solutions treating criminology as:

1 an effective politics of crime control
2 part of a 'master' discipline
3 critical practice

We will look at each of these in the following sub-sections.

6.1 Criminology as an effective politics of crime control

The domain of criminology as a politics of crime control is constituted by criminal justice institutions. Criminologists working within this approach share with practitioners and policy-makers key analytical and research questions about these institutions and their functioning. These include questions about problems within the system, explanations of such problems and solutions with which to address them. This form of discourse, or criminology-as-knowledge, about 'effective politics of crime control' predominates in the discipline and is typical of what has been described earlier as 'criminology on the inside'. Ericson and Carriere identify three main versions. The first of these is right realism which gained ascendancy in the USA but which has its variant in this country in what has been termed administrative criminology. It has certain key assumptions. One of these is that there is consensus and unified interest in society, especially in relation to the protection of individuals and property from the 'underclass' of urban poor, and another is that the role of criminal justice institutions is to afford such protection by methods of deterrence and incapacitation. Such a criminology is 'the ideological and technological arm' of criminal justice institutions.

A second version is left realism which is described as consumer- and victim-orientated, grounded in the collection of survey data and in favour of strategies of crime control which are accountable to the community, especially those sections of the community which are most likely to be victims of crime:

> Identifying with the consumers of criminal justice, especially crime victims who are poor and otherwise disadvantaged, left realism asks how the criminal justice system can meet their needs more adequately. In contrast to right realists who believe that the police are already in touch with essential community interests, left realists challenge state definitions by documenting community interests through victimization and fear of crime surveys. Survey data are treated as indicative of essential community interests. They are used as a template for rationalizing formal policing practices, and for making the police more accountable to the urban poor and other minorities.

> (Ericson and Carriere, 1994, in the Reader, pp.509–10)

As indicated earlier, Young's position is that left realism emerged out of, and remains part of, the radical tradition in criminology. For him it represents a response within that tradition to the problems of idealism. Ericson and Carriere, however, see left realism as much more institutionally orientated and therefore locate it differently (as, indeed, does Smart): 'Led by criminologists who appeared more radical in the 1970s, left realists have adjusted to a 1980s and 1990s "realism" that really entails joining the ranks of those who take a pragmatic, piecemeal, administrative approach to the field on behalf of particular interests' (Ericson and Carriere, 1994, in the Reader, p.510).

Between Left and Right lies a liberal approach which 'is essentially concerned with the just administration of criminal law conceived in terms of due process of law, and efficiency and humaneness in its administration' (Ericson and Carriere, 1994, in the Reader, p.510). The argument is that Left, Right and Liberal actively defend their positions against one another and also against a second essentialist position, that which treats criminology as part of a 'master' discipline.

6.2 Criminology as part of a 'master' discipline

Academic purists who populate this position do not start with the pragmatic and policy questions relating to criminal justice institutions, their functioning, efficiency and humaneness. Instead, problems, theories and methods derive from 'master' disciplines such as history, psychology and sociology. For example, for some, criminology is positivist sociology which concerns itself with the causes of crime; others reduce criminological problematics to the sociological problem of order at the same time as castigating those who focus on explanations of crime or on the operation of the criminal justice institutions for being politically, as opposed to academically, driven. In terms of the previous discussion in this chapter, the academic purist position is one of 'criminology-on-the-outside', although it is not one of a 'critical-outsider' in so far as there is no sense of endeavouring to produce a critical analysis of power and social control in relation to criminal justice institutions, nor of a political praxis aimed at such institutions. The latter is much more typical of a third essentialist position – namely, that belonging to those who represent the radical or critical tradition in criminology.

6.3 Criminology as critical practice

Ericson and Carriere portray this in idealist terms: 'Such attempts to unify the field betray a nostalgia for the Enlightenment fantasy of the pursuit of freedom through the collection and synthesis of truth, as well as the Marxist fantasy of a united revolutionary class' (Ericson and Carriere, 1994, in the Reader, p.512).

However, radical criminology is not just grounded in idealistic 'Marxist fantasies' as Ericson and Carriere describe. For example, considerable theorizing and research has been concerned with connections between crime and criminal justice and ethnicity and gender, and not just class relations (**Scraton and Chadwick, 1991**). Feminist criminology, and various strands within it, can be viewed as radical and critical in terms of the ways in which it challenges theoretical and methodological orthodoxy (including the 'gender-blindness' of Marxist criminology) and is critical of the functioning of the criminal justice system in relation to women. These include what **Smart (1990)** describes as 'feminist empiricism' and 'standpoint feminism'. Her case for feminist postmodernism is a case for ways of thinking beyond these.

One important strand within feminism has been concerned with addressing crime and criminal justice in the context of conformity of women in society which, in turn, had encouraged a viewpoint that the women–crime equation is too narrow and too constraining. Within this lies an argument for thinking, not in terms of feminist criminology, but in terms of redirecting all issues into a wider analysis of social control. This challenges established 'ways of thinking' inside criminology. In turn, there is a link to the postmodernist case for the deconstruction of the core concepts of 'insider criminology'. Such developments represent an argument for theorizing and research outside and beyond criminology.

The contemporary scene of the 1990s, then, is one of internal debate (even 'scorn'!), diversity, fracture and fragmentation. What, then, is the value of a fragmented criminology? Ericson and Carriere make the case for a criminology which is tied neither to disciplinary bases, their problems and preferred theoretical and methodological approaches, nor to particular institutional bases and their problems and preferred theoretical and methodological approaches. The crux of their argument is that those who represent any given position seek justification by criticizing other, alternative, positions as being reductionist and essentialist. However, in order to do so, justifications typically descend into reductionism and essentialism themselves. For example, the 'sociological academic purist' seeking to criticize radical criminology as reducing all explanations to capitalism, class relations and conflict, and portraying all truth in these terms, tends to do so by putting forward an alternative 'truth' which can only be accessed in terms of other formulations of social order which are equally reductionist and essentialist. Ericson and Carriere portray criminology as an enterprise which is not only fractured and fragmented, but also overly populated by those activities which are characterized as reductionist and essentialist challenges and defences (or what elsewhere has been described as 'warring and intransigent fortresses' – Jupp, 1989, p.178): 'The only problem with the fragmentation of criminology is criminologists who fret about it. Problems arise when criminologists essentialize the field within their preferred template of political and/or academic correctness' (Ericson and Carriere, 1994, in the Reader, p.512).

Fragmentation, they argue, is inevitable and even desirable. Criminologists should not start from the assumption that a diversity of positions is a temporary phase before academic consensus is achieved. Only when this is recognized will energies be diverted from a concern with defending essentialist positions while attacking others. Instead, fragmentation – and the recognition of its inevitability – can be used creatively. For example, it can be used to examine the ways in which interdisciplinary work can open up enquiry and understanding. It can also be used to encourage reflexiveness about criminology. In terms of the research agenda questions posed at the beginning of this chapter, it is fruitful, for example, to ask questions about what particular criminological positions see as problematic, how they seek to explain these problems, what kind of data they admit as being valid and what kind of solutions are put forward. This is not simply to be endlessly reflexive but to facilitate further understanding by considering the relationship between forms of criminology-as-knowledge, institutional bases and power. Why, for example, do forms of knowledge associated with particular institutional bases take the shape that they do? Which forms of knowledge are ranked in high positions in the hierarchies of credibility? And how are 'rankings' linked to the institutional bases from which forms of knowledge emerge and which they represent?

Further, as this book is especially concerned with methods of research in crime and criminal justice, we can recast such questions in terms of the use or non-use of particular methods. For example, what kind of research is carried out, by whom, for what purpose and with what effect?

> One important way of uncovering institutional policies and practices is via an examination of the institutional reactions to criminological research in terms of what is and is not constrained; what is and is not facilitated; and what is and is not favoured. This is suggestive of a criminological enterprise which is not solely concerned with criminals as objects of enquiry but which also embraces an examination of the research process itself in terms of what it can tell us about the interests of different groups, the relations of power which exist between them and the way in which they seek to promote and protect such interests by the mobilization of the relations of power.

(Jupp, 1989, p.176)

This is what is meant by being methodologically reflexive about criminological research in order to understand further the institutional bases of criminology, their functioning and the forms of knowledge which are part of their functioning.

7 Conclusion

This chapter has been concerned with mapping some of the major contours of criminology-as-knowledge. This has been done by adopting a reflexive approach to past and contemporary criminology, using a research agenda which encourages questions about what, in any form of criminology-as-knowledge, is viewed as problematic and why; how it is explained; how it is researched; and what kinds of policy solutions are put forward. Distinctive constellations of types of problem, theory, method and policy represent distinctive forms of criminology-as-knowledge. Such an agenda has been used to examine the development of British criminology from the turn of the century to the mid 1990s and has helped to chart the ascendancy and demise of forms of knowledge and also the contemporary variety and fragmentation. An important theme has been that contemporary contours of criminology have been shaped by forces in the historical development of the discipline. These include forces within the discipline (for example, significant theoretical and methodological developments; importation of ideas from other countries); forces outside the discipline (for example, the development of postmodernist thinking); and wider social and political forces (such as drives for law and order campaigns or for greater efficiency in the criminal justice system).

A further aspect of the agenda involves locating the institutional bases of different forms of knowledge. A broad distinction has been made between the production of criminological knowledge 'on the inside' (for example, knowledge about the efficient functioning of the criminal justice system), production of knowledge 'on the outside' (for example, knowledge which is critical of the fundamental principles underpinning that system) and production of knowledge 'beyond criminology' (for example, knowledge based on a deconstruction of established ways of thinking within criminology, whether these be 'insider' or 'outsider' ways). Each of these has its own research agenda. The relationship between institutional bases, research agendas and the production (and dissemination) of knowledge is closely linked to power and to the politics of criminological research discussed in the next chapter.

Further reading

Those who wish to study developments in British criminology in further detail can consult a number of sources. *A History of British Criminology*, edited by Paul Rock (1988) contains a compilation of articles which chart developments from the beginning of the twentieth century up to the mid 1980s. In addition, contributors comment on the state of criminology in the 1980s and strands within the discipline at that time. Stanley Cohen has written a number of essays reflecting on criminology and the sociology of deviance. These are brought together in his volume *Against Criminology* (Cohen, 1988). David Garland's 'Of crimes and criminals: the development of criminology in Britain' (Garland, 1994), which is part of *The Oxford Handbook of Criminology* (Maguire *et al.*, 1994), offers a further historical commentary and provides a selection of further reading.

A useful starting point for examining contemporary criminology is consultation of journals such as the *British Journal of Criminology* and *The Howard Journal of Criminal Justice*. Each contains articles, but also, perhaps more usefully, reviews of recent books. Recent writings in book form can also be monitored by checking publishers' catalogues. This will provide access to radical writings outside the mainstream of criminology. Journals outside criminology occasionally publish articles dealing with crime and criminal justice. For example, *Youth and Policy* takes articles and publishes reviews relating to youth and crime.

The Home Office Planning Unit produces *Research Bulletins* comprising short summaries of commissioned research and the *Home Office Research Series* produces longer, more detailed research reports. The Home Office Research and Statistics Department publishes regular statistical 'briefings' in *Research Findings*. Pressure groups such as the Prison Reform Trust and NACRO produce pamphlets and other publications which detail the findings of their, and others', research.

References

Becker, H. (1963) *Outsiders: Studies in the Sociology of Deviance*, New York, Free Press. (Extract reprinted as 'Outsiders' in Muncie *et al.*, 1996.)

Becker, H. (1967) 'Whose side are we on?', *Social Problems*, vol.14, no.3, pp.239–47.

Bennett, T. and Wright, R. (1984) *Burglars on Burglary*, Aldershot, Gower.

Bryman, A. (1988) *Quantity and Quality in Social Research*, London, Allen and Unwin.

Bulmer, M. (ed.) (1986) *Social Science and Social Policy*, London, Allen and Unwin.

Campbell, D.T. (1969) 'Reforms as experiments', *American Psychologist*, vol.24, pp.409–29.

Clarke, R.V.G. (1980) '"Situational" crime prevention: theory and practice', *British Journal of Criminology*, vol.20, no.2, pp.136–47. (Reprinted in Muncie *et al.*, 1996.)

Clarke, R.V.G. and Cornish, D.B. (eds) (1983) *Crime Control in Britain*, New York, State University Press.

Cohen, S. (1981) 'Footprints in the sand: criminology and the sociology of deviance', in Fitzgerald, M., McLennan, G. and Pawson, J. (eds) *Crime and Society: Readings in Theory and History*, London, Routledge and Kegan Paul.

Cohen, S. (1988) *Against Criminology*, New Brunswick, NJ, Transaction.

Cornish, D.B. and Clarke, R.V.G. (eds) (1986) *The Reasoning Criminal: Rational Choice Perspectives on Offending*, New York, Springer-Verlag.

Croft, J. (1982) 'The Research and Planning Unit', *Home Office Research Bulletin*, no.13, pp.4–5.

Durkheim, E. (1952) *Suicide: A Study in Sociology*, London, Routledge and Kegan Paul. (First published in 1897.)

Durkheim, E. (1964) *The Rules of Sociological Method*, New York, Free Press. (First published in 1895.) (Extract reprinted as 'The normal and the pathological' in Muncie *et al.*, 1996.)

Ellis, H. (1890) *The Criminal*, London, Walter Scott.

Ericson, R. and Carriere, K. (1994) 'The fragmentation of criminology', in Nelken, D. (ed.) *The Futures of Criminology*, London, Sage. (Extract reprinted in Muncie *et al.*, 1996.)

Farrington, D. (1989) 'The origins of crime: the Cambridge Study of Delinquent Development', *Research Bulletin*, Home Office Research and Planning Unit No.27, pp.29–33.

Farrington, D. and West, D. (1990) 'The Cambridge study in delinquent development', in Kerner, H.J. and Kaiser, G. (eds) *Criminality: Personality, Behaviour and Life History*, Berlin, Springer-Verlag.

Field, S. (1990) *Trends in Crime and Their Interpretation*, Home Office Research Study No.119, London, HMSO. (Extract reprinted as 'Crime and consumption' in Muncie *et al.*, 1996.)

Garland, D. (1988) 'British criminology before 1935', *The British Journal of Criminology*, vol.28, no.2, pp.1–17. (Extract reprinted in Muncie *et al.*, 1996.)

Garland, D. (1994) 'Of crimes and criminals: the development of criminology in Britain', in Maguire *et al.* (1994).

Glueck, S. and Glueck, E. (1950) *Unravelling Juvenile Delinquency*, New York, Harper and Row.

Goring, C. (1913) *The English Convict: A Statistical Study*, London, HMSO.

Harvey, L. (1990) *Critical Social Research*, London, Allen and Unwin.

Home Office (1984) *Tougher Regimes in Detention Centres: Report of an Evaluation by the Young Offender Psychology Unit*, London, HMSO.

Hough, M. and Mayhew, P. (1983) *The British Crime Survey: First Report*, Home Office Research Study No.76, London, HMSO.

Jones, T., Maclean, B. and Young, J. (1986) *The Islington Crime Survey: Crime Victimisation and Policing in Inner City London*, Aldershot, Gower.

Jupp, V.R. (1989) *Methods of Criminological Research*, London, Allen and Unwin.

Jupp, V.R. and Norris, C. (1993) 'Traditions in documentary analysis', in Hammersley, M. (ed.) *Social Research: Philosophy, Politics and Practice*, London, Sage.

Kinsey, R. (1985) *Merseyside Crime and Police Surveys: Final Report*, Liverpool, Merseyside County Council.

Klein, D. (1973) 'The etiology of female crime: a review of the literature', *Issues in Criminology*, vol.8, no.2, pp.3–30. (Extract reprinted as 'The etiology of female crime' in Muncie *et al.*, 1996.)

Lea, J. and Young, J. (1984) *What Is To Be Done About Law and Order?*, Harmondsworth, Penguin. (Extract reprinted as 'Relative deprivation' in Muncie *et al.*, 1996.)

Lombroso, C. (1876) *L'Uomo Delinquente*, Milan, Hoepli.

Lombroso, C. and Ferrero, W. (1895) *The Female Offender*, London, Fisher Unwin. (Extract reprinted as 'The criminal type in women and its atavistic origin' in Muncie *et al.*, 1996.)

Maguire, M., Morgan, R. and Reiner, R. (1994) *The Oxford Handbook of Criminology*, Oxford, Oxford University Press.

Mair, G. and Nee, C. (1990) *Electronic Monitoring: The Trials and Their Results*, Home Office Research Study No.120, London, HMSO.

Mannheim, H. and Wilkins, L.T. (1955) 'Prediction methods in relation to Borstal training', *Home Office Studies in the Causes of Delinquency and the Treatment of Offenders*, London, HMSO.

Martin, J.P. (1988) 'The development of criminology in Britain, 1948–60', *British Journal of Criminology*, vol.28, no.2, pp.35–44.

Merton, R.K. (1957) *Social Theory and Social Structure*, New York, Free Press.

Morris, T. (1988) 'British criminology: 1935–48', in Rock (1988).

Muncie, J., McLaughlin, E. and Langan, M. (eds) (1996) *Criminological Perspectives: A Reader*, London, Sage in association with The Open University.

Quetelet, M.A. (1842) *A Treatise on Man*, Edinburgh, Chambers. (Extract reprinted as 'Of the development of the propensity to crime' in Muncie *et al.*, 1996.)

Rock, P. (ed.) (1988) *A History of British Criminology*, Oxford, Oxford University Press.

Rutter, M. and Smith, D. (1995) *Psychosocial Disorders in Young People*, Chichester, John Wiley and Sons.

Scraton, P. and Chadwick, K. (1991) 'The theoretical and political priorities of critical criminology' in Stenson, K. and Cowell, D. (eds) *The Politics of Crime Control*, London, Sage. (Extract reprinted in Muncie *et al.*, 1996.)

Shaw, C.R. (1930) *The Jack Roller*, Chicago, IL, University of Chicago Press.

Sim, J., Scraton, P. and Gordon, P. (1987) 'Crime, the state and critical analysis', in Scraton, P. (ed.) *Law, Order and the Authoritarian State*, Milton Keynes, Open University Press.

Smart, C. (1990) 'Feminist approaches to criminology or postmodern woman meets atavistic man', in Morris, A. and Gelsthorpe, L. (eds) *Feminist Perspectives in Criminology*, Buckingham, Open University Press. (Extract reprinted in Muncie *et al.*, 1996.)

Taylor, I., Walton, P. and Young, J. (1973) *The New Criminology*, London, Routledge and Kegan Paul. (Extract reprinted in Muncie *et al.*, 1996.)

West, D.J. (1982) *Delinquency: Its Roots, Careers and Prospects*, London, Heinemann.

Wilson, J.Q. (1983) *Thinking About Crime* (2nd revised edn), New York, Basic Books. (Extract reprinted as 'On deterrence' in Muncie *et al.*, 1996.)

Wootton, B. (1959) *Social Science and Social Pathology*, London, Allen and Unwin.

Worrall, A. (1990) *Offending Women: Female LawBreakers and the Criminal Justice System*, London, Routledge.

Young, J. (1971) *The Drugtakers*, London, Paladin.

Young, J. (1986) 'The failure of criminology: the need for a radical realism', in Matthews, R. and Young, J. (eds) *Confronting Crime*, London, Sage. (Extract reprinted in Muncie *et al.*, 1996.)

Young, J. (1988) 'Radical criminology in Britain: the emergence of a competing paradigm', in Rock (1988).

Appendix 1.1

Jupp: 'Gaining access: research in prisons'

All social research involves gaining access to data. Access involves being able to obtain data which is considered relevant or appropriate to the research aims of the investigation. The individuals who are most closely associated with problems of gaining access to data are usually known as gatekeepers. The 'gate' can be exercised in a number of ways. For example, the gatekeeper may have formal powers to exclude researchers from the research situation or he or she may be able to exercise informal management of social situations such that researchers are unwittingly, but effectively, denied access to particular informants and particular forms of data. Often there are layers of gatekeepers to be negotiated, with hierarchies of authority and power between them. For example, in police research, the superintendent of a police sub-division can prevent access to officers. However, whatever his wishes or desires, his decisions as to access are worthless if overruled by a chief constable.

The difficulties of obtaining formal access have been most graphically highlighted in relation to some research in prisons. In England and Wales prisons are the responsibility of the prison department within the Home Office. This is headed by the Director General of the Prison Service who is a senior civil servant and who is responsible for the formulation of overall policy, subject to the ratification of the Home Secretary and ultimately Parliament. Individual prisons are administered by a governor. The prison system in Scotland is the responsibility of the Secretary of State for Scotland and civil servants within the Scottish Home and Health Department of the Scottish Office. Within this department there is the equivalent of the prison department in England and Wales, headed by a director. The day-to-day running of Scottish prisons is in the hands of prison governors.

Over the past two decades research in prisons has been decreasing, partly because of cutbacks in the research activities of the HORPU but also because of the suspiciousness of the Home Office towards social science research following the publication of writings about Durham's E Wing by Cohen and Taylor (1972). Such suspiciousness has led to problems of gaining access for researchers. Nevertheless, some research has taken place. For example, King and Elliott (1977) distinguish four types of research: *independent,* where the social scientist is carrying out his or her own research (see, for example, Morris and Morris, 1962); *officially sponsored* (see, for example, Emery, 1970); research based upon *mutual staff and researcher interests* (see, for example, Bottoms and McClintock, 1973); and research based upon *mutual prisoner and researcher interests* (see, for example, Cohen and Taylor, 1972). It is with the last type of research that the problems of gaining access are most likely to occur.

Long-term imprisonment

A central concern of research in prisons has been the problem of long-term prisoners. In England and Wales long-term male prisoners are those sentenced to over four years and long-term female prisoners are those sentenced to over three years imprisonment. In Scotland long-term refers to a sentence of over eighteen months for both sexes. There have been personal accounts of the effects of long-term imprisonment by prisoners themselves (see, for example, Boyle, 1977; McVicar, 1979; and Probyn, 1977). In the late 1960s two social scientists, Stanley Cohen and Laurie Taylor, started research work which was also concerned with the effect of long-term imprisonment and which also sought to describe it from the point of view of prisoners. Their work developed out of classes about sociology with long-term prisoners in the maximum security E-Wing of Durham prison. The classes soon developed into exchanges and conversations about a whole range of issues of mutual concern. Cohen and Taylor refer to these exchanges and conversations as 'talk' (Cohen and Taylor, 1977, p.68). This 'talk' was to become an essential component of research which Cohen and Taylor subsequently published in their book *Psychological Survival: The Experience of Long Term Imprisonment* (1972).

Psychological survival in Durham's E Wing

The use of 'talk' as a central pillar of the early researchers was in complete contrast to the more formal research protocols of a group of Home Office researchers, who, coincidentally, had arrived at the prison to carry out psychological research – using structured questionnaires and personality and other psychometric tests – to examine the effects of long-term imprisonment. Their research design was cross-sectional and involved formal interviews with prisoners serving different lengths of imprisonment with a view to testing hypotheses that the effect of imprisonment was to damage intellectual and other faculties. Findings of this research were published in a series of articles in the 1970s. One of these reports that length of imprisonment was not correlated with a reduction in intellectual faculties as measured by intelligence tests (Banister *et al.*, 1973). Further papers gave results derived from the administration of a large battery of standard personality inventories and showed that length of imprisonment was associated with a decrease in extraversion and an increase in hostility particularly as directed against the self. There did not, however, appear to be any effect on neuroticism, emotional stability or spontaneity (Heskin *et al.*, 1973, 1974). A retesting of prisoners and comparisons with an outside control group confirmed the changes in extraversion and in self-directed hostility (Bolton *et al.*, 1976). Overall, the research was highly statistical and within that tradition which emphasizes measurement, hypothesis-testing and explanations in psychological terms.

Theoretical and methodological commitments

To act as a balance to what they saw as an overly psychological approach, Cohen and Taylor suggested embarking on a collaborative research project on exactly the same topic as the Home Office researchers but with different theoretical and methodological thrusts. For example, Cohen and Taylor's aim was to focus on the way in which inmates subjectively interpreted and experienced long-term imprisonment with particular reference to the passage and marking of time, the significance of inmate subculture and the nature of inmate solidarity. Their work was to be discovery-based, being concerned with the description and formulation of ideas about these aspects rather than with the formal testing of hypotheses which is a feature of much of the psychological research which characterized the Home Office project. What is more, they were concerned with prisoners' deterioration in a much wider sense than could be measured by formal tests of cognitive ability. Cohen and Taylor's research was intended as inherently naturalistic, that is, concerned with uncovering the subjective experiences of the inmates in their natural surroundings and as they typically experienced them. As they point out:

> Our research did not look at a specifically constituted experimental environment – like the McGill coffin or the Ames room – but looked rather at a natural one which had been assembled in the real social and political world for a set of specific purposes over a long period of time. The environment, unlike its standard experimental counterpart, was already rich in symbolism, it had a known history and a forseeable future. In all these respects and others, it was unique.

(Cohen and Taylor, 1977, p.71)

Although 'talk' was central to the research, the data Cohen and Taylor collected gradually became more structured. For example, they asked the inmates to respond to specific questions and encouraged them to produce stories, essays and poems on particular topics. Such structured forms of data became the basis for further 'talk' and exchange of mutual interpretations. They also entered into a form of collaborative research in which subjects and researchers are viewed as equal partners and have some equal contribution to make to the final product. The rationale for such collaboration is that if subjects recognize themselves in research accounts this provides one way of establishing the validity of such accounts.

The recognition that the research act is a form of social interaction which all participants endow with meanings and definitions is of fundamental methodological significance since it is relevant to the debate about whether social scientists can, or should, be viewed as objective observers. In this case, however, it was also of critical political significance in terms of whether or not Cohen and Taylor would subsequently be allowed to continue with their research. The unstructured and informal methods of data collection and the recognition of, and use of, the subjects in the research were vital to the theoretical and methodological commitments of Cohen and Taylor. But it was perceived by Home Office officials as the antithesis of what they viewed as the correct protocols of more formal research methods such as experiments and surveys, and was used to justify the claim that Cohen and Taylor were not engaging in legitimate research. There was another way in which a concentration on informal methods, and on 'talk' in particular, contributed to the downfall of the project. Not only was 'talk' open to accusations of being 'unscientific' by prison authorities but it was also an activity over which these authorities have formal control. They have the power to prevent prisoners from talking to researchers and sought to do so partly under the cloak of arguing that the methodological justifications for such talk were not legitimate.

History of the project

So much for the theoretical and methodological underpinnings of Cohen and Taylor's work and the important part they played in its subsequent abortion. The following is a brief history of the research project (the description of events is largely drawn from the only comprehensive accounts available, those by Cohen and Taylor (1975, 1977). As indicated earlier, Cohen and

Taylor began their work with the inmates in the late 1960s and in 1969 formally outlined to the governor of the prison the way in which they hoped to develop their research and announced their intention to publish an article in the journal *New Society*. Cohen and Taylor believed that he was happy with these developments. The Prison Department of the Home Office were not. The department wrote to Cohen and Taylor outlining objections to the research largely on the grounds that their work was too concerned with particular aspects of long-term imprisonment and that its methodological approach was journalistic. Nevertheless, they continued with their classes and with collecting their material. The *New Society* article, entitled 'The experience of time in long term imprisonment', was published in 1970. It emphasized the ways in which prisoners experience and structure time and the way in which inmates seek to mark time in order to combat what for them is a major fear of deterioration during their imprisonment. The Home Office objected to the article because the authors had failed to get official clearance before publication, because of their belief that the research was too subjective and based on too small a number of inmates, and because of the failure, as they saw it, of the researchers to recognize that prison conditions were improving.

In 1971 E Wing was closed and the men were transferred to other prisons. The classes were obviously at an end. Cohen and Taylor had hopes of maintaining contact with the inmates. However, permission to visit them was refused and letters sent to inmates were returned on the grounds that such communications should not be used for research. Cohen and Taylor tried to retrieve their research programme by addressing one of the complaints that had been levelled at their work, namely, that it was based upon a small and unrepresentative sample. They proposed a follow-up project which would include two sub-samples, the original E-Wing inmates and another group of long-termers, but the Home Office rejected the idea of continuing with the original sample. The response of Cohen and Taylor was to publish their work to date in *Psychological Survival: The Experience of Long Term Imprisonment* (1972). The book re-emphasized the inmates' fear of deterioration and further elaborated their earlier analysis of the way in which prisoners handle time and seek to maintain their self-identity. It also contained a detailed rebuff of the accusation that they were referring to conditions which were no longer relevant and a critique of the methodological approach adopted by the Home Office sponsored researchers coupled to a justification of the methods of research they had themselves adopted. The publication of the book led to a further cooling of relations between the Home Office and the researchers. All was not lost, however, and negotiations were renewed at a later date. One positive development was a research proposal submitted by Cohen and Taylor which involved following the original Durham group and another group and included the use of more conventional questionnaire and interview methods. At one point Cohen and Taylor believed that their proposal had been accepted in principle and they even obtained a grant from the (then) Social Science Research Council to cover research costs. However, the Home Office subsequently insisted upon a number of controls upon the way in which the research was to be carried out, including restricted access and proposed censorship of the interview material by the Prison Department's officials. At this point, and in the face of these constraints, Cohen and Taylor abandoned their work.

No doubt the precise story of what did or did not happen in relation to this project can be the subject of differing interpretations and differing claims and counter-claims. This is not the place to enter into some adjudication of these. Rather, we can use the story, as told by Cohen and Taylor, to exemplify and further elaborate the dynamics and the interplay between subjects, researchers, gatekeepers and sponsors. There can be overlaps between the different categories of individuals who have an interest in the research, and in certain instances they can be one and the same. For example, where the Home Office commissions research into, say, the psychological effects of long term imprisonment, there is a considerable overlap between sponsor and gatekeeper and no doubt the researchers' problems of gaining formal access to subjects can be considerably eased. There is no reference, for instance, in the writings of Banister *et al.* (1973) to the problems of gaining access to prisoners at Durham nor in commissioned research carried out at other prisons at the same time (see, for example, Emery, 1970).

In some cases, alliances between different individuals or groups can emerge because such alliances are to the benefit of these individuals or groups, even where the respective interests are not necessarily the same. For example, the inmates of E Wing were concerned to tell their own story on their own terms and in the way in which they wanted, no doubt to alleviate the conditions in which they were imprisoned. In part, this complemented the aims and interests of the researchers who for theoretical reasons (to capture the subjective experiences) and methodological reasons (to do so as naturalistically as possible) were also interested in encouraging the men to tell their story in the way in which they wanted. The researchers also had an interest in alleviating the conditions for long-term prisoners but differed from the inmates in so far as they were concerned with following the well-established means of developing academic careers, that is, by making contributions to the existing stock of knowledge by the publication of books and papers. These differences apart, the subjects and the researchers formed an alliance of interests – albeit a relatively powerless alliance – in terms of wanting to continue with the project and see its conclusions published.

This is in contrast to the relationship between the inmates and the Home Office sponsored researchers where there is some evidence of conflicts of interest. The prisoners were interested in publishing the conditions which prevailed in E Wing and their effects upon those who endured them. They did not feel that these aims could be facilitated by the kind and style of research which was envisaged, and no doubt antagonisms were fuelled by the official sponsorship of the research. Cohen and Taylor described the reactions of the men as follows:

> In their many years of experience of the penal system, the men had built up a cynical attitude towards research in general and psychological research in particular. Psychologists 'come in and use you for other things they are doing outside', as one of them remarked. It was not therefore surprising to us that these researchers were met by a partial boycott; one member of the class was apparently delegated to inform them as politely as possible that the approach they were adopting did not meet with the approval of most of the men and would they therefore find some other subject.

(Cohen and Taylor, 1977, p.72)

Much more fundamental, however, was the clash of interests between Cohen and Taylor and the Prison Department of the Home Office. This highlights the importance of the role of gatekeepers in the pursuit of social research. In our preceding discussion we referred to 'gatekeeper' as if it were some single unitary position to be negotiated. In fact, there are often layers of gatekeepers to be negotiated and the gatekeepers are themselves in some hierarchical relationship with differentials of power between them. For example, what this case study reveals is two main gatekeepers – the prison governor and the Prison Department of the Home Office in London. Cohen and Taylor refer to keeping the governor fully informed of their work at all times and of their intentions to publish. The picture that is portrayed is of a local gatekeeper who had the power to prevent access but who was reasonably happy with the progress of the project, at least in its early stages. Of governors and other local officials Cohen and Taylor write:

> Throughout these years we had had many sympathetic contacts with Governors, Assistant Governors and prison psychologists. But this local support has counted for little. Such individuals are unable to give any public indication of their approval or disapproval; they may not even enter the public debate about prison life. This blanket of silence (justified by reference to the all-embracing Official Secrets Act) immunizes the system from criticism and positively encourages the type of 'sensation revelation – official denial' sequence which characterizes public information on our penal institutions.

> (Cohen and Taylor, 1977, p.85)

More crucial gatekeepers in prison research are officials within the Prison Department of the Home Office in London who are able to exercise power over local governors because of their position in the organizational hierarchy. The clash of interests between Cohen and Taylor and the Prison Department was fundamental to the eventual outcome of the project. The researchers wanted to carry out and publish research which was predominantly discovery-based, naturalistic and grounded in unstructured forms of data collection. They also wanted to be free of the constraints which surround official controls on data collection, analysis and publication. The Prison Department objected to the subject matter on several grounds. They felt that the research was focusing on what they perceived as the lurid aspects of long-term imprisonment; that Cohen and Taylor were not giving sufficient recognition to the viewpoint that conditions were improving; and that they were distorting official policy on long-term imprisonment. What is more, the very theoretical and methodological commitments at the centre of the research served to justify the claim by the Home Office that it was unscientific and therefore could not be relied upon to provide a valid picture and assessment of these aspects. The Prison Department held the power *vis-à-vis* the researchers who had little scope for bargaining. Cohen and Taylor summarize the sources of this power, and the means by which it was exercised, as follows:

(1) *Centralisation of power:* power centralised in the prison department with few discretionary powers given to local governors.

(2) *Legalisation of secrecy:* the use of the Official Secrets Act to prohibit the publication of anything discovered in the course of prison talk or observation.

(3) *Standardisation of research:* either carrying out its own research – through such bodies as the Home Office Research Unit – or using its definition of 'proper' research to exclude outsiders.

(4) *Mystifying the decision structure:* the impenetrability of civil service decision making.

(5) *Appealing to the public interest:* applying moral pressure by presenting a viewpoint of representing public interests.

Commentary: rights of subjects and researchers

The claims and counter-claims which surrounded the research at Durham prison, and its eventual outcome, illuminate aspects of the politics of social research. These relate to problems of gaining access to subjects who are in closed situations and where there are gatekeepers who have interests to protect – interests which are not the same as the subjects of the research – and who have the formal power to deny such access. In this instance, the gatekeepers had powers over the activities of both the subjects and the researchers. In addition to these formal powers they were able to mobilize informal mechanisms to abort the research (or at least to make it, in the eyes of the researchers, difficult to complete). In providing an illustration of the different parties at work – subjects, researchers, sponsors and gatekeepers – and the way in which they are able to protect their interests, the case study gives an insight into 'what is' or 'what can be'. However, it also raises issues about 'what should be', that is, about how power *should* be exercised in relation to research, with particular reference to the rights of different individuals and groups who are either central to the research or who are in some way affected by it. Here we restrict ourselves to brief comments about issues raised by the case study with particular reference to subjects and researchers.

The rights of the subjects of research are often discussed with reference to the doctrine of informed consent, a doctrine which asserts that subjects should be aware of any research and should give their consent to the part they play within it. The information which is given to subjects can vary. For example, they may simply be aware that the research is taking place; they may be told that they are the subjects within the research; they may be given details of the research procedures to be used; and they may be forewarned of the potential consequences, say, on publication. There is considerable discussion as to how far and over how many of these aspects the doctrine should extend. Let us take the basic right, that is, the right to know that one is participating in research and to have the option as to whether or not to participate in it. It has been argued by some (see, for example, Berreman, 1972) that deceit is a part of everyday life and therefore the social researcher who is interested in studying aspects of this life should not feel bound by ethical principles which dictate that subjects should know of their participation in such research. A fundamental assumption which is made here is that, whether or not such deceit is a part of everyday life, the researcher should grant to all citizens the right of letting them know that they are to become the subjects of research and thereby facilitate the opportunity to opt out of this role. This basic tenet becomes complicated when one is talking about inmates in a prison for they are not everyday citizens who have basic human rights. Some human rights have been removed from them because they have been convicted of criminal offences. However, there is no reason why suspension of such rights should extend to rights which are given to everyday citizens to know about their participation in social research and thereby choose whether or not to participate. The removal of the rights to freedom of liberty are very much part of the prisoner's role. Once that right is taken away prisoners should have the rights of everyday citizens and these should include rights in relation to the principle of informed consent. They have given up the positive freedom of liberty because of criminal actions but that does not mean that they should surrender the negative freedom to be free from the interference of others and particularly in this context the interference of social researchers. (For a discussion of the distinction between positive and negative freedom see Sir Isaiah Berlin's *Two Concepts of Liberty* (1958).)

The inmates in Durham's E Wing were told of the officially-sponsored research carried out by Banister *et al.* and had their own means of non-participation. A much more difficult question, however, is raised by the Cohen and Taylor project. This is whether inmates should have the positive rights to be involved in research which they see as being in their interests, say, in permitting them to express their feelings about the effects of long-term imprisonment, even where the authorities feel that it is not in the interests of the 'system' or of security and where authorities take decisions about participation in research on behalf of the inmates and without consulting them. Prisoners who have committed serious crimes quite rightly lose the most fundamental right of all, the fight to freedom. Provided their inclusion in properly conducted research does not threaten the curtailment of this freedom, prisoners should not be denied the right to participate in such research. Taking away an individual's freedom by incarceration should not take away that individual's freedom to know about research and to opt out of it. Equally, it should not take away that individual's positive right to know about research and to take part in it if he or she so wishes. Where authorities believe that there is a real danger that research may threaten prison or state security then they have an obligation to the researchers to make quite explicit the way in which such security is likely to be threatened. Hiding behind a cloak of secrecy is not sufficient. Equally, there is an obligation on the researcher not to undertake any work which is likely to result in the reduction of such security.

Reference to 'properly conducted research' raises the question of what is, and is not, legitimate methodology, and it touches upon the rights of researchers to carry out their trade in the way in which they feel most appropriate according to the theoretical and methodological commitments of the disciplines they represent. A fundamental tenet of this book is that criminological research is pluralistic and that it benefits from such pluralism because of the range of problems it addresses and the range of theoretical paradigms it uses to address them. The researcher should have the right to choose methods appropriate to what he or she is examining and to the theoretical ideas upon which he or she wishes to draw. There should be no constraint in terms of what gatekeepers or sponsors perceive as legitimate or properly conducted research. The value of contributions of any project, and any methodological approach adopted within such a project, can be assessed on publication of findings and should not be used at the point of entry into the research field to deny access to willing subjects.

References

Banister, P.A., Smith, F.V., Heskin, K.J. and Bolton, N. (1973) 'Psychological correlates of long-term imprisonment I: cognitive variables', *British Journal of Criminology*, vol.13, no.4, pp.312–23.

Berlin, Sir I. (1958) *Two Concepts of Liberty*, Oxford, Clarendon.

Berreman, G.D. (1972) *Hindus of the Himalays: Ethnography and Change*, Berkeley, CA, University of California Press.

Bolton, N., Smith, F.V., Heskin, K.J. and Banister, P.A. (1976) 'Psychological correlates of long-term imprisonment IV: a longitudinal analysis', *British Journal of Criminology*, vol.16, no.1, pp.38–47.

Bottoms, A.E. and McClintock, F.H. (1973) *Criminals Coming of Age*, London, Heinemann.

Boyle, J. (1977) *A Sense of Freedom*, London, Pan.

Cohen, S. and Taylor, L. (1972) *Psychological Survival: The Experience of Long Term Imprisonment*, Harmondsworth, Penguin.

Cohen, S. and Taylor, L. (1975) 'Prison research: a cautionary tale', *New Society*, vol.31, no.643, pp.253–5.

Cohen, S. and Taylor, L. (1977) 'Talking about prison blues', in Bell, C. and Newby, H. (eds) *Doing Sociological Research*, London, Allen and Unwin.

Emery, F.E. (1970) *Freedom and Justice Within These Walls: The Bristol Prison Experiment*, London, Tavistock.

Heskin, K.J., Bolton, N., Smith, F.V. and Banister, P.A. (1974) 'Psychological correlates of long-term imprisonment III: attitudinal variables', *British Journal of Criminology*, vol.14, no.3, pp.421–30.

Heskin, K.J., Smith, F.V., Banister, P.A. and Bolton, N. (1973) 'Psychological correlates of long-term imprisonment II: personality variables', *British Journal of Criminology*, vol.13, pp.323–30.

King, R.D. and Elliott, K.W. (1977) *Albany: Birth of a Prison – End of an Era*, London, Routledge and Kegan Paul.

McVicar, J. (1979) *McVicar by Himself*, London, Arrow.

Morris, T. and Morris, P. (1962) *Pentonville: A Sociological Study of an English Prison*, London, Routledge and Kegan Paul.

Probyn, W. (1977) *Angel Face: The Making of a Criminal*, London, Allen and Unwin.

(Source: Jupp, 1989, pp.138–48)

Chapter 2
The Politics of Criminological Research

by Gordon Hughes

Contents

1 Introduction

When you read about criminological research in texts and newspapers it may often appear that the research process follows a very systematic and detached logic informed by the particular epistemological and methodological premises of its line of enquiry. There is, of course, much truth in this broad impression which the reader gleans from studying the 'finished product' of criminological research. However, this rather antiseptic and tidy picture may, by itself, give students of criminology a dangerously skewed and false impression of the realities of actually 'doing research'. All too often research publications fail to tell us about the hidden outcrops on the apparently smooth surface of the research process. What, for example, are the realities of doing research on humans in social groups and institutions where political and ethical dilemmas cannot be neatly sanitized and controlled, unlike doing research in the purified atmosphere of the physical scientist's laboratory?

In order to answer this question this chapter will take you on a chronological journey through the major stages of the research process from inception to completion. In this way, we will attempt to uncover the various ways in which politics not only impacts upon research, but in part may be said to constitute the very form that research agendas take. The aim of this chapter, then, is to help you gain an informed and critical understanding of the varying political and moral contexts which impact on criminological research in contemporary society.

In pursuing this general aim, the chapter will focus on a number of influential research projects which have both 'opened up' the criminal justice system and categories of crime to investigation and highlighted the political nature of criminological research. These range, *inter alia*, from studies of rank-and-file police sub-cultures and explorations of the meanings of delinquency among contemporary youth to the investigation of penal regimes. It will be suggested that much criminological research in the UK since the 1970s has played a significant role in partially opening up the worlds of 'the criminalized', 'the criminal' and the workings of the often secretive parts of the criminal justice system. This noted, we will also consider the politics of what Cohen (1981) has termed 'mainstream criminological' research which has been constituted by a very different agenda from much critical social scientific research (see Chapter 1). In particular, we will examine the extent to which the hidden political agendas of technocratic, positivist and current 'administrative' criminology have been the historical construction of 'the criminal' as pathological object and the legitimation of dominant criminal justice practices. Here again it will be argued that the influence of politics cannot be avoided in any adequate understanding of criminological research, both past and present. As a consequence, the overall thrust of this chapter is that the development of criminological research is inherently and integrally bound up with wider political conflict and debate, whether or not this is overt (see, for example, Reiner, 1989). Finally, the chapter will explore the different political and ethical issues thrown up by research studies from the plurality and diversity of 'perspectives' to be found in contemporary criminology (as introduced in Chapter 1).

2 Defining 'political'

All social science has a political dimension, in the non-party political sense. All aspects of research necessarily involve the researcher in both the analysis and practice of power and, in turn, have the potential to generate conflicts of interest between a whole host of potentially interested parties.

ACTIVITY 2.1

Take the example of one aspect of research, namely publication. Think of all the potential parties who may have an interest in, and a potential source of conflict/power struggle over, a project on why young people break the law with regard to under-age drinking.

Draw up a list of the different interest groups potentially affected by the publication of the research findings and the differential impact of research findings on each group.

COMMENT

Amongst the myriad of interest groups, the following immediately come to mind:

- Young under-age drinkers may find that their activities are perhaps subject to unwelcome surveillance and may be even more concerned about the effects of the publication of the results and any media-generated 'moral panic' which may ensue.

- Parents are likely to be affected by any publicity about the deviant behaviour of youth and may meet pressure to monitor and 'police' the leisure activities of their children.

- Schools may come under heightened pressure to teach children morally acceptable practices and thus come into conflict with some of their pupils.

- The police and the courts may be encouraged to deal proactively and more harshly with young offenders and guilty licensees should the study show high levels of under-age drinkers.

- Licensees of public houses and off-licences are another interest group affected by any publicity about the issue, who may, as a result, engage in more strict control and monitoring of their customers.

- The local authority may come under pressure to improve leisure facilities, should lack of alternative modes of recreation be cited as a factor.

- Health agencies may wish to run health promotion campaigns to try and deter under-age drinking.

- The government itself may have to respond with legislation should high rates of criminality around under-age drinking be discovered.

- Finally, the mass media is a powerful secondary definer of social problems and the link between youth and crime is a traditional and successful newsline for the press, television and radio.

No doubt more groups could be cited, but this selective list conveys the complex nature of the audiences which may greet any published criminological research.

It becomes clear that the study of people and institutions may necessarily intrude on privacy at times, may subvert deeply held moral beliefs and practices, and may uncover unwelcome truths for some groups which may be very welcome truths for others. As we will see later, research into the attitudes and potential prejudices among agents of the criminal justice system has highlighted the inevitability of political and, thus, ethical controversy in a very clear and explicit fashion. No criminological research takes place in a political and normative vacuum. If it did so, how very dull the criminological enterprise would be.

All social settings and institutions (not just 'total institutions' with closed doors and barred windows) raise questions of access (such as whether you will be permitted entry), questions of confidentiality of your findings, and ethical dilemmas (such as gaining the trust of people and uncovering and publishing disturbing truths). This is the broad meaning of criminological research being necessarily *political* in character. When 'political' is conceptualized as concerning questions of control, authority, conflict and power alliances and struggles, it becomes obvious that criminological research cannot avoid the epithet of being political. As Arber notes, research cannot be context-free and 'in reality, research takes place in a political context, including the micropolitics of interpersonal relationships and the politics of research units' (Arber, 1993, p.33).

More obviously and no less importantly for criminological research is the second sense of the word 'political', relating to explicit political ideologies and organized coercive institutional power, most apparent in the modern state. This second meaning of political is of crucial importance for research agendas and projects in criminology, given that so much criminological investigation is *de facto* the study of state power in its starkest form. As a student of the social sciences, you will be aware that much of our work both challenges and subverts the dominant taken-for-granted assumptions about the world. Hudson's comparative research into penal policy in contemporary societies provides us with an illustrative example of how research may be given extra impetus by its opposition to the prevailing dominant political climate (in this case that of the UK in the mid 1980s) (Hudson, 1993). Hudson recounts her experience of a senior Home Office official discussing the new 'twin-track' or bifurcated approach to punishment whereby only the most serious offenders would be sent to prison for punishment, whilst punishment in the community would be used for offenders of 'middle range' seriousness (see **Book 2, Chapter 5**). This dominant political view that prisons were to be filled by only serious offenders departed from Hudson's own initial survey findings in that 'the people I saw going into custody were very different from the serious offenders who so monopolized the attentions of managers and policy-makers' (Hudson, 1993, p.2). Hudson's subsequent research thus, in part, grew out of a conscious reaction to current dominant thinking on crime which was predicated on what she termed 'penological' thinking rather than on a 'welfare' approach to crime and justice. As a result of her research, Hudson effectively shows that, while there may be disparity and temporal variability in offences producing imprisonment, there was clear consistency and stability in the vulnerability of those who were homeless, mentally ill or unemployed and especially in the vulnerability of unemployed black offenders across most European countries (Hudson, 1993, p.3). Such a finding across different societies challenged the dominant discourse of the nature of the offender and offered a radical critique of existing penal and social policy.

However, we must recognize that criminological knowledge may also be used to lend 'scientific' credibility to prevailing dominant ideological assumptions. We will thus encounter examples of criminological research which have supported dominant ideological discourses on, for example, 'race' and gender inequality (see **Lombroso and Ferrero, 1895**). Indeed, Cain and Smart (1989) suggest controversially that the whole *raison d'être* of criminology is that of being part of society's regulatory discourses.

However, it is also common for criminological research, particularly its critical tradition, to question dominant ideologies of human nature and human behaviour. If a clamp-down on political rights and dissent does arrive, it is likely that *critical* social science would be subject to censorship, if not to legal ban. The social science that does survive repressive control may wither on the branch as an independent, reflexive and critical activity. An example which comes to mind of such withered fruit was the crude functionalism which ironically dominated criminological thinking in both the former Soviet Union and the USA in the 1950s across the Cold War divide. In both countries, a crude emphasis was placed on crime being understood as a pathological condition standing outside and opposed to the consensual majority's 'normality'.

On the basis of the foregoing discussion, it will be apparent that it is difficult to separate out the necessarily interrelated political dimensions to the research process in criminology. Indeed, criminology itself is arguably a politically contested term, given the discipline's own sullied history. In the words of Theodor Sellin, criminology is 'a bastard science grown out of the public preoccupation with a social plague' (Sellin, 1938, quoted in Bottomley, 1979). You will already be aware that many contemporary theorists of crime and criminalization reject the term 'criminology' as a description of their own theorizing and research activities for the very reason that much 'positivist' criminology in particular has, arguably, been on the side of the 'overdog' rather than the 'underdog' in much of its research (see Chapter 1 and **Reader Guide 1, section 7**).

This section will have alerted you to the definitional complexities surrounding the phrase 'the politics of criminological research'.

3 Doing research in a political world

It is a basic tenet of this chapter that criminological research, in its variety of perspectives, does not take place in a political and moral vacuum despite the silence of positivist and traditional criminology with regard to questions of political bias and power. To paraphrase Bell and Newby, criminological research is a 'deeply *"political"* process' (Bell and Newby, 1977, our emphasis). However, this deeply political process is often hidden in the 'finished' published product of research. At best, we may have a chapter or an appendix on the realities of research; more often it is in the brief preface that the reader may get a hint of the sponsor and the important contacts which underpin the research project.

In what follows we will work our way, chronologically, through the key stages of the research process, drawing on illustrative examples from influential research projects. In the course of this metaphorical journey you will be asked to adopt the role of the fictitious researcher confronted by challenges at the various stages through which you hypothetically pass.

For the sake of analytical clarity, the following stages may be distinguished (in reality, it is not possible to 'pigeon-hole' these stages so neatly):

- getting started
- gaining support/sponsorship
- gaining access
- gathering the data
- publishing the results
- utilization of the research

3.1 Getting started: seeing the problem and asking the question

All research involves the asking of questions about a particular problem and even at this initial point of departure for criminological enquiry we cannot avoid politics. There are instances, for example, when we may not be allowed to ask certain questions, as in a situation defined as involving 'national security'. Thus, the role of the British Forces' Special Air Service (SAS) in Northern Ireland, and its possible links to assassinations of suspect 'terrorists', might have been a potential research problem which would have been extremely difficult and dangerous to try to investigate. Brewer, writing of his research assistant, Magee's, own research into routine policing by the Royal Ulster Constabulary (RUC) in Northern Ireland during the 1980s, admits that the original plan to study public order policing proved impossible 'in the midst of the province's continuing conflict' (Brewer, 1991, p.13). This may be due to the risks to both researcher and researched, but it is also likely that the British government would not have officially countenanced such sensitive research. Of course, the influence of state power is often not so transparent. Adopting Lukes' three-dimensional view of power (Lukes, 1974), power is often most effective when decisions are not explicit but, rather, when the influence over others is hidden. Political influence may often be most telling when no decision has been made. In the context of research, the influence of dominant ideologies and institutional practices may be most evident when researchers do not even think to ask 'awkward' questions! With the privilege of retrospect, we may see how the early criminology of Italian positivism effectively took on board the hegemonic political agenda of the late nineteenth century in theorizing the significance of the 'inherited' attributes of class, 'race' and sex (see **Reader Guide 1, section 3.1.1**).

The very formulation of a research question or hypothesis is surrounded by the political constraints noted above and the obverse of this, namely political opportunities. Political currents and counter-currents do not just wash over a research culture but instead help construct its agenda. The rise of labelling perspective research in the 1960s (see **Reader Guide 1, section 5.1**) would, of course, be inexplicable without some awareness of its debt to the radical libertarian politics of the period. Another very obvious example of a political current which has drastically reshaped the research agenda of late in criminology is the rise of feminist movements since the late 1960s (see **Reader Guide 1, section 5.3** and **Reader Guide 2, section 8**).

ACTIVITY 2.2

Referring to Reader article 41, 'Feminist approaches to criminology or postmodern woman meets atavistic man', by Carol Smart; article 42, 'Towards transgression: new directions in feminist criminology', by Maureen Cain; and article 43, 'Criminal women and criminal justice: the limits to, and potential of, feminist and left realist perspectives', by Pat Carlen, outline how feminism has affected:

1   the research agenda;
2   the focus of research; and
3   the methods of enquiry used in contemporary criminology.

COMMENT

Perhaps most critically, where not so long ago criminology was largely 'gender-blind', it is now acknowledged that gender differences in criminalization and victimization are crucial to criminological analysis. Furthermore, with regard to the nature of professional decision-making, the existence of distinct gendered discourses is now foregrounded in much current criminology (see, for example, Newburn and Stanko, 1995). New questions are now being asked – to the point of questioning criminology itself. It is arguable that the counter-current of feminism against the dominant political tide in modern society has even caused some changes of viewpoint in such places as the Home Office and other portals of the crime industry's establishment (for example, publication of data on gender and ethnic monitoring for the criminal justice system is now mandatory following the Criminal Justice Act 1991). Finally, qualitative and autobiographical data have been given renewed authority as valuable methods of enquiry in criminology (for example, Carlen's work *Criminal Women*, 1985, is structured around conversations and interviews with ex-women prisoners who 'tell' their life stories).

Any undue optimism does need to be tempered by the awareness of the political constraints which continue to impact on criminological research. For example, research on gun-related crimes in Manchester or Los Angeles of the so-called 'underclass' is much more likely to be looked upon favourably by official sponsors than any research on state-related crimes and misdemeanours. An example of the latter was the 1994 controversy involving the British government, British arms dealers and the provision of aid to the Malaysian government. As a result of what was called the Pergau Dam deal with the Malaysian government, the provision of aid and the sale of weapons were not so subtly merged by the British government (Pilger, 1994; see also **Book 1, Chapter 7**).

The difficulty of starting research in the face of opposition from the state is graphically illustrated by the example of police research in the 'old' South Africa. Commenting on the paucity of research on the South African police and their own reliance on secondary data from the media, Brogden and Shearing (1993) clearly show the immense influence of political power on the nature of the research process. Noting that in South Africa most state practices have been defined as beyond legitimate public concern and, thus, academic enquiry, Brogden and Shearing go on to note that there was a methodological impasse with regard to obtaining reliable data on the South African police: 'It is no fault of critical South African academics that research on policing in South Africa is notable for its relative barrenness ... Parliamentary debates have indicated that the line between criticizing the police and subverting the "national interest" has been a very thin one' (Brogden and Shearing, 1993, p.192). As a consequence, Brogden and Shearing had to rely largely on newspaper reports as a major source of illustrative material in putting together their analysis of the operation and *raison d'être* of the 'old' South African police force.

Most criminological research in contemporary democracies does not encounter such obvious or overt opposition as that which faced these researchers. However, extreme examples or *causes célèbres* are important in revealing the limits of open government. The classic example of state control and censorship from British research into the criminal justice system remains that of Cohen and Taylor's study of life-sentence prisoners at Durham Prison (Cohen and Taylor, 1972). We will discuss this research study more fully in section 3.2.2 below which concerns the issues of gaining support and sponsorship. Suffice it to say that Cohen and Taylor encountered state opposition (particularly from the Home Office) towards both the further development of the research project and publication of their provisional results. As a consequence, they were unable to get started on the fuller research project which they hoped would grow out of their original investigation. Here, then, is an example of not being allowed to ask questions which may threaten the legitimacy of the state, albeit that in the view of one leading criminologist, 'the freedom of access to information and the freedom to interpret and publish findings [is] a prerequisite for any really incisive and honest research' (Radzinowicz, 1994, p.103). The melancholy but salutary lesson, from this and other research studies of the criminal justice system, is that the authorities may wield great power over the nature of the research that it is possible to undertake.

3.2 Gaining support and sponsorship

What, then, are the routine channels through which to gain sponsorship for research? It should be noted that different theoretical approaches tend to generate specific research strategies and, in turn, look to different 'sponsors'. Nor should we assume that research strategies are created outside 'sponsor' and gatekeeper influence. As Lee notes: 'the agendas themselves arise as the by-product of a set of preferences by funding gatekeepers for research having a particular character' (Lee, 1993, p.25).

These preferences, Lee continues, typically include a concern for 'relevance' or utility to the policy process, individualistic explanations which locate 'pathology' at the level of the individual rather than at the structural level and, finally, quantitative findings which have a 'hard' scientific appeal (Lee, 1993). There is a danger of exaggerating the one-way nature of the relationship between academic research and the sponsor, which Lee himself acknowledges. Too much emphasis is thus often given to the 'demand' side of the relationship (that is, the sponsor) and not enough to the 'supply' side (that is, the researcher).

Given the principle of academic autonomy, researchers do not always 'supply' their sponsors with what they may wish to hear. Indeed, not all sponsored research is uncritical of the status quo or subservient to the interests of the sponsor. The research programme of the government-funded Economic and Social Research Council (ESRC) on criminal justice in the 1980s produced explicitly critical findings on government and Home Office criminal justice policy in virtually all its projects, ranging from studies of penal policy to those of community consultation and policing (Downes, 1992). In his introduction to the collection of ESRC research studies, Downes criticizes the 'myth' (associated with the Conservative government) that academic research is an ivory tower pursuit with little connection with the 'real world' of wealth creation and practical affairs. According to Downes, this myth helped fuel the contraction of the necessary public investment in the sector in the 1980s.

To take one illustrative example from the programme, King and McDermott's study 'Security, control and humane containment in the prison system in England and Wales' (1992) clearly shows the critical possibilities opened up by state-funded research. King and McDermott investigated five representative prisons in the Midlands in order to compare current conditions with those in the 1970s. Drawing on such indicators as length of time in cell and amount of time available for work, training and education, the study showed a depressing picture of deterioration in conditions: 'In every comparison much less time was spent in work or similar activities today than had been the case fifteen or more years ago' (King and McDermott, 1992, p.104). Their policy recommendations were suitably critical of current government policy on sentencing and penal policy. King and McDermott recommended a 'minimum-use-of-custody' principle for government and the courts which would bring the prison population into line with existing resources; a 'minimum-use-of-security' principle to alleviate the deterioration of conditions within prison; and, finally, legally enforceable standards of custody to ensure that resources were maintained at levels appropriate for the tasks of the prison service (King and McDermott, 1992).

Although such research stopped short of calling for the abolition of the prison, there is little doubt that this example illustrates the relative autonomy of academic-sponsored research from the ideological preoccupations of the dominant authorities. We shall see later, however, that it is quite another thing to argue that such well-informed and objective research-based recommendations will have any noticeable effect on government policy on law and order.

Having noted the important qualification about academic autonomy and critique, let us now explore how the different means of gaining support may involve different political constraints and opportunities for the researcher. The typical sponsors for criminological research range from direct state sponsorship (for example, Home Office and Royal Commissions) to relatively autonomous government research councils (for example, ESRC) through to local government support (for example, borough and county councils), private charitable organizations (for example, the Joseph Rowntree Foundation), university departments and employer organizations (Bulmer, 1982). Each of these sponsors will bring different political agendas to the researcher–sponsor relationship.

3.2.1 The changing institutional context

As a backdrop to the whole research process, the broad changes in the institutional context of criminological research during the twentieth century need to be pencilled in. Our starting point is to offer an outline of the political economy of criminological research.

May notes that: 'The majority of social research in Britain is sponsored by governments, or other agencies with a vested interest in the results. This is not to say that this necessarily invalidates any conclusions because the work is "interested" as opposed to "disinterested" (often assumed to be a characteristic of scientific activity)' (May, 1993, pp.34–5). May's general point and qualifying remark at the end of the statement are both important. Sponsored research is not necessarily a latter-day myrmidon or obedient servant of its 'boss'. However, we do need to be aware of the issues which surround the production of research. Questions such as who funds or requests the research, what is the main aim of the research, and how might the results be disseminated and publicized all need to be kept in mind when looking at the finished product. As May notes again: 'This enables an understanding of the context in which research takes place and the influences upon it, as well as countering the tendency to see the production and design of research as a technical issue uncontaminated by political and ethical questions' (May, 1993, p.35). Such an understanding does not make the research process invalid, but will heighten one's awareness and knowledge of the whole research process in criminology.

3.2.2 Excursus on the 'secret state': the closed world of criminal justice

Most criminological research may be defined as 'sensitive' research in that it has potentially serious consequences for both research participants in, or the individuals represented by, the research (Lee, 1993). Much of criminology's findings may also be surrounded by political and moral controversy in that it 'illuminates the dark corners of society' (Lee, 1993, p.2). Not least among our society's 'dark corners' is that of the criminal justice system itself! Thus the Official Secrets Act (OSA) of 1911 effectively established certain research terrains which were 'no-go areas' for independent scholarly work. The OSA was amended in 1989 and the infamous catch-all section 2, whereby it was made an offence to receive any information covered by the Act, was removed. However, as Lee notes, anything defined as officially protected information is arguably subject to even tighter control and the impact of this amendment remains to be seen (Lee, 1993, p.23).

The most famous example of criminological research in the UK to come under the withering gaze of this 'secret state' is the previously mentioned research of Cohen and Taylor on life-sentence prisoners in Durham Prison's E Wing (Cohen and Taylor, 1972; see also Chapter 1, Appendix 1.1). This much-discussed project may act as a useful exemplar to illustrate the highly charged political climate in which penal research in particular has to operate.

The research project focused on prisoners' 'talk' about how they coped with long-term imprisonment and it departed from the positivist psychological work previously carried out on 'psychological deterioration'. The research pointed to the brutalizing effects of institutionalization which are compounded by the tyranny of a sense of endless time, unbroken by the escape routes available to most of us 'outside'. For the Home Office, such a project was 'unscientific' given its qualitative methodology, its small sample and its subjective approach. It was also suggested by the Home Office that the research ignored the fact that conditions in prisons were improving (Cohen and Taylor, 1977).

At the end of their 'battle' with the Home Office, Cohen and Taylor offered an analysis of the political power of the Home Office over criminological research which arguably still resonates to this day. Five sources of power are distinguished by the authors, namely:

1 centralization of power in the prison department
2 legalization of secrecy, particularly through the OSA
3 standardization of research
4 mystification of the decision structure, given the impenetrability of civil service decision-making
5 appeal to public interest

(as adapted from Jupp, 1989, p.146).

The power of the Home Office to set limiting criteria in terms of a customer–contractor basis for deciding on the agenda of research to be funded has been questioned by Radzinowicz (1994). Radzinowicz repeats the warning of other academics that this development:

> can lead to the agenda for research being set in relation to the administrators' (and ultimately the Minister's) conception of what kind of knowledge is needed. Moreover, it will also lead to a preference for short-term inquiries on matters of immediate concern which are regarded as politically or administratively urgent.

> (Radzinowicz, 1994, p.101)

In like vein, Holdaway has expressed fears about the recent pressure to give the 'customer'/patron what they want: '"relevance", "evaluation" and "monitoring" form the sacred canopy of this academic age' (Holdaway, 1989, p.66). The dangers to criminology of this institutional pressure for 'policy-relevant' research are multifold, but, most pressingly, they may lead to a dissolution of genuine analytical questions due to the pressure again of giving the 'customer' what it narrowly defines as relevant.

3.2.3 A grudging 'Perestroika'? The partial opening of the criminal justice system to criminological research

It would be inaccurate to exaggerate the closed nature of the criminal justice system in the UK. For example, in the early 1990s there was some evidence of the Home Office's willingness to have parts of the system monitored. In part, this was due to the legal requirements of the Criminal Justice Act of 1991 whereby 'race' and gender monitoring of the criminal justice system was required to be published annually. To some extent, this partial opening up of the system to research arose out of a concern for the legitimacy which external 'audits' (to use the language of 'new managerialism' – Clarke *et al.*, 1994) offered public services.

An illustrative example of a research study which has been the beneficiary of a limited 'Perestroika' (or the opening up of a previously closed world) is Genders and Player's study *Race Relations in Prisons* (1989). This study was commissioned and funded by the Home Office Research and Planning Unit (HORPU) on the basis of a senior academic's suggestion. As the authors note, research on race relations has been absent from studies of

British prisons and their own study was thus mapping out 'largely unchartered territory' (Genders and Player, 1989, p.v). In their two-year study of (primarily) three prison establishments they were granted access to interview 140 inmates and 83 prison officers, to observe the daily routines in the prisons and, finally, to analyse over 1,000 classification records to check for disparaging language and racial stereotyping in the formal assessments of prisoners. Their findings were perhaps unsurprising in that they showed the existence of racial stereotyping and discrimination. Black prisoners did get differential (and lesser) opportunities compared with white prisoners. Furthermore, staff used racial stereotyping to:

> justify and rationalize the belief that it is only possible to go so far in pursuing the goal of fairness and equality before a conflict arises with the goals of maintaining order or organizational efficiency. In choosing the latter, staff reinforce the advantage of the White majority to the relative disadvantage of ethnic minority inmates.

> (Genders and Player, 1989, p.134)

This research study ends with several recommendations to the Prison Department to help overcome the stumbling blocks they identify for the successful implementation of the Department's anti-discriminatory policy.

It is debatable how influential such independent studies are on actual policy and practice in the Prison Service, but this example does show that the Home Office is not a monolithic bastion whose every gate is forever closed to academic scrutiny.

3.3 Gaining access

In order to carry out criminological research you often need to get into an institution or an informal grouping and make contact with the people you wish to study. The problem of access does not end, however, once you are 'in'. Instead, gaining access involves an on-going process of negotiation and renegotiation. In particular, a crucial role is played by key individuals (termed 'gatekeepers' in the academic literature). Burgess defines gatekeepers as follows: 'those individuals in an organisation that have the power to grant or withhold access to people or situations for the purposes of research' (Burgess, 1984, p.48).

It is important to note that such gatekeepers are not necessarily synonymous with being formally in charge of a given institution or group. As with many sites of research, there are often multiple points of entry into an institution or social setting. Thus any research into the existence of an informal sub-culture among police officers would need to have access to the rank-and-file 'canteen culture' rather than the formal policy statements of senior police managers if it is to explore the issue in an adequate fashion (Smith and Gray, 1983; see also **Book 2, Chapter 2**). Formal access will thus often be only the start of the real access process in criminological research.

It is also important to clarify the differences of degree in the relative openness of access. As Hornsby-Smith notes, openness of access 'relates to questions of power of those being studied to exclude intrusive enquiry, and the overtness or covertness of the research methods being employed' (Hornsby-Smith, 1993, p.52).

ACTIVITY 2.3

Taking an example of two starkly different phenomena, write notes on the different problems of accessing information about the incidence of criminality among London's homeless youth as against that of the unreported crimes of City financiers. Note that 'studying down' (that is, of vulnerable minority groups) is much easier and commonplace in criminology than is 'studying up' of powerful élites.

COMMENT

Homeless youth is subject to much more public scrutiny than City financiers, whether we are referring to the policing of their behaviours, to media reportage or, indeed, to academic research. The young homeless as a vulnerable group also lack formal protection from academic scrutiny. It would be quite straightforward to investigate known offenders among homeless youth with likely high levels of subsistence crime, such as shoplifting, vagrancy and begging. However, there may be significant social barriers to studying, in an ethnographic manner, the everyday activities and motives of youth on the street. Such young people are likely to be highly suspicious of intruders, especially middle-class and middle-aged criminologists!

In contrast, City financiers possess a great many resources for maintaining their privacy and freedom from intrusion from academic researchers who may wish to study such crime as unreported fraud. Closed doors and many gatekeepers will confront any rare researcher who wishes to study business-suite crime. Undercover research would be possible but very difficult given the problem of 'passing' as a financier due to the technical knowledge required of the researcher (see **Book 1, Chapter 6**).

The gaining of access ('getting in') may also be highly procedurized or personalized (Lee, 1993, p.124). An example of a highly procedurized relationship would be the conditional access associated with conditions laid down by the Official Secrets Act in the UK. Much of the research undertaken for the Home Office Research and Policy Unit would fall into this category of procedurized access, with HORPU maintaining the right to examine and modify any material to be published. To take another example from research which has already been mentioned in section 3.1, Brewer, in commenting on the difficulties of gaining access to members of the Royal Ulster Constabulary due to the general concern over security, both personal and statist, has noted that members of the RUC need to obtain official permission before they are allowed to talk to strangers about their role. If RUC officers break this rule they are likely to face dismissal from the force. Covert research, Brewer suggests, is in this case unethical: 'no researcher should expose respondents to that possibility [of the sack]' (Brewer, 1991, p.16).

Accordingly, Brewer argues that it was necessary for his researcher, Magee, 'to undertake an overt study and to obtain permission for the research from the Chief Constable' (Brewer, 1991, p.17). The obvious question to ask is whether the research was subsequently constrained by having such procedurized access granted by top officialdom. To this question, Brewer responds that: 'once permission was granted, no limits were laid down by senior officers and no censorship role has been retained by the RUC over the final manuscript' (Brewer, 1991, p.17).

In contrast, a more personalized mode of access often involves a designated chaperone to escort the researcher down the metaphorical corridors of the research process. Such access may also be very restricted in that the apparent openness may, in practice, mean that the researcher gets sent down wrong corridors and the personalized chaperone may control the nature of the information gathered.

There is also likely to be an imbalance of power between gatekeeper and researcher which in turn will lead to bargaining between the two parties: the so-called 'research bargain'. If researching is viewed as being potentially threatening, the process may generate what is often termed 'the politics of distrust' whereby each side is suspicious and secretive about the activities of the other. Perhaps unsurprisingly, gatekeepers tend to prefer methods which are thought to deliver 'hard facts' and which as a result offer some scope for scrutiny and control by themselves, thus explaining the attraction of quantitative surveys and questionnaires rather than qualitative observation and interviews (Lee, 1993, p.124).

3.3.1 Social access ('getting on' after 'getting in')

ACTIVITY 2.4

Imagine that you are a researcher who has been given formal approval by the Chief Probation Officer in your region to conduct research on a probation office, investigating how the staff respond to the government initiative on electronic tagging of offenders. In other words, you are 'physically' through the gate. What 'social' barriers to access are you likely to encounter?

COMMENT

The first barrier is the problem of being a stranger in a world in which much knowledge is taken for granted. Thus, even if there is no opposition to the research from the staff, it may be difficult to gain access to the occupational practices and beliefs of the probation workers.

Second, there may well be opposition from the rank-and-file staff to what may be perceived as a 'top-down' initiative and thus the researcher may well experience a form of 'chilling out' from the researched.

Third, the staff may put up informal barriers to revealing the truth about their practices and beliefs about the implementation of electronic tagging. Probation workers may, for example, give the 'policy line' on the initiative whilst operating differently with their clients in situations of 'low visibility discretion'.

There is a hierarchy of consent in all formal organizations. It would be very dangerous to assume that 'superiors' (that is, formal gatekeepers) have the right to allow 'subordinates' to be investigated. It is not uncommon for researchers to get formal physical access without the accompanying informal social access. We may term this 'the micro-politics of research'. This situation should alert us to the significance of informal gatekeepers who may erect non-official barriers or fronts. To cite the example of Magee's ethnographic research on the RUC once more (Brewer, 1991), access to the force was granted eventually by senior officers since allowing such research to take place would look good as a form of public relations exercise and would show that the RUC was open to public scrutiny. There was thus a pay-off for senior echelons of the RUC in terms of their professional ethos. However, it was likely that the research would be less popular with the rank-and-file police officers who ran the risks of answering awkward questions and being observed doing their often 'messy' work. Having dealt with the first gate of the senior 'gatekeepers', Magee had a much more difficult task gaining 'social' access through the informal gate of the rank and file. Gaining the trust of this group was to prove a long drawn-out process, in Brewer's words 'a result of a progressive series of negotiations ... continually negotiated' (Brewer, 1991, p.19).

One illustrative example of the officers' fears of being observed by a 'stranger' concerned explicitly the religious affiliation, and implicitly the gender, of the key researcher Magee. One officer in the overwhelmingly protestant RUC confronted Magee quite early on in the research process with the question: 'How do we know we can trust you? What religion are you? How do I know I can trust you if I don't know what religion you are?' (Brewer, 1991, p.22). When informed by Magee that she was a Catholic, the general response of the officers was to define her as a 'good' Catholic who proved herself largely by her willingness to do all the anti-social shifts which officers themselves least liked.

Another classic illustration of this phenomenon of informal gates and obstacles to access arose in Punch's research on the Amsterdam police (Punch, 1993). Punch describes his own approach to doing beat patrol research as follows: 'The researcher's task becomes, then, how to outwit the institutional obstacle-course to gain entry and how to penetrate the mine-field of social defences to reach the inner reality of police work' (Punch, 1993, p.184). Punch's preferred strategy for penetrating this mine-field was prolonged participant observation which would enable him to tap into the discretionary activities of the beat officer. Even with such a sensitive approach to observational research, Punch only discovered a depth of corruption to policing in Amsterdam at the very end of the research process at a party when several officers talked of the corruption which Punch had missed: 'a subterranean police culture which had largely escaped me suddenly emerged' (Punch, 1993, p.192).

The personal hazards of detailed ethnographic research are humorously well stated by Hobbs with regard to his experiences of studying policing and working-class crime in the East End of London:

> For the most part I spoke, acted, drank and generally behaved as though I was not doing research. Indeed, I often had to remind myself that I was not in a pub to enjoy myself but to conduct an academic enquiry and repeatedly woke up the following morning with an incredible hangover facing the dilemma of whether to bring it up or write it up.
>
> (Hobbs, 1988, p.6)

Through the illustrative example of the police, we have noted that it is very difficult to negotiate successful access to the routine operation of the criminal justice system and its practitioners. The growing body of research on the rank-and-file police officer (for an overview see Reiner, 1992) has uncovered some important findings with regard to such phenomena as the role of discretion in routine police decision-making and the importance of the informal occupational 'cop culture' in moulding rank-and-file attitudes.

However, very little is known of the life of the men and the (few) women at the top. Access to élites in the criminal justice system is rare for researchers. An exception to this rule is Reiner's study of chief constables in England and Wales (Reiner, 1991). As Reiner himself observes:

> The police research literature is replete with studies of canteen-cop culture, seen as the key to understanding street-level policing. Nothing, however, was known of the top-cop culture, presumably the key to understanding suite-level policing. It was my intention to investigate this, but the denouement – their personal subordination to the Home Office – is not what I anticipated at the outset.
>
> (Reiner, 1991, p.344)

Reiner's findings were undoubtedly important in opening up a still murky area of policing politics in which the existence of a *de facto* national police force appears to be under construction from central government. It may be a salutary lesson to any budding 'élite studies' researcher to read Reiner's frank reflections on the attenuated process of negotiating access to the chief constables which accompanied his research proposal.

ACTIVITY 2.5

Now read the extract from Robert Reiner, 'Assisting with inquiries: studying a criminal justice élite', which is reproduced as Appendix 2.1 at the end of this chapter. As you do so, address the following questions:

1   What major problems of 'access' did Reiner encounter from the Home Office?
2   In what ways did Reiner use informal means of 'social access' to gain chief constable support for his interviews?

It is highly probable that researchers are 'checked out' by information-gathering institutions such as the police in terms of their previous work and political affiliations. In what has been termed the era of 'late modernity' (Giddens, 1991), the institutions of the criminal justice system are likely to be knowledgeable and reflexive and quite often the researcher's reputation will precede him or her. This may create complex problems for the researcher in 'passing over' as a legitimate person. There is the likelihood that he or she will be tested and face unofficial rites of passage. The extract from Reiner in Appendix 2.1 will have illustrated some of these issues relating to access.

As a researcher, it is not uncommon to hear stories from the researched about the character and outcomes of previous research. In my own experience I have heard a comment from a senior police officer with regard to a researcher on victims' and offenders' treatment by the police who is now commonly known in the particular police force as the 'study and snitch' researcher since she seemed friendly during the research and then produced a damning written report. Whatever the rights and wrongs of the particular case, it is a useful illustration of the possible informal barriers to access which may be erected by institutions following earlier research experiences.

3.4   Collecting data and the question of 'informed consent'

The above example of a sense of betrayal felt by the researched leads us on to the next stage of the research process, namely the gathering of data and the extent to which 'informed consent' is required for ethically sound research. Informed consent has been defined as follows by the British Sociological Association:

> As far as possible sociological research should be based on the freely given informed consent of those studied. This implies a responsibility on the sociologist to explain as fully as possible, and in terms meaningful to participants, what the research is about, who is undertaking and financing it, why it is being undertaken, and how it is to be promoted.

(British Sociological Association, 1992, in Appendix 2.4, p.102)

Once again, we are made aware that the collection of data is far from being a purely technical exercise, but is itself a form of political activity.

3.4.1 Whose side are we on?

> The social scientist ... cannot remain true to the ethical principles of his science and at the same time refuse to take a stand on the wider ideological and ethical issues of the societal processes in which he is involved as a practitioner. ... It is not a question of science versus politics, but of one kind of science-in-politics versus another.

(Stavenhagen, 1993, p.63)

Few would dissent from the above general statement but there are, nevertheless, important differences of emphasis between competing methodological positions on the continuum from detachment to involvement in the stage of collecting data during the research process.

Most research, as we have previously argued, is carried out on the relatively powerless. Exposé research of dominant élites and institutions is the exception rather than rule, but it is alive and well in a strand of critical criminology dubbed 'critical interventionism' (for example, Scraton, 1987) as well as journalistic, documentary research. A highly committed stance is put quite starkly by Mies in her discussion of feminist methodology when 'She argues that feminism, as a critical approach to research, implies that the researcher must adopt a conscious partiality towards the people being studied' (cited in Hammersley, 1993, p.x). In similar vein, Hudson argues that one of the defining characteristics of critical social science is 'that it is to be working on behalf of those on the downside of power relations' (Hudson, 1993, p.7). In Hudson's case, this has meant the championing of the rights of the most oppressed sections of the community who end up criminalized and incarcerated. Worrall's research on the regulatory discourses surrounding female law-breakers also deliberately avoided asking such questions as why certain women offend since this may perpetuate dominant practices and ideologies with regard to what Worrall argues are oppressed women. Instead of retreading the traditional path of searching for causation and aetiology, Worrall's research sought, in collecting her data, to 'examine the ways in which the authorization of professionals and experts to define certain women as being the type of woman who requires treatment, management, control, or punishment serves to perpetuate the oppression of all women' (Worrall, 1990, p.4). Worrall's study of 15 female law-breakers, together with 'experts' such as magistrates, solicitors, psychiatrists and probation officers, questioned the gender neutrality of the exercise of authority and showed the criminal justice system to be 'bewildering, degrading and unjust' to the female offender (Worrall, 1990, p.160). Here we have a clear illustration of research which explicitly seeks to correct what it sees as a bias in previous criminological theorizing whereby female offenders have been pathologized, and it seeks to give voice to the otherwise silenced women who are criminalized by current practices and discourses in the criminal justice system (see also Eaton, 1993).

Arguably, the most influential attempt to produce a committed and partisan 'criminology from below' in the UK is work associated with Scraton (Scraton, 1987; Scraton and Chadwick, 1987; Scraton et al., 1991). The research and independent enquiry carried out by Scraton et al. (1991), following the protests at Peterhead Prison in Scotland in 1986, will provide us with a flavour of the political thrust of this critical research. Commenting on the study, the famous ex-prisoner and penal reformer, Jimmy Boyle, has noted that the book is to be applauded in that it was 'unequivocably about the unheard voice of the underdog', namely the inmates, and it uncovered another story to the prison protests in Scotland which official reports have sanitized (Scraton et al., 1991, p.vii). The study itself offered an unofficial history of Peterhead Prison, both before and after the 1986 protests, drawn from press reports and official papers. In conclusion, the authors make out the case that, by the early 1970s, Peterhead had become institutionally and structurally 'a prison regime of extreme brutalization and alienation' (Scraton et al., 1991, p.15). The research also drew on evidence from current inmates in Scottish prisons in the shape of 45 completed questionnaires (out of a total of 76 which were sent out to the Scottish prisons). Throughout the study, these 'voices from below' (evidence rarely collected) are given a central place in the story which is told. Thus, for example, in discussing the lives of prisoners 'within the machine', Scraton et al. pointed to the concentration in the media and official statements on the violent activities of the prisoners themselves, but the 'violence of institutions has been marginalized in the majority of accounts about prison' (Scraton et al., 1991, p.59). In contrast, this research went out of its way to allow the prisoners to articulate their own analysis of the situation as epitomized in the following comment from an inmate on the physical conditions in Peterhead: 'There will always be trouble at Peterhead and other prisons unless the government radically changes its policy of wanting to give out American-type sentences but only wants to pay for Russian-type conditions' (Scraton et al., 1991, p.47). In concluding their study, the identification of the 'problem' involves a neat reversal of the orthodox explanation: 'In a sociological sense, the disturbances can be understood as conscious and structured resistance to penal domination rather than as pathological responses to a regime which is fair, just and benevolent' (Scraton et al., 1991, p.133). Here is a clear example of ideologically committed research which self-consciously sought to write an alternative history of the prison. Its position with regard to the question of 'Whose side are we (criminologists) on?' was, unequivocably, that of the 'oppressed'.

At the opposite end of the continuum from such critical research is the type of research which is fully supported by the agency being investigated. Waddington's research (Waddington, 1991) into the weapons and public order policing policy of the Metropolitan Police offers an interesting illustration of what Scraton et al. (1991) would term 'criminology from above'.

ACTIVITY 2.6

Now read the extracts from Peter Waddington's *The Strong Arm of the Law*, 'Acknowledgements', and Roger Grimshaw and Tony Jefferson's *Interpreting Policework*, 'Foreword and Acknowledgements', in Appendices 2.2 and 2.3 at the end of this chapter. As you do so, address the following question:

What major differences are apparent in the relationship of the researcher(s) to the subjects of their research in the two acknowledgements?

COMMENT

Reading Waddington's acknowledgements and contrasting them with those of Grimshaw and Jefferson, we see a very different experience of research from that undergone by most 'outsiders'. Waddington appears very much an 'insider' with easy access to the normally hidden world of armed and riot control policing, receiving, as he notes, 'the fullest co-operation from … all ranks of the Metropolitan Police'. There is obviously much to recommend in this study 'from the inside' of changing police policy and practice. At the same time, questions may be raised as to the detachment and objectivity of a researcher who becomes very closely involved with, and on the side of, the research participants and, in Waddington's case, appears to have committed himself to the 'police side' in the manner that much of Waddington's narrative appears to imply. That said, the study is an interesting antidote to much prominent critical research on paramilitary policing. In the course of his overt participant observational research and analysis of current policing policy, Waddington arrives at the conclusion that there are distinct advantages both for the police and citizens in the existence of a professional and specialized paramilitary policing strategy. He rejects the notion that 'minimum force' has ever been a principle of British policing, suggesting that it has instead been a style used for most occasions but not all eventualities. The professional and competent use of force thus remains an inevitable feature of policing which cannot be avoided but in turn creates distrust and hostility among the public (Waddington, 1991, p.271; see also **Book 2, Chapter 2**).

By way of contrast, Grimshaw and Jefferson's observations of the complex problems and tensions associated with doing research on traditionally closed institutional practices such as operational policing is, arguably, more typical of the 'outsider' researcher's experience. In particular, they note that there were 'divergent institutional interests' between that of the university and the Home Office as to what the primary concern of research in this instance was. For the former, research was about explaining policies *of* the police whereas the latter was interested in policy *for* the police. As Grimshaw and Jefferson also note, this differential expectation regarding the purpose of research was to be the seedbed for later disagreements over the submitted report to the Home Office.

Compared with the partisan approach of both Scraton (1987) and Waddington (1991) a more common stance throughout criminology is the attempt to appreciate the world inhabited by those researched by becoming familiar with what previously was unfamiliar and perhaps unappealing, whether this be offenders (Parker, 1974) or agents of social control (Brewer,

1991). Punch again notes that most researchers do develop a social relationship with the subjects of their research and in his case Punch ended up with a more positive attitude to the police at the end of the research compared with his views at the beginning. Rejecting what he terms the 'espionage' model (that is, spy and then inform), Punch admitted that: 'to a large extent I accepted police work as an enterprise and "morally" approved of most of its activities' (Punch, 1993, p.196).

The question of 'Whose side are we on?' as criminological researchers is unlikely ever to be resolved in the plurality of approaches that is contemporary criminology. Traditionally, criminology has been on the side of the criminal justice system and much research continues to adopt this (often) unstated political position. Perhaps it is a sign of criminology's vibrancy that the question of allegiance is now openly aired and debated.

3.4.2 The issue of informed consent

The informed consent of the people being researched with regard to the nature of the research and its likely dissemination may seem an undeniable right to which any human is entitled. Indeed, there are now codes of practice in most of the social sciences which seek to establish this entitlement as part of the working philosophy of researchers. Certain approaches such as that of feminism would go even further than the rather woolly notion of informed consent and argue for a fundamentally non-hierarchical relationship between researcher and researched so that the latter's invisibility and reification is overcome.

May (1993) suggests that there are two extreme opposed positions in the debate on the politics and ethics of research which he terms 'deontology' and 'consequentialism'. Put briefly, deontology argues for a set of principles which must be universally followed. This position is often encapsulated in ethical guidelines set up by professional research associations and such like. By way of contrast, consequentialism is not concerned with following a set of inviolate rules but focuses instead on the specific situations in which the researchers find themselves and with the likely consequences of their acts. In other words, consequentialism involves a much more pragmatic approach to issues of ethics compared to that of deontology.

ACTIVITY 2.7

Now read the extract from the British Sociological Association's 'Statement of ethical practice' reproduced as Appendix 2.4.

Having looked at the guidelines, list both the advantages and disadvantages of such guidelines for the researcher, the researched and the public at large.

COMMENT

The value of such guidelines is that they acknowledge explicitly the power relations between researcher and researched. They are particularly helpful in protecting the vulnerable from exploitation by researchers. Furthermore, they have the ethically powerful appeal of being open and honest about the actions and outcomes of the work undertaken by the researcher. It is likely that research run along these lines will maintain a reasonable level of public trust.

Critics of such guidelines would point to the danger that the gathering of data organized on the basis of informed consent may not uncover important data since the co-operation of the research participants should be sought and those with things to hide may be unwilling to allow research to be undertaken. This would then limit the capacity for exposé research. More generally, it might be argued that life itself involves lies and distrust and, as a consequence, such codes are a denial of reality.

3.4.3 Subterfuge, complicity and deception

Not all research in criminology has been characterized by openness and informed consent in the manner of its data collection. Covert or undercover research clearly negates the principle of informed consent as the researched cannot refuse involvement. One might argue that, of necessity, certain research needs to be covert. This claim applies in particular to research on the powerful and the privileged. Overt research, according to this argument, only favours the rich and the powerful. As Benyon has remarked: 'Historically the rich and powerful have encouraged hagiography, not critical investigation' (quoted in Lee, 1993, p.8).

It is important to note that studies of élites in the criminal justice system are extremely thin on the ground (Griffith, 1977; Reiner, 1991) when compared to studies of the system's rank-and-file workers, not to mention its euphemistically termed 'customers'! An explicitly adversarial and exposé approach to research is evident in the work of some critical criminologists like Scraton and Chadwick (1987) on deaths in custody, which aimed to open up previously closed milieux to critical scrutiny and champion the rights of the 'underdog'. Such research is unlikely to attract funding from formal state bodies. There are limitations to this radical research strategy in that outrage and hostility to the 'system' and the 'authorities' may itself lead to bias and myopia. There is a strong argument that, whether investigating violent criminals or prison officers, criminological research needs to 'appreciate' even unloved groups.

Lee observes that, where research is threatening, the relationship between the researcher and the researched is likely to become hedged about with mistrust, concealment and dissimulation (Lee, 1993, p.2). This statement is not just relevant to studying the very powerful but any group with vested interests such as bakery workers and their perks (Ditton, 1977; see also **Book 1, Chapter 1**). Indeed, Ditton argues that all participant observational research is inevitably unethical 'by virtue of being interactionally deceitful'. Nor is Ditton concerned by the accusation of subterfuge with regard to his own undercover gathering of data on the routine fiddling in the 'Wellbread' bakery: 'Without reliance on some subterfuge the practices of subterfuge will not be opened to analysis' (Ditton, 1977, p.10).

Acknowledging the strength of Ditton's assertion, other commentators remain concerned about the ethics of such deceitful research. Killian has noted the danger of 'sociological sadism' (Killian in Lee, 1993, p.58) in the sense that human suffering tends to fade with sociological abstraction. We are thus faced with a difficult balancing act between the quest for greater human knowledge and harm done to individuals in the pursuit of this goal. For philosophers this represents the classic means/ends dilemma for which there is no easy answer.

It may be argued that researchers need to compromise or we end up seeking 'to understand how angels behave in paradise' (Klockers quoted in Lee, 1993, p.139). Such compromises may involve the researcher in some complicity in wrong-doing – for example, the witnessing of malpractice among the police, or witnessing illegalities whilst being a participant observer of juvenile delinquency (Parker, 1974). Some accommodation to, and appreciation of, the world of the deviant/wrong-doer may thus be a necessary feature to the successful gathering of data in some criminological research.

3.5 Publishing the results

'Publish and be damned' or 'the pen is mightier than the sword'.

3.5.1 Confidentiality and the politics of exposure

When we publish research findings we enter another political arena in which the researcher has to take account of a variety of audiences including research participants, sponsors, funders, the public, and other academics. It is highly probable that all these audiences have distinct and differing expectations.

ACTIVITY 2.8

You have been given £20,000 by your local authority to conduct research into the characteristics of lone-parent households on income support in your area. At the same time, you are also told that an 'informal economy' thrives in the area and to remember this fact when designing and analysing your research (adapted from May, 1993).

What ethical dilemmas would you face in both the execution and, more importantly, the publication of the research data?

COMMENT

The research may identify criminal offences among some very vulnerable groups whose trust you may have gained in the pursuit of the research. With the publication of the findings it is also possible that a 'moral panic' may be generated about the 'informal economy' through the media drawing selectively on your evidence and analysis (see **Book 1, Chapter 1**). Such a panic may in turn lead to greater targeting of lone-parent households by Social Security fraud officers and the police in the area in question.

Lee has noted that: 'Frankness may be the final indiscretion of a never very welcome guest' (Lee, 1993, p.128). It is likely that there will be people who feel damaged and hurt by the release of criminological research findings. We have already discussed the inevitable ethical dilemmas that surround the issue of how data can and should be collected. There are no easy answers to the problem of balancing particular group interests and the pursuit of knowledge as the goal of criminological research. However, Jupp is surely correct in pointing to criminology's commitment to the principle of validity: 'that is to ensuring that conclusions derived from any investigation are true to what is being described and explained' (Jupp, 1989, p.132). Exposure is thus an inevitable and at times painful part of the research process to which all criminological researchers must be sensitive.

3.5.2 Censorship

Criminological research has in the past been subject to legal writs regarding defamation. In the British context, Baldwin and McConville's research into 'plea-bargaining' (1977) remains the most famous example of research which met pressure for censorship of its findings.

Briefly, their research uncovered worryingly high rates of informal bargaining and negotiation as to the plea despite the formal denial in law of such practices in England's adversarial system of justice. In particular, evidence was found of defendants being persuaded to change their plea from innocent to guilty as a result of pressure often from their own legal representatives. The project unearthed significant evidence that the formal processes of due process and adversarial justice were routinely undermined in practice in the Crown Courts. There thus appeared to be a gulf between what is often called the 'law in books' and the 'law in action' (see also **Book 2, Chapter 3**).

Baldwin and McConville's *Negotiated Justice* remains an instructive exemplar of the politics of publishing. Prior to its publication, the authors were confronted with a public controversy emanating from the Senate of the Inns of Court and representatives of the Bar. In other words, the legal establishment was set against the publication of the study. Given its status as a Home Office-commissioned piece of research, the Home Secretary was even asked to stop publication as a result of a question in the House of Commons. Only after a prolonged series of negotiations in which external academic consultants were commissioned to check the validity of the research findings did the research get the go-ahead for publication. In the longer term, the importance of the work has been undeniable in opening up the criminal justice system to critical scrutiny and making the closed world of criminal justice more visible to the public.

3.6 Really useful knowledge?: the utilization and non-utilization of criminological research by policy-makers

3.6.1 Getting research used

Most commentators on the issue of research utilization in the social sciences accept that the effects of social science are often negligible in the sense of exciting public interest. Like the rest of the social sciences, criminology has 'a low level of visibility in the public consciousness' (Lee, 1993, p.32). That noted, the highest profile utilization (and non-utilization) of criminological research is that associated with royal and other government commissions in the UK. Bulmer defines commissions as follows: 'The term "commission" is used here to refer to special *ad hoc* bodies set up to advise on specific political problems' (Bulmer, 1982, p.94).

Routinely, commissions collect evidence, analyse the problem, report publicly and make recommendations for governmental action (Bulmer, 1982, p.96). In arriving at their conclusions, Royal Commissions on Criminal Justice do draw on criminological research evidence, although the extent of academic research influence is a matter of some controversy. The possibility of a consensus at times appears to be a more important factor than the most accurate explanation of events. We have a long history of political neglect of research-based policy recommendations. Indeed, the body of literature on government commissions suggests that very often their recommendations are not acted upon by government (Bulmer, 1982, p.101).

The Royal Commission on Criminal Justice (RCCJ) published in July 1993 is a very pertinent example to use in our discussion of how research may or may not be utilized in the policy-making and implementation process in the UK. To help put the RCCJ in its political context, it should be noted that the Home Secretary announced the establishment of a Royal Commission on Criminal Justice in March 1991 on the day when the 'Birmingham Six' – six individuals wrongly convicted for 'terrorist' bombings – were released after 16 years of imprisonment. The brief of the Commission seemed to be that of addressing the many problems associated with unsafe convictions and there is little doubt that the setting up of a commission was an exercise in addressing a perceived crisis of legitimacy in the criminal justice system in the UK. When eventually established, the terms of reference of the RCCJ were to examine the workings of the system from the stage at which police investigations of alleged criminal offences occur right through to the point at which the defendant has exhausted his or her rights of appeal (Vennard and Brown, 1994). Furthermore, the emphasis moved from that of wrongful convictions to encompass effectiveness in securing convictions and the efficient use of resources. As Field and Thomas note, 'the Government effectively defused a political crisis about imprisonment of the innocent by setting up a Royal Commission that was only in part directed at that issue – nifty footwork indeed' (Field and Thomas, 1994, p.2).

To assist the Commission in its work, a programme of research was commissioned and organized by the Home Office Research and Statistics Department. In all, 22 commissioned reports were published. When the Commission came to make its 352 recommendations the response from much of the academic community, and including some of the commissioned researchers, was that of anger and disappointment over the neglect of its research, as we shall see shortly. However, this controversy over the 'politics' of the RCCJ and its selective use of research would not be apparent if one only read the Home Office Research and Statistics Department's Research Bulletin on the research undertaken for the RCCJ. This Bulletin noted in rather bland language: 'From the very beginning of the Royal Commission's life, it was clear that research would have an important part to play in providing empirical data about the working of various aspects of the criminal justice system and in helping to evaluate different options for change' (Vennard and Brown, 1994, p.1).

Viewed more critically, the RCCJ has been termed a commission which 'normalizes injustice' (Bridges, 1994). In order to understand the controversy over the apparent non-utilization of (critical) research (such as that of Bridges himself) by the RCCJ, we will first briefly outline its key recommendations.

The Runciman Commission (named after the chairman) in fact rejected most of the radical academic suggestions put to it which were aimed at reducing the likelihood that the innocent would be convicted (Field and Thomas, 1994, p.2). That noted, the RCCJ did make some important recommendations with regard to the 'efficiency' of the criminal justice system such as that, in cases of either-way offences, the defendant should no longer have a right to trial by jury. Pre-trial disclosure of defence evidence was extended and plea-bargaining was more overtly accepted with a higher discount for an early plea. More scope for pre-trial procedures which clarified issues before trial was also recommended. As Field and Thomas note, the Commission's most radical proposals went in the opposite direction of greater safeguards against miscarriages of justice given the focus on greater efficiency (Field and Thomas, 1994, p.4). This said, higher standards for both police and defence lawyers were recommended and an end to the right to silence was rejected. However, the RCCJ did reject calls for a corroboration requirement for confession evidence from academic researchers, although it recommended that the trial judge should warn the jury of the dangers of convicting on the basis of uncorroborated evidence. Finally, the establishment of a completely independent forensic service was not recommended (Field and Thomas, 1994, p.3).

Since the publication of its report, the utilization by the government of the RCCJ's recommendations has been selective and illustrates the complex ways in which research and its policy recommendations are liable to be refracted, if not ignored, within dominant political discourses. Addressing the Conservative Party Conference on 6 October 1993, the Home Secretary, Michael Howard, announced the unveiling of a dramatic and draconian 'law and order package'. As Field and Thomas again note:

> All the penal lessons that had been painfully learnt in the early 80s were lost in a scramble for a law and order rhetoric with popular appeal. Inconvenient evidence was simply ignored. In this process, the Runciman Commission was cannibalized: anything that could be presented as a contribution to cost-effective crime control became an urgent political priority. Other issues could wait. Some of the announced changes follow the Runciman Report closely; others flatly reject the majority view or simply cut across the Commission's assumptions.

(Field and Thomas, 1994, p.7)

The broad message seems to be that governments are able to pick and choose which pieces of informed recommendations are appropriated and which are banished from the populist 'law and order' discourse.

The response of the academic community to the recommendations of the RCCJ has on the whole been negative and Bridges, himself a participant in the sponsored research for the Commission, notes disapprovingly how the goal of efficiency became the co-equal to convicting the guilty and acquitting the innocent. Summarizing his own criticisms of the report, Bridges suggests:

> The overall effect of the specific proposals reviewed here – to abolish a defendant's right to elect jury trial, to introduce open 'plea-bargaining' and other procedural inducements toward guilty pleas in the Crown Court, and to safeguard and extend the police's opportunities to obtain and use confessions and other physical and psychological pressures against suspects – will all normalize miscarriages of justice.

(Bridges, 1994, p.35)

As a consequence, Bridges argues that this and other commissions on criminal justice have a specific political function (and so, by implication, do those who carry out research for such commissions) which is that of 'crisis management' for the state. Such a 'crisis management' function involves the provision of 'a space in which the impetus for reform can be quelled' (Bridges, 1994, p.35). In conclusion, it would seem that the Runciman Report has been used to help bolster a new reactionary law and order campaign in contemporary Britain.

From the above outline of the history of the utilization of research for the most recent RCCJ, it should be clear that politics plays a quite central and determining role in the way in which research will be utilized, or not, as the case may be.

ACTIVITY 2.9

Now read the article 'Ministers suppress research' by Alan Travis, reproduced below from *The Guardian*, 4 July 1994, and compare the 'facts' given there to the above discussion on the RCCJ.

Ministers suppress research

Findings contradict Howard crackdown

Alan Travis
Home Affairs Editor

HOME Office research projects are being systematically shelved by ministers because their findings do not support Michael Howard's law and order crackdown, according to Whitehall sources.

The Guardian has learned of eight pieces of completed Home Office research whose publication has been delayed or postponed by ministers.

Ministers have become so concerned about the direction of the research and planning unit that its head, Dr Roger Tarling, has been asked to give a presentation in the next few days to the Home Secretary detailing the relevance of its past programme and future plans to the development of government policy.

The political crackdown on the 75-strong unit, which was set up in 1957 and is internationally renowned for work free of political bias, is a precursor to moves to a full-blown 'market test' of the Home Office's internal research function next spring.

An exercise is to be undertaken in October to examine the potential for hiving off the work to universities and institutes.

The unpublished research includes:

❑ Refugees: A study in collaboration with the University of Salford which looked at the experiences of 263 asylum-seekers who had been granted refugee status or been given exceptional leave to remain. Half had to wait more than 16 months for a decision on their cases.

It also found that most were well educated – more than a third at degree level – but had had great difficulty getting work. The research undermined popular Conservative Party beliefs that most asylum-seekers are poverty-stricken economic migrants.

❑ Help and Assistance to Refugees: A study of voluntary agencies also painted a positive image of asylum seekers and was critical of the difficulties the organisations experienced in helping them.

❑ Vietnamese Refugees: Looked at the particular problems faced by the Vietnamese boat people since they arrived in Britain in the early 1980s.

❑ Black Youth and Crime: A study across several European countries which looked at the connection between crime and young offenders and their ethnic origin. The Home Office contribution concluded that people of West Indian origin were less likely to be involved in crime, including drug crime, than their white counterparts. The research is not being published in Britain.

❑ Bail: Concluded that there had been no change over the last 10 years in the proportion of people granted bail who went on to commit further offences. The study looked at how many courts actually had access to the criminal's previous convictions when they were sentenced. Its conclusions tend to undermine the importance of the Government's crackdown on 'bail bandits' which has loomed large in ministers' rhetoric in the past 18 months.

❑ Probation: Research into the effectiveness of different intensive supervision schemes. Although some schemes were identified as 'aimless and unstructured' the study gave high marks to the effectiveness of intensive probation as an alternative to prison.

❑ Reconviction Rates: A study of criminals released in the mid-1980s comparing different forms of punishment, including prison. Used a 'scientific test' to compare predicted with actual reconviction rates. Highly controversial since the Home Office's historic shift in policy from trying to develop alternatives to custody when Douglas Hurd was Home Secretary to Michael Howard's 'prison works' policy.

❑ Criminal Justice Agencies: A study using in depth interviews with different parts of the criminal justice system, including judges and magistrates, on their views on the 1991 Criminal Justice Act. Apart from criticism of the now dropped unit fines system and the restrictions on taking previous convictions into account, it found much support within the criminal justice system for the act's promotion of punishment in the community and probation.

Many of the projects which have been shelved were initiated more than two years ago when Douglas Hurd's emphasis on developing alternatives to custody was official Home Office policy. Some observers fear the research unit is being attacked for its failure to keep up with the speed at which the Government is undertaking U-turns on criminal justice policy.

A Home Office spokesman denied there had been any suppression of research reports but made clear that ministers insisted on the right to decide what was published when.

'There has been no suppression of research by ministers. Research is constantly prioritised and allocated accordingly. Ministers safeguard taxpayers' money and set priorities and objectives throughout the department, including the research unit so it can make the best possible contribution to policies,' he said.

The Home Office denied that the heads of the unit had been specially called in to give a demonstration of its work. However the spokesman added: 'There are regular meetings between officials and ministers to discuss departmental work.

'It would be worse if ministers made decisions about research without the input of officials and for them to set out their work.'

(The Guardian, 4 July 1994)

ACTIVITY 2.10

Next, read the article 'Home Office crime' by Simon Jenkins, reproduced below from *The Times*, 28 September 1994. As you do so, make notes on how crime statistics may be used selectively by government (see also **Book 1, Chapter 1**).

Home Office crime

Fear of crime is self-fulfilling, but scare stories about rising lawlessness no longer suit the police and politicians

Read that headline carefully. Revel in it. 'The biggest fall in crime for 40 years.' There is no crime wave after all. There is a crime trough. Help is at hand for embattled ministers. Come Master Shallow, come Bardolph and Pistol, we must hasten to court. Jack Falstaff will hear the chimes at midnight.

Yesterday's British crime figures are indeed a surprise, but not the surprise suggested above. The phoney ones have fallen. The real ones have risen. Anybody listening to the BBC yesterday will have heard the opposite, but that is what the Government hoped. Most of the press bought the same story. I sense that the Home Secretary, Michael Howard, knew the truth. He shrewdly absented himself from yesterday's press conference, leaving his junior minister, David Maclean, to issue one of the most mendacious press releases I have ever read.

Let me say it again. Crime figures gathered at local police stations are a hopeless index of public or private wrongdoing. They record just a third of actual crime, and they distort its rise or fall over time. They are meaningless. Yet policemen bidding for resources, newspapers bidding for headlines and politicians bidding for votes still find them a happy hunting-ground. The worst culprit was Tony Blair as Labour home affairs spokesman. Let one police statistic drop from the sky and the jackals pounce, salivating.

Nothing in even the sordid history of crime statistics equals yesterday's farrago. The fall of 5.5 per cent in total crimes recorded at police stations over the past year is due to a steep fall in theft and burglary, which comprise 94 per cent of the total. There is no evidence that this reflects any fall in crime. The biggest reduction came in the last two quarters, when most people renew their insurance. Premiums soared last year, leading to reduced cover, higher 'excess' exclusions and restricted payments by insurers. Property crime victims were less widely insured (by at least 5 per cent), and when burgled they made fewer claims that required a report to a police station. There has been an extraordinary 6 per cent fall over the past two years in insurance claims by victims.

Another reason for the fall could be the trauma that most police forces have been through this past year. Criticism of police productivity and the imminence of performance measures have led policemen to be more chary of putting reported crimes into their incident books. A fall in recorded crime can mean success for a police division and a rise in the clear-up percentage. More crime used to mean more resources, whereas now less crime can mean higher pay. For the first time, policemen have a financial incentive to record less crime. The politics of law and order no longer feeds on higher crime figures. It demands the opposite. And surprise, surprise, the police figures have fallen.

The police may say that the new 'targeting' policy for burglary is working; for instance Operation Bumblebee in London. It would be nice if this were true, but recorded burglary has fallen equally in areas with no targeting, such as Manchester. Nobody knows whether targeting works. Meanwhile, property crime bulks so large in the national crime total that it overwhelms more serious crimes, such as violence against the person, which continue to rise. The Government might as well lump together cancer and in-growing toenails to get an index of the nation's health. Such aggregation is an insult to public intelligence. Yesterday's much-trumpeted fall in crime was 'technical'. There was no fall in crime.

For proof, we need only turn to another document issued yesterday from the Home Office. It was the official twice-yearly British Crime Survey. In contrast to the police figures, this survey is reputable and authoritative, a costly investigation into how much crime Britons experience each year. Normally it would merit a press conference of its own. Yesterday, Mr Maclean barely mentioned it. His release nowhere indicated what the survey said: that far from falling, crime actually rose faster over the past two years than during the 1980s. These press officers should be ashamed of such *suppressio veri, suggestio falsi*. Are they professionals or political hacks?

The British Crime Survey flatly contradicted the technical fall indicated by the police figures. Throughout the 1980s, it showed a slow rise in the public's experience of crime, at a time when police figures were going through the roof. Now, in the 1990s the British Crime Survey suggests that all categories of crime are rising faster, not slower. Yesterday's figures were not good at all.

Over the latest survey period – 1991 to 1993 – crimes experienced by the public rose by 18 per cent across all categories of offence – vandalism, burglary and violence against the person. Rises were strong in vandalism and in property crime in the non-metropolitan South of England. Car crime has risen fast, though better security has led to the biggest rise being in attempted rather than actual theft. Fewer people bother to report attempted thefts to the police.

The police figures over the same two-year period, comparing like with like, show a rise of just 7 per cent (including the past year's fall). The Home Office's own research document is emphatic about the reason for this blatant divergence. The public is less inclined to report trivial offences to the police, and the police are less inclined to record them when reported. Police figures have fallen, says the Home Office, 'because the proportion of crimes reported to the police has fallen'. This was not the impression created yesterday by the minister, David Maclean.

Where does this leave a thesis beloved of this column, that 'there is no crime wave'? The answer is that I stand on the only remotely solid ground visible above these quicksands, the British Crime Survey. This has always shown a rise in experienced crime, but not an exponential one. It is now showing a slight increase in that figure. Britons appear to be more conscious of criminality, and claim to have suffered more of it with

each passing year. They are certainly more fearful. That is all we know.

At such times, most citizens fall back on hunch, and pretend that hunch is not prejudice. I believe that crime is not 'out of hand', but that misbehaviour changes its character with time. Each year we define more antisocial but legal behaviour as crime, never the reverse. We know that fewer young people are becoming criminals, but that those who do go on to commit more crimes. (This perhaps vindicates Mr Howard's view that police and magistrates should concentrate on fewer, tougher young offenders; in which case the criminal justice system needs urgent reform.)

Each year we are more protective of our property, of which we have more, and are less tolerant of vandals, rowdies, sneak thieves, and foulmouths. When asked by a pollster if we have encountered more such people, we are likely to say yes. We are more aware of areas of rising crime – better roads bring urban villains into the countryside – than of falling crime elsewhere. Publicity alerts us to crime and helps us to recall incidents that we might have forgotten.

What to do about all this nobody has the faintest clue. Stuffing jails with petty thieves, debtors and drug addicts is costly lunacy. The huge increase in policing – 50 per cent in real terms – that has been brandished at crime over the past 15 years has had no effect, nor has similar spending on prisons. A sensible observer would have to conclude that current crime policies are not just hopeless but counterproductive. They are the Tory equivalent of Labour's industrial subsidies in the 1970s. Policing does not work. Prison does not work. Probation does not work. Villains go about their business like locusts immune to pesticide. They always have. I imagine they always will.

The best face to be put on the Home Office's statistical juggling is that its apparent belief that crime is now falling faster than for 40 years should at least mean reduced pressure on police and prisons and less money squandered on law and order. The television companies might lay off their crime-scarer programmes. Politicians might stop fostering fear of crime. This benighted subject might drop back down the political agenda. Then, who knows, crime might really start to fall.

(The Times, 28 September 1994)

Simon Jenkins

COMMENT

These press cuttings support much of our previous discussion about both the selective use of evidence and data by policy-makers and the ability of politicians and policy-makers to ignore or, indeed, conceal research findings which do not resonate comfortably with the dominant political ideologies of law and order. This noted, we can argue that everyone uses crime statistics selectively.

The research approach most often utilized by policy-makers is that which is generally termed 'evaluation' research, often carried out by 'market researchers' rather than academic researchers (Bulmer, 1982). This approach is also often called 'relevant research' which itself is a contested term given the implicit emphasis on pragmatic, action-oriented and managerially driven recommendations for alleviating a sponsor-defined problem.

There are obvious dangers in research findings being used selectively for political purposes. Perhaps most notoriously, data on 'race' and crime have been used to lend support to moral panics with regard to the 'race problem' in the UK. As Ahmed and Sheldon point out, we have witnessed a 'racialization of statistics' and even with the good intention of monitoring 'race' discrimination '[u]ncritical collection and use of "ethnic" data will aid racialization and stereotyping and thus reinforce oppression of the very minorities which the data were ostensibly meant to support' (Ahmed and Sheldon, 1993, p.129). Once again, it is clear that the use of statistics in such areas as the debate on crime and discrimination is never free of political interpretation.

3.6.2 Non-utilization of research

It will come as no surprise that the more conventional criminological approaches, such as the positivist and 'administrative', have tended to be viewed as more useful by policy-makers than the findings of, say, critical criminology. However, even officially commissioned research may be of only limited influence in the political decision-making process on criminal justice.

Jupp (1989) cites a particularly interesting example of the non-utilization of officially sponsored research into the treatment and punishment of young offenders. In the light of the government's decision in the early 1980s to make juvenile offender regimes tougher, two new regimes were evaluated by the Prison Department's Young Offender Psychology Unit and the Home Office's Statistics Department. The evaluation study also compared the two new regimes with a control group of old regime centres. Its findings were that the new 'short, sharp shock' regimes had a negligible effect on recidivism. Despite the findings, the then Home Secretary, Leon Brittan, announced in parliament that tougher regimes would be extended. The research also showed that compulsory drill and physical education had proved attractive to young offenders and this element was discontinued. The main hypothesis of the evaluation research was to assess 'whether spending a period of weeks in a detention centre with a more rigorous and demanding regime could effectively deter offenders from committing further offences' (quoted in Jupp, 1989, p.169). The study's conclusion was 'no'. This negative finding was subsequently ignored in the political decision-making process, no doubt because such a finding was out of step with the ideology of the government. Such a case once more highlights the importance of the wider ideological currents at work on politicians in making decisions over policy implementation which may drown and dwarf the influence of academic research findings.

Another illustration of this lack of concern over whether certain crime management strategies are 'successful' or not can be found in Muncie's analysis of the repeated failures of the 'get tough on young offenders' initiatives in Britain since the 1970s. When the political imperative is foremost it would appear that 'failure never matters' (Muncie, 1990). More recently, we have also witnessed the resurgence of the 'short, sharp shock' approach towards young offenders with the establishment of 'boot camps' in 1996 based on US retributionist penal policy, despite both Home Office and academic warnings of the past failure of such initiatives.

4 Conclusion: the 'enlightenment' model of the research–policy interface

It is clear that criminological research does not offer politicians and policy-makers 'quick-fix' answers. However, the long-term influence of research on both the policy and political process should not be lost. In the following quotation, Bulmer puts the case for an 'enlightenment model' rather than an 'engineering model' of the research–policy relationship: 'Social scientific research may exercise its most important influence through affecting the general frameworks that policy-makers employ to look at issues, the implicit theories that they use' (Bulmer, 1982, p.163). Broadening out Bulmer's thesis, it may be argued that criminological research helps redraw the frameworks employed in political discourses on law and order.

Some writers such as Cohen (1985) and Jefferson (1990) explicitly reject a policy orientation for academic research. Following the original proposition of Cohen, Jefferson, in concluding his critique of the rise of paramilitarism in the British police, argues that it is not the job of the sociologist 'to advise, consult, recommend or make decisions … . Recommendations and similar tasks, as Cohen says, belong to others' (Jefferson, 1990, p.136). Not all academics would go along with this position, but it does offer an alternative viewpoint to those researchers who at times may be in danger of serving their sponsor at the cost of academic autonomy and the right to be critical.

This chapter has explored the realities of doing criminological research in what is a highly politicized world. For some, our 'warts and all' outline may represent a depressing tale, but only if the reader has a naive view of how social scientific research happens in the real world. Research does not occur in a metaphorical germ-free zone. Instead, criminological research is infected – or rather, enriched – by the political and ethical dilemmas and challenges which we have described. Be wary of the talk of the end of politics and rise of non-political technical fixes for research – such talk is likely to usher in very restricting research agendas for criminology. Similarly, it is impossible to envisage a time when criminological research will not generate the types of ethical dilemmas discussed in this chapter. Bronfenbrenner puts the matter quite bluntly: 'The only safe way to avoid violating principles of professional ethics is to refrain from doing social research altogether' (cited in Burgess, 1984, p.207).

When you come to construct your own research ideas for the research outline you will be asked to write in TMA 06, many of the issues raised in this chapter should be remembered, not least to forewarn you of some of the pitfalls and complexities that await any criminological research project (see Figure 2.1). In particular, the following questions may be worth remembering:

- What constraints may face the initial construction of the research problem?

- Is it possible, or indeed desirable, to seek institutional support and sponsorship for the project?

- How would you negotiate access, both formal and informal, to your chosen research site?

- What politico-ethical issues are likely to emerge during the process of gathering the data, such as that of informed consent as against subterfuge?

- What may be the consequences, for yourself and other interested parties, of publishing the research findings?

- How might the research findings be utilized, or alternatively ignored, by other parties?

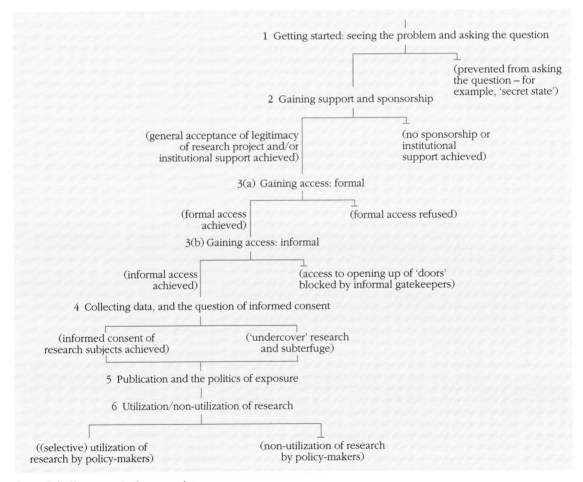

Figure 2.1 Key stages in the research process

Further reading

Very little has been written on the politics of criminological research. Vic Jupp's *Methods of Criminological Research* (1989) is the most comprehensive account of the political contexts within which criminological research needs to be contextualized. A useful essay on the history and ideological underpinnings of British criminology is Stanley Cohen's 'Footprints in the sand: criminology and the sociology of deviance' (Cohen, 1981).

For a general introduction to the politics of social research see Tim May's *Social Research* (1993) and Martin Hammersley's edited collection of papers, *Social Research: Philosophy, Politics and Practice* (1993). The best introduction to the specific political and ethical dilemmas associated with research on 'sensitive issues' is Michael Lee's *Doing Research on Sensitive Topics* (1993).

References

Ahmed, W.I.U. and Sheldon, T.A. (1993) '"Race" and statistics', in Hammersley (1993).

Arber, S. (1993) 'The research process,' in Gilbert (1993).

Baldwin, J. and McConville, M. (1977) *Negotiated Justice*, Oxford, Martin Robertson.

Bell, C. and Newby, H. (eds) (1977) *Doing Sociological Research*, London, Allen and Unwin.

Bottomley, A. (1979) *Criminology in Focus,* Oxford, Martin Robertson.

Brewer, J. (with Magee, K.) (1991) *Inside the RUC: Routine Policing in a Divided Society*, Oxford, Oxford University Press.

Bridges, L. (1994) 'Normalizing injustice', *Journal of Law and Society*, vol.21, no.1, pp.20–34.

British Sociological Association (1992) 'BSA statement of ethical practice', *Sociology*, vol.26, no.4, pp.703–7.

Brogden, M. and Shearing, C. (1993) *Policing for a New South Africa*, London, Routledge.

Bulmer, M. (1982) *The Uses of Social Research*, London, Allen and Unwin.

Burgess, B. (1984) *In the Field*, London, Allen and Unwin.

Cain, M. (1990) 'Towards transgression: new directions in feminist criminology', *International Journal of the Sociology of Law*, vol.18, no.1, pp.1–18. (Extract reprinted in Muncie *et al.*, 1996.)

Cain, M. and Smart, C. (1989) Preface to Worrall (1990).

Carlen, P. (1985) *Criminal Women*, Cambridge, Polity.

Carlen, P. (1992) 'Criminal women and criminal justice: the limits to, and potential of, feminist and left realist perspectives', in Matthews, R. and Young, J. (eds) *Issues in Realist Criminology*, London, Sage. (Extract reprinted in Muncie *et al.*, 1996.)

Clarke, J., Cochrane, A. and McLaughlin, E. (eds) (1994) *Managing Social Policy*, London, Sage.

Cohen, S. (1981) 'Footprints in the sand: criminology and the sociology of deviance', in Fitzgerald, M., McLennan, G. and Pawson, J. (eds) *Crime and Society*, London, Routledge and Kegan Paul in association with The Open University.

Cohen, S. (1985) *Visions of Social Control: Crime, Punishment and Classification*, Cambridge, Polity.

Cohen, S. and Taylor, L. (1972) *Psychological Survival: The Experience of Long Term Imprisonment*, Harmondsworth, Penguin.

Cohen, S. and Taylor, L. (1977) 'Talking about prison blues', in Bell and Newby (1977).

Ditton, J. (1977) *Part-time Crime*, London, Macmillan.

Downes, D. (ed.) (1992) *Unravelling Criminal Justice: Eleven British Studies*, Basingstoke, Macmillan.

Eaton, M. (1993) *Women After Prison*, Buckingham, Open University Press.

Field, S. and Thomas, P. (1994) 'Justice and efficiency? The Royal Commission on Criminal Justice', *Journal of Law and Society*, vol.21, no.1, pp.1–19.

Genders, E. and Player, E. (1989) *Race Relations in Prisons*, Oxford, Clarendon.

Giddens, A. (1991) *Late Modernity and Self-identity*, London, Polity.

Gilbert, N. (ed.) (1993) *Researching Social Life*, London, Sage.

Griffith, J. (1977) *The Politics of the Judiciary*, London, Fontana.

Grimshaw, R. and Jefferson, T. (1987) *Interpreting Policework*, London, Allen and Unwin.

Hammersley, M. (ed.) (1993) *Social Research: Philosophy, Politics and Practice*, London, Sage.

Hobbs, D. (1988) *Doing the Business: Entrepreneurship, the Working Class and Detectives in the East End of London*, Oxford, Oxford University Press.

Holdaway, S. (1989) 'Discovering structure: studies of British police occupational culture' in Weatheritt (1989).

Hornsby-Smith, M. (1993) 'Gaining access' in Gilbert (1993).

Hudson, B. (1993) *Penal Policy and Social Justice*, London, Macmillan.

Jefferson, T. (1990) *The Case Against Paramilitarism*, Buckingham, Open University Press.

Jupp, V.R. (1989) *Methods of Criminological Research*, London, Allen and Unwin.

King, M. and McDermott, K. (1992) 'Control, security and humane containment in the penal system in England and Wales', in Downes (1992).

Lee, R.M. (1993) *Doing Research on Sensitive Topics*, London, Sage.

Lombroso, C. and Ferrero, W. (1895) *The Female Offender*, London, Fisher Unwin. (Extract reprinted as 'The criminal type in women and its atavistic origin' in Muncie *et al.*, 1996.)

Lukes, S. (1974) *Power: A Radical View*, London, Macmillan.

May, T. (1993) *Social Research*, London, Sage.

Muncie, J. (1990) 'Failure never matters: detention centres and the politics of deterrence', *Critical Social Policy*, 28, pp.53–66.

Muncie, J., McLaughlin, E. and Langan, M. (eds) (1996) *Criminological Perspectives: A Reader*, London, Sage in association with The Open University.

Newburn, T. and Stanko, E. (eds) (1995) *Just Boys Doing Business? Masculinities and Crime*, London, Routledge.

Parker, H.J. (1974) *View from the Boys: A Sociology of Down-town Adolescents*, Newton Abbott, David and Charles.

Pilger, J. (1994) 'Pergau Dam', *New Statesman/Society*, 4 March, p.89.

Punch, M. (1993) 'Observation and the police: the research experience', in Hammersley (1993).

Radzinowicz, L. (1994) 'Reflections on the state of criminology', *British Journal of Criminology*, vol.34, no.2, pp.99–104.

Reiner, R. (1989) 'The politics of police research', in Weatheritt (1989).

Reiner, R. (1991) *Chief Constables*, Oxford, Oxford University Press.

Reiner, R. (1992) *The Politics of the Police*, Brighton, Harvester.

Scraton, P. (ed.) (1987) *Law, Order and the Authoritarian State*, Milton Keynes, Open University Press.

Scraton, P. and Chadwick, K. (1987) *In the Arms of the Law: Coroners' Inquests and Deaths in Custody*, London, Pluto.

Scraton, P., Sim, J. and Skidmore, P. (1991) *Prisons Under Protest*, Buckingham, Open University Press.

Smart, C. (1990) 'Feminist approaches to criminology or postmodern woman meets atavistic man', in Morris, A. and Gelsthorpe, L. (eds) *Feminist Perspectives in Criminology*, Milton Keynes, Open University Press. (Extract reprinted in Muncie *et al.*, 1996.)

Smith, D. and Gray, J. (1983) *The Police and the People in London,* London, Policy Studies Institute.

Stavenhagen, R. (1993) 'Decolonializing applied social sciences', in Hammersley (1993).

Vennard, J. and Brown, D. (eds) (1994) 'The research programme of the Royal Commission on Criminal Justice' *Home Office Research Bulletin*, no.35.

Waddington, P. (1991) *The Strong Arm of the Law*, Oxford, Clarendon.

Weatheritt, M. (ed.) (1989) *Police Research*, Aldershot, Gower.

Worrall, A. (1990) *Offending Women: Female Lawbreakers and the Criminal Justice System*, London, Routledge.

Appendix 2.1

Reiner: 'Assisting with inquiries: studying a criminal justice élite'

Élites need to be interviewed. The best way of finding out about people is by talking to them. It cannot guarantee the truth, especially from people well practised in the arts of discretion. But it is superior to any alternative way of discovering what they believe and do.

(Crewe, I. 'Studying Élites in Britain', pp.42–3)

The history of the project

The idea of studying chief constables first occurred to me in 1980. There were a number of factors which made it an attractive and interesting project. Above all, there was the growing prominence of some chief constables as vocal and controversial public figures. Although this was before the urban riots which made policing issues absolutely central to political consciousness and debate, many commentators were already pointing to a growing politicization of the police, spearheaded by the more vocal chief constables and ACPO[1] [Association of Chief Police Officers]. The accountability of the police was already becoming a central issue, with many critics arguing that the police were not adequately controlled by democratic and legal institutions.[2] This controversy was to become more intense after 1981 as several radical Labour local authorities elected in that year began to engage in conflict with their chief constables over the question of police accountability.[3] Chief constables were thus public figures of growing prominence and interest in 1980.

At the same time, a study of chief constables seemed a logical progression to plug a clear gap in the burgeoning field of police studies. In the 1960s and even more rapidly and extensively in the 1970s systematic social research on police organizations developed rapidly, first mainly in the USA, but then in Britain too.[4] However, all the research concentrated on the lower ranks of the police. Knowledge of the senior ranks was sketchy and anecdotal, a pot-pourri of chance revelation and reminiscence, titbits of scandal, and the much-publicized remarks of probably unrepresentative police superstars on the rent-a-quote circuit. This led me to conclude at the time that: 'The character of police work at the senior levels of the organisation is the greatest gap in the growing body of knowledge which social scientists have accumulated about the police ... While we have some knowledge of the social origins and previous careers of recruits, we do not have this information for senior officers' (Reiner, 1982, pp.165–74).

Having previously published a study of the backgrounds, careers, and occupational perspectives of the Federated ranks of the police (Reiner, 1978), it seemed a logical step to attempt to conduct similar research on the élite levels. The immediate trigger for my attempting to launch such a study was a 1979 *Newsnight* programme on which I was supposed to debate new tactics of riot control with the President of ACPO. Much to the consternation of the presenters, who were clearly hoping for some more televisual sparks of conflict, consensus broke out between us. This encouraged me to write to him seeking ACPO approval for an interview study of all forty-three chief constables then in office, aiming to ascertain their background, careers, and philosophies of policing. (The dates and precise terms of this correspondence cannot be checked now, as my file containing all the preliminary material about the research was stolen from my office shortly before I began to conduct the present interviews.)

I did not receive any reply at all from ACPO concerning my request. Instead, about six months later I received a letter from a senior official in the Home Office. This informed me that my request had been passed onto them by ACPO. After due deliberation it had been decided that my research would not be officially supported by them in any way. They did not see any value in a study compiling information about chief constables which was available to them already in their files.[5] There would also be no possibility of collecting demographic data about chief constables from these files on an anonymous basis, as I had requested as an alternative. The letter did say I was free to approach individual chief constables to seek an interview with them, but it would be for them to decide whether to grant it. The whole purpose of my research was to gain a representative picture of chief constables, and it seemed likely to me that without any official blessing the only chiefs who would respond positively would be a self-selected few. I therefore shelved the project at that time.

In 1986 I thought the moment might be right to make another attempt at the same project. Policing matters had become even more prominent and politically controversial. However, in the wake of the 1981 Scarman Report attempts were being made on a broad front to restore public confidence in policing and to professionalize the service. One aspect of this was a much greater degree of openness to outside (as well as internal) research. My 1985 book on *The Politics of the Police* had received a positive response from a number of prominent chief officers, who I hoped might therefore look more favourably on my research proposal than their 1980 counterparts had done.

During 1986 I applied successfully for a Nuffield Foundation Social Research Fellowship, to run from the autumn of that year for twelve months. I am most grateful to them not only for providing me with the time and the money to conduct the fieldwork, but for showing their trust in the project before I had been able to secure research access.

Once I had obtained the Fellowship I set about trying to mobilize support for the project in official circles. I discussed it with members of the Home Office Research and Planning Unit and Her Majesty's Inspectorate of Constabulary. Both groups were favourable to the research, so I then approached the Home Office Police Department for official permission to interview all chief constables. They replied in July 1986, implying they would support the project if ACPO did, and informing me they had already communicated this to the then president, Sir Stanley Bailey, Chief Constable of Northumbria. Sir Stanley was well known to me as a champion of police research from his participation in the series of influential seminars organized by Professor Michael Banton at Bristol University in the early 1970s (Banton, 1971, 1973, 1975). I approached him for ACPO support, and was interviewed by him and the late Harry Ross (then ACPO secretary) in September 1986.

Prior to the interview, I discussed the matter with several chief officers with whom I had a good relationship. All were keen on the idea of the research, but indicated that their own participation would be conditional on ACPO support. This underlined to me that ACPO approval was vital, and several chiefs subsequently told me in the interviews that they would not have seen me without it.

It was during this period that my research file was stolen. A number of chiefs I spoke to at the time expressed concern about it. A couple wondered whether Special Branch was involved, while some were worried about it being found and passed to the media. They tried to recall what correspondence had gone on between us, and whether its appearance in the *Guardian* would cause them any embarrassment!

The interview with Sir Stanley Bailey and Harry Ross was successful, and the proposal was approved at the ACPO Conference that year. Subsequently Harry Ross wrote a letter to all chief constables informing them that the project enjoyed the support of ACPO and the Home Office. ... It was made clear that the participation of individual chief constables was entirely a matter for them to decide upon. However, armed with this official blessing, I began to approach the forty-three chief constables.

I decided to write to the chiefs in batches of about a dozen. In the first wave I wrote to those chief constables whom I knew and by the time I approached the second batch of twelve, I had successfully completed ten interviews. Of the twelve chiefs in the second batch, four immediately refused to be interviewed. Three communicated this to me through their secretaries over the phone, while one wrote to me attributing his refusal to a reading of my *The Politics of the Police*. 'Having now read your book (which I found very informative) and considered the request in the your letter, I regret that I am unable to accept your invitation to interview me on this occasion.' While pleased to learn that my book had an audience, I was less happy about its effect! Shortly after this, one of my first batch of chiefs, who had given me an appointment, withdrew his consent to be interviewed following a visit to the Home Office concerning some controversial public statements he had made. Sadly for me this meeting at the Home Office coincided with my scheduled interview with him, and after first postponing our interview he cancelled it altogether.

I grew alarmed about the prospects of the research at this stage, for if the rate of refusal of the second batch continued in subsequent ones I would end up with only about a 70 per cent sample. While a fairly respectable response rate, I was concerned about whether I would be systematically missing a substantial body of opinion. In the event these anxieties proved completely groundless. All the chief constables in the last two batches I approached agreed to be interviewed. I suspect that the high refusal rate in the second batch was due to these being the first group of chief constables I approached without any previous relationship to build upon. By the time I contacted the last two batches, I had already completed nearly twenty interviews. Word had evidently got around about the nature of the interviews, and it was clear that I could be seen without the chief constable's thoughts being plastered across the front page of the *Guardian* the next morning. It was my distinct impression that the later interviews were altogether more relaxed, not only because I was more fluent in handling them but because people were seeing me in the knowledge that I already had a substantial number of interviews under my belt.

After completing the thirty-eight interviews with those who agreed to see me when I first approached them, I was subsequently able to add two more interviews to achieve a final total of forty. The chief who had originally agreed to see me but then changed his mind was prevailed upon to reconsider yet again when I met him at a public lecture. He is one of the most prominent of all chiefs and I successfully argued that his participation was crucial to the project. The other change of heart was a chief I met when I attended a set of extended interviews for the Senior Command Course as an observer. He overheard me discussing the research interviews with another chief, and asked what they were about. I told him I had approached him for an interview, but his secretary had told me over the phone that he was unwilling. He maintained he had not heard of this approach, and that his secretary was probably performing her gate-keeping function with exceptional zeal. At any rate, he granted me an interview bringing the completed total to forty.

The interviews amount to a sample of 93 per cent of chief constables, a virtual census. It is possible that if I had approached the three remaining refusals, they would have changed their minds. However, they were all fairly low-profile individuals, and indeed, when one was subsequently appointed to head a controversial investigation, the newspaper reports all mentioned his retiring personality. In any event, I rested content with the forty interviews.

Notes

1   The politicization of the police is more fully analysed in Hall (1979); Thompson (1980); Kettle (1980); Reiner (1980).

2   Pioneering discussions of the issue of police accountability were Brogden (1977, 1981, 1982); Cain (1977, 1979); Hain (1979, 1980); Bowden (1978).

3   Case studies of such conflicts can be found in Jefferson and Grimshaw (1984); Loveday (1985); McLaughlin (1990).

4   Fuller accounts of the development of police research are Reiner (1989, 1991).

5   Towards the end of my fieldwork, I came across a somewhat galling confirmation of this. My penultimate interview was with a former president of ACPO. He was keen to know some of my findings. I read him some of the data on the background and careers of chiefs, which it had taken me over a year, numerous train journeys all across England and Wales, and some £15,000 of the Nuffield Foundation's money to assemble. As I was doing this he pulled open the top drawer of his desk, and pulled out some sheets of paper from which he read out identical numbers. Unfortunately, the contents of ACPO presidents' desks are not in the public domain, so I had to expend considerable resources to reproduce them by the scenic route.

References

Banton, M. (1971) 'The sociology of the police', *Police Journal*, 44, pp.227–43.

Banton, M. (1973) 'The sociology of the police II', *Police Journal*, 46, pp.341–62.

Banton, M. (1975) 'The sociology of the police III', *Police Journal*, 48, pp.299–315.

Bowden, T. (1978) *Beyond the Limits of the Law*, Harmondsworth, Penguin.

Brogden, M. (1977) 'A police authority – the denial of conflict', *Sociological Review*, 25, pp.325–49.

Brogden, M. (1981) 'All police is conning bastards', in Fine, B., Hunt, A., McBarnet, D. and Moorhouse, B. (eds) *Law, State and Society*, London, Croom Helm.

Brogden, M. (1982) *The Police: Autonomy and Consent*, London, Academic Press.

Cain, M.E. (1977) 'An ironical departure: the dilemma of contemporary policing', in Jones, K. (ed.) *Yearbook of Social Policy in Britain*, London, Routledge.

Cain, M.E. (1979) 'Trends in the sociology of police work', *International Journal of the Sociology of Law*, 7, pp.143–67.

Crewe, I. (1974) 'Studying élites in Britain', in Crewe, I. (ed.) *British Political Sociology Yearbook I: Élites in Western Democracy*, London, Croom Helm.

Hain, P. (ed.) (1979) *Policing the Police*, London, Calder.

Hain, P. (ed.) (1980) *Policing the Police 2*, London, Calder.

Hall, S. (1979) *Drifting into a Law and Order Society*, London, Cobden Trust.

Jefferson, T. and Grimshaw, R. (1984) *Controlling the Constable*, London, Miller.

Kettle, M. (1980) 'The politics of policing and the policing of politics', in Hain (1980).

Loveday, B. (1985) *The Role and Effectiveness of the Merseyside Police Committee*, Liverpool, Merseyside County Council.

McLaughlin, E. (1990) 'Community, policing and accountability: a case-study of Manchester 1981–1988', PhD Thesis, Faculty of Law, University of Sheffield.

Reiner, R. (1978) *The Blue-Coated Worker*, Cambridge, Cambridge University Press.

Reiner, R. (1980) 'Fuzzy thoughts: the police and law and order politics', *Sociological Review*, 28, pp.377–413.

Reiner, R. (1982) 'Who are the police?', *Political Quarterly*, 53, pp.165–80.

Reiner, R. (1989) 'The politics of police research', in Weatheritt, M. (ed.) *Police Research: Some Future Prospects*, Aldershot, Avebury.

Reiner, R. (1991) 'Chief constables in England and Wales: a social portrait of a criminal justice élite', in Reiner, R. and Cross, M. (eds) *Beyond Law and Order: Criminal Justice Policy and Politics into the 1990s*, London, Macmillan.

Thompson, E.P. (1980) 'The state of the nation', in Thompson, E.P. (ed.) *Writing By Candlelight*, London, Merlin Press, pp.189–210. (Originally published in *New Society*, 8 Nov.–13 Dec. 1979.)

(Source: Reiner, 1991, pp.39–43)

Appendix 2.2

Waddington: *The Strong Arm of the Law*, 'Acknowledgements'

The research upon which this book is based was undertaken under the auspices of the Police Foundation, without whose help, support, and assistance it could not have been successfully completed.

This book addresses one of the most controversial and sensitive issues in modern policing – the use of force by what we have been traditionally proud to describe as our unarmed and non-aggressive police. The research has only been made possible by the fullest co-operation received from all ranks of the Metropolitan Police. I am, therefore, indebted to Sir Kenneth Newman, the Commissioner of the Metropolitan Police at the time the research commenced, and to Sir Peter Imbert, who was then Deputy Commissioner and has now succeeded Sir Kenneth, both of whom supported and encouraged the research from the beginning. Their willingness to grant complete access to hitherto confidential internal documentation, to allow me to interview serving police officers, and to permit my participation in training courses for armed officers and those engaged in riot control is ample testimony to their confidence in the Metropolitan Police.

I am particularly grateful to all members of the Force Firearms Unit, formerly known as D11 and now, following reorganization, known as PT17. All members of the unit welcomed me, and tolerated my inquiries with good humour and friendliness. My thanks go especially to Chief Superintendent Bob Wells for his courtesy and frankness, and also to his successor, Rick Johnson; also to Chief Inspector Mike Waldren for taking time to educate me in some of the technicalities of firearms and firearms tactics, and correcting an earlier draft of this book; and to all the instructors on the various courses in which I participated who treated me as just another trainee. I am equally grateful to my fellow trainees on those courses who treated me as one of them, despite the fact that I would never have to face the dangers and dilemmas that they might face.

I am equally indebted to all those involved in public-order policing, especially those who work in the Public Order Forward Planning Unit, New Scotland Yard, and the instructors at the Public Order Training Centre, Hounslow. I am particularly indebted to Commander Robinson for allowing me such freedom, and to Chief Superintendents Mike Shadrack, George Crawford, Ian Hurd, and Roger Barr and Superintendent Syd McKay, for their time and advice. I am equally grateful to Chief Inspector Peter Buck and Inspector Peter Power for their help and assistance in finding relevant documentary material. All the instructors at 'riot city' earned my thanks and respect, not least for demonstrating just how many muscles can be made to ache simultaneously! They, like their colleagues in PT17, accepted my intrusions with good grace and humour, and for that I am more than grateful. To the many ordinary police officers whom I joined, huddled together behind shields, and to those others who threw wooden blocks at me with no less force than at anyone else, go my gratitude and the hope that they will not face such a situation 'for real'.

Although this research concentrates upon policy and training, it proved immensely valuable to have been allowed to observe actual police public-order operations. I am, therefore, most grateful to Deputy Assistant Commissioner Douglas Cree for permitting me to observe the Gold control room at Wood Green during the weekend following the conviction of Winston Silcott and others for the murder of PC Keith Blakelock. I am similarly grateful to Deputy Assistant Commissioner Hunt for allowing me to observe the policing operation on the occasion of a major reggae concert on Clapham common in the summer of 1987. Most of all, I am indebted to Assistant Commissioner Paul Condon, who twice allowed me to observe the policing of the Notting Hill Carnival and see anything I wished, from the briefings for senior officers to rioting at close quarters. At Clapham I accompanied Chief Superintendent George Crawford and at Notting Hill I twice spent two very long days with Chief Superintendent Rod Havard. I must thank them not only for willingly accepting the additional burden of my presence but for ensuring that I lived to tell the tale!

Writing this report has been a labour I have shared with others. I have already expressed my thanks to Mike Waldren for the technical assistance he gave me. My thanks also go to Professor Tony Smith and Peter Schofield, both of the Department of Law, and to Malcolm Hamilton and Ken Robertson, from the Department of Sociology, all at the University of Reading, and to Mollie Weatheritt, Deputy Director of the Police Foundation and Robert Reiner of the London School of Economics, for reading various sections of the manuscript and helping me translate my thoughts into English. I am particularly indebted to Peter Schofield who, as a pacificist, read this account of guns and rioting with repugnance, but was the more able, thereby, to challenge any ill-thought-out arguments. However, the prize for dedication, as well as staying power, must go to my wife, Diane, who read the entire manuscript whilst maintaining order in the Waddington household.

I would also like to thank the Police Foundation for permission to base much of the discussion in Chapters 3 and 4 and Appendix 1 on my interim report, *Arming an Unarmed Police*. I am also grateful to the Rt. Hon. Sir Leon Brittan for permission to quote from a letter written to Dr David Owen; also James Anderton, Chief Constable of the Greater Manchester Police, for permission to quote from his report of the 1981 riot in Moss Side. My thanks also go to Mike Hoare, for permission to reproduce a figure from his unpublished M.Sc. dissertation, 'The Pattern of Experience in the Use of Firearms by Criminals and the Police Response'. I must thank the Policy Studies Institute for granting permission ,to quote a lengthy extract from volume iii of their report *Police and People in London.*

P.A.J.W.
June 1990

(Source: Waddington, 1991, pp.vii–ix)

Appendix 2.3

Grimshaw and Jefferson: *Interpreting Policework*, 'Foreword and acknowledgements'

Conducting research on the police is not easy. To get off the ground at all involves bringing together institutions, such as the police, universities and the Home Office whose interests are not coincident. To continue to a mutually satisfactory conclusion, therefore, involves the maintenance of a sometimes 'teeth gritting' harmony. And to write up involves bearing in mind one's debt to all the divergent institutional interests that made it possible, one's responsibilities to the next generation of researchers, and finally, and by no means least, one's responsibilities to one's conscience. Moreover, there is an (understandable) temptation, 'when it's all over', to remember, like summers of yesteryear, only the days when the sun shone brilliantly all day and long into the evening. In truth, past summers were always more variable than selective memory allows – as was the route taken by the research project upon which this book is based.

The project had its origins in a Home Office research fellowship, instituted at the Centre for Criminological and Socio-Legal Studies, Sheffield University, and taken up by Tony Jefferson in October 1977. Since the normal relationship between the Home Office and the research it funds is via direct contracting, this indirect form of arrangement, via a university fellowship, was an unusual initiative, only the second of its kind. As beneficiaries of that bold initiative, and the freedom it granted to plan and execute research completely untrammelled by Home Office policy-dominated interests, we are extremely grateful for the opportunity it gave us. Yet there is no doubt that that same freedom, given the Home Office's interest in policy *for* the police, and the universities in *explaining* (in our case and among other things) policies *of* the police, was the seed bed for later disagreements over our submitted report (Jefferson and Grimshaw, 1981).

By that time, Roger Grimshaw had long been a member of the research team (since October 1978); but also the status of the project had changed, when Tony Jefferson secured a lectureship in January 1980, to a piece of traditional contract research. So, whilst gratefully mindful of our opportunity, and not unaware of shifts taking place within the Home Office Research Unit itself, we were led to perceive a crucial axis of differentiation between the two institutions – the Home Office and the university – which could not be dissolved by good intentions. It is a difference which is, to anticipate a key theme of the book, *structural*. Not surprisingly then, our disagreements with the Home Office focused around the 'relevance *for* (rather than *of*) policy' of the submitted report; difficulties which led, in the event, to the completion of a supplementary Appendix drawing out the policy implications.

Similarly, the divergence of interests between the university and the police is structural. Any conjunction of an institution given the power to uphold order in a society undergoing profound and painful economic and social transformations, and one with the responsibility for examining and explaining the exercise of that power, can hardly be easily harmonious. It is not, therefore, paranoia that causes police to resist observation and examination on the grounds that whatever emerges will not be 'for them';

sociology of the police, as police know too well, *is* always critical – even when not conducted within a radical tradition. Since police apparently have so little to gain from opening their doors, we wish to express our real gratitude to the Chief Constable for the facilities and access granted us. It was unique in its extent, and, like the Home Office, bold in the current context which gives chief constables absolute powers over access decisions. Whilst we feel exceptionally privileged in the access we were granted, allowing us to reach into areas that other researchers hardly dared dream of, and enabling us to fully pursue the generality of our research, two points need also to be made; such access was not granted without considerable negotiations, and was not without some (albeit small) losses of particular access locations requested, a point we make not out of churlishness but to remind those who follow not to expect that doors will simply open, Ali Baba-like, on the production of some magic words. Secondly, to remind our readers of the important political point that, ultimately, such decisions, so crucial to the success or otherwise of a research project, lie with an unelected public official – a chief constable. It is this latter point which renders us ambivalent about our 'privilege'; quite simply, grateful though we are, it ought not to be a privilege in a society claiming the mantle democratic, but should be an expectation that researchers and others subject the exercise of power to objective and critical scrutiny. Hopefully our work, like that of other researchers, will help to demonstrate the value of that access.

Thanks are also due to those individuals within the force who fulfilled a contact and liaison role during the period of the research. And officers whom we accompanied on patrol and visits, etc., as well as those who consented to be interviewed, are owed our thanks for their co-operation. We hope that they will understand that our primary sociological interests are expressed in what might otherwise be seen as individious scrutiny of their daily work.

Studying the police in action always requires that a deep breath be taken before committing the findings to paper. The sharp splash of new experience, after entry to a normally closed world, is invigorating but transition to the stage of written report needs careful consideration, the more so the deeper the penetration of an uncharted territory. The writer's responsibility lies in handling this difficult process of making the invisible visible, all the while with the consent of those who usually maintain that invisibility in place. For such reasons our lengthy main report to the Home Office was preoccupied with theoretical clarification and general description; its completion, however, was delayed until a year after the project had formally ceased. In particular we had embarked on a further joint project that took up those theoretical lines of investigation but was applied specifically to the pressing issue of police accountability. Though material from the Home Office Report was published at around the same time (Jefferson and Grimshaw, 1984a), it was the accountability study that found book length form first (Jefferson and Grimshaw, 1984b). The involution of two research themes within the limiting scope of our work schedules meant that this more substantial, analytical version of our work on organization and control has taken some years to appear. While the intellectual fruits of longer consideration may be significant, we are aware that the presentation of particular empirical facts is sometimes felt to suffer from the passage of time, as identifiable changes serve to freeze some detailed patterns into the glacier of history. The major institutional innovation that has supervened in the interim is probably the Police and Criminal Evidence Act 1984; whose significance receives some attention in the latter part of the text. However, our concerns are not with the documenting of recent police history but with the elucidation of sociologically-defined structures that underwrite the development of modern policing. For this purpose the detail of observed policing more than retains its relevance into the mid-80s. Consequently after some consultation we have normally adopted the 'historical' or 'continuous' present tense in recounting our observations and in general discussion.

We should, however, draw attention to the fact that the Home Office advised the consistent use of the past tense because, like the researched force, they felt that inferences about subsequent events should not be drawn from data collected some years earlier. This point had been raised in connection with the final draft of our discussion of policy on community policing and racial attacks in particular, now slightly amended. Though we obviously cannot comment on empirical changes that may have taken place in the force's consideration of policy, nor any other changes for that matter, we must reiterate our concern to produce a structural analysis. The resolution of structural questions is not necessarily affected by the mere passage of time. The vital issue is whether any observed change would lead us to conclude that a structural alteration had occurred. On this point our material remains singularly relevant to any structural assessment of the present state of affairs, as Chapter 9 in particular seeks to demonstrate.

From the beginning the research process was overseen by a Steering Committee chaired by Professor Tony Bottoms, then Director of the Centre, now of the Institute of Criminology, Cambridge. We should like to thank him and other members of that Committee – Keith Bottomley, Maureen Cain, Ken Lidstone, Ian Taylor, John Westergaard, Paul Wiles, Sir John Wood and Ron Broome – for their sympathetic advice and support throughout the period of research. We also wish to acknowledge the long-standing counsel of others who have ventured into the hinterlands of police sociology, notably Stuart Hall, Mike Brogden, Joe Sim and Robert Reiner. These helped to sustain our belief in the validity and relevance of a sociology closely pursuing the detail of the police organization.

The crucial dimension of administrative and secretarial support was provided by Barbara Holland, Shirley Peacock, Lynn Rance, Vera Marsh, Annie Lutwama and Connie Goodwin. Family and friends endured the many phases of production in the making of this book; to them apologies, as well as thanks, would seem most appropriate.

We are grateful to the publishers of the *International Journal of the Sociology of Law* for allowing us, in Chapter 8, to draw substantially on our article 'The problem of law enforcement policy in England and Wales: the case of community policing and racial attacks', *IJSL*, vol.12, no.2, pp.117–35.

Finally we must always turn to 'the public', especially people in police contact who tolerated our presence at times of anger or distress. We did not give them anything resembling succour. But we can offer, now, a form of knowledge that opens up for inspection some of the foundations of power in this society. Indirectly, the fulfilment of one duty to the public has therefore been attempted.

We are not the first academic researchers to reflect upon discords – as well as harmonies – between universities and the police, as Jerome Skolnick can testify. What we hope above all is that the fruits of the research will on balance be felt to justify the efforts, stresses and sacrifices of all the various parties. But that judgement, of course, rests above all with the readers.

August 1986

References

Jefferson, T. and Grimshaw, R. (1981) 'The organisation and control of policework', unpublished report to the Home Office (Centre for Criminological and Socio-Legal Studies, University of Sheffield).

Jefferson, T. and Grimshaw, R. (1984a) 'The problem of law enforcement policy in England and Wales: the case of community policing and racial attacks', *International Journal of the Sociology of Law*, vol.12, no.2, pp.117–35.

Jefferson, T. and Grimshaw, R. (1984b) *Controlling the Constable: Police Accountability in England and Wales*, London, Muller/Cobden Trust.

(Source: Grimshaw and Jefferson, 1987, pp.ix–xiii)

Appendix 2.4

British Sociological Association: 'BSA statement of ethical practice'

Ratified by the Annual General Meeting of
The British Sociological Association, April 1992

Styles of sociological work are diverse and subject to change, not least because sociologists work within a wide variety of settings. Sociologists, in carrying out their work, inevitably face ethical, and sometimes legal, dilemmas which arise out of competing obligations and conflicts of interest. The following statement aims to alert members of the Association to issues that raise ethical concerns and to indicate potential problems and conflicts of interest that might arise in the course of their professional activities.

While they are not exhaustive, the statement points to a set of obligations to which members should normally adhere as principles for guiding their conduct. Departures from the principles should be the result of deliberation and not ignorance. The strength of this statement and its binding force rest ultimately on active discussion, reflection, and continued use by sociologists. In addition, the statement will help to communicate the professional position of sociologists to others, especially those involved in or affected by the activities of sociologists.

The statement is meant, primarily, to inform members' ethical judgements rather than to impose on them an external set of standards. The purpose is to make members aware of the ethical issues that may arise in their work, and to encourage them to educate themselves and their colleagues to behave ethically. The statement does not, therefore, provide a set of recipes for resolving ethical choices or dilemmas, but recognizes that often it will be necessary to make such choices on the basis of principles and values, and the interests of those involved.

Professional integrity

Members should strive to maintain the integrity of sociological enquiry as a discipline, the freedom to research and study, and to publish and promote the results of sociological research. Members have a responsibility both to safeguard the proper interests of those involved in or affected by their work, and to report their findings accurately and truthfully. They need to consider the effects of their involvements and the consequences of their work or its misuse for those they study and other interested parties.

While recognizing that training and skill is necessary to the conduct of social research, members should themselves recognize the boundaries of their professional competence. They should not accept work of a kind that they are not qualified to carry out. Members should satisfy themselves that the research they undertake is worthwhile and that the techniques proposed are appropriate. They should be clear about the limits of their detachment from and involvement in their areas of study.

Members should be careful not to claim an expertise in areas outside those that would be recognized academically as their true fields of expertise. Particularly in their relations with the media, members should have regard for the reputation of the discipline and refrain from offering expert commentaries in a form that would appear to give credence to material which as researchers they would regard as comprising inadequate or tendentious evidence.

Relations with and responsibilities towards research participants

Sociologists, when they carry out research, enter into personal and moral relationships with those they study, be they individuals, households, social groups or corporate entities. Although sociologists, like other researchers are committed to the advancement of knowledge, that goal does not, of itself, provide an entitlement to override the rights of others. Members must satisfy themselves that a study is necessary for the furtherance of knowledge before embarking upon it. Members should be aware that they have some responsibility for the use to which their research may be put. Discharging that responsibility may on occasion be difficult, especially in situations of social conflict, competing social interests or where there is unanticipated misuse of the research by third parties.

1   Relationships with research participants

(a) Sociologists have a responsibility to ensure that the physical, social and psychological well-being of research participants is not adversely affected by research. They should strive to protect the rights of those they study, their interests, sensitivities and privacy, while recognizing the difficulty of balancing potentially conflicting interests. Because sociologists study the relatively powerless as well as those more powerful than themselves, research relationships are frequently characterized by disparities of power and status. Despite this, research relationships should be characterized, whenever possible, by trust. In some cases, where the public interest dictates otherwise and particularly where power is being abused, obligations of trust and protection may weigh less heavily. Nevertheless, these obligations should not be discarded lightly.

(b) As far as possible sociological research should be based on the freely given informed consent of those studied. This implies a responsibility on the sociologist to explain as fully as possible, and in terms meaningful to participants, what the research is about, who is undertaking and financing it, why it is being undertaken, and how it is to be promoted.

(i) Research participants should be aware of their right to refuse participation whenever and for whatever reason they wish. They should also not be under the impression that they are required to participate.

(ii) Research participants should understand how far they will be afforded anonymity and confidentiality and should be able to reject the use of data-gathering devices such as tape-recorders and video cameras.

(iii) Where there is a likelihood that data may be shared with other researchers, the potential uses to which the data might be put may need to be discussed with research participants.

(iv) When filming or recording for research purposes, sociologists should make clear to research participants the purpose of the filming or recording, and, as precisely as possible, to whom it will be communicated. Sociologists should be careful, on the one hand, not to give unrealistic guarantees of confidentiality and, on the other, not to permit communication of research films or records to audiences other than those to which research participants have agreed.

(v) It should also be borne in mind that in some research contexts, especially those involving field research, it may be necessary for the obtaining of consent to be regarded, not as a once-and-for-all prior event, but as a process, subject to renegotiation over time. In addition, particular care may need to be taken during periods of prolonged fieldwork where it is easy for research participants to forget that they are being studied.

(vi) In some situations access to a research setting is gained via a 'gatekeeper'. In these situations members should adhere to the principle of obtaining informed consent directly from research participants to whom access is required, while at the same time taking account of the gatekeeper's interest. Since the relationship between research participants and the gatekeeper will continue long after the sociologist has left the research setting, care should be taken not to inadvertently disturb that relationship unduly.

(c) It is incumbent upon members to be aware of the possible consequences of their work. Wherever possible they should attempt to anticipate, and to guard against, consequences for research participants which can be predicted to be harmful. Members are not absolved from this responsibility by the consent given by research participants.

(d) In many of its guises, social research intrudes into the lives of those studied. While some participants in sociological research may find the experience a positive and welcome one, for others the experience may be disturbing. Even if not exposed to harm, those studied may feel wronged by aspects of the research process. This can be particularly so if they perceive apparent intrusions into their private and personal worlds, or where research gives rise to false hopes, uncalled-for self-knowledge, or unnecessary anxiety. Members should consider carefully the possibility that the research experience may be a disturbing one and, normally, should attempt to minimize disturbance to those participating in research.

It should be borne in mind that decisions made on the basis of research may have effects on individuals as members of a group, even if individual research participants are protected by confidentiality and anonymity.

(e) Special care should be taken where research participants are particularly vulnerable by virtue of factors such as age, social status and powerlessness. Where research participants are ill or too young or too old to participate, proxies may need to be used in order to gather data. In these situations care should be taken not to intrude on the personal space of the person to whom the data ultimately refer, or to disturb the relationship between this person and the proxy. Where it can be inferred that the person about whom data are sought would object to supplying certain kinds of information, that material should not be sought from the proxy.

2 Covert research

There are serious ethical dangers in the use of covert research but covert methods may avoid certain problems. For instance, difficulties arise when research participants change their behaviour because they know they are being studied. Researchers may also face problems when access to spheres of social life is closed to social scientists by powerful or secretive interests. However, covert methods violate the principles of informed consent and may invade the privacy of those being studied. Participant or non-participant observation in non-public spaces or experimental manipulation of research participants without their knowledge should be resorted to only where it is impossible to use other methods to obtain essential data. In such studies it is important to safeguard the anonymity of research participants. Ideally, where informed consent has not been obtained prior to the research it should be obtained *post hoc*.

3 Anonymity, privacy and confidentiality

(a) The anonymity and privacy of those who participate in the research process should be respected. Personal information concerning research participants should be kept confidential. In some cases it may be necessary to decide whether it is proper or appropriate even to record certain kinds of sensitive information.

(b) Where possible, threats to the confidentiality and anonymity of research data should be anticipated by researchers. The identities and research records of those participating in research should be kept confidential whether or not an explicit pledge of confidentiality has been given. Appropriate measures should be taken to store research data in a secure manner. Members should have regard to their obligations under the Data Protection Act. Where appropriate and practicable, methods for preserving the privacy of data should be used. These may include the removal of identifiers, the use of pseudonyms and other technical means for breaking the link between data and identifiable individuals such as 'broadbanding' or micro-aggregation. Members should also take care to prevent data being published or released in a form which would permit the actual or potential identification of research participants. Potential informants and research participants, especially those possessing a combination of attributes which make them readily identifiable, may need to be reminded that it can be difficult to disguise their identity without introducing an unacceptably large measure of distortion into the data.

(c) Guarantees of confidentiality and anonymity given to research participants must be honoured, unless there are clear and overriding reasons to do otherwise. Other people, such as colleagues, research staff or other employees, given access to the data must also be made aware of their obligations in this respect. By the same token, sociologists should respect the efforts taken by other researchers to maintain anonymity. Research data given in confidence do not enjoy legal privilege, that is they may be liable to subpoena by a court. Research participants may also therefore need to be made aware that it may not be possible to avoid legal threats to the privacy of the data.

(d) There may be less compelling grounds for extending guarantees of privacy or confidentiality to public organizations, collectivities, governments, officials or agencies than to individuals or small groups. Nevertheless, where guarantees have been given they should be honoured, unless there are clear and compelling reasons not to do so.

4   During their research members should avoid, where they can, actions which may have deleterious consequences for sociologists who come after them or which might undermine the reputation of sociology as a discipline.

Relations with and responsibilities towards sponsors and/or funders

A common interest exists between sponsor, funder and sociologist as long as the aim of the social enquiry is to advance knowledge, although such knowledge may only be of limited benefit to the sponsor and funder. That relationship is best served if the atmosphere is conducive to high professional standards. Members should attempt to ensure that sponsors and/or funders appreciate the obligations that sociologists have not only to them, but also to society at large, research participants and professional colleagues and the sociological community. The relationship between sponsors or funders and social researchers should be such as to enable social enquiry to be undertaken as objectively as possible. Research should be undertaken with a view to providing information or explanation rather than being constrained to reach particular conclusions or prescribe particular courses of action.

1   Clarifying obligations, roles and rights

(a) Members should clarify in advance the respective obligations of funders and researchers where possible in the form of a written contract. They should refer the sponsor or funder to the relevant parts of the professional code to which they adhere. Members should also be careful not to promise or imply acceptance of conditions which are contrary to their professional ethics or competing commitments. Where some or all of those involved in the research are also acting as sponsors and/or funders of research the potential for conflict between the different roles and interests should also be made clear to them.

(b) Members should also recognize their own general or specific obligations to the sponsors whether contractually defined or only the subject of informal and often unwritten agreements. They should be honest and candid about their qualifications and expertise, the limitations, advantages and disadvantages of the various methods of analysis and data, and acknowledge the necessity for discretion with confidential information obtained from sponsors. They should also try not to conceal factors which are likely to affect satisfactory conditions or the completion of a proposed research project or contract.

2   Pre-empting outcomes and negotiations about research

(a) Members should not accept contractual conditions that are contingent upon a particular outcome or set of findings from a proposed enquiry. A conflict of obligations may also occur if the funder requires particular methods to be used.

(b) Members should try to clarify, before signing the contract, that they are entitled to be able to disclose the source of their funds, its personnel, the aims of the institution, and the purposes of the project.

(c) Members should also try to clarify their right to publish and spread the results of their research.

(d) Members should be prepared to clarify with sponsors the methods of analysis to be used.

3   Guarding privileged information and negotiating problematic sponsorship

(a) Members are frequently furnished with information by the funder who may legitimately require it to be kept confidential. Methods and procedures that have been utilized to produce published data should not, however, be kept confidential.

(b) When negotiating sponsorships members should be aware of the requirements of the law with respect to the ownership of and rights of access to data.

(c) In some political, social and cultural contexts some sources of funding and sponsorship may be contentious. Candour and frankness about the source of funding may create problems of access or co-operation for the social researcher but concealment may have serious consequences for colleagues, the discipline and research participants. The emphasis should be on maximum openness.

(d) Where sponsors and funders also act directly or indirectly as gatekeepers and control access to participants, researchers should not devolve their responsibility to protect the participants' interests onto the gatekeeper. Members should be wary of inadvertently disturbing the relationship between participants and gatekeepers since that will continue long after the researcher has left.

4   Obligations to sponsors and/or funders during the research process

(a) Members have a responsibility to notify the sponsor and/or funder of any proposed departure from the terms of reference or proposed change in the nature of the contracted research.

(b) A research study should not be undertaken on the basis of resources known from the start to be inadequate, whether the work is of a sociological or inter-disciplinary kind.

(c) When financial support or sponsorship has been accepted, members must make every reasonable effort to complete the proposed research on schedule, including reports to the funding source.

(d) Members should be prepared to take comments from sponsors or funders or research participants.

(e) Members should, wherever possible, spread their research findings.

(f) Members should normally avoid restrictions on their freedom to disseminate research findings.

Acknowledgements

The British Sociological Association gratefully acknowledges the use made of ethical codes produced by the American Sociological Association, the Association of Social Anthropologists of the Commonwealth and the Social Research Association.

(Source: British Sociological Association, 1992, pp.703–7)

Chapter 3
Reading Quantitative Research

by Roger Sapsford

Contents

1 Introduction

esearch, quite simply, is systematic enquiry: that is, 'researching' consists in doing more systematically what we all do in our everyday lives. As part of our normal lives, we have to make sense of what is going on around us, on the basis of the evidence available to us and how it interacts with what we already understand (with 'theory'). This is precisely what 'research' also involves. The difference between formal research and our everyday common-sense enquiries lies in the more extensive and rigorous use of 'rules of evidence'. In everyday life, we commonly generalize from imperfectly understood single cases, act on untested assumptions and form deductions on the basis of local prejudices, group beliefs, what our parents told us and what we see on television and in the newspapers – often without examining the factual content or the origins of these premises. To a large extent, it is necessary to do so: in ordinary life we often cannot wait 'until all the evidence is in' before reaching even the most trivial decision. Further, we cannot continually be reflecting on our beliefs and actions to see what assumptions are implicit within them and whether we approve of the source and nature of these assumptions. Researchers, however, do try to stand outside their day-to-day lives, and they try to assure themselves that the available evidence clearly supports their conclusions, that they have not overlooked or failed to explore any relevant source of information, and that they are not being misled by an apparently logical chain of argument which expresses prejudice or taken-for-granted ideology cloaked as a set of neutral 'facts'.

In this and the following chapter we explore the activity of social research, looking at the different approaches which can be taken. All evidence is valuable, and all reports should be taken seriously. The key question we hope you will come to ask is whether the conclusions of a given research report do follow from the evidence presented:

- Is what has been studied appropriate, and was it sensibly selected?

- Are the measures used valid ones – do they mean what the researcher says they mean – or have the interview and/or observational data been collected and presented in a valid way?

- Are the analysis and interpretation of the data adequate – can we see how the conclusions have been reached, and are alternative interpretations equally plausible?

The underlying logic of all research reports is the same: they start with questions or problems, finish with answers or solutions, and in between come the arguments supporting the answers, the evidence which is adduced, and the arguments as to what the evidence means and what it can show. Thus theory and research practice are intertwined: the answer is supported by arguments from theory, arguments based on past research, and arguments based on current evidence. It is important to understand from the outset that no research report just 'gives the facts'. A report of research is always an *argument*: 'Here is what I conclude, on the basis of this research evidence, and here is why you should agree that the evidence supports the conclusion'.

This chapter is concerned with the 'quantitative' or 'scientific' style of research – research which most nearly approaches the popular stereotype of research in the physical sciences. It is concerned with three problems which are most evident in such research and into whose solution the researchers often put great effort and ingenuity:

- problems of measurement and classification;

- problems of sampling and representation; and

- problems of drawing conclusions about causal relationships from observed correlations.

Each of its three substantive sections begins with a discussion of some aspect of research results as evidence for conclusions, raises some problems about the mechanics of how they were arrived at and offers some criteria for assessment and evaluation. Through the activities, you are invited to apply these criteria, first on a brief summary description of a piece of research, and then on an actual research paper. I shall offer my own responses to these exercises following each activity. These are not necessarily the *right answers*, because we may well differ on what we consider important and what we consider acceptable; but they offer you a chance to reflect on your own responses, perhaps from a different perspective.

The 'problems' discussed in this chapter are presented as problems of 'scientific' research, and indeed this style of research has been very much concerned to devise solutions to them. As we will see in Chapter 4, however, similar problems occur in all research, and while the 'quantitative' solutions may often not be appropriate for other styles of research, the thinking which led to them is relevant to all research.

2   Counting cases

Perhaps the simplest form of research is to define something of interest and then count it. If you wish to know how many children in a particular school are boys, you count the total number in the school and the number of boys – 450 boys out of a total of 1,000 pupils in the school, say, or 45 per cent. This might be the starting point for research which evaluates the need for a particular service or provision. Research into housing needs in a local government area might logically start by counting the number of available houses and the number of people or families not currently housed. Research into the prevention of domestic burglary logically starts by counting where the burglaries occur – by area, by type of property, by level of anti-theft precautions. Such information can then perhaps help the police or other services determine how their resources could best be deployed.

Sometimes it is not even necessary to do your own counting for this kind of research: you can use counts made by other agencies, often government departments. For example, the decennial UK Census of Population attempts to obtain a complete count of every person in every household in the UK on a particular night. A substantial questionnaire is completed, covering every person in the houshold at that time, giving details of age, gender, marital and family status, education, work, housing, facilities available, such as cars for example, and other information. Census-like

Glossary of some useful terms in quantitative research

case	a counted instance; generally the measurements taken on one person or situation. In quantitative research, if the cases are people, they are generally referred to as *subjects*, or as *respondents* if the data are collected by means of a questionnaire or interview schedule.
data	numbers gathered by the research.
correlation	an association between two variables such that the values of one can be predicted to some extent from the values of the other. A *causal connection* is said to exist where there is not only correlation, but also the supposed cause precedes the supposed effect in time and a mechanism can be shown to exist (or is strongly suspected on the basis of evidence) by which the one is connected to the other.
experiment	a systematic study aimed at identifying causal connection between variables.
population	the whole group to which the results of research are claimed to apply – everyone in the UK, or everyone in a given town, or all prisoners, or all people under the age of 15, or all houses without burglar alarms, for example.
questionnaire	a structured list of questions to be filled in by the respondent in person.
sample	a subset of cases, picked to be representative of the population. In general, the best samples are *random* – picked in such a way that every case in the population has an equal chance of selection, chance being the principle on which the selection is carried out.
schedule	an *interview schedule* is a list of questions to be asked by the interviewer; an *observation schedule*, similarly, is a structured form on which a researcher fills in systematically what has been observed.
survey	the systematic collection of data from a population, often information on people's attitudes, knowledge or beliefs, by means of questionnaires or interview schedules; but a systematic observation project in which researchers measure aspects of behaviour or environment for each case without asking verbal questions is also a survey.
variable	one item of data, recorded for all cases: for example, age, IQ score, or previous convictions. Where a causal connection is claimed, the *independent variable* or *explanatory variable* is the supposed cause. The *dependent variable* is the one whose variation we are trying to explain, arguing that changes in the dependent variable are produced by changes in the independent variable(s): for example, that average driving speed (*independent* variable) has a causal effect on incidence of fatal traffic accidents (*dependent* variable).

figures – that is, complete counts of all cases – are often available from the administrative statistics collected and reported as a matter of routine by government departments. The Prison Department, for example, publishes an Annual Report and a volume of associated statistics based on complete counts of people in prison. This volume enumerates every prisoner in every prison, by type of prison, and gives a range of descriptive information such as type of offence and length of sentence. Various other useful statistics are also included (sometimes in separately published appendices), such as counts of disciplinary charges and punishments awarded. Similar figures are published by other major agencies in the criminal justice system, such as the probation service. The 'annual reports' of the police and of the courts are given in the form of tables in the annual government publication *Criminal Statistics*, which also includes complete counts of all crimes recorded and criminals apprehended during the year and of their disposal.

Despite their apparently objective and authoritative status, all such counts need to be treated with considerable caution: they may be 'factual', but paradoxically they may not represent 'the facts' (or at least, not the *desired* facts). The Prison Department's reports on the number of prisoners received or size of the prison population, for example, may for the most part be taken as reliable and valid counts of those cases; occasional clerical errors do creep in, but in the long term they are corrected by the various checking mechanisms built into the system. Counts of discipline offences, however, must be seen as a construction rather than a straightforward report of prison indiscipline: what counts as a disciplinary offence and what merits a given grade of punishment are subject to the decisions of particular prison officers (who bring the charge), of particular governors or other decision-making bodies (who adjudicate on it), and policy decisions, either specific to particular prisons or general within the prison system at that time. The figures are a precise report of a class of administrative events – the bringing of discipline charges – but their value as a measure of prisoners' behaviour may be disputed.

Similarly, the assessment of whether a given incident in the real world is to be counted in *Criminal Statistics* as a crime, and its perpetrator as a prosecuted and sentenced offender, is not straightforward but depends on a series of decisions. It is dependent on the choice of the public as to whether to report it (in some cases); the discretion of particular police officers as to whether it shall be recorded; their discretion as to which cases to follow up; the policy of the force on the deployment of personnel and on charging; and the discretion of the courts as to conviction and sentence. What is reported is not a raw record of events, but rather the record of what has emerged from a long chain of decision-making. It does not accurately reflect the absolute level of crimes committed, and it certainly does not reflect the balance of *types* of crime because there is differential under-reporting of offences. Virtually all car theft is reported, because reporting is a condition of recovering the value from the insurers, but not all burglaries are reported – people say they see no point in reporting small losses, given that there is little the police can do. Both rape and violent assaults appear to be seriously under-reported – people say they are embarrassed and ashamed to report them. We have to be careful, therefore, of conclusions based on criminal statistics as *evidence* and to think carefully about the quality of the statistics as measures of crime in the context of how they are used in particular research (see also **Book 1, Chapter 1**).

2.1 Validity of measurement

What is at stake here is a very common problem with research – *validity of measurement.* In the scientific approach to research, questions of measurement are of key importance. The aim is to measure independent (explanatory) variables, to measure their effect on a dependent variable (the aspect or quality to be explained), and to eliminate alternative possible explanations or to measure their effects so that they may be allowed for (controlled) in the analysis. For example, a probation researcher might set out to evaluate the effects of a particular form of psychologically designed casework on the subsequent behaviour of probationers. To argue that the treatment has an effect, three kinds of measurement will be needed:

1 A clear specification of what the independent variable (the treatment) *is*, and probably a way of quantifying the amount that a person receives, at least into 'some' versus 'none' (see section 4).

2 A clear specification of the dependent variable (the outcome) and how it can be measured.

3 Measurement of other variables which might be thought to have a greater effect (for example, aspects of personality, or degree of departmental support for the initiative).

A key part of the evidence which the evaluation report would have to present is a convincing rationale for the measurements taken, demonstrating that they do measure what the researcher says they measure, and with some degree of accuracy.

A minor but necessary part of this evidence will concern *reliability* – that is, showing that the measuring technique produces reasonably consistent results. Using the probation officer's 'impression of whether clients had become more stable' would not be very convincing; his or her impression could be influenced systematically by knowing which people had received the treatment. The impressions of another probation officer might be more useful, particularly if the judgements were made 'blind', without knowledge of which were the treatment cases, but the measuring technique would still be liable to human variability. The impressions of several probation officers working independently would be more convincing, because random fluctuations are likely to 'even out' when several judges are used. Best of all might be scores on a basket of 'objective' measures – for example, whether the person was in employment three months after the end of treatment, whether the employers described themselves as satisfied with the work, whether the client turned up punctually for work, whether he or she had been in any trouble with the police in the three months. Whatever strategies are adopted, the value of the evidence is greatly increased if it can be shown that the measures are being applied consistently.

However, it would be relatively useless to demonstrate that your test was measuring *something* consistently unless you could also demonstrate *what* it was measuring. The *validity* of a measurement technique is the extent to which it demonstrably measures what the researcher says it measures. So the outcome measure in our fictional probation study, for example, must be *justified* as a measure of 'good outcome', before a link between scoring highly on it and having been exposed to the new form of casework can be taken as evidence that the treatment has the desired effect.

The simplest and weakest guarantee of validity is what is called *face validity*; that is, the researcher's assertion that 'on the face of it, it certainly *looks* as though it ought to measure what I want'. Sometimes this will be sufficient. In the fictional probation research, for example, we should not quibble at accepting as valid evidence of improvement the fact that people who had been through the new form of casework were more likely to hold down a job and less likely to get into trouble with the police. More often, however, this kind of researcher's impression is not of much value as evidence. If a subsidiary argument of the paper was that extroverts did better than introverts, for example, we should want more than face validity from the measure of extroversion; we should want evidence that people who are classed as extroverts or introverts on other agreed measures, or whose behaviour is demonstrably extrovert or introvert, are correctly classified by the researcher's measuring instrument.

2.2 Example 1: Grendon Prison

As a first example of what can be done by just counting and examining the counts, we will consider research on the effectiveness of Grendon Prison, which runs a psychiatric regime based on the principles of psychotherapeutic communities (see **Audio-cassette 2, Side 2**). Eric Cullen published an analysis of a sample of 277 randomly selected men who were in therapy between January 1984 and December 1988 (Cullen, 1992). (A *random sample* is one where every member of the population has an equal chance of being selected, so that the sample is not biased towards a particular kind of person.) The average age of these men on reception into Grendon was 31.2 years. The average number of previous convictions was about 10 but it ranged from none (16 men) to 34. More than a quarter of the sample were in prison for offences of violence, another quarter for sex crimes, about a third for theft, robbery and fraud, with a few men convicted of a range of other crimes.

Two measures of success or failure are discussed in Cullen's article. In terms of reconviction, 33 per cent were reconvicted within two years of release from prison, compared with between 42 and 47 per cent of all adult males (Home Office, 1989, Table 9.3). Of those who had completed over 18 months of therapy, however, only 20 per cent re-offended. The percentage re-offending was smaller still if we look only at those released directly from Grendon after 18 months or more of therapy, as opposed to being transferred to another prison. As a second measure, a smaller sample of the most recent releases (41 men) were rated by the prison wing psychologist as 'success' or 'failure' in terms of clinical judgements. Of those who had completed 18 months in therapy and were rated as successful by the psychologist, only one man out of 14 (7 per cent) was reconvicted within two years of release, but a third of the men rated as failures were reconvicted.

ACTIVITY 3.1

Write a brief synopsis of Cullen's research based on the outline given above.

1   Summarize briefly what he is trying to show.
2   Look at the measures he uses in his research.
3   Outline his conclusions and assess the extent to which they are established beyond doubt by the research.
4   Take into account any alternative explanations of the results which might be possible.

You should not spend more than 20 minutes on this Activity.

Cullen sets out to show that the Grendon regime does have some beneficial effect on those sent to the prison (and therefore, implicitly, that it is worth continuing). His main outcome measure is reconviction: whether released inmates are reconvicted within two years of release. He finds that the Grendon reconviction rate is markedly lower than that of released prisoners as a whole. Those who have undergone 18 months or more of the regime are even less likely to be reconvicted within two years, and those on whom the treatment has had a successful impact, in the opinion of their prison wing psychologist, are even less likely to be reconvicted. (This last finding is based on a rather small number of cases, however, and should be treated with caution, as suggestive rather than conclusive, pending further evidence.) Cullen concludes that the Grendon regime works.

Three points of caution occur to me:

1   As we know, not all offences finish up as criminal statistics, so it is *possible* that former Grendon prisoners are less likely to be caught rather than less likely to re-offend; they could, indeed, be re-offending at the same rate. (This is unlikely to be the case, but it is logically possible. To disprove it we would look for associated differences between the Grendon prison population and other prisoners, and between those who last out in therapy and those who do not – higher measured intelligence, for example.)

2   The difference between the overall reconviction rate of Grendon released prisoners and that of released prisoners as a whole is due at least in part to differences in age: the Grendon prison population is older than the average for all prisoners, and it is known that older people are less likely to offend (or at least, to be caught).

3   There could be differences among Grendon groups which are not explored in the brief paper from which this account was taken, which could form an alternative explanation of the results. For example, those who last out in therapy may be older, on average, than those who do not.

2.3   Example 2: 'Black and blue'

ACTIVITY 3.2

Let us look at another kind of counting exercise – a structured observational survey of police behaviour. Read Appendix 3.1, 'Black and blue: an analysis of the influence of race on being stopped by the police', by Clive Norris *et al*. Make notes for an evaluation of the evidence:

1   What is being counted?
2   How?
3   What is concluded from the counts?
4   How adequate is the evidence to sustain these conclusions?

When you have finished, compare your notes with my comments.

This Activity will probably take about 2 hours.

Three of the authors of Appendix 3.1 spent several hundred hours accompanying police officers on routine patrols in the Metropolitan Police district and in Surrey. They observed 213 instances of officers stopping a member or members of the public (involving 319 people in total), where 'stopping' is defined as 'non-elective' and 'potentially adversarial': the police initiated the encounter, and those stopped were suspected of some kind of legal or at least moral/behavioural offence. The observer recorded (among other things) demeanour of police and citizen(s) at the start of the encounter and during it, and the age and ethnic group of those stopped. The major findings were that black people were substantially more likely to be stopped than their prevalence in the local population would suggest (this was particularly true of younger people), but there was little or no difference between black and white people in their behaviour towards the police or in the behaviour of the police towards them. The authors warn the reader to be cautious about generalizing on the basis of a single study, but conclude tentatively that even if racist attitudes are prevalent in the police, as the research literature suggests, the police do not necessarily treat black people any differently from white people in face-to-face interaction (though they are more likely to stop them in the street in the first place).

To the extent that the counts are accurate, the conclusions would seem well supported by the evidence provided. Two 'points of caution' occur to me, however:

1   Would the police have behaved differently if they had not been accompanied by a researcher? (This is the problem of reactivity – that is, the effect of the research on the situation it is examining – which is discussed further in Chapter 4.)

2   Were the measures of 'demeanour' entirely accurate? We should note that:

   (a) to minimize reactivity – to make the police less conscious that their behaviour was being observed – records were not made at the time of the encounters, but after the end of the shift. The accuracy of the information therefore depends on the memory of the observers.

   (b) the decision as to whether one party or the other was 'calm or agitated', 'civil or antagonistic', for example, was made entirely by single observers; undoubtedly the decision was made on the basis of agreed criteria, but nonetheless it can hardly be counted as an exact method of measurement.

Two other points should be noted, to which we shall return later in the chapter:

1   There are apparently differences in other sets of figures, for example Table V in the paper, which are ignored by the authors as of no account, being too small to be significant. There are in fact 'statistical' ways of testing this.

2   There is very little mention in the paper of the gender of those stopped.

3   The logic of representation

The initial question of a piece of research quite often may be not 'Why does this happen?' or 'Does this work?', but '*What* is it that happens?' or '*How many* of these are there out there?' (This may very quickly lead to 'Why?' questions in most cases – '*Why* are black men stopped more often by the police than white men?' – but this may not be the initial way in which the problem presents itself.) Description is often the first stage of social or criminological research. We set out, for example, to see how many crimes occur, committed by whom and with whom as victim; how many released offenders might benefit from a particular service or be suitable for control in a particular way; or how many prisoners of a particular kind there are and what their ages and backgrounds are.

If you are doing a survey of a very restricted locality, it may be easy to count every case: if you have the access (if you work in the institution where the research is being conducted) it is not too difficult to look at every person on a prison landing, for example, or every medical report made during a one-month period. It may not be *necessary* for the researchers themselves to look at every case because sufficient information is contained in published and available statistics collected on a national basis – *if* these cover the precise topics with which the research is concerned. Most often, however, we have to generalize to a *population* from information collected about a *sample* – generalizations about the practicalities of policing from interviews with just a few police officers studied in depth, for example, or from the opinions of a larger sample of police officers asked to answer a questionnaire. How, then, does the researcher convince the reader that the cases picked for study were typical of the population, so that what is true of the sample is likely to be true of the population?

A technology has grown up around the question of generating representative samples of populations in surveys – that is, samples from which inferences about the population can be drawn with a calculable likelihood of error. The basis of this technology is the concept of *randomness*. The survey researcher selects cases randomly in order to be able to argue that the sample does not differ significantly from any other random sample which might have been drawn, or from the population as a whole. If it is possible to list every member of a population and select a sample of them at random, the only constraint on representativeness is the *size* of the sample: from a very large population consisting of equal numbers of women and men it is obviously absurdly easy to draw a sample of two people which does *not* have equal numbers of women and men, and still very easy with a sample of 10, but equality is more likely to be approached with a sample of 100 and even more likely with a sample of 10,000.

The mathematics of random numbers (statistics) is well enough worked out that the probable confidence limits for the relation of your sample to the population may be stated. Thence it is possible to work out the likelihood of a relationship or a difference found in a sample being spurious – that is, the probability that you have drawn an unrepresentative sample, in this respect, from a population in which the relationship or the difference is not true. The reader does not have to understand how to calculate this probability (and even the researcher does not need to understand the mathematics of it).

You will find a great range of statistics quoted in different research papers. For example:

- Differences between means (average values) on some variable.

- Correlation coefficients (which express the extent to which two variables *co-vary*, so that the value on one helps to predict the value on the other).

- Statistics such as chi-squared (χ^2) which test the extent to which there is a 'pattern' in data expressed in tables.

- Analysis of variance (which, as the name suggests, estimates the amount of the total variance in the data 'explained' by a given variable).

- More complex *multivariate* statistics, such as multiple regression and multivariate analysis of variance, which offer 'explanations' in terms of *several* possible explanatory variables.

Whichever of these or many other statistical techniques is used, the basic process is the same; it is a kind of 'model-fitting' in reverse. We test the hypothesis that the relationship or the difference which we observe in the sample is there because we have picked a peculiar sample and that it does not exist in the population as a whole.

Suppose we had a population in which, say, age and likelihood of reconviction are *not* correlated; what is the likelihood of drawing a random sample in which there *does* appear to be a correlation? If we were to draw sample after sample, randomly, from the population in which no correlation existed, many samples would show no correlation; and a majority would show, at most, a very slight correlation in one direction or another. If we drew enough samples, however, by chance alone we would be bound to draw a few which would show a very strong correlation in one direction or the other, even though there was none in the population. (With 10 black balls and 20 white balls in a hat, if you draw out a set of 10 balls it is perfectly possible that all the balls in your 'sample' will be black – but this is *very* unlikely to happen often!) If our sampling is random, the probability of drawing a very untypical sample, in which there is a strong correlation, is precisely calculable, however, and we can offer odds on (assign a probability to) the likelihood of drawing a sample which exhibits an association of a given degree of extremity, from a population in which there is no overall association.

The question then becomes just *how* unlikely it has to be that the model of 'no association' fits (that we have drawn a totally untypical sample) before we reject the model and say that probably the difference is a real one in the population. If it is highly probable that a difference or a correlation as large as the observed one could occur in a random sample from a population which did *not* exhibit it, then we do not accept the difference as worth building arguments on but dismiss it as within the bounds of sampling error. If, however, such a result is reasonably unlikely, then we describe it as 'statistically significant' and treat it as worth interpreting. Typically, we assign odds of 19:1, a 5 per cent probability, as the 'significance level' at which we decide that the 'model of no association' is just not plausible (or we can assign the more demanding odds of 99:1, a 1 per cent probability). In other words, we start calling a result 'significant', and accepting that what the sample shows may well hold true for the population, when we would have to draw 20 random samples of this size from the population in order to get *one* which misled us by showing this result (or 100 samples, using the more stringent test).

When a result is described in a research report as 'statistically significant at the 0.05 level' or 'at the 5 per cent level' or 'with p<.05', what is being claimed is that the probability of having drawn an unrepresentative sample is only one in 20 – 5 per cent. That is, we would expect to draw a sample which showed a relationship or a difference as strong as the observed one, from a population in which this relationship or difference did *not* hold, only one time in 20. (If the claim is for significance 'at the 1 per cent level' or 'with p<.01', then this means that such a sample should be drawn, from a population in which the relationship or difference does not hold, only one time in 100.) Statistics deal with how likely it is that the observed results do *not* represent what is true about the population; and it is by showing that the probability of a *spurious* relationship or difference is low that the researcher is able to assert that the sample probably represents the population fairly accurately. We should be suspicious of quantitative research which generalizes from a sample to a population but does not use statistical tests to strengthen the claims made.

Statistical methods are totally appropriate only when the sample *is* a random one – that is, where every member of the population has a known, equal chance of being selected. Often survey researchers have to work with samples which are not randomly selected. Random sampling may not be feasible, for instance; there may be no complete list of the population from which to draw a sample. Many surveys (particularly in market research) have therefore depended on other means to obtain arguably representative samples. A very common method is the 'quota' sample, where the researcher instructs interviewers to obtain so many cases in each cell of a table which represents the population on variables known to be important; for example, so many young women in middle-class jobs, so many older ones in middle-class jobs, so many young men in middle-class jobs, and so on. The sample which is finally obtained matches the population in terms of gender, age and class. This at least guarantees that the sample will be representative of the population in respect of the variables used to construct the quotas. However, it leaves the selection of the cases to the convenience of the interviewers. Sometimes the method can provide usable samples – it has been used quite successfully in political research – but sometimes quite bad errors may creep in because the interviewers have selected groups which are not representative of the population on 'non-quota' variables. For example, market research surveys frequently over-sample full-time housewives and under-sample women who go out to work, because interviewers prefer to do their work during the day-time.

Thus with a non-random sample the likelihood of error – that is, of picking a sample which is *not* typical of the population – is much increased, and it may not always be possible to predict the respects in which it will be untypical. Worst of all is the 'sample of opportunity': people stopped in a particular street on a particular day, or people in a particular school class, or people on a particular course, selected because it happens to be convenient (or sometimes because there is really no other way of drawing a sample with the resources available). Here there are almost certain to be in-built selection biases. The people in the street at that time are those who are free to leave home and who are not at work, the children in that class are in a middle-class or a working-class school, the people on the course are all motivated to take part in it because they have come voluntarily; these are all factors which mean the samples are predominantly from only one section of the population and are not representative of the whole of it. In these cases, researchers still use statistical tests as if the sample were random, but they cannot put a great deal of faith in them.

Most importantly, what should be considered is the kinds of people likely to be in the sample and the kinds likely to be excluded from it, and the effect their presence or absence is likely to have on the conclusions. For example, in any interview project where one writes to all possible respondents and interviews those who respond, one should be aware that those being interviewed are volunteers and that the sample will be seriously deficient in people who cannot be bothered or do not wish to talk to a researcher – who may be different from the rest of the population in important ways. Indeed, even with random sampling it is important to take note of the extent of non-response/refusal and to consider what effects it may have on the sample. A famous study of car workers by John Goldthorpe and his colleagues, for example, picked a representative sample of people to interview and came to interesting conclusions about their attitudes to work and home, the dominance of money in their lives and the low likelihood of worker solidarity developing in this kind of industry (Goldthorpe *et al.*, 1969). Not long after the results were published, the factory experienced the longest and most bitter strike of its history. One explanation which has been put forward for the discrepancy between this event and what would be expected from Goldthorpe's research is that not everyone agreed to be interviewed (though they had a 79 per cent response rate). There may have been a pattern in the refusals; if it were true that those who refused were the committed and active union members, the fact that their views were not represented might explain the outcome.

However, random sampling is not a 'magic technology' guaranteed to produce the most appropriate sample for the researcher's purpose. When drawing samples for interview research with life-sentence male prisoners, for example, I wanted to contrast groups at different stages of sentence to examine the effects of their sentence on them and to talk to them about how they coped with it (Sapsford, 1983). I quickly found that samples randomly selected from newly received men, men in mid-sentence and men who had served longer than the average term before release were typical of the men in those sentence bands, but so different from each other that they could not validly be compared. Because certain kinds of offence (for example, sexual offences) lead to men serving longer on indeterminate sentences than other kinds of offence (for example, domestic murder), the long-serving group were almost entirely composed of men who represented only a small proportion of the 'newly received' group. To obtain groups that could fairly be compared I had to construct *matched* samples – samples which had the same composition on the key variables which differentiated the sentence groups – even if this meant they were not typical of the population as a whole.

Whenever we talk about survey research, we tend to think of attitude questionnaires or opinion polls, and indeed it is true that a great deal of survey work is concerned with collecting data about people's attitudes, feelings, opinions, beliefs and intentions. However, the same methods are used when carrying out structured observation research (as we saw in Activity 3.2) or studying organizations or settings rather than people, or even analysing text by quantitative means. It will still be necessary to show that the sample of situations or texts or whatever is typical of the population. There is no point, for example, in carrying out detailed analysis of the contents of Tuesday's edition of *The Guardian* (which carries the educational supplement) and expecting the results to be typical even of *The Guardian* in general, let alone newspapers as a whole.

3.1   Example 3: The South-East Prison Survey

The South-East Prison Survey was a large-scale sample survey of prisoner characteristics in one prison region, carried out over twenty years ago by staff at the Home Office Research Unit, under the direction of Charlotte Banks (Banks and Fairhead, 1976). The study has been chosen as an example here, despite its age, because it is a classic of its kind and because it exemplifies a particular kind of measurement in survey research, in which subjective judgement masquerades to some extent as scientific precision. (Also, as I was involved in the data collection and analysis, I can say more about how these activities were conducted than is apparent from the two short reports which emerged from the survey.)

A 10 per cent random sample of male prisoners on a particular day in 1972 was identified, and research staff worked through their prison files (including medical records) and their records in New Scotland Yard to try to build up a comprehensive picture of their personal and criminal histories. The New Scotland Yard records yielded data on the number of their previous convictions, the kinds of offences for which the men had been convicted, the total value of property involved in their crimes over a lifetime (including 'TICs', offences 'taken into consideration', to which the offender had confessed but for which he was not formally tried and sentenced), and whether the men had 'known criminal associates'. In addition, it was usually possible to find details of injuries caused by offences of sex and violence. The prison and prison hospital files provided demographic details such as age, employment history, marital status and type of accommodation at arrest, and reports on the man's character, behaviour and mental state throughout sentence.

One of the reports to emerge from this survey pays particular attention to those men in prison who some might think could be diverted from the prison system without great danger to the public (Banks and Fairhead, 1976). Of the 811 men in the sample, 300 (37 per cent) were serving sentences of 18 months or less. Four researchers made judgements about which of these men might be considered by magistrates and the general public as 'petty offenders' – people whose *lifetime* of crime had gained them less than £600 overall (or less if the criminal career was a short one), who had not been involved in 'aggravated' burglaries, who had no record of serious violent or sexual offences, and who were not recorded as having criminal associates with substantially worse records than their own. The researchers identified 93 such cases (31 per cent of the men serving 18 months or less, and 11 per cent of the prison population as a whole). Of these 93 cases, nine had no property offences, and a further 44 had succeeded in obtaining less than £50 during their entire criminal careers. When the 'petty offenders' were compared with the others, the largest difference was in type of accommodation: the petty offenders were substantially and significantly more likely to be homeless at the time of arrest. They were also likely to have been described as 'unable to settle' and to be somewhat older on average than the rest of the prisoners; the homeless petty offenders were particularly likely to be older than the average. About a quarter of the petty offenders were recorded as having a drink problem. Many short-term prisoners tended to have poor work histories. The petty offenders were no different from the others in this respect, but more of them were described as in some way psychologically maladjusted (though not necessarily displaying outright disorder). Forty-two per cent of the petty offenders were reconvicted within one year of release from prison (60 per cent of the homeless ones and 26 per cent of the others) – a substantially higher rate than for other short-term prisoners. The authors concluded that in this one prison region, on any given day, there were probably between 750 and 1,000 men in prison who would be considered 'petty offenders' even on this restricted and conservative criteria; about 350 of them were probably homeless on arrest and had nowhere to go on release; and, because of the rate of conviction:

> It seems that, if alternative methods could be found of dealing with such 'petty' prisoners so that they were not returned to custody, then the burden on the prisons of receiving and discharging them would be reduced by a greater proportion than the number of men involved would suggest – particularly in the case of homeless men.

> (Banks and Fairhead, 1976, p.23)

ACTIVITY 3.3

Write a brief evaluation of this research. To what extent do the conclusions follow from the evidence?

This Activity should not take more than 20 minutes.

The main contention of the Banks and Fairhead report was that a substantial group of the men in prison do not need to be there; the public would be safe if they were not incarcerated. Implicit is the idea that they therefore *should* not be there, on humanitarian grounds – that prison ought not to be used for these people. Thus the implicit justification for prison in this report is that its role is to protect the public by segregating dangerous offenders. Explicitly made is the point – which is undoubtedly true – that a great deal less work would be involved for those who run prisons if this 'revolving door' group were diverted from prison. (The growing cost of prison places was an issue in the 1970s, and it became so again in the 1990s with record levels of prison population.)

In terms of methods, the sampling pattern is entirely sound and the sample reasonably large, so the estimates of the size of the various groups may be accepted as probably accurate (if we accept the classification used to assign people to groups). What is more doubtful is the nature of the data. For reasons of cost it was not possible to interview the prisoners and have them psychologically examined; the sole source of the data was documents in files. File data, prepared for a range of purposes which do *not* include the research, are notoriously unreliable. The 'factual' material is probably reasonably accurate – previous convictions, the details of offences, accommodation on arrest – though some of it will come from brief official interviews with the offenders and some from what the police or probation service could find out. Even 'value of property stolen', though necessarily only approximate, is probably a reasonable indicator of whether or not they have made a profit from their criminal careers or merely constituted an expensive nuisance.

What is in doubt, however, is the rating of mental state as disordered, maladjusted or normal. This is based on reports in files from psychologists, general practitioners and others less qualified in psychology, and indeed, on occasion, it was inferred by the researchers from reported behaviour alone. The reports were not always made *in order* to classify the offenders psychologically; we are relying in a number of cases on stray remarks in the middle of reports about something else. The offenders themselves had no access to their files during this period, so there was no way that a report could be contradicted. Further, if they had known they were being classified in terms of psychological condition, and if some administrative action such as remission of sentence or even transfer to lower security conditions had been at stake, the men might have acted quite differently and therefore received quite different reports. In other words, their mental state is being judged from conditions in which they were 'off guard' and may have felt free to behave in ways which did not at all reflect their true mental and emotional capacities. Most of all (and this is important for the validity of the classification into 'petty') we cannot tell what *might* have appeared in a report but did not – what informal diagnosis of dangerousness might have been made on an offender but was never formally required for a report in the file.

On the whole I am inclined to agree with the authors that there are men in prison whom we need not bother to incarcerate, both in their own interests and in ours. A great deal of time and money is spent locking up and guarding people who are not even much of a nuisance and certainly very little danger. However, we ought to regard the Banks and Fairhead estimates of their numbers as at best suggestive; the validity of the measure of 'pettiness' must necessarily be open to question, even if we accept the criteria which the authors use, because some of the constituent data are inherently unreliable.

The criticism of this kind of measurement applies not only to the Banks and Fairhead report, but also more generally to a wide range of research studies. It is all too easy for the seemingly authoritative numbers of 'scientific measurement' to conceal the fact that what is being presented does not have the authority of science at all but represents the considered but subjective judgement of the authors. Many classifications in daily use by prison officers, police, social workers and other practitioners, as well as by researchers, are 'performative' rather than just descriptive (they consist in assigning a person to a category *for the purpose of directing policy or practice*) and are done by the best means possible – which may not always be very systematic or based on anything better than informed opinion. This does not invalidate such measurements; the good judgement of experienced researchers and practitioners has a place in the scheme of things. However, they should not be given more weight than they deserve, and the reader of research reports should always examine what is presented, to separate what is literally descriptive from what rests on the judgement of the authors or of other involved parties.

3.2   Example 4: Concern about crime

ACTIVITY 3.4

Now read Appendix 3.2, 'Measuring concern about crime: some inter-racial comparisons', by Monica Walker. Summarize her methods and conclusions and comment on the extent to which her evidence is adequate for the purpose for which it is used.

This Activity should probably take about 2 hours.

Walker reports on a survey of fears, worries and problems about crime, which was carried out in Leeds in 1987. The households sampled were in Census Enumeration Districts in which, according to the 1981 Census, more than 10 per cent of 'heads of household' were born in the New Commonwealth and Pakistan. (The sample was restricted to men aged 16–35 because 'females and older men were thought to be less likely to have had experience of crime'.) Whether this was a wise decision may be debated, but we must in any case remember that it limits the breadth of the population to which the results can legitimately be generalized.) The sampling fraction – the proportion of households approached – was adjusted according to the ethnic origin of the respondents, to give reasonably sized groups of black, Asian and white men within a total sample of over 600. Thus the sample is not representative of Leeds as a whole, let alone the UK, for two reasons:

1   The different ethnic groups were sampled differentially, so their numbers do not represent their frequency in the population. (This would not be a problem, however. We could 'reconstruct' the population proportions by weighting; that is, by multiplying the figures for each group by the proportion it formed of the total population.)

2   More fundamentally, the white males in the survey live in the same deprived areas as the black and Asian males, and are not representative of white males in general.

Thus if the purpose of the survey were to find out the extent of problems and worries in the general population, or even in Leeds, this sample would be quite unsuitable. Its main purpose, however, is to examine problems and worries experienced by young male black and Asian citizens, with the white males included only for the purpose of comparison. For this purpose the sampling design is entirely suitable; the comparison can be made with white males living in the same area and, to a large extent, sharing economic and social circumstances. This underlines the point made earlier, that sampling is not a mechanical process but is carried out for a particular purpose.

Walker reports clear differences between the three ethnic groups on all the measures used. Black males were least, and Asian males most, in fear of crime; the same was true for fear of being a victim of robbery, burglary, vandalism or insulting behaviour. The Asian and white males gave a similar rating to crime, seeing it as more of a problem than did black males. However, white males saw sex assaults and the pestering of women as a disproportionately serious problem. From the pattern of the figures, the author claims that a single measure of 'fear of crime' is shown not to be sufficient to encompass the different worries and problems of different groups and the different emphases they place on aspects of the fear of crime.

The conclusions seem to me to follow quite soundly from the evidence as presented. The only problem is a general one, not specific to this survey but common to all survey research which uses questionnaires. What the researchers collect in such studies is not what people do or what they feel, but what they *say*. Thus the results may reflect fear of crime; they may, on the other hand, reflect the rhetoric of fear of crime, which is different in different groups for political reasons. They may even reflect what is seen as acceptable to say to a research interviewer, what image is seen as acceptable to present. Thus the 'science' of the method cloaks a considerable and fundamental degree of uncertainty about what is being measured, as in the Banks and Fairhead (1976) study which we considered above. (See also **Book 1, Chapter 1** for a discussion of these measurement problems.)

4   The logic of comparison

Most survey research is not just descriptive, but uses some kind of comparison as evidence that something causes or has an effect on something else: to use the language of experiments, that an *independent variable* (or *explanatory variable*) explains variation in a *dependent* variable. This is not inevitably the case: in Banks and Fairhead (1976), for example, the inbuilt comparison was essentially descriptive: it was shown that one group of prisoners differed from others (in the extent to which they might be regarded as dangerous), and from this it was argued that they *could* and therefore *should* be treated differently. In many studies, however, the comparison is made to point to a possible causal influence. In order to argue that Grendon's regime reduces reconviction after release, Cullen's study compared male prisoners who had been through Grendon with male prisoners in general, and men who had undergone at least 18 months' therapy with those who had not lasted out that long. There is some of the logic of the experiment here –

differences in an independent variable (type of treatment) produce differences in a dependent variable (reconviction) – and indeed, such comparisons are often called *quasi-experimental*.

The point of the comparison groups is that without them little can be demonstrated about causal influences. If Cullen had only presented reconviction figures for Grendon prison, declared that they were low and therefore that Grendon was successful, we should not be very convinced. A minimum requirement is that he should state with what they are *compared* in determining the 'low' rating. Even then, the argument is a weak one; its logical form is:

- this group differs from that one,
- so I must be right about *why* they differ,

which is clearly not a very strong argument for the effectiveness of a treatment. Admittedly, one essential element of causal explanation is also present, as it can be argued that the cause precedes the effect. So the argument is actually of the form:

- this (independent variable) changed and then that (dependent variable) changed,
- and I can find no other change that occurred in between,
- so this caused that.

Cullen's comparison with released prisoners as a whole establishes that there actually is something worth talking about: Grendon prisoners do have a lower reconviction rate. His comparisons of people who completed 18 months of treatment with those who did not, and of those judged as 'successes' by the psychologist with those not so judged, are attempts to establish that it is the treatment and not something else which makes the difference.

When you are relying just on temporal succession to argue your case, you are in the same kind of weak position as when using correlation to 'prove' causation – the evidence is just not logically sufficient. It may be true that many heroin users started on cannabis, or even that *all* heroin users started on cannabis, but they all also preceded their heroin use by hanging around with their mates, going to school, growing up, eating bread and butter, and many other activities. More evidence is needed before we can assert with confidence that it is cannabis and nothing else which influences them to take up heroin. The search for other things that changed in between is an attempt to rule out the 'anything else': if you could really show that nothing else changed, then the argument for a causal effect would be a strong one. Unfortunately, it is impossible even in principle to show that nothing else changed; if nothing else happened to the people over time, they certainly grew older. So how do we proceed?

The key method of the natural sciences for handling this problem is the *experiment*, where, for example, a theory is tested by taking a substance, measuring its condition, applying a treatment (heat, say) and measuring its condition afterwards. This has the same logic as the statement above: I applied this treatment and avoided making any other changes, so the effects are due to the treatment. The logic works in the physical sciences, which have the great advantage over the social ones that it can reasonably be assumed that their 'subjects' do not vary among themselves. Copper sulphate is copper sulphate, unproblematically. The same cannot be said for people, however: they may vary in their make-up and their past experience and learning, and they are continually developing and changing. The social researcher has therefore to demonstrate that what has occurred is genuinely a result of the treatment administered and not something that might have occurred anyway. The notion of control by comparison is thus central to social experimentation.

Typically, there are *two* groups: 'experimental' (or 'treatment') and 'control' groups. We administer treatment to the one and not the other, making sure beforehand that the two groups are as alike as possible in other respects. We may do this by taking the whole available 'population' of subjects and assigning them randomly to one group or the other; this will mean that all differences are likely to even out between the groups, including ones we did not know about, provided the groups are fairly large. Alternatively, we may 'match' groups: we may pick pairs of subjects as near identical as possible on the variables we know might be important, and randomly assign one of a pair to the treatment group and the other to the control group. We then inflict precisely the same procedures on the two groups, except that the experimental group receives the treatment and the control group does not. To the extent that we can show that the experience of the two groups was *identical* except for the treatment and that they were precisely alike beforehand, we are able to make a much stronger statement:

- this group, who received the treatment, changed like this;
- the other group, identical except for the treatment, did not;
- therefore the treatment caused the change.

Sometimes, rather than a control group, we will have several groups receiving different levels of the treatment, but the principle remains the same.

In one 'classic' experiment, Farrington and Kidd (1977) posited that financial dishonesty was a rational decision and would therefore increase as the pay-off increased and decrease as the cost to the offender rose. The experimenters went to a central shopping street and offered coins to people in circumstances where the people approached had the opportunity to claim, dishonestly, that they had dropped them. The coin was either a 10-pence or a 50-pence piece (low or high pay-off, a contrast of two treatments, rather than a treatment and a control group). The approach to the subject was either 'Excuse me, I think you dropped this' or 'Excuse me, did you drop this?'. This provided a further contrast between two treatments, as it varied the 'cost' to the potential offender; in responding positively to the second question he or she was not just accepting someone else's interpretation of the situation (as in the first approach) but was asserting ownership of the coin. If the subject refused the coin, the experimenter prompted with 'Are you sure?', and if it was still refused the experimenter walked away. One of the four possible experimental conditions was chosen randomly for any given subject; and after the 'trial' the experimenter would take a note of the gender of the subject, estimated age, style of dress, estimated social class, place, day, time and anything said by the subject. Some of the trials were observed by another experimenter to make sure that the 'scenario' was working as desired. A further variable was the gender of the experimenter who proffered the coin.

Some of the main results are outlined in Table 3.1. There was no sign of dishonesty being related to any characteristic of the subjects, but there was some effect of the type of statement used (cost to the potential offender) and the gender of the experimenter, and a weaker effect of the value of the coin. As Table 3.1 shows, there is a substantial difference, by the type of statement used, for male experimenters but not for female ones. (The 'p<0.01' at the end of the first row signifies that a difference this large would be expected, for this size of sample, less than one time in 100 if we were sampling from a population where the difference did not occur – where the gender of experimenter who approached the subject did not matter.) There is a smaller difference by type of statement for the high value coin but not the low value one – $p<0.05$, a difference large enough that it would be expected less often than one time in 20 if sampling from a population where the difference did not occur. (The 'not significant' against the two other rows means that one could get a difference of this size by chance alone as often as one time in 20, so the researchers are not prepared to reject the idea that it is just sampling error.)

Table 3.1   Extent of dishonesty in a 'dropped coin' experiment

Condition	Percentage accepting coin		Significance of difference
	Low cost	High cost	
Male experimenter	71.4	21.1	$p<0.01$
Female experimenter	22.7	31.8	Not significant
Low utility (10p)	37.5	33.3	Not significant
High utility (50p)	57.9	20.0	$p<0.05$

Source: Farrington and Kidd, 1977, Table 2

The researchers conclude:

> The results of this experiment do not wholly support the theory that financial dishonesty involves a rational decision. In agreement with theory, decreasing the cost of the act resulted in the expected increase in dishonesty, but only with the male experimenter … Contrary to the theory, increasing the utility of the act did not result in the expected uniform increase in dishonesty … Contrary to the theory, cost and utility did not have additive effects.
>
> (Farrington and Kidd, 1977, p.143)

On the whole the experiment is well conducted, and only four points of caution occur to me:

1   It is possible that some of the subjects genuinely accepted that the coin was theirs – a possibility the experimenters note but think unlikely from their observation of behaviour.

2   The experimenters consisted of one man and one woman, so the gender findings are open to doubt – they could be due to some other characteristic of the particular experimenters and should be replicated using different experimenters.

3   The 'utility' manipulation (the type of statement used) was very weak – the difference in 'cost' to the subjects is very slight – and indeed, the whole situation could be considered a trivialization of the concept of financial dishonesty.

4   The conclusions assume that all financial dishonesty is one thing – that these findings hold not just for coins in the street but also for shoplifting, stealing from houses, major fraud and so on – which is not established by the evidence offered here and, in the extreme form in which I have stated it, would seem to me to be a very dubious proposition.

4.1   Example 5: The Connecticut Crackdown Study

The 'Connecticut Crackdown Study' is another 'classic' research study, this time from the 1960s. In 1955 the Governor of Connecticut responded to a particularly bad year of road traffic fatalities by introducing a programme of administrative orders which made it more certain that those who drove excessively fast on the state's roads would be caught and, when caught, punished. The result was a 12 per cent drop in road traffic fatalities. In the late 1960s, Donald Campbell and his colleagues (Campbell and Ross, 1968; Campbell, 1969) used this event as a powerful illustration of how such public events can be evaluated. Clearly they were not content with the argument that because the drop in deaths followed the Governor's action it was caused by it; stronger proof than this was needed. For example, it is natural that a lower figure would follow the higher one because of a phenomenon known as *regression to the mean* – when figures vary randomly around a trend, some will be higher and some lower, so there could be a decrease in a year following a particularly sharp increase, even if the underlying trend were still upwards. The researchers therefore looked at a longer time-series (the black line in Figure 3.1) to assess the trend overall. As you can see, it is upward on the whole to 1955, and thereafter downward; it continues to fall from year to year. More importantly, there could be a whole range of alternative explanations for a decrease in deaths: changed weather, changes in petrol prices, changes in drinking habits, changes in the capabilities of the emergency health services – anything, in other words, which might change driving behaviour or the likelihood of victims surviving. What the researchers did, therefore, was to compare fatalities in Connecticut with figures over the same period from four states where the 'Crackdown' had not occurred (the coloured line in Figure 3.1). There was a slight decrease in this comparison group over the period, but not as marked as in Connecticut and certainly not inflected at the time when the policy change took effect. The researchers therefore felt able to conclude that it *was* the Governor's action which had affected the fatality figures.

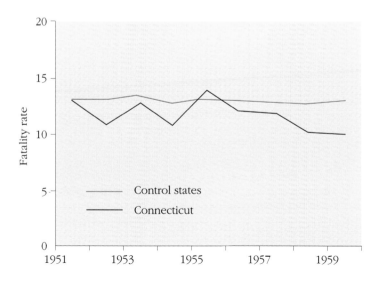

Figure 3.1   The Connecticut Crackdown: traffic fatalities 1951–59
(Source: Campbell, 1969, Figure 11)

The design of the study mimics the design of a true experiment, which is why this kind of analysis is sometimes called *quasi-experimental*. It differs from true experimental design in two very important respects, however:

1   The researchers could not allocate people to 'treatment' or 'control' groups, nor could they compare two contrasted treatments which they themselves applied to the same group. They had to study, *post hoc,* what actually happened to people living in the five states. However careful they were, therefore, they could never discount the possibilities that the comparison group differed from the experimental state *before* the change was introduced in some way which would account for the results.

2   The researchers did not introduce the treatment but rather studied it *post hoc* and therefore had no control over its nature. It is possible, indeed quite likely, that more changed than was specified in the Governor's orders. In particular, it is likely that the behaviour of the traffic police changed, with the new orders directing their attention towards speeding, and that they therefore intervened more often *before* fatal accidents could occur. The researchers were well aware of this possibility. Though in their opinion (and mine) it would not be sufficient to explain the change by itself, it cannot be discounted.

Thus the study benefits from some of the logic of experimentation, but it provides weaker evidence than a true experiment might have done. (On the other hand, a true experiment on this topic would be impossible, at least on the scale of this study.)

4.2   Example 6: Probation practice

This paper reports on the application in one probation area of a perspective on probation work which has been labelled the 'non-treatment paradigm'. This takes the view that the purpose of casework should be not the moral or psychological reform of offenders but to enable them to think more clearly and skilfully about what works in their lives and how they might profitably stay out of trouble. The idea was implemented in the form of an intensive programme of 35 two-hour group sessions in which probation officers led discussions and practice sessions on problem-solving, social skills, management of emotions, negotiation skills, critical reasoning, creative thinking and 'value enhancement'. The authors comment: 'Although many of the methods used were familiar to probation officers with experience of running offending behaviour groups ... the systematic and intensive nature of the programme was qualitatively different (Raynor and Vanstone, 1994, in Appendix 3.3, p.164).

The report compares the re-offending during the first year of 107 probationers sentenced to the programme (described as 'persistent offenders with a high risk of reconviction') with that of 164 people who received custodial sentences, and with a separate analysis of the 59 who actually completed the 'experimental' programme. Expected reconvictions are computed using an established and validated prediction inventory, with which the rate of actual reconviction is compared. The main findings are that those sentenced to the programme were reconvicted at about the expected rate; the comparison group of men receiving custodial sentences had more reconvictions than the prediction instrument suggested; and those who completed the programme had fewer reconvictions than expected. A correction is also applied for reconvictions occurring during the period which were actually for offences committed before it, but this does not change the pattern of the results. There was also a strong suggestion that those who completed the programme were less likely to be reconvicted for serious offences (violence, sexual offences, burglary).

The design of the study is a *field experiment*, something between a true experiment and a quasi-experimental comparison. The researchers do have control of the programme, and they do have a comparison group to whom the programme was not administered. However, they were obviously not able to allocate people randomly to programme or control group, so differences could again, in principle, be due to pre-existing differences between the people who made up the groups, not to the differential treatment.

The first question we have to ask, therefore, is about the sampling. These are clearly 'samples of opportunity' – groups who happened to be available at the time when the study started – and they are not particularly large. The authors suggest that the 'custodial' group is *probably* fairly comparable to the 'programme' group, but they offer little evidence to back up this assertion. However, differences are to a large extent 'controlled' by comparing not the rates of conviction between groups but the differences from *expected* reconviction rates. To the extent that the prediction instrument is valid (that is, it does indeed predict reconviction adequately and accurately), this will take care of most relevant differences between the groups. The one outstanding difference – that it is easier to be 'brought to book' for previously committed offences if you are serving a custodial sentence than during a community sentence – is separately 'controlled' by applying a correction to the figures. Thus the argument of the paper does not founder on questions of sampling or comparability. However, the programme is applied in a single area, by a particular group of probation officers. Further research, from other areas and using other 'administrators', would increase our confidence that the programme 'worked' universally. Overall, though, the argument of the paper is sound and the evidence is suitable to support it.

Where the research is more open to doubt is in the nature of the measures used; this is not a problem specific to this particular research, but one which tends to be general to the *kind* of research:

1 The outcome measure is reconviction, and, as we know, reconviction statistics are open to question. A 'filtering process' occurs between the commission (or non-commission) of offences and the conviction for them of a defendant, and this could have been affected by the nature of the research. It is possible that the police or the courts are more likely to apprehend, prosecute and convict someone whose last sentence was a custodial one than someone on a known 'experimental' probation programme. This does not seem to me particularly likely, but it *is* a possibility which cannot be discounted.

2 More to the point, while I do not see what the authors could have used other than official reconviction figures, their use does tend to redefine the research problem. The major interest is in the effect of the programme on *re-offending*; what is actually shown, however, is its effect on *reconviction*, which is not the same thing. This kind of tacit redefinition brought about by choice of measures is a very common feature of quantitative experimental studies and one of its major weaknesses.

3 As is also very common in real-life experiments, the treatment measures are also ill-defined. The researchers are quite clear about what programme was applied, but we do not know what else was occurring at the same time. For example, one difference between the two groups was that one was in the community and the other in custody during the treatment period, which could have had some effect irrespective of the nature of the treatment programme. (This objection is largely answered, however, by the separate analysis of the programme completers. The figures show that those sentenced to a community measure did indeed 'do better' than those sentenced to custody, but that those who completed the programme did better still.)

4 More importantly, however, we do not know what aspect of the programme was effective. There is a great deal of research to suggest that just paying attention to people and letting them know they are on an experimental programme can affect their behaviour, *irrespective of what the programme actually contains*. For a fully convincing argument, we should need a fully experimental design in which a matched comparison group was given a similar amount of attention but not the specific contents of the programme, and/or perhaps one where the members were told they were on an experimental programme but received effectively no 'treatment' at all.

5 Conclusion

In this chapter, we have focused on the extent to which research evidence in a report may be taken as sustaining the report's conclusions: that is, the extent to which conclusions *can* logically be based on such evidence. In the process, we have looked at:

- The *generalizability* of the results – the extent to which the subjects or informants can be taken as 'standing for' some population.

- The *nature* of the measurements used.

- The *validity* of the measures used – whether the numbers which have been collected do indeed measure what the researcher would wish to assert they measure.

- The *appropriateness* of the measures – whether the numbers collected are the 'right' ones for the job (a topic obviously connected to the last one).

- The extent to which *like is being compared with like* – where comparison is at the heart of the argument; and particularly whether all explanations other than the one which the researcher wishes to put forward have been eliminated by the design or subsequent analysis; so that differences between groups or over time can fairly be attributed to the sources to which the researcher attributes them.

The research examples in this chapter all have been in the 'scientific' tradition of social research and all cast within a fundamentally positivist discourse. That is, they tend to take 'what is out there' or 'what goes on' for granted – facts about the world are taken as existing in a fundamentally unproblematic sense. This being so, the problem becomes how best to get at these facts and produce convincing evidence that what you are offering in the research report *is* the truth. The problems of research therefore become problems of measurement, with theory being something which happens *outside* the research process. Not all researchers take this stance, however, and not all social research is grounded in it. Objections grounded in a different way of looking at how research results are produced have already been raised above, in the comments on Activities 3.4 and 3.6. The next chapter will take a different perspective and look at different ways not just of doing research but of conceptualizing what 'collecting evidence' is all about.

Research methods considered in Chapter 3

experiments	the systematic examination of a 'treatment' by, for example, applying it to one group (the experimental group or treatment group) and not to another (the control group or comparison group), making sure that everything else is identical in the experience of the two groups and that the groups are as near identical as possible at the start of the experiment. Both the treatment (independent variable) and the outcome (dependent variable) are carefully measured. In *quasi-experimental analyses* (often of naturally occurring changes) the similarity of the groups cannot be guaranteed, and often the treatment cannot be precisely measured and controlled.
surveys	the systematic collection of data from an existing population – often data about attitudes or beliefs, for example, but the systematic observation of behaviour can also use survey methods.
secondary sources	much criminological and other social research does not collect fresh data but presents fresh analyses of existing figures which were collected by survey methods (for example, the Census, General Household Survey) or as a by-product of departmental administration (for example, criminal statistics, prison statistics).

Further reading

Introductory texts in this area include Davidson and Layder (1994) on research methods generally; Jupp (1989) on criminological research, and Sapsford and Jupp (1996) on data collection. Any of these books would expand on the points made here, with a more extensive range of examples, and for the most part, they offer enough instruction and practice exercises to enable you to think about carrying out research of your own. They also raise ethical and political questions about the conduct of research.

More advanced texts include Oppenheim (1992) on questionnaires, De Vaux (1991) on surveys, and Bausell (1994) on experiments. These are the kinds of books which are read (or *should* be read) by researchers themselves, as they look in great detail at aspects of the research process, and suggest refinements of common methods.

References

Banks, C. and Fairhead, S. (1976) *The Petty Short-Term Prisoner,* Chichester, Barry Rose/Howard League for Penal Reform.

Bausell, R.B. (1994) *Conducting Meaningful Experiments: 40 Steps to Becoming a Scientist,* London, Sage.

Campbell, D.T. (1969) 'Reforms as experiments', *American Psychologist,* vol.24, pp.409–29.

Campbell, D.T. and Ross, H.L. (1968) 'The Connecticut crackdown on speeding: time-series data in quasi-experimental analysis', *Law and Society Review,* vol.3, pp.33–53.

Cullen, E. (1992) 'The Grendon Reconviction Study Part 1', *Prison Service Journal,* vol.90, pp.35–7.

Davidson, D.O. and Layder, D. (1994) *Methods, Sex and Madness,* London, Routledge.

De Vaux, D.A. (1991) *Surveys in Social Research,* London, UCL Press.

Farrington, D.P. and Kidd, R.F. (1977) 'Is financial dishonesty a rational decision?', *British Journal of Social and Clinical Psychology,* vol.16, pp.139–46.

Goldthorpe J.H., Lockwood, D., Bechhofer, F. and Platt J. (1969) *The Affluent Worker in the Class Structure,* Oxford, Oxford University Press.

Home Office (1989) *Prison Statistics: England and Wales 1988,* London, HMSO.

Jupp, V. (1989) *Methods of Criminological Research,* London, Allen and Unwin.

Norris, C., Fielding, N., Kemp, C. and Fielding, J. (1992) 'Black and blue: an analysis of the influence of race on being stopped by the police', *British Journal of Sociology,* vol.43, no.2, pp.207–24.

Oppenheim, A.N. (1992) *Questionnaire Design, Interviewing and Attitude Measurement,* London, Pinter.

Raynor, P. and Vanstone, M. (1994) 'Probation practice, effectiveness and the non-treatment paradigm', *British Journal of Social Work,* vol.24, pp.387–404.

Sapsford, R.J. (1983) *Life-Sentence Prisoners: Reaction, Response and Change,* Milton Keynes, Open University Press.

Sapsford, R.J. and Jupp, V. (1996) *Data Collection and Analysis,* London, Sage.

Walker, M.A. (1994) 'Measuring concern about crime: some inter-racial comparisons', *British Journal of Criminology* ,vol.34, no.3, pp.366–78.

Appendix 3.1

Norris *et al.*: 'Black and blue: an analysis of the influence of race on being stopped by the police'

Abstract

This article addresses the debate over the disproportionate representation of black people in the criminal justice system, with particular reference to the link between a person's race and the process of being stopped on the street by the police. On the basis of a participant observation study of routine police patrol in inner city London, the article explores the influence of race in relation to citizen and officer demeanour, and on the actions taken by police in initiating, processing and terminating a stop. Demeanour and process variables are derived from quantified observational data recorded on codified observation schedules from 213 police stops involving 319 members of the public. Among the findings reported, blacks prove over two and a half times more likely to be stopped than their presence in the local population would suggest, with a higher disproportion in the case of young black men. However, blacks and whites prove equally likely to be calm and civil to police at contact and during processing, and there are scant differences in police demeanour and action toward the two groups.

Introduction

In a recent article reviewing the literature on race[1] and the criminal justice system, Reiner argues that the disproportionate representation of black people in the criminal justice system has become 'the single most vexed, hotly controversial and seemingly intractable issue in the politics of crime, policing and social control'.[2] It is also an issue which the limitations of official statistics and census data make difficult to examine. Nor are alternative statistics a ready substitute; for instance, although more accurate figures on the racial compostion of the population can be derived from the annual Labour Force Surveys, these cannot be used to calculate local arrest rates for different ethnic groups where police figures are available.[3] In this paper we seek to contribute to one area of this debate: the link between a person's race and the process of being stopped by the police. Although there is a growing body of literature which shows the markedly higher stop and arrest rate for blacks than for the population as a whole, there is no systematic, British data as to the precise effects of race on the behaviour of police and citizens during a stop. Here we explore the influence of race both in relation to the demeanour of citizens and police and in terms of the actions taken by police to initiate, process and terminate a stop.

British research has consistently shown a markedly higher stop rate for blacks. Willis' study[4] of people stopped in four contrasting areas found that, in each district, blacks were more than twice as likely to be stopped as whites. Such findings are supported by the Islington Crime Survey,[5] which shows that, among young black males aged under twenty five, some 52.7 per cent had been subject to a police stop in the previous year as opposed to only 31 per cent of whites. Not only are blacks more likely to be stopped than their proportional presence in the population would suggest but they are also likely to be stopped more frequently. Smith[6] found that young black males (15–24) had, on average, been stopped four times by police in the preceding twelve months, compared with just over two and a half times for whites.

Numerous studies of policing, on both sides of the Atlantic, also document the heavily disproportionate arrest rate of blacks by police[7] and recent figures from the Home Office show that, in the Metropolitan Police District, 18 per cent of those arrested are 'black skinned' even though blacks make up only about 5 per cent of the population.[8] However, with regard to arrests resulting solely from stops, in Britain there is no concrete evidence that police arrest blacks at a higher rate than whites. The arrest rate resulting from stops for both blacks and whites stands at about 10 per cent.[9] Furthermore, although research is unequivocal about the disproportionate rate at which blacks are stopped, there is no such consensus about why this is so. Previous studies have offered three contrasting explanations for the differential stop rate: racial prejudice of officers; more disrespectful demeanour of blacks, and the differential offending rates of blacks and whites. We will examine each of these in turn.

Police prejudice

For the past 25 years, research on the British police has consistently documented the prevalence of deep-seated racial prejudice amongst street level police officers.[10] Racist language and hostile attitudes toward blacks, in particular, have an everyday and common currency within the culture of the lower ranks[11] and, as the PSI [Policy Studies Institute] study of the Metropolitan Police showed, 'racist language and racial prejudice were prominent and pervasive'.[12] However, documenting racist attitudes and language is not the same as demonstrating the link between those attitudes and discriminatory behaviour. Given the complexity of policing and the wide discretionary powers available to police officers, it is difficult to isolate whether race or some other factor leads to a particular police action. Indeed, the PSI researchers conclude, despite the prevalence of racist attitudes,

> our more general impression is very strongly that police officers rarely behave badly in such a way as to make it obvious that a person's ethnic group is the reason for their bad behaviour … we are fairly confident (in routine policing) that there is no widespread tendency for black or Asian people to be given greatly inferior treatment. [13]

Citizen behaviour

Waddington[14] argues that it is not police prejudice which leads to the differential arrest rate of blacks and whites. Rather, this is due to the disproportionate degree of disrespect shown towards the authority of police officers by blacks. Given the wide discretionary powers available to police, they are more likely to arrest blacks for an offence rather than deal with them informally because blacks are more likely to be disrespectful. In Britain, there is little direct observational research data to back up Waddington's claims although other data offer some partial support. For instance, the survey of Metropolitan police officers carried out by the PSI found that, 'where the person stopped was of West Indian or African origin, the officer was distinctly more likely to judge that he (*sic*) was uncooperative than when he was white'.[15] Further, research on attitudes towards the police has consistently shown that 'blacks are more hostile to them than other groups, and more critical of police performance'.[16] In the USA, numerous studies on suspect demeanour have shown that 'disrespectful' or 'uncooperative' suspects are more likely to be arrested than those who are 'cooperative' and 'civil'.[17] But whether race is a key factor in explaining disrespect remains open to debate. The original analysis of the Black–Reiss data[18] showed that the higher black arrest rate, even when offence seriousness was controlled for, could be explained because blacks were more disrespectful towards the police. Yet, as has been pointed out by critics, this analysis is flawed because the authors fail to show whether disrespect occurred before or after the arrest.[19]

Differential offending rates

The third explanation of racial disparities in stop rates is that blacks have a higher rate of offending than whites and, therefore, they are more likely to be stopped and arrested.[20] This argument has been subject to fierce and heated debate between Lea and Young in their guise as 'radical realists' and writers associated with the Institute of Race Relations such as Gilroy,[21] Bridges,[22] and Gutzmore.[23] Lea and Young argue that, given the socio-economic position of the black population, particularly during the recession of the mid-seventies to mid-eighties which impacted more harshly on the black population, it would be hardly surprising if black crime was not higher than that for whites. The disproportionate stop and arrest rate partially reflects this reality. In the eyes of their critics, Lea and Young have merely become apologists for police racism. They see the higher black arrest rate as purely a function of police prejudice which subjects blacks to more intensive surveillance and arrest. But as Reiner has argued in his review of the literature on black crime and police prejudice, 'it seems clear that the disproportionate black arrest rate is the product of black deprivation, police stereotyping and the process by which each of these factors amplifies each other'.[24]

The complexity of this process is demonstrated by the contradictory findings of North American research about the relationship between race and the treatment people receive once they have been stopped by the police. For instance, Skolnick suggests that blacks are routinely subject to more uncivil treatment[25] whereas Reiss[26] found that, while lower-class youth who challenged police authority were more likely to be subject to excessive force, this was not related to race. However, Black and Reiss[27] indicated that blacks were more likely to be searched and interrogated than whites but that whites were subject to a greater degree of excessive force, although Fyfe[28] has shown that blacks were far more likely to be shot and wounded, or even killed, by police.

The data

In this analysis we draw on an observational study of routine police patrol work carried out over a fifteen-month period during 1986 and 1987. Our observations were conducted in three police divisions: two in the Metropolitan Police District and one in Surrey. In all, some 807 hours were spent accompanying officers on routine patrol. The observational fieldwork was carried out by three members of the research team (N. Fielding, C. Kemp and C. Norris). Each field researcher worked with a separate group of officers and, therefore, only one researcher was present at any given incident; there were, however, extensive discussions of coding conventions and frequent team meetings with a view to inter-rater reliability. In order to differentiate 'stops' from other forms of police/public interaction, two criteria had to be met for inclusion in our sample. First, encounters had to be non-elective or police-initiated. Second, they had to be potentially adversarial in that the person stopped was suspected of a legal or normative infraction, however minor. For each encounter which satisfied these criteria we filled in an observational schedule[29] which codified basic details relating to the characteristics of those stopped; citizen and police demeanour at contact and processing; and police action at contact, processing and exit. Given the physical constraints of observing ongoing police work, for example, the problem of one observer having to record the details of complainants, informants, bystanders and all the police officers involved, it was not always possible to record complete information for each participant, so that sample sizes vary in the tables which follow; column totals are 100 plus or minus one due to rounding. To minimize the problem of reactivity, no recording devices were used in the field. The observational schedules were compiled immediately after each period of observation (usually an eight hour police shift).

Before looking at the data in more detail, we should be clear about the scope of this study. Its focus is on routine relief and home beat patrolling. We are not concerned with the activities of the CID [Criminal Investigation Department], the plainclothes crime squads comprised of uniformed officers on secondment, or the Territorial Support Units. All of these units may have a specific effect on how black people, both quantitatively and qualitatively, experience policing. For instance, during our fieldwork, the TSU was deployed at one of the principal research sites at the request of the divisional Chief Superintendent. Their task was specifically to target the problem of theft from motor vehicles. The local crime squad staffed from uniform officers was strengthened at the expense of the Home Beat Officers to combat what was seen as an increasing problem of theft with violence ('mugging') on the division. While the deployment of the TSU had no explicitly racial dimension, the crime squad's brief was seen by several officers as being targeted specifically at what they saw as the rising tide of black crime. These factors may have a direct bearing on the issue of race and policing, but were outside the scope of the present study.

In all, we observed 213 police stops which involved 319 people whose racial composition is shown in Table I. Note that in this and the other tables figures have been rounded to the nearest whole per cent. Percentages may not sum to 100 due to rounding.

Table I Persons stopped by racial group in numbers and percentages

Race	Number	Per cent
White	225	72
Black	81	26
Asian	5	2
	311	100

Missing observations = 8

To assess whether the police are more likely to stop blacks as opposed to whites in relation to their proportional presence in the population, we need an independent measure of population characteristics. For such a measure we were able to use the 1981 Census but only in relation to the two research sites located in the single London borough (see Table II). We have excluded data derived from the other research site for this part of the analysis because the small number of stops recorded (N = 33) would not enable meaningful comparison with the Census data.

Table II Persons stopped by racial group in London borough compared with 1981 Census and expected versus actual stop rate from sample

Race	No. and % stopped	1981 Census	Expected stop rate per 100 of pop'n	Actual stop rate	Actual stop rate as % of expected stop rate	% of pop'n stopped
White	192 (71)	81	8.1	7.1	90	9
Black	76 (28)	10	1.0	2.8	280	28
Asian	4 (2)	0.9	0.9	0.2	20	2
	N = 272					

The results of the Islington Crime Survey and the Policy Studies Institute's 'Survey of Londoners' have indicated that about one in ten of the population will have been stopped in the previous twelve months. If we assume that the stop rate in our research site is also 10 per cent, and we have no reason to believe otherwise, then the expected number of stops per hundred of the population, based on the 1981 Census, should be 8.1 for whites, 1.0 for blacks and 0.9 for Asians. However, on the basis of our data, we would calculate stop numbers of only 7.1 for whites, fewer than 2 for Asians and 2.8 for blacks. Whites are thus being stopped at 90 per cent of the expected rate, Asians at less than 20 per cent, and blacks at 280 per cent of the expected rate. While the average stop rate for the population as a whole is 10 per cent, only 9 per cent of the white, less than 2 per cent of the Asian, but 28 per cent of the black population, would be stopped. In other words, black people are two and a half times more likely to be stopped than their presence in the local population suggests.

The Islington Crime Survey[30] has shown that this imbalance is compounded by considerations of age and gender. In their survey, over half of young black males were stopped in the previous year. Using the Census data we can also calculate the effect of age and gender. For both blacks and whites the Census indicates that around 25 per cent of the population are males under 35 years. However in our sample of those stopped, 91 per cent were male, and 89 per cent under 35 years old; in total 81 per cent of our sample were males under 35 years old. In Table III we have calculated what the effect of this stop rate would be for one thousand black and one thousand white people in the population.

Table III   Expected and actual number of stops per 1000 of the population by race taking into account age and gender

Race	Base	Sample estimate of total no. stopped per 1000 pop'n	No. and % of pop'n under 35	Expected no. of stops of males under 35 per 1000 pop'n	Estimated no. of males under 35 stopped and % in terms of presence in pop'n
White	1000	90	250 (25%)	23	82 (29%)
Black	1000	280	250 (25%)	70	255 (91%)

Note: Asians have been omitted due to small number in sample.

Table III shows that, for every thousand whites and thousand blacks in the community, we would estimate from our data that 90 white and 280 black persons respectively would be stopped. Given that only 25 per cent of the population are males under 35 years, if stops were spread evenly over the population in terms of age and gender we would expect 23 white and 70 black males under 35 to be stopped. However, police do not stop all sections of the population at the same rate – we have calculated that 81 per cent of those stopped are males under 35 years old. While for every 1000 white persons and every 1000 black persons, 90 white persons overall would be stopped, and 280 blacks, of the 90 whites 82 would be males under the age of 35 and of the 280 blacks 255 would be males under 35 years old. In other words, between a quarter and one third of white males under 35 are subject to police stops during the course of a year, and for black males under 35 the figure is nine out of ten.

Of course, even amongst young males the probability of being stopped is not equally spread and certain individuals in the area who are well known to the police will be stopped more frequently and others less often, thus diluting the individual experience of being stopped. However, in terms of the collective experience of policing which young males share in a particular community, race is a key structural determinant and it is the relative intensity of surveillance that the two groups experience which is important. For whites, police surveillance is diluted – even for males under 35 the majority will not have been stopped by police in the last year. In contrast, it will be a minority of young black males who have not been stopped. It is this concentrated intensity of surveillance that black male youths collectively experience which contributes to the high level of negative attitudes towards the police revealed by survey research.

From our data we cannot, of course, discern whether police select candidates for stops on the basis of their racial characteristics alone. Nevertheless, we can categorically challenge the assertion that differential treatment of blacks and whites is due to transmitted discrimination; that is, the tendency of victims and witnesses to call the police more often in incidents involving black offenders. The over-representation of black persons stopped in our sample has to be the result of police differentiation.

In view of the higher stop rate for blacks than whites, in Tables IV and V we pursue two further questions: first, whether blacks are stopped for different types of offence; and second, whether police reasons for making stops vary in terms of the degree of tangible evidence used to warrant the stop. In Table IV, we classify stops into three offence categories: traffic, crime-related and order maintenance. Under traffic, we include all car stops arising from infractions of the highway code, erratic driving or defective vehicles; under crime-related, all stops which were directly related to investigation of a specific offence like car theft or criminal damage; and under order maintenance, stops resulting from low level disturbances, for example rowdy youths. It should be noted that in our sample, all crime-related incidents related to crimes against property. No stops were recorded as a result of crimes against the person such as assault. Table IV shows the difference in the proportion of black and white persons involved in the three types of stop. Table V shows whether the stop was carried out on the basis of tangible evidence or more general suspicion.

Table IV shows quite clearly that there is little overall difference in the proportion of black and white persons involved in different types of stop. However, we are also able to see whether these stops occurred on the basis of tangible evidence that an offence had taken place or on more speculative grounds. For instance, officers may stop a car because it has faulty headlights or because the occupants of the car look 'suspicious'. This is important because one possible explanation for the differential stop rate is that police stop blacks on more speculative grounds in the hope that they may discover evidence of an offence. In our observation of incidents we recorded whether, in our view, stops were made for tangible or less tangible reasons. This data is displayed in Table V. We can see that blacks are, indeed, more likely to be stopped on speculative grounds than whites. However, although this may give us some evidence that racial stereotypes are being used as the basis for stops, it only partially explains the difference in the stop rate for blacks and whites.

Table IV   Persons stopped by race in relation to type of stop in percentages

Type of stop	White %	Black %
Traffic	51	48
Crime related	9	4
Order maintenance	40	48
	100	100
	N = 220	N = 80

Note: Asians are excluded in all subsequent tables because of the small number stopped.

Table V   Persons stopped by race in relation to police reasons for stop in percentages

Reason for stop	White %	Black %
Obvious enforcement	58	44
General suspicion	42	56
	100	100
	N = 220	N = 89

Citizen demeanour at contact and processing

In the previous section we established that although there is little significance in the type of stop (traffic, crime-related and order maintenance), blacks are more likely to be stopped than whites and often for less tangible reasons. Here we examine the behaviour of persons stopped during the contact and processing stages of an incident in order to see if a person's race influences the dynamics of the encounter. We have used three separate measures of a person's demeanour: first, whether their general state is calm or agitated; second, whether their manner towards the police is civil or antagonistic; third, whether they display signs of insobriety. The chi square test of independence was carried out on all tables and significance levels less than 0.05 are presented where appropriate.

Surveys on public attitudes have shown that blacks and, in particular, black youth are most likely to hold negative and hostile attitudes towards the police.[31] Of course, our data does not give us access to what people think about policing. It does, however, allow us to record the outwardly visible and publicly-expressed attitudes of the person stopped. Accordingly, we are able to examine whether widely held black feelings about the police are displayed in actual behaviour during routine police stops. This is important because it is implicit in much of the literature that the high black arrest rate can, in part, be explained by the contempt shown towards police authority by young blacks.[32] Waddington, for instance, argues that young blacks represent the equivalent of the Victorian dangerous classes and the police an army of occupation in the ghetto. Waddington believes that non-compliance with police authority by this new black underclass has the result that officers use their extensive discretionary powers to arrest as a means of imposing control and punishing those who do not comply.[33]

However, our data do not support this view of demeanour. Tables VI and VII indicate that during contact and processing, a person's race is not a statistically significant predictor of demeanour shown towards the police. Blacks and whites are equally likely to be calm and civil towards police at both contact and processing. Despite the negative attitudes that young black males have of the police, as revealed by survey research, it would seem that in routine policing these attitudes are not translated into overt behaviour. However, it is worth noting that while race plays no part in determining a person's general demeanour and their demeanour towards police, whites are over two and a half times more likely than blacks to show signs of insobriety. This may partially explain the more negative police demeanour towards whites, which we examine in the next section.

Police demeanour at contact and processing

The literature on policing reminds us that police–public encounters are a special form of focused interaction. As Sykes and Clarke have noted, in such encounters 'persons come together to give their attention to a particular activity and then disperse; they do not attribute any enduring identity to their joint endeavours'.[34] In police stops there are strong contrasts in the roles assumed by the various participants. On the one hand, police officers are well versed and well rehearsed in the improvised drama which is to unfold. They also have special power and obvious authority at their disposal. On the other hand, citizens who have been stopped are reluctant and irregular performers in a drama which may be of their own making but is unlikely to have been of

Table VI Persons stopped by race in relation to demeanour shown at contact in percentages

Person's demeanour	White %	Black %	
General			
calm	77	82	
agitated	23	18	
	N = 210	N = 74	n.s.
Towards police			
civil	89	90	
antagonistic	11	10	
	N = 205	N = 73	n.s.
Sobriety			
no effect	80	92	
some effect	20	8	
	N = 193	N = 64	p<0.05

Note: n.s. not significant.

Table VII Persons stopped by race in relation to demeanour shown at processing in percentages

Person's demeanour	White %	Black %	
General			
calm	82	85	
agitated	18	15	
	100	100	
	N = 216	N = 75	n.s.
Towards police			
civil	91	85	
antagonistic	9	15	
	100	100	
	N = 212	N = 73	n.s.
Sobriety			
no effect	81	92	
some effect	19	8	
	100	100	
	N = 194	N = 66	p<0.05

Note: n.s. not significant.

their own choosing. Further, the interaction is almost always between strangers who have not been party to any joint rehearsal. Although police officers are well rehearsed in the general art of stopping people, they have no advance knowledge as to how this particular stop will progress.

One of the consequences of such informational uncertainty is the perceptual heightening of the threat of danger and violence related to on-the-job trouble. It gives rise to what Manning[35] has termed the 'threat-danger-hero' notion of police work and the development of a set of working rules which classify various groups and classes as more dangerous than others. In Skolnick's[36] terms, police officers develop a shorthand classification of people who represent 'symbolic assailants'; as Holdaway[37] has shown, in Britain the category of 'symbolic assailant' is extended to include not only those who threaten the police with potential violence, but those who, by virtue of their authority or status, can challenge or disarm police authority. Lawyers, doctors and social workers are 'challengers'; while women and young children are 'disarmers'. When police initially stop people, they have very few clues as to whether their authority is likely to be challenged or whether the encounter may become dangerous. Clues which are immediately available concern the personal characteristics and the demeanour of the persons stopped. Brogden, Jefferson and Walklate[38] argue that the key sociological determinants of policing derive from age, race, sex and class and, as Holdaway has demonstrated, in the context of urban Britain, these variables are directly related to shared assumptions contained within the police occupational culture as to the moral worth of people. With regard to race, there is overwhelming evidence of hostile and prejudiced attitudes towards blacks on the part of street level officers.[39] However, the link between prejudice and practice which can be found in, for example, the translation of negative attitudes into discriminatory action, is not necessarily straightforward. In this section, we explore whether police prejudice has a discernible effect on the demeanour of police officers towards black persons during stops. We classify police demeanour as positive (informal), neutral (business-like or formal) and negative (brusque, rude or authoritarian). In Tables VIII and IX, we can see the relationship between a person's race and police demeanour at contact and processing.

Table VIII Persons stopped by race in relation to police demeanour at contact in percentages		
Police demeanour	**White** %	**Black** %
Positive	7	7
Neutral	66	83
Negative	27	10
	100	100
	N = 178	N = 60	p<0.05

Table IX   Persons stopped by race in relation to police demeanour at processing in percentages

Police demeanour	White %	Black %	
Positive	17	12	
Neutral	64	81	
Negative	18	7	
	99	100	
	N = 207	N = 68	$p < 0.05$

It would appear that race has little impact on whether a person is positively treated. For example, 7 per cent of both whites and blacks are treated in a polite, friendly way at the beginning of an encounter. At processing the equivalent percentages are 17 per cent of whites and 12 per cent of blacks. While we might predict that blacks would be more likely to receive more negative treatment, the data suggests the opposite. At contact, 27 per cent whites, as opposed to 10 per cent of blacks, were subject to negative and hostile demeanour from police. In other words, whites are over two and a half times more likely to be subjected to negative demeanour than blacks and this relationship holds at processing. Rather than attitudes being simply translated into action the reverse seems to apply. One reason for this may be that because whites are more likely to have been drinking than blacks, police are more likely to treat them negatively. However, even where whites and blacks display no signs of insobriety, whites are still four times more likely to be subject to negative police demeanour than blacks. We would suggest that one possible explanation for this unexpected finding is that given the police view that blacks represent a particularly problematic group,[40] there may be a conscious or semiconscious decision not to 'up the ante' by being hostile or brusque. In routine encounters, therefore, where police have little to gain from antagonizing people, they may tend to adopt a neutral manner.

Police control strategies at contact and processing

The adoption of a neutral demeanour by police officers does not rule out the possibility that black people are subject to qualitatively and quantitatively different forms of policing than whites. For example, whilst remaining polite and businesslike, police may nonetheless subject blacks to more coercive and intrusive strategies of control at contact and processing. In this section, we look at the strategies employed by officers when dealing with stops.

In Table X, following Skyes and Brent,[41] we classify strategies used by police at contact into three types according to their level of forcefulness: coercive (involving some element of physical control); imperative (orders and commands); and interrogative (the asking of questions). In Table XI, we provide a similar threefold classification for processing based on the degree of intrusiveness of police action. At the lowest level of intrusiveness, police may merely question people. At the next level, they may ask to see documentary evidence such as a driving licence or other means of identification and/or run a check via their personal radio to the Police National Computer to ascertain whether the car has been reported stolen or a person has a criminal record. At the highest level, they may search a person or their property or, where there is suspicion of drink driving, breathalyse the driver of a vehicle. We have termed these strategies 'interrogative', 'corroborative', and 'search'.

Table X Persons stopped by race in relation to police supervisory strategy at contact in percentages

Supervisory strategy	White %	Black %
Coercive	8	10
Imperative	34	36
Interrogative	55	51
None apparent	4	2
	101	99
	N = 155	N = 41

For the purposes of the analysis of contact, processing and exit actions, we have only been able to classify the race of the first person stopped in an incident, although the actions that police take apply to all the people stopped. This means that some police actions refer to incidents where the first person stopped was black while the second, third, fourth or fifth person could have been white. However, only 7 per cent of stops involve both blacks and whites. Furthermore, we have taken the highest level of forcefulness or intrusiveness in situations where the police may have had recourse to one or more strategies. For example, in one incident three people were stopped: two black and one white. No coercive strategies were used at contact but the police employed two interrogative and two imperative strategies. In Table X the stop would be classified as 'black' because the first person stopped was black and as 'imperative' because that was the highest level of forcefulness used.

Looking at Tables X and XI, we can see that blacks and whites are subject to almost identical treatment in terms of the level of forcefulness used to control them at contact; and that, during processing, there is a difference with regard to corroborative and interrogative strategies but not search. However, the difference is relatively slight.

Table XI Persons stopped by race in relation to level of intrusiveness of police strategy at processing in percentages

Level of intrusiveness	White %	Black %
Search	34	36
Corroborative	18	26
Interrogative	49	38
	101	100
	N = 146	N = 42

Police actions on exit

In order to terminate a stop, police may resort to a number of exit actions. At one extreme, they may simply allow those they have stopped to go, whilst at the other, they may make arrests. Research has consistently shown that blacks are, in general, subject to disproportionately high levels of arrest,[42] and that they are arrested for particular types of offence.[43] Although the number of arrests in our sample makes direct comparison difficult (N = 25), we can shed some light on this debate. In Table XII, we have once more classified police actions on exit into three types: formal, informal and no action. Formal actions include issuing a fixed penalty notice, requesting documentation be produced at a police station at a later date, filling in a crime report, officially recording a person's name and address, and arrest. Informal actions comprise warnings and more or less pointed advice.

Table XII Persons stopped by race in relation to police action at exit in percentages		
Police action	White %	Black %
Formal	31	40
Informal	27	19
No action	42	40
	100	99
	N = 158	N = 42

Table XII indicates that incidents involving black persons are subject to a slightly higher formal action rate by the police. This difference cannot readily be explained by the type of stop (traffic, crime related and order maintenance) or by the demeanour of the person stopped. However, neither do our data clearly support the assertion that, once stopped, blacks are more likely than whites to be subject to formal police action, such as arrest. Nonetheless, because blacks are disproportionately stopped in relation to whites, it is important to note that our data do not necessarily contradict other findings which suggest more strongly that blacks are subject to significantly higher rates of formal police action, including arrest.

This last observation is especially pertinent in the light of our earlier discussion on the implications of differential stop rates for how different groups experience policing. Blacks are far more likely to be stopped than would be expected from their proportionate presence in the population, and they are also more likely to be subject to formal police action. For example, we suggested earlier that over the course of a year, up to 90 per cent of black males aged less than 35 would be stopped. From our exit data we can see that 40 per cent of incidents where the first person stopped was black resulted in formal police action. Over the course of a year, this means that, approximately one in three of the black male population under 35 would be involved in a stop resulting in formal police action in contrast to only one in ten of white males under 35. Interestingly, while we might expect that this would lead to more negative attitudes being displayed by blacks at the termination of the stop, this is not the case. Blacks are no more likely to be observably negative in their attitude towards police at termination than whites.

Conclusion

In this paper, our aim has been to use quantified observational data to explore the complex linkage between racial prejudice and discriminatory police action. For example, do police treat black people differently, in line with widely documented negative racial attitudes? And, if so, is such discrimination compounded by the fact that blacks are more disrespectful of police authority? A single study cannot provide definitive answers to these questions but our analysis does, at least, clarify aspects of the highly controversial race–policing debate.

Our data confirm that blacks (and especially young blacks) are more likely to be stopped by the police than whites, although they are, on average, stopped for the same types of offences. It would also appear that blacks are stopped on more speculative grounds than whites. However, once stopped, the demeanour of blacks towards the police is no different to that displayed by whites, except that blacks are less likely to show signs of insobriety.

On the police side, officers are, if anything, more negative towards whites at contact and processing, and remain largely neutral in their dealings with blacks. Although the levels of forcefulness demonstrated by officers on contact are much the same, there is a slight difference in the degree of intrusiveness displayed towards blacks and whites during processing. This is reflected in the tendency to seek more corroborative information from blacks, although this does not seemingly lead to a higher incidence of search. Similarly, at exit, blacks are subject to a slightly higher rate of formal action which may or may not include arrest.

Despite the considerable body of literature documenting the prevalence of racist attitudes within the police occupational culture, our data suggest that, in routine patrolling by relief and home beat officers, prejudice does not significantly lead to differential or discriminatory police action *once a stop is underway*. Equally important to establish, nor does our data support the view commonly expressed by police that encounters with blacks resulting from stops are especially difficult, troublesome or conflictual. However, any assessment of the different experience of policing felt by various racial or other groups in the community must take into account the implications of the disproportionate number of stops affecting the black community and, in particular, black males under thirty five, and the differential rate of formal police action on exit. It may be that most police stops of black persons are neutral. Yet, overall perceptions of police behaviour will remain unfavourable because blacks feel, for understandable reasons, that they are subject to excessive levels of police surveillance.

(Date accepted: November 1990)

Clive Norris
Department of Applied Social Science, Newcastle Polytechnic

Nigel Fielding
Department of Sociology, University of Surrey

Charles Kemp
Faculty of Law, University of Bristol

Jane Fielding
Department of Sociology, University of Surrey

Notes

1   We have used the term 'race' throughout, rather than its alternatives, which are generally unwieldy and subject to fashion (e.g., we understand 'minority ethnic group' is now preferred to 'ethnic minority' in some quarters). 'Race' remains the term in public and police use. Similarly we have preferred 'black' to 'Afro-Caribbean', 'white' to 'Caucasian' and so on.

2   Reiner, R. (1989) 'Race and criminal justice', *New Community,* vol.16, no.1, p.5.

3   Fitzgerald, M. (1990) 'Crime: an ethnic question', *Home Office Research Bulletin 28,* London, HMSO.

4   Willis, C. (1983) *The Use, Effectiveness and Impact of Police Stop and Search Powers,* London, Home Office Research Unit.

5   Jones, T., MacLean, B. and Young, J. (1986) *The lslington Crime Survey,* Aldershot, Gower.

6   Smith, D.J. (1983) 'A survey of Londoners', *Police and People in London,* London, Policy Studies Institute.

7   Black, D. and Reiss, A. (1967) *Studies of Crime and Law Enforcement in Major Metropolitan Areas,* Washington, DC, Government Printing Office; Bogolmony, R. (1976) 'Street patrol: the decision to stop a citizen', *Criminal Law Bulletin,* vol.12, no.5; Lundman, R., Sykes, R. and Clarke, J.P. (1978) 'Police control of juveniles', *Journal of Research in Crime and Delinquency,* vol.15; Stevens, P. and Willis, C. (1979) *Race, Crime and Arrests,* Home Office Research Study 58, London, HMSO; and Smith, D.J. and Gray, J. (1983) *Police and People in London,* vol.IV 'The Police in Action', London, Policy Studies Institute.

8   Cited in Reiner, 1989, *op. cit.*

9   Willis, 1983, *op. cit.,* and Smith, D.J. (1983) *The Police and People in London*, vol.III, 'A Survey of Police Officers', London, Policy Studies Institute.

10 Cain, M. (1973) *Society and the Policeman's Role,* London, Routledge and Kegan Paul; Reiner, R. (1978) *The Blue-Coated Worker*, Cambridge, Cambridge University Press; Smith and Gray, 1983, *op. cit.*; Norris, C.A. (1987) *Policing Trouble: An Observational Study of Police Patrol Work in Two Police Forces,* unpublished PhD Thesis, University of Surrey; and Graef, R. (1989) *Talking Blues*, London, Collins.

11 Norris, 1987, *op. cit.*

12 Smith and Gray, 1983, *op. cit.*

13 Smith and Gray, 1983, *op. cit*, pp.127–8.

14 Waddington, P.A.J. (1983) *Are the Police Fair?* Research Paper 2, London, Social Affairs Unit; and Waddington, P.A.J. (1984) 'Black crime, the "racist" police and fashionable compassion', in Anderson, D. (ed.) *The Kindness that Kills,* London, SPCK.

15 Smith and Gray, 1983, *op. cit.*, p.101.

16 Brogden, M., Jefferson, T. and Walklate, S. (1988) *Introducing Police Work*, London, Unwin Hyman, p.126.

17 Piliavin, I. and Briar, S. (1964) 'Police encounters with juveniles', *American Journal of Sociology*, vol.70; Black, D. and Reiss, A. (1970) 'Police control of juveniles', *American Sociological Review*, vol.34; and Lundman, Sykes and Clark, 1978, *op. cit.*

18 Black and Reiss, 1967, *op. cit.*

19 Sykes, R. and Clarke, J. (1975) 'A theory of deference exchange in police civilian encounters', *American Journal of Sociology,* vol.81.

20 Stevens and Willis, 1979, *op. cit.*

21 Gilroy, P. (1982) 'The myth of black criminality', *Socialist Register,* London, Merlin.

22 Bridges, L. (1983) 'Policing the urban wasteland', *Race and Class,* vol.XXV, no.2, pp.31–4.

23 Gutzmore, C. (1983) 'Capital, "black youth" and crime', *Race and Class,* vol.XXV, no.2, pp.13–30.

24 Reiner, R. (1985) *The Politics of the Police,* Brighton, Wheatsheaf.

25 Skolnick, J. (1966) *Justice Without Trial,* New York, Wiley.

26 Reiss, A.J. (1971) *The Police and the Public,* New Haven, CT, Yale University Press.

27 Black and Reiss, 1967, *op. cit.,* p.81.

28 Fyfe, J. (1981) 'Toward a typology of police shootings', in Fyfe, J. (ed.) *Contemporary Issues in Law Enforcement,* London, Sage.

29 A copy of this instrument may be obtained by contacting the authors.

30 Jones, MacLean and Young, 1986, *op. cit.,* p.149.

31 Small, S. (1983) *Police and People in London,* vol.II 'A Group of Young Black People', London, Policy Studies Institute; and Reiner, 1985, *op. cit.*

32 Reiner, 1985, *op. cit.*; Black, D. (1980) *The Manners and Customs of the Police,* New York, Academic Press.

33 Waddington, 1983, *op. cit.,* p.5; and Waddington, 1984, *op. cit.,* p.47.

34 Sykes and Clarke, 1975, *op. cit.,* p.587.

35 Manning, P.K. (1977) *Police Work,* Cambridge, MA, MIT Press.

36 Skolnick, 1966, *op. cit.*

37 Holdaway, S. (1983) *Inside the British Police: A Force at Work,* London, Blackwell.

38 Brogden, Jefferson and Walklate, 1988, *op. cit.*

39 Norris, 1987, *op. cit.*; and Smith and Gray, 1983, *op. cit.*

40 Norris, 1987, *op. cit.*; and Holdaway, 1983, *op. cit.*

41 Sykes, R. and Brent, E. (1983) *Policing: A Social Behaviourist Perspective,* New York, Rutgers.

42 Black and Reiss, 1967, *op. cit.*; and Lundman, Sykes and Clark, 1978, *op. cit.*

43 Stevens and Willis, 1979, *op. cit.*; and Blom-Cooper, L. and Drabble, R. (1982) 'Police perception of crime', *British Journal of Criminology,* vol.22, no.1.

(Source: Norris *et al*., 1992, pp.207–24)

Appendix 3.2

Walker: 'Measuring concern about crime: some inter-racial comparisons'

Concern about crime can be examined in many ways, and a survey carried out in certain areas of Leeds in 1987 incorporated items on three different aspects which have been labelled 'fear', 'worries', and 'problems'. The survey compared the reactions of three ethnic groups – black, Asian, and white. These groups all lived in the same areas, so their experiences of crime were to some extent controlled for. There were clear differences between the groups on each of the measures. However, the measures varied and showed that any one measure does not sensibly summarize differences between the groups. On the other hand, within each group the three measures were to some extent correlated, showing there was some consistency between the types of concern.

Several victim surveys of the general population in certain areas of Great Britain have been carried out over the last few years. The impact of crime on people's lives has also been incorporated to some extent, mainly in the form of a question about 'fear of crime'. This has been operationalized by a question such as 'do you think it is safe to go out alone in this area at night?'. The limitations of this simple question have been realized (see for example, Maxfield, 1984). It only relates to reaction to a single situation, which may, in any case, not be relevant to some people's experience. Other types of concern about crime have been investigated in some surveys, such as whether people worry about being burgled, and whether crime is a problem in the area in which they live.

A study in the United States (Lewis and Salem, 1986) compared ten areas which differed considerably on many socio-economic variables and also the crime rate. They found that areas with social deprivation and higher crime rates tended to have higher scores on 'fear of crime'. Since areas of social deprivation tend to have higher offender rates (Baldwin and Bottoms, 1976) and non-whites tend to be socially deprived and live in these areas (see below), it would not be expected that, taken over larger areas, whites and non-whites would have the same fear and general concern about crime. Surveys in this country which have compared ethnic groups have mainly been of large areas in which there is considerable variation in social class and other socio-economic variables. The British Crime Survey was carried out in the whole of England and Wales [Hough and Mayhew, 1983], and Box *et al.* (1988), in their analysis of survey data, examined 'fear' in relation to several variables, including a white/non-white dichotomy. Surveys of London boroughs (with populations of over 300,000) have also reported on this variable (Hammersmith and Fulham by Painter *et al.*, 1989 and two surveys in Islington by Jones *et al.*, 1986 and Crawford *et al.*, 1989). A survey in the whole of London by the Policy Studies Institute (Smith, 1983), which was mainly concerned with attitudes to the police, also compared ethnic groups on 'fear of crime'. In none of these studies were adequate controls made in the design or analysis to enable comparisons to be made between ethnic groups living in similar conditions.

The study reported here[1] was carried out in Leeds in 1987, and incorporated a survey in which the sampling scheme enabled comparisons to be made between blacks, Asians, and whites *living in the same small areas* (enumeration districts (EDs)) who would therefore be living in roughly the same circumstances as each other. Differences between them are therefore more likely to be due to ethnicity *per se*, rather than differences in the environment. The areas sampled were those where most of the non-whites in Leeds lived and tended to be socially deprived, so the results cannot be extrapolated to all areas (see Table 1). Besides this, only males aged 16–35 were included in the main questionnaire, since females and older men were thought to be less likely to have had experience of crime. Their attitudes to the police have been reported elsewhere (Jefferson and Walker, 1993); here the results of analysing three measures of 'concern about crime' labelled 'fear', 'worries', and 'problems' are reported.

Table 1 Socio-economic characteristics of survey areas

Percentage	Survey areas > 10% non-white	Other areas < 10% non-white	All[a]
Social class 1,2	8.7	14.2	12.4
Social class 4,5	37.2	28.4	31.3
Unemployed	18.2	10.8	13.2
Overcrowding[b]	2.5	0.6	1.2
Privately rented	23.9	13.1	16.6
No. of EDS	212	436	648

a 'All' excludes outer wards of Leeds. These were excluded from the main study as they contained so few non-whites that arrest rates could not be calculated satisfactorily.

b 'Overcrowding' means percentage of households with over 1.5 persons per room.

Source: 1981 Census

Comparisons with other surveys addressing these topics are difficult to make because their results are seldom presented broken down by age and sex. In addition, in other studies blacks and Asians have sometimes been combined as 'non-white', which is shown here not to be justified since there were clear differences between them. However, extrapolation from the Leeds survey to other towns should only be undertaken with care, since the experiences of Asians and blacks (and of course, whites) may well differ in other parts of the country.

Full details of the survey are given in the Main Report (Walker *et al.*, 1990). Jefferson and Walker (1992) give an overview of the research.

The Leeds Survey

The sample was selected from EDs (which contain about 150 houses), estimated to have over 10 per cent households which were non-white.[2] These areas contained over 50 per cent of blacks and Asians, but only 6 per cent of the whites in the city, and clearly the sample could not be regarded as representative of the whole city. The areas included in the survey, compared with the rest of Leeds, had fewer in Social Classes 1 and 2; more in Social

Classes 4 and 5; more people unemployed; more overcrowding, and more households which were privately rented. These data (from the 1981 Census) show that non-whites tend to live in areas which are socially deprived – see Table 1. EDs were stratified into five groups as follows: A contained EDs with over 50 per cent non-white households, B contained 33–50 per cent, C contained 20–33 per cent, D contained 15–20 per cent, and E contained 10–15 per cent non-white. A random sample of households was selected from EDs in A, and an interview was requested if there was a male aged 10–35 (one aged under 16 and one aged 16 or over, if possible). Households selected in B were asked 'are there any men/boys of West Indian, African, or Asian descent?' and if the answer was 'yes' an interview was requested in the appropriate age group and the ethnic origin stated by the respondent was recorded. If the answer was 'no', only one in three households were asked for an interview. In stratum C all non-white but only one in five white households were asked for an interview; in strata D and E the sampling fraction was one in eight.

The response rate overall was 77 per cent and did not differ significantly between ethnic groups. The number of black men aged 16–35 interviewed was 171; there were 199 Asian men and 271 white men, totalling 641. Altogether 225 boys were interviewed; their results are presented in the Main Report (Walker *et al.,* 1990) and will not be discussed here.

Fear of crime

Respondents were asked: 'How safe do you feel walking about in this area after dark on your own?' The percentages giving the answers 'very safe', 'fairly safe', 'a bit unsafe' and 'very unsafe' are given in Table 2. Those saying 'a bit unsafe' or 'very unsafe' will be referred to simply as feeling unsafe and it can be seen that more Asians felt unsafe (at 31 per cent), next were whites (21 per cent) and fewest blacks (10 per cent): the three races all differing significantly. If we look at the proportions feeling 'very safe', the figures are Asians 23 per cent, whites 35 per cent, and blacks 54 per cent, showing the same trend but even bigger differences. The four answers were scored, for the purposes of analysis, as 1, 2, 3, 4 (the score being labelled Fear or F) and as would be expected, the mean F scores differed significantly, Asians being highest and blacks lowest.

The relationship with age was explored and only for Asians was it found that more older men (those aged 31–35) felt unsafe than younger men; for the other groups there was no correlation with age. It should be remembered that, unlike other studies, the highest age here was only 35, so we know nothing about those aged over 35. Maxfield (1984), for example, found that those aged over 35 were more likely to feel unsafe.

The number of times people went out the previous week was examined in relation to 'fear'. The correlation was not significant for any race group, unlike Maxfield's finding that those who tended to go out more tended to feel unsafe. The Leeds study incorporated a question on victimization, and found significantly fewer blacks had been victims in the preceding 12 months (blacks 23 per cent, Asians 37 per cent, whites 42 per cent). Fear was correlated with the number of times people had been victimized only for blacks (for burglary <.05) and Asians (for car theft <.05), so victimization, in general, does not appear to have affected fear in the street.

Table 2 Fear of crime

	Percentages		
	Black	**Asian**	**White**
Very safe[a]	54	23	35
Fairly safe	36	46	44
A bit unsafe	8	21	15
Very unsafe	2	10	6
n = 100%	167	198	271
F score[b]	1.6	2.2	1.9

a   Answers to: 'How safe do you feel walking about in this area after dark on your own?'

b   F = Fear; for scoring see text. Asians are significantly higher than whites and blacks ($p<0.05$).

Differences between any 2 ethnic groups of 10 or more in the percentages are significant at $p<0.05$ or higher.

In an examination of data from the 1984 British Crime Survey, Box *et al.* (1988) found that the percentage feeling unsafe among all non-whites was similar to that for whites in inner-city areas (for which our areas would qualify), but no breakdown was given by age and sex, and all non-whites were taken together, so satisfactory comparisons cannot be made.

The wording of the question in the PSI study was slightly different. Respondents were asked, first, if there were risks to women going out alone after dark. They were then asked if they sometimes worried for themselves (the figures being blacks 28 per cent, Asians 52 per cent, and whites 48 per cent) (Smith, 1983, p.32). This study indicated that blacks felt less afraid than whites and Asians, and this was true for all age groups. Smith (p.33) suggests this is because blacks 'may wish to deny that a serious problem exists because their own group is held responsible for the problem', but this is clearly hypothetical.

The other London studies, in Islington and Hammersmith, had rather different results. The Islington study (Jones *et al.,* 1986) found about 50 per cent 'feeling worried' about going out alone, with no significant differences between races, and this figure seems remarkably high compared with other studies; the explanation of these findings is not clear. The Hammersmith report does not give the percentages of respondents who themselves felt unsafe going out alone after dark, but gives the percentages of blacks and whites who felt it was risky for several specified groups to go out on their own after dark. For each group blacks had higher percentages than whites thinking it was risky. For example 13 per cent of blacks thought black people were at risk and only 6 per cent of whites thought this (Painter *et al.,* 1989, Table 61). There is no indication that in Hammersmith or in Islington blacks were less afraid than other racial groups, as we found in Leeds, and as Smith (1983) found for the whole of London. There is a possibility that respondents do not interpret feeling 'unsafe' about going out alone after dark as the same as being 'worried' about it and that might account for differences in the results. This will be explored in the next section.

Worries about crime

A second indication of people's concern about crime was obtained from their answers to the question: 'How much do you yourself worry about the possibility of (a) your home being broken into and something stolen (burglary); (b) being mugged or robbed (robbery); (c) having your home or property damaged by vandals (vandalism); or (d) being insulted or bothered by strangers (being insulted or bothered may be unpleasant but are, of course, not necessarily offences)?'

Comparisons between races showed, again, that Asians differed from blacks and whites, with higher percentages worried about each item. However, in this case blacks and whites did not differ significantly. Table 3 shows the percentages saying 'quite a bit' or 'a lot' for each item. In particular about two-thirds of Asians worried about burglary and only half of blacks and whites; twice as many Asians (36 per cent) worried about robbery as did blacks and whites (about 18 per cent). On the whole people who worried about one offence tended to worry about the other offences and the answers referring to different offences were significantly correlated (the average correlation within race being about 0.5). This justified the calculation of an overall worries score (W)[3] from the individual scores for the three offences. Worry about insults from strangers was also significantly higher for Asians, and correlated highly with worries score (W).

Table 3 Worries about crime

Percentage who worry[a]	Black	Asian	White
Burglary[b]	50	66	52
Robbery[b]	19	36	18
Vandalism[b]	41	60	36
Insults from strangers[b]	15	33	12
Mean of first three	37	54	35
W score[c]	6.5	7.7	6.7

a   Percentage saying they worry quite a bit or a lot about being victims.

b   Offences with significant differences.

c   W = Worries: for scoring see text. Asians are significantly higher than whites and blacks ($p<0.05$).

Differences between any 2 ethnic groups of 10 or more in the percentages are significant at $p<0.05$ or higher.

Comparing our results with those of others, the Islington study gave figures ranging from 15.5 per cent (worried about attacks by strangers) to 26.6 per cent (for burglary). The Hammersmith study reported that considerably more Asians (about 73 per cent) worried about burglary and property damage than did whites and blacks (averaging 63 per cent for burglary and 53 per cent for damage), who did not differ. These differences and similarities are consistent with those found in Leeds (see Table 3).

Correlations of worries with age were not significant except for a slight tendency, among blacks, for older people to worry more about burglary and *less* about insults from strangers than the other groups. Maxfield (1984) found (using British Crime Survey data, which covers the whole of England and Wales) an increase in the percentage of males with a 'big worry about crime' with age, which is not confirmed in the current study. His figures increased from about 2 per cent at age 16 to 10 per cent at age 35 – considerably fewer than in Leeds. The London studies did not give results in relation to age.

Correlations of worries with actual victimization in our study were not significant for blacks or whites; for Asians there was a low (just significant) correlation ($r = 0.19$), those having been victims of more offences tending to be more worried.

Relationship between worries and fear

Were those who worried about being a victim of an offence the same as those who felt unsafe in the area at night? It is perhaps surprising to find that the correlations of 'fear' with worry about *robbery* are about the same as those with worry about *burglary* and (for Asians and whites) with worry about *vandalism* (see Table 4, first three columns). It might be expected that fear in the streets would only be associated with worry about being robbed, rather than worry about burglary or vandalism. Correlations were low (of the order of 0.3), but in the main significant.

Table 4 Fear related to worries

Worries about:	Correlation[a]. Fear score (F) with worries score (W)			% bit or very unsafe[b]					
	Black	Asian	White	Black		Asian		White	
				High[c]	Low[c]	High	Low	High	Low
Burglary	0.23	0.28	0.28	14	4	37	19	28	13
Robbery	0.22	0.29	0.37	19	7	44	23	43	16
Vandalism	(0.16)	0.23	0.40	13	6	36	24	30	16
Insults	(0.02)	0.19	0.22	8	9	41	26	29	19

a   Correlations are significant at $p<0.05$ or more except those in parentheses.

b   For interpretation see text.

c   High = worried quite a bit or a lot. Low = worried not much or not at all.

Table 4 illustrates the meaning of these correlations by also showing that the percentages feeling very or a bit unsafe tend to be higher for those having high as compared with low values of 'worry'. For example, of those Asians who say they worry about being a victim of burglary quite a bit or a lot, 37 per cent feel a bit or very unsafe while only 19 per cent of those who do not worry about being a victim of burglary do so.

The low correlations between fear on the street and worry about robbery suggest the questions addressed are to some extent tapping *different* types of concern. On the other hand the fact that there are many *significant* correlations between the fear and the worry scores for *each* of the three offences (in the main of the order of 0.3 for Asians and whites) suggests there is a diffuse feeling of 'concern' about being a victim of any of the three types of crime.

Crime as an area problem

Another approach to respondents' concern about crime was to ask them whether they thought certain features (including crime) were a problem in the area they lived in. This is a less personal concern and invokes a more general perception of the area. The items were in four main groups: these are briefly described as relating to (1) crime; (2) attacks on women; (3) people (incivility); and (4) civic problems. They were intermingled in the questionnaire. Those related to crime were: 'crime', 'burglary', 'robbery', and 'vandalism'. There were two items referring to women: 'sex attacks on women' and 'women being pestered' (which is unpleasant but not necessarily an offence). The other items (3) and (4) are described in the following section. Possible answers were 'a big problem', 'a slight problem', and 'not really a problem'. The percentages in the first and last categories are given in Table 5, where it can be seen that the ethnic groups differed significantly on only three items. First, in relation to 'burglary', fewer blacks thought it a big problem: 38 per cent compared with an average of 51 per cent for Asians and whites, who did not differ significantly. For the two items involving women as victims (assaults and pestering women), significantly more whites thought these a problem: about a quarter compared with about 12 per cent for blacks and Asians. This is consistent with Smith (1983) who found considerably more whites thought so (42 per cent) than did blacks (24 per cent) or Asians (30 per cent) (the statement was 'risks to women are serious'). He also found, as did we, that Asians and blacks did not differ. These groups included men and women respondents, and all ages, so no direct comparison is possible. Older people and women tended to have higher percentages. This was one of the few variables, in the Leeds survey, where blacks and Asians did not differ. It is possible that Asian women go out less than black or white women, and therefore the men do not regard them as being at risk.

	Table 5 Crime a problem in area					
	Percentage a big problem			Percentage not really a problem		
	Black	Asian	White	Black	Asian	White
'Crime'	38	46	44	23	26	25
Burglary[a]	38	50	52	25	18	16
Vandalism	36	42	44	24	28	25
Robbery	25	26	24	51	47	48
Mean of last three (Crime problems)	33	39	40	33	31	30
P score[a,b]	3.9	4.3	4.3			
Sex assaults[a]	9	1	23	77	65	53
Women pestered (not a crime)	14	13	25	67	62	45
S score[a,b]	0.7	0.8	1.1			

a   Significant differences between ethnic groups (p<0.05 or higher).

b   P = Problems, S = Sex attacks, for scoring see text.

Differences between any 2 ethnic groups of 10 or more in the percentages are significant at p<0.05 or higher.

The average inter-correlations between the four crime scores were fairly high, being over 0.5 for each ethnic group, and an overall crime problem score (P) was calculated.[4] The two items referring to women had correlations (within races) of over 0.7 and were scored together as SP (crime) was fairly highly correlated with S (problems for women), the correlations averaging 0.47 for the three ethnic groups. The overall scores on crime problems (P) showed whites and Asians as having slightly and significantly higher scores respectively (<0.05), while for 'problems for women' the difference between whites and the rest was more highly significant (<0.01). On average about a third of blacks and about 10 per cent of whites and Asians thought the crime items a big problem, but the proportion saying these items were 'not really a problem' did not differ significantly, averaging just under one third.

Neither age nor number of times people went out were significantly correlated with these two problem scores. However, for Asians and for whites the number of times people had been a victim of an offence was significantly correlated with the problem score (P) (r = 0.29 and r = 0.19 respectively), those who had been victims of an offence, perhaps not surprisingly, tending to regard crime as a problem.

The report on the Islington study does not give full details of the different ethnic groups' perception of specific offences as a problem. However, for 'crime' generally, the percentages thinking it a big problem are given by sex, age group, and race (Jones *et al.*, Table 23). For men aged 16–24 only 18.9 per cent of Asians thought so, compared with 31 per cent of whites and 35.7 per cent of blacks (for those aged 25–44 the figures are slightly higher for whites and Asians but lower for blacks). These figures are quite the opposite from those in the Leeds study, where blacks had the *lowest* problem scores.

In the Hammersmith and Fulham study (Painter *et al.*, 1989), figures are not given by age group and sex, so they cannot be compared directly. Here Asians had figures *similar* to those of blacks, and both had a higher proportion than whites thinking vandalism and crime generally 'a big problem' (36 per cent thinking so, compared with 26 per cent of whites). This is at variance with their finding that Asians had considerably more saying they worried quite a bit or a lot about burglary and vandalism (nearly 75 per cent or three quarters compared with about 58 per cent of the rest). Without knowing more about the characteristics of the Asians and the populations involved it is difficult to interpret these very diverse results.

Crime problems and fear

The relationships between fear and regarding offences as a problem are shown by the correlation coefficients in Table 6 (first three columns). The correlations between 'fear' and regarding robbery as a problem are significant but perhaps surprisingly low (averaging 0.30); correlations with burglary are of about the same magnitude. The correlations of fear and regarding vandalism as an area problem were significant for Asians and whites (0.28), but were not significant for blacks.

Table 6   Correlation of 'crime problems' with 'fear' and 'worries'

| | | | | Worries about | | | | | | | | |
| | Fear | | | Burglary | | | Robbery | | | Vandalism | | |
Problems	Bl	As	Wh	Bl	As	Wh	Bl	As	Wh	Bl	As	Wh
Burglary	0.24	0.23	0.32	0.42	0.34	0.33	0.22	(0.15)	(0.13)	0.41	0.47	0.19
Robbery	0.23	0.30	0.37	(0.12)	0.27	0.22	0.28	0.34	0.30	(0.17)	0.40	0.24
Vandalism	(0.15)	0.28	0.28	(0.16)	0.23	0.23	(0.11)	(0.15)	0.17	0.19	0.41	0.31

Figures in parentheses are not significant.

Underlined figures are those expected to be high, as they relate to same offence.

Crime problems and worries

The correlations between problems and worries for the individual offence types – burglary, robbery, and vandalism – are also shown in Table 6. While those for the same offences (underlined in the table) are undoubtedly significant, they were not as high as would be expected if they were tapping the same type of concern. The average correlation (over the three ethnic groups) between the worry score and problem score for burglary was 0.37, and that for robbery 0.31. For the vandalism items blacks had a correlation of only 0.19, significantly lower than that of Asians (0.41), whites having a value of 0.31. Several of the correlations between regarding an offence as a problem and worrying about a *different* offence were also significant. In particular Asians and blacks had correlations of 0.47 and 0.41 respectively between 'burglary a problem' and 'worrying about vandalism'; this is perhaps not surprising as both are attacks on the home. On the other hand, considering that blacks had over a third (36 per cent) thinking vandalism a big problem and 41 per cent saying they worried about vandalism, the low correlation (0.19) with 'worries' scores (bottom line) is puzzling.

Overall, it is clear that the three measures of concern: 'fear' of attack, 'worries' about different offences, and regarding different offences as 'problems' in the area are all inter-correlated, if not highly.

Correlations between *overall* scores for the four measures 'fear' (F), 'offences a problem' (P), 'problems for attacks on women' (S), and 'worries about offences' (W) are shown in Table 7. The only non-significant one is for blacks, between fear and attacks on women being a problem. (It should be borne in mind that the sample was for males only.) Twelve of the 18 coefficients in the table are between 0.32 and 0.52 indicating that *within* each race group the scores were to some extent, but by no means entirely, measuring the same concept. For each pair of variables the correlations were lower for blacks, perhaps indicating a slightly less generalized concern, and a *consequence* of their mean scores on each measure tending to be lower than the *rest*.

Table 7   Correlations between overall scores for fear, worries and problems

	Black	Asian	White
F.W	0.24	0.33	0.40
F.P	0.21	0.35	0.28
F.S	(0.08)	0.26	0.23
P.W	0.36	0.49	0.37
W.S	0.26	0.37	0.32
P.S	0.45	0.52	0.48

P = crime problems score.

W = worries about crime score (for scoring see text).

S = attacks on women score.

F = fear score.

General area problems

As already mentioned in the Leeds survey the question on problems in the area included general topics intermingled with those related to crime discussed above. They have been divided into two main groups. The first group, named 'people problems', had four items and consisted of 'race relations', 'general unfriendliness', 'rowdiness among teenagers', and 'fights and disturbances'. The score obtained from this group was labelled PP. The second was named 'civic problems' (CP). There were five items consisting of housing, schools, public transport, street lighting, and play space. (These groups are similar to, but not identical with, those of Box *et al.*, 1988 named 'Incivilities', 'Cohesion', and 'Housing conditions'.) There were three additional items relating to unemployment, lorry noise, and 'activities for young people'. The percentages thinking each item 'a big problem' or 'not really a problem' are given in Table 8.

Differences between ethnic groups were small. In the PP group there were no differences between races except that fewer whites and more blacks thought race relations were 'not really a problem' and blacks had a lower problem score (PP)[5] (but not significantly lower). On the CP items significantly more whites than Asians thought housing a big problem but the overall scores (CP) were almost the same. The correlation between PP and CP scores were blacks 0.52, Asians 0.47, and whites 0.27, and it is apparent that people had general feelings of satisfaction or dissatisfaction about problems in their areas, although this was true to a lesser extent for whites. The fact that the ethnic groups did not differ significantly on the overall scores may be a consequence of the samples being taken from the same areas. Painter, in contrast, found in Hammersmith and Fulham that more blacks than whites found nearly every one of 19 items a big problem, but it is not clear if they lived in the same areas as the whites. Jones *et al.* (Islington survey) did not give details for ethnic groups.

Table 8 Area problems

	% a big problem			% not really a problem		
	Black	Asian	White	Black	Asian	White
People problems:						
race relations[a]	14	15	20	64	61	53
general unfriendliness	10	7	10	71	68	67
rowdiness by teenagers[a]	25	29	26	45	35	38
fights and disturbances	14	19	14	62	47	58
Mean %	16	18	18	60	53	54
PP score	0.1	0.5	0.5			
Civic problems:						
poor housing[a]	58	53	65	16	24	24
poor schools	34	30	33	40	39	39
public transport	14	12	15	74	67	66
street lighting	12	7	11	72	72	70
play space	44	45	52	28	26	21
Mean %	32	29	35	46	46	44
CP score	1.0	0.9	1.0			
Other items:						
unemployment	76	68	70	8	8	8
lorry noise	14	17	14	67	62	65
activities for young	57	49	54	18	21	20

a   Significant differences between some groups.

Differences between any 2 ethnic groups of 10 or more in the percentages are significant at $p<0.05$ or higher.

Relationship between area problems and concern about crime

The correlation between the area problem scores PP and CP with each of the four measures of concern about crime are shown in Table 9. The 'fear' score was significantly correlated with PP (people problems) for all three races, but the correlation was low for blacks (blacks r = 0.19, Asians r = 0.31, whites r = 0.27). The correlation between fear (F) and crime problems (CP) was only significant for Asians (r = 0.29).

Table 9   Correlations between area problems and concern about crime

	Black	Asian	White
PP.F	0.19	0.31	0.27
PP.W	0.37	0.27	0.27
PP.P	0.62	0.57	0.56
PP.S	0.45	0.53	0.38
CP.F	(0.12)	0.29	(0.10)
CP.W	0.19	0.17	0.21
CP.P	0.52	0.44	0.41
CP.S	0.22	0.32	0.44
CP.PP	0.52	0.48	0.27

PP = people problems score.
P = crime problems score.
W = crime worries score.
CP = civic problems score.
S = attacks on women score.
F = fear score.
All correlations are significant (p<0.05 or higher) except those in parentheses.

Worry about crime items was significantly correlated with PP (people problems) for all three ethnic groups, the average of the three correlations being r = 0.30. Correlations with CP (civic problems), however, are again considerably lower, being less than 0.22, but are just significant.

However, the problem scores for crime (P) and attacks on women (S) were consistently and fairly highly correlated with the area problem scores (CP and PP), straight averages from correlations being 0.45 (blacks), 0.45 (Asians) and 0.45 (whites). This is of considerable interest because it suggests concern about crime as a problem is part of a general pattern of perception of problems in the area.

Summary and conclusions

The survey reported here differed from many other similar surveys in that it was restricted to areas of Leeds where over 10 per cent of the people were estimated to be non-white; these contained over half the Asian and black population of Leeds but only 6 per cent of the white population. This had the advantage that comparisons between those of different ethnic origin were between those having roughly the same living conditions, although there were some differences in their socio-economic status, which have been described in the Main Report (Walker *et al.*, 1990). Useful comparisons cannot be made with the results of other surveys which covered large areas, and where the non-whites would be more likely than whites to be living in socially deprived areas. It was interesting to find, however, that none of our measures was correlated with the percentage of non-whites in the areas included in the survey. This varied from 10 per cent to 60 per cent.

The respondents of the main survey were all males aged 16 to 35, which is another reason why it is difficult to compare the results with other surveys, where breakdowns by sex and age, in relation to ethnic origin, are often not given. Besides this, sometimes Asians and blacks are taken together as non-white, and differences between them have not been presented.

'Concern about crime' has been examined here in three different ways, and while the results of sample surveys can only give indications of underlying reactions to crime, those presented here suggest that the subject is a complex one. The three measures, which we have named 'fear', 'worries', and 'problems', were in the main, significantly correlated with each other *within* each race group, so to some extent they were measuring the same thing. But, insofar as the correlations were small, it is clear that all three are measuring slightly different concepts and these should all be examined separately.

Differences and similarities between the three ethnic groups are a further indication that the three measures should be examined separately. For, while blacks are evidently less fearful than whites about walking on the streets at night (Table 2), they did not appear to worry about crime any less than whites (Table 3). With regard to problems, more whites than blacks thought burglary a problem (in spite of living in the same areas), and that attacks on women were a problem (the reaction of women to this question would be of considerable interest). About the same proportion (a quarter) thought robbery a problem.

Asians tended to differ from both blacks and whites on both 'fear' (having considerably more who were fearful) and on 'worries' (with more who worried a lot). This ties up with their reaction to the police (Jefferson and Walker, 1993), which was generally favourable, and their believing there were not sufficient police around. On the other hand, they did not differ from whites in regarding crime a problem, the figures were fairly high, with, on average, about 40 per cent thinking this was the case (Table 4). Significantly fewer Asians than whites thought attacks on women a problem (possibly because Asian women are unlikely to go out on their own).

Perception of particular features as being problems in the area did not differ greatly between ethnic groups. Under 20 per cent regarded what we called 'people problems' (see Table 8) as being big problems, and about a third, on average 'civic problems'. It was interesting to find that there were mainly significant correlations between these measures and the three measures of 'concern' (Table 9). This suggests that 'crime' is one of a constellation of factors which people regard as part of life's problems.

Overall, it is clear that just one measure of 'concern about crime' is inadequate. It is also clear that deconstructive work on the meanings of the terms used, for the different ethnic groups, could be usefully undertaken.

Notes

1   This was part of a research project entitled 'Ethnic minorities, young people and the criminal justice system', funded by the Economic and Social Research Council, Ref. E 06250023.

2   The 1981 Census included a question on place of birth and EDs were selected in which the head of household was born in the New Commonwealth or Pakistan.

3   The answers coded were 'not at all' (scored 1); 'quite a bit' (scored 2) and 'a lot' (scored 3) ('don't know' was also scored 1).

4   For the analysis these were scored as: a large problem = 3; a slight problem = 2; not really a problem = 1.

5   Scoring: big problem = 3; not really a problem = 1; other = 2.

References

Baldwin, J. and Bottoms, A.E. (1976) *The Urban Criminal: A Study in Sheffield,* London, Tavistock.

Box, S., Hale, C. and Glen, A. (1988) 'Explaining fear of crime', *British Journal of Criminology,* vol.28, pp.340–56.

Crawford, A., Jones, T., Woodhouse, T. and Young, J. (1989) *Second Islington Crime Survey,* Middlesex Polytechnic.

Hough, M. and Mayhew, P. (1983) *The British Crime Survey: First Report,* Home Office Research Study No.76, London, HMSO.

Jefferson, T. and Walker, M.A. (1992) 'Ethnic minorities and the criminal justice system', *Criminal Law Review,* February, pp.83–95.

Jefferson, T. and Walker, M.A. (1993) 'Attitudes to the police of the ethnic minorities in a provincial city', *British Journal of Criminology,* vol.33, no.2, pp.251–66.

Jones, T., Maclean, B. and Young, J. (1986) *The Islington Crime Survey,* Aldershot, Gower.

Lewis, D.A. and Salem, G. (1986) *Fear of Crime, Incivility and the Production of a Social Problem,* New Brunswick, NJ/Oxford, Transaction Books.

Maxfield, M.G. (1984) *Fear of Crime in England and Wales,* Home Office Research Study No.78, London, HMSO.

Painter, K., Lee, J., Woodhouse, T. and Young, J. (1989) *Hammersmith and Fulham Crime and Policing Survey,* Middlesex Polytechnic, Centre for Criminology.

Smith, D. (1983) *A Survey of Londoners: Police and People in London 1,* London, Policy Studies Institute.

Walker, M.A., Jefferson, T. and Seneviratne, M. (1990) *Ethnic Minorities, Young People and the Criminal Justice System,* Main Report, Centre for Criminological and Legal Research, University of Sheffield.

I wish to thank my colleagues Tony Jefferson, Mary Seneviratne, and Halina Szulc for their co-operation in this research project, and Tony Jefferson for his comments on a draft of this article.

Monica Walker is at the Centre for Criminological and Legal Research, University of Sheffield.

(Source: Walker, 1994, pp.366–78)

Appendix 3.3

Raynor and Vanstone: 'Probation practice, effectiveness and the non-treatment paradigm'

Summary

This paper reports interim and largely positive results from the continuing evaluation of 'Straight Thinking on Probation', a substantial intensive probation programme in Mid-Glamorgan based on the work of Robert Ross *et al.* (1988) in Canada. The potential effectiveness of this type of programme is then discussed in relation to the influential model of the probation service's role advanced by Bottoms and McWilliams in their 1979 'non-treatment paradigm'. Are such programmes 'treatment', based on a model of offender pathology and therefore in conflict with the paradigm; or are they 'help', based on a model of empowerment? An attempt to answer this question also requires consideration of how far the 'non-treatment paradigm' was itself a response to perceived ineffectiveness requiring revision in the light of new evidence. It is argued that such revision need not threaten the underlying moral philosophy of the paradigm.

'Reasoning and rehabilitation': the model and its critics

The Reasoning and Rehabilitation (R & R) programme originated in Canada from a series of systematic research studies of successful programmes of intervention with offenders (Ross *et al.*, 1988). Of particular interest to the researchers was what contributed to that success, and thereby distinguished these programmes from the generality of offender based work. They discovered, perhaps not surprisingly, that the programmes tended to be properly planned; systematically and consistently delivered; owned by both practitioners and management; and resourced at an appropriate level. However, the single unifying characteristic was that the focus of the programmes was on people's thinking. More traditional therapeutic goals were eschewed or given lower priority, and replaced by attempts to enhance offenders' thinking skills.

Ross and his colleagues also reviewed forty years of experimental work with people who continually offend whatever the response of the courts, and isolated a range of thinking skills deficiencies. These included a failure to think actions through, and a lack of awareness of the impact of their behaviour on other people. Such problems are not confined to persistent offenders and the researchers did not argue that crime is caused by lack of thinking skills; they recognized social and economic conditions as significant contributory factors which, if ignored, would undermine any attempt to influence or change individuals (Ross and Fabiano, 1985). Instead they concluded that training in thinking might increase the range of choices for people whose usual response to problems was offending. Accordingly they gathered a number of cognitive training methods and exercises from successful programmes, and organized them into a carefully constructed training manual.

The programme itself is subdivided into several different modules which in their turn are divided into specific skill categories. The modules are: problem solving; social skills; management of emotions; negotiation skills;

critical reasoning; creative thinking; and values enhancement. Within these a wide range of skills is taught: for example, the problem solving sequence consists of problem recognition; problem identification; conceptualizing; non-verbal communication; verbal communication; assertiveness; and consequential thinking. Inherent in this is an attempt to teach the programme participants to stop and think before acting, to consider the consequences of their behaviour for themselves and others, and to help them develop a greater range of alternative ways of responding to personal, inter-personal and social problems.

The programme model has been subject in Britain to wide-ranging criticisms, notably by Neary (1992a; 1992b) who indicts it on the following alleged grounds:

a   the language and the material are racist;

b   the manual provides a script which officers have to read to participants;

c   innovative effort is constrained by the demand that the programme should be delivered as intended (programme integrity);

d   the ethos of the programme undermines the essential humanity of social work interactions (as Neary put it: 'The fact that everything that constituted our living humanity was to be subordinated to everything that constituted life as machines');

e   the focus on teaching skills to individuals diverts attention away from the capitalist system's deficiencies, in particular poverty and disadvantage;

f   based as it is on liberal social theory, the programme itself is the product of 'irrational cognitive processes'.

More generally, Pitts (1992), in a considered and discerning critique of the 'something works' bandwagon, whilst not specifying the Reasoning and Rehabilitation model, argues that effective programmes need to be adaptive and based on knowledge of the needs of offenders; and that they should not be prescriptive, directive and requiring technicians.

The point that crime needs to be addressed from both an individual and a wider social perspective, and in a way that challenges discrimination and disadvantage, is very important, and there is an important debate surrounding the location and relevance of programmes like Reasoning and Rehabilitation in society's response to crime and its related problems. It is a pity that some of the contributions to that debate are marred by overstatement; Neary, for instance, refers to the programme writers' emphasis on the management of emotions rather than their exploration as 'Clockwork Orange'. The structural dimension to people's anger and frustration is appropriately highlighted by Neary, but if this argues against any attempt to help people control anger or potential violence, then it fails to take account of the victims' perspective. Feminist criminology (Horley, 1990) and the rediscovery of the victims' perspective (e.g. Maguire and Pointing, 1988) have effectively exposed the frailty of such ideological positions. In saying this we are not denying the relevance of understanding and exploring the reasons for anger, but rather arguing that, along with self-control techniques, they have a place in a strategy which might have different emphases in different contexts. Moreover, the implied criticism that the programme is a form of brainwashing which focuses attention away from the structural problems faced by offenders needs to be balanced against a perspective within which teaching people to think creatively, to solve problems, and to challenge attempts to manipulate and mislead them, is a form of empowerment.

Nevertheless the anxiety that programmes of this kind will focus exclusively on the individual, and will be seen as *the* only strategy available to reduce crime and help offenders, is justified, and Pitts sounds a useful cautionary note in his paper. The 'Reasoning and Rehabilitation' programme also needs to be scrutinized in the light of his argument that effective programmes need to be run by thoughtful, imaginative people who work in the light of new knowledge and who respect people enough to shape their own efforts to meet their needs. Moreover, the programme needs to be looked at critically in the light of charges of racism. There is, on the one hand, little attempt in the programme to address the specific needs of black people, and this criticism needs to be taken seriously; on the other hand, the emphasis on awareness of other people's views and experience which permeates the programme, and the specific focus in a section of the programme on the challenging of prejudice and stereotyping, suggest a sensitivity to cultural difference. The point we make is that this particular issue is too important to be reduced to generalization.

One way to focus the debate about the place of such programmes in British probation practice is to consider them in the light of past theoretical work on the distinctions between 'help' and 'treatment'. Fifteen years ago Bottoms and McWilliams wrote a very influential paper which presented a paradigm for working with offenders based essentially on respect for persons (Bottoms and McWilliams, 1979). We think that the debate about 'Reasoning and Rehabilitation' can be taken forward constructively by reflecting on the relevance of that paradigm in the light of new evidence about what works, and by exploring the degree to which the approach accords with the moral philosophy of the paradigm.

Implementing 'reasoning and rehabilitation' in one probation area

Before doing that, it might help to inform the discussion if we briefly outline how 'Reasoning and Rehabilitation' has been implemented in one probation area in Britain (for another example see Weaver and Bensted, 1992). The original experimental project in Canada, after an admittedly limited follow-up of nine months, reported reconviction rates which were significantly lower in the experimental group compared to two control groups (Ross *et al.*, 1988). These results, coupled with two British studies of enhanced probation orders (Raynor, 1988; Roberts, 1989) were sufficiently encouraging for the Mid-Glamorgan Probation Service to commit itself to the first UK application of this approach. The decision to involve all six field teams was based on a desire not only to help field team officers to address the quality and effectiveness of their work with high risk offenders but also to impact on the 'practice culture' of the whole organization.

The experimental period of twelve months started on 1 June 1991, and during that period probation officers delivered a groupwork programme based on the original manual designed by Robert Ross and his colleagues. It comprised 35 two-hour group sessions which incorporate the programme modules. Although many of the methods used were familiar to probation officers with experience of running offending behaviour groups (McGuire and Priestley, 1985), the systematic and intensive nature of the programme was qualitatively different. A non-therapeutic teaching model involving incremental learning of thinking skills required early adjustments for all of the officers who led groups. Within the programme, the traditional concern with personal problems is deliberately avoided; the emotional and material problems of offenders are not ignored, but are dealt with as part of the wider supervision process rather than within the group programme. This programme is known in Mid-Glamorgan as 'Straight Thinking on Probation', or STOP. More detailed descriptions of the STOP programme itself can be found in Raynor and Vanstone (1992) and in a paper produced by Mid-Glamorgan Probation Service (1991).

Interim results from the STOP evaluation

In the initial planning stage care was taken to ensure that a continuing staff development strategy and a detailed evaluation study were in place. The evaluation study, which broadly follows a pluralistic design (Smith and Cantley, 1984) and uses a variety of outcome measures, considers both the programme's influence on probationers and the impact of its introduction on the probation service concerned. The results of the study so far are covered in the second and third interim reports (Lucas *et al.,* 1992; Raynor and Vanstone, 1994) and readers interested in the full detail are referred to these. In this paper we aim only to present those interim results and conclusions which appear most relevant to the 'effectiveness' debate and which have caused us, as researchers, to reflect further on the non-treatment paradigm.

Briefly, the second interim report considered the organization and delivery of the programme; recruitment, attendance and completion; and the reactions to it of probationers and probation staff. Information on the first 133 probationers sentenced to the programme showed that they were, as intended, persistent offenders with a high risk of reconviction. With an average age of twenty-three and an average of nine previous convictions, they presented a higher risk profile than the non-custodial comparison groups in the study ('standard' probation, Community Service and suspended sentences) and were directly comparable to those receiving custodial sentences; three-quarters of them had already served a custodial sentence. Nearly two-thirds (62 per cent) of those sentenced to the programme completed it; this proportion rises to three-quarters (75 per cent) if we discount those who found work. became ill, moved out of the area, or were sentenced to custody for offences committed before the probation order was made. This completion rate for the eighteen-week programme is comparable to those for other community sentences: for example, the most recent national figure for non-completion of Community Service Orders is reported as 28 per cent (Home Office, 1993). Random sampling of video-recorded sessions showed a high level of programme integrity, i.e. that the programme was being delivered as intended. The feedback from probationers completing the programme was predominantly positive and suggested changes in thinking. Most staff involved in the programme viewed it positively, and sentencers supported it by making a substantial number of orders. The first results from before-and-after administration of a questionnaire on attitudes to offending (Frude *et al.,* 1990) showed more positive change in the STOP group than in the Community Service group.

These early results, broadly positive though they were, primarily concerned the development and implementation of the programme rather than its impact, if any, on the subsequent behaviour of those who were involved in it. The third report (Raynor and Vanstone, 1994) presents the first reconviction data from the STOP group and the comparison groups, based on a 12-month follow-up of 655 offenders sentenced in the first nine months of the experiment. The data on offending were provided by the Home Office from the National Identification Bureau and covered standard list offences. Reconvictions were counted from the date of sentence for non-custodial sentences and the date of release for custodial sentences. Readers interested in the full detail of the follow-up are advised to consult the report; further analysis will in due course cover 2-year reconviction rates, and will incorporate post-programme as well as post-sentence comparisons. For the purposes of this paper we concentrate on comparisons between the STOP group and those who received custodial sentences, both of which represent higher-risk offenders than those who received other community sentences. For all groups expected reconviction rates at the point of sentence were calculated using the Home Office 'National Risk of Reconviction Predictor' based on Copas (1992) and modified by a standard formula to yield expected one-year reconviction rates. Standard correction factors for both expected and actual rates were also calculated from local file studies to allow for 'false positives', i.e. apparent reconvictions for offences committed before the order or sentence started, but not dealt with until afterwards. These are more common in non-custodial than in custodial sentences, since in the latter case outstanding offences are more likely to be cleared up before release and less likely to affect apparent post-release reconviction rates. (The correction factor for 'false positives' is likely to vary from area to area as a result of different police and prosecution practices: for Mid-Glamorgan it was calculated that both predicted and actual rates should be multiplied by 0.90 for community sentences and 0.97 for custodial sentences to give a more accurate estimate of actual and expected 'true' reconviction.) Some cases were eliminated from the study by incomplete Home Office data but these were spread fairly evenly across the groups and so have only a limited effect on comparisons.

Also included in the study was a separate analysis of those who actually completed the STOP programme. These are not strictly comparable to other groups based on sentence rather than completion: those who receive a custodial sentence have little option but to complete, whilst those who complete community-based programmes are always likely to have a lower reconviction rate than those who start them if the follow-up period includes the period of the programme, since reasons for non-completion include reoffending during the programme when this results in a different sentence. However, the subsequent experience of those who complete a programme is relevant to consideration of its impact when delivered as intended, as a full programme. Table 1 sets out expected and actual 12-month reconviction rates for STOP and for custodial sentences. These figures must be interpreted with caution, as most differences between groups are not statistically significant at this stage. One observed difference (between STOP completers and a Young Offender Institution comparison group in which 46 out of 82 offenders reconvicted within 12 months of release) did reach significance ($\chi^2 = 4.02$, p = <0.05), but this is subject to the reservation about comparability noted above. It will not be possible to draw conclusions with full confidence until after a longer follow-up period incorporating comparisons between STOP completers and offenders who complete comparable proportions of other forms of supervision. However, the observed differences so far are clearly not inconsistent with the intention that STOP should result in lower levels of reconviction than custodial sentences for comparable offenders.

Table 1   Expected and actual reconviction rates

	Expected	Actual % (and number)	
Those sentenced to STOP (N = 107)	49%	49%	(52)
Custodial comparison group (i.e. Young Offender Institutions and adults sentenced to up to 12 months) (N = 164)	44%	51%	(83)
Those who completed a STOP programme (N = 59)	47%	39%	(23)
Expected and actual rates incorporating 'false positive' correction:			
Sentenced to STOP	44%	44%	
Custodial comparison group	43%	49%	
Completed STOP	42%	35%	

Some other features of the subsequent behaviour of those who completed the programme are also interesting. Table 2 compares the groups in respect of the proportions originally convicted and subsequently reconvicted for the more serious offence categories (violent and sexual offences and burglaries), and also compares the proportions of each group who, when reconvicted for any offence, received an immediate custodial sentence.

Table 2   Serious offences (violence, sexual offences and burglary) and custodial sentences on reconviction

	Serious offences on original conviction	Serious offences on reconviction	Custodial sentences on reconviction
Sentenced to STOP (N = 107)	42 (39%)	19 (18%)	19 (18%)
Custodial comparison group (N = 164)	67 (41%)	34 (21%)	21 (13%)
Completed STOP (N = 59)	21 (36%)	5 (8%)	0 (0%)

It is clear that those who completed STOP were not only less likely to be reconvicted, but also less likely to be reconvicted for an offence in the serious range, and much less likely to receive a custodial sentence if they were reconvicted. (The absence of custodial outcomes was also a finding of Ross *et al.,* 1988.) The reduction in seriousness of offences is likely to be a factor in the low incarceration rate, perhaps alongside other factors such as more favourable pre-sentence reports or sentencers' favourable view of past efforts. A detailed analysis of further offences committed by STOP completers confirmed that in comparison with other groups, they were tending to commit fewer offences of the kind which are obviously damaging to other people (violence and burglary), with signs of a shift towards offences which damaged objects (criminal damage) or perhaps themselves (possession of drugs). It is interesting in this context to note that one aim of the STOP programme is to increase awareness of other people's needs and feelings, particularly those of victims.

So far, then, the findings are mixed, but with some encouraging results for STOP clients in comparison with those receiving custodial sentences, and some quite positive outcomes for those who complete the programme. Bearing in mind that these figures are based on the first nine months of the programme when most staff had little experience of it, there are also some interesting implications for practice: for example, is it possible to increase completion rates, and what consequences would this have? Further evaluation will seek to address this and other questions. Such programmes cannot in any case solve all the problems of daily survival in a local economy of limited opportunities, but the evidence so far suggests that they may have a place among a range of strategies for helping people to reduce their offending.

At this stage, then, we are not making a premature claim that the programme 'works', but only that there are some early indicators of effectiveness. Readers will have an opportunity to judge for themselves as more follow-up data become available from the continuing evaluation. However, even on the basis of these interim results, we have had to think seriously about the possibility that the programme might 'work'. As long-term advocates of non-treatment approaches, we are now confronted with cognitive problems of our own: are we encountering here a successful 'treatment'? Such a description would present no problems to the originators of the programme: working within the discipline of psychology, they would find no philosophical problems in the idea of 'treatment', only in treatments unethically applied. In social work, however (and we still, perhaps unfashionably, regard probation practice as part of social work), the critique of 'treatment' has been the basis of opposition to hidden agendas, covert coercion, manipulation of clients, and the dehumanization of service users through the 'objective attitude', in which clients become objects of intervention rather than persons seeking help. Most informed commentators on recent probation practice would, we think, welcome the contribution of the 'non-treatment paradigm' to probation practice, as it has encouraged styles of work based on honest and open negotiation, informed consent, and client involvement in determining the agenda of supervision; whilst these are not universally practised, they seem at least to have replaced, as desirable features of practice, earlier probation aspirations such as one-sided psychosocial diagnosis and psychodynamically based interpretation of hidden drives (see, for example, Raynor, 1985).

We would argue that the non-treatment paradigm has been largely beneficial in its impact on social work with offenders, but it was founded on a scepticism about treatment which was both empirical and philosophical. If programmes like STOP begin to produce evidence of effectiveness, does this weaken the fundamental arguments of the paradigm, or do they still essentially stand? We are not attracted by the possibilities of a retreat into crude psychologism – 'if it works, why worry? – and there is some force in the argument that a purely psychological orientation, by focusing on the individual cognitive skills of probationers, can involve some insensitivity to social context. (In Mid-Glamorgan, for example, the programme required some adaptation both to ensure cultural sensitivity and to produce a version suitable for women probationers.) However, a review of the non-treatment paradigm to assess its contemporary relevance requires some re-examination of its basic assumptions.

Reviewing the non-treatment paradigm

The context of the non-treatment paradigm stretches back to the history of the professionalization of social work, and in particular probation, between the First and Second World Wars. Status gained through training and qualifications required theoretically informed practice; uncomplicated help in itself was not enough. Psychoanalysis, handily placed in current vogue as it was, neatly fitted an approach to criminal behaviour premised on the notion of curing a disease. Offenders, even if they didn't know it (and invariably they didn't), were suffering from a pathological condition.

By 1979 the edge had been taken off the excesses of the medical model, although offenders were still suffering from authority problems and lack of insight (Foren and Bailey, 1968), and the IMPACT experiment with its assumption about the efficacy of increased doses of case-work was only a few years distant (Folkard *et al.*, 1976). However, it still permeated practice sufficiently for the authors of the paradigm to declare the need for:

> a new paradigm of probation practice which is theoretically rigorous; which takes very seriously the exposed limitations of the treatment model; but which seeks to redirect the probation service's traditional aims and values in the new penal and social context.

(Bottoms and McWilliams, 1979, p.167)

Fourteen years on its main features make interesting and relevant reading, but its foundations, built as they were out of a mixture of doubt and scepticism about the crime-reducing potential of rehabilitation, have produced cracks in the structure. Before examining these cracks, and indeed what is still in sound condition, we shall summarize the authors' main arguments. In developing a critique of the treatment model which highlighted its theoretical fault lines, discriminatory processes and inequities, they argued that the model was theoretically incoherent and led to injustice. Inevitably, a summary will fail to do justice to the complexity of the arguments, but in essence they argued that crime is voluntary whereas disease is involuntary; that crime is not pathological but has social causes; and that enforced treatment is inherently unjust. These enduringly persuasive conclusions formed the basis of their conviction that a new framework for practice was needed, incorporating four basic aims.

The first, *the provision of appropriate help* for offenders, was described as something which the client rather than the worker defines. In other words, the appropriateness of the help is governed by the expressed needs of the client, and is separate from the crime reduction component of rehabilitation. Paradoxically, Bottoms and McWilliams suggested that the needs of the client were to be clarified within a process of joint assessment and collaboration; and furthermore, by a passing reference to successful work with offenders released from prison (Berntsen and Christiansen, 1965), that there might be evidence that help could reduce crime.

The second, *the statutory supervision of offenders,* was ensconced in acceptance of the reality that probation officers are law enforcement agents who must provide help which is consistent with agency function. Inevitably, this means that the transactions between officer and client occur within a context of authority and power imbalance. In order to resolve the problem created by that tension between client-defined needs and the statutory requirements of supervision, the paradigm draws on Raynor's exposition of the difference between coercion and 'choices made under constraint' (Raynor, 1978); within this conceptualization of the exercise of authority constrained choices are acceptable, but manipulative coercion is not.

The third, *diversion of appropriate offenders from custody,* required probation officers to abandon treatment, to eschew recommendations for custody or suspended sentences, and to think creatively about alternatives to custody. These changes in turn would facilitate the use of community resources to hold offenders as effectively as prison but at less cost.

The fourth, *reduction of crime,* positioned uneasily as it is within an analysis which denies the reductive potential of rehabilitation, focused on crime prevention activity based on the expressed wishes of the community, and directed at increasing social cohesion. To help them in this, the authors draw on Abrams' (1978) notion of reciprocity (i.e. there is a mutual pay off for helper and helped alike), and Christie's (1977) ideas of structural change in criminal justice processes (such as a 'conflict-based, victim-orientated, non-professional neighbourhood court'). So, in the light of National Standards (Home Office, 1992), the Criminal Justice Act 1991, and the current social and economic context of crime, how do these four pillars of the paradigm stand up? Perhaps we should first clear the ground and state which of them remains firm. Statutory supervision of offenders premised on maximizing choice with due regard to the function of the agency, and the development of imaginative community sentences, both seem as relevant today as they were then. The problem lies in their relationship with activities which may both help offenders and reduce crime, which because of *a priori* assumptions were almost unavailable for consideration by the authors of the paradigm.

The non-treatment paradigm was written at a time when the received wisdom about work with offenders aimed at reducing their offending was that at best it was a waste of energy and commitment, and at worst it was counter-productive. It was also written before any published revision of the analysis of the causes of crime by the school of 'new criminology' (Taylor *et al.,* 1973). The more recent 'left realist' position (Young, 1988) takes account of *all* of the actors in the criminal justice process, including victims and potential victims. As a result Bottoms and McWilliams follow lines of reasoning which significantly affect the persuasiveness of some of their key arguments.

The acceptance that 'nothing works' confined them to consideration of crime prevention strategies which had a social focus, to the exclusion of any concern with influencing individuals. Such a connection between the reinforcement of social bonds and a reduction in individual offending could plausibly be made, as in Kevin Haines' recent application of Hirschi's control theories (Haines, 1990; Hirschi, 1969) to explain the possible greater success of after-care provision which achieves the social reintegration of offenders; however, such arguments play a minor role in the original non-treatment paradigm. By uncoupling 'helping offenders' from 'crime reduction', the paradigm is prevented from exploring whether work with individuals on their thinking, behaviour and attitudes has any relevance to crime reduction. Current knowledge of research into effectiveness necessitates, therefore, a redefining of the concept of appropriate help in a way which retains the principle of collaboration, and the stress on client needs, but which incorporates informed practice focused on influencing and helping individuals to stop offending (Raynor, 1988; Roberts, 1989; Lipsey, 1992). This should not detract from the need to address the social and economic context of crime. A further problem for Bottoms and McWilliams stemmed from the fact that their only alternative to attacking the social causes of crime is the treatment model, which they very effectively demolished. Not only, therefore, as we have argued above, were they unable to consider individual offence-focused work, they were also inclined to write about offenders as if they were a homogeneous group. Consequently their main argument fails to address either the degree to which crime harms victims and communities as well as offenders, or to attempt to explain why the majority of poor, disadvantaged people do not become persistent offenders. This requires some acknowledgement of individual differences, and of patterns of thinking or behaviour which increase the risk of some people becoming involved in crime. The habits of thought and behaviour which STOP tries to influence could be included here. …

Acknowledgements

We are grateful to the Mid-Glamorgan Probation Service for collaboration in the STOP research, and to the Home Office Research and Planning Unit for support of the staff survey and assistance with the reconviction study.

References

Abrams, P. (1978) 'Community care', in Barnes, J. and Connelly, N. (eds) *Social Care Research*, London, Bedford Square Press.

Berntsen, K. and Christiansen, K.O. (1965) 'A resocialization experiment with short-term offenders', in Christiansen, K.O. (ed.) *Scandinavian Studies in Criminology*, vol.1, pp.35–54.

Bottoms, A.E. and McWilliams, W. (1979) 'A non-treatment paradigm for probation practice', *British Journal of Social Work*, vol.9, pp.159–202.

Christie, N. (1977) 'Conflicts as property', *British Journal of Criminology*, vol.17, pp.1–15.

Copas, J.B. (1992) *Statistical Analysis for a National Risk of Reconviction Predictor* (report to the Home Office), University of Warwick.

Folkard, M.S., Smith, D.E. and Smith, D.D. (1976) *IMPACT Vol.II*, London, HMSO.

Foren, R. and Bailey, R. (1968) *Authority in Social Casework*, Oxford, Pergamon.

Frude, N., Honess, T. and Maguire, M. (1990) *Crime PICS*, Cardiff, Michael Associates.

Haines, K. (1990) *After-Care for Released Prisoners: A Review of the Literature*, Cambridge, Institute of Criminology.

Hirschi, T. (1969) *Causes of Delinquency*, Berkeley and Los Angeles, CA, University of California Press.

Home Office (1992) *National Standards for the Supervision of Offenders in the Community*, London, Home Office.

Home Office (1993) *Probation Statistics England and Wales*, London, Home Office.

Horley, S. (1990) 'Responding to male violence against women', *Probation Journal*, vol.37, no.4, pp.166–70.

Lipsey, M. (1992) 'Juvenile delinquency treatment: a meta-analytic enquiry into the variability of effects', in Cook, T. *et al., Meta-Analysis for Explanation: A Casebook*, New York, Russell Sage.

Lucas, J., Raynor, P. and Vanstone, M. (1992) *Straight Thinking on Probation One Year On*, Bridgend, Mid-Glamorgan Probation Service.

Maguire, M. and Pointing, J. (eds) (1988) *Victims of Crime: A New Deal*, Milton Keynes, Open University Press.

McGuire, J. and Priestley, P. (1985) *Offending Behaviour*, London, Batsford.

Mid-Glamorgan Probation Service (1991) *Straight Thinking on Probation*, Bridgend, Mid-Glamorgan Probation Service.

Neary, M. (1992a) 'Robert Ross probation and the problems of rationality', unpublished paper distributed at 'What Works?' conference, Salford University.

Neary, M. (1992b) 'Some academic freedom', *Probation Journal*, vol.39, pp.200–2.

Pitts, J. (1992) 'The end of an era', *Howard Journal of Criminal Justice*, vol.31, pp.133–49.

Raynor, P. (1978) 'Compulsory persuasion', *British Journal of Social Work*, vol.8, no.4, pp.411–24.

Raynor. P. (1985) *Social Work, Justice and Control*, Oxford, Blackwell (2nd edn, 1993, Whiting and Birch).

Raynor, P. (1988) *Probation as an Alternative to Custody*, Aldershot, Avebury.

Raynor, P. and Vanstone, M. (1992) 'STOP start', *Social Work Today*, 16 February, pp.26–7.

Raynor, P. and Vanstone, M. (1994) *Straight Thinking on Probation: Third Interim Evaluation Report*, Bridgend, Mid-Glamorgan Probation Service.

Roberts, C.H. (1989) *Hereford and Worcester Probation Service Young Offender Project: First Evaluation Report*, Oxford, Department of Social and Administrative Studies, Oxford University.

Ross, R.R. and Fabiano, E.A. (1985) *Time to Think: A Cognitive Model of Delinquency Prevention and Rehabilitation*, Johnson City, Academy of Arts and Sciences.

Ross, R.R., Fabiano, E.A. and Ewles, C.D. (1988) 'Reasoning and rehabilitation', *International Journal of Offender Therapy and Comparative Criminology*, 32, pp.29–35.

Smith, G. and Cantley, C. (1984) 'Pluralistic evaluation', in Lishman, J. (ed.) *Evaluation*, Aberdeen, University of Aberdeen.

Taylor, I., Walton, P. and Young, J. (1973) *The New Criminology*, London, Routledge and Kegan Paul.

Weaver, C. and Bensted, J. (1992) 'Thinking for a change', *Probation Journal*, 39, pp.196–200.

Young, J. (1988) 'Radical criminology in Britain: the emergence of a competing paradigm', *British Journal of Criminology*, vol.28, pp.289–313.

Peter Raynor is Reader in Applied Social Studies at the University of Wales, Swansea. Maurice Vanstone has a split post between the University of Wales and the Mid-Glamorgan Probation Service.

(Source: Raynor and Vanstone, 1994, pp.387–99)

Chapter 4
Reading Qualitative Research

by Roger Sapsford

Contents

1 Introduction

*I*n this chapter we continue to explore methods of research used in criminology. The methods discussed in Chapter 3 were largely informed by *positivism* as a theoretical approach: research studies adopting such an approach aim to describe and eventually predict the behaviour of individuals and groups by similar means to those of the physical sciences, or even control it. The scientist (or researcher) is perceived as being 'outside' the area of study, able to do the research without affecting the nature of what is studied, and with a duty not to impose value judgements or preconceptions on the results. In this chapter we look at research methods which emanate from an interactionist or constructionist stance, in which the nature of social reality is not taken for granted but seen as actively *constructed* by its participants.

Researchers in this tradition are well aware of the dangers of *personal reactivity* – the inevitable changing of the situation brought about by the researcher's presence. If meanings are to any extent situation-specific and negotiated, then the presence of the researcher changes the situation and he or she becomes a party to the negotiation. We have also seen, in Chapter 2, that the actual process of research is often an intensely *political* act; issues of politics and power arise at every stage.

Beyond this, it is not even clear that what the social scientist wishes to examine is 'there', in the simple, unproblematic way that elements in chemistry may be taken to be 'there'. Rather, in forming hypotheses to test and explore, we *abstract from* the social world in ways which are not value-free but embody our cultural preconceptions, and which may unwittingly reinforce the very social structures which we wish to study, by writing power inequalities into 'scientific laws'. We are *in* the world that we wish to study, and *of* it, and so our research cannot be neutral (that is, value-free); it necessarily has some kind of political element to it, however remote.

One basic way of working in the physical sciences, which the positivistic stance brings over into social research, is *reductionism* – the attempt to isolate 'pure' elements whose 'laws' we can determine when the intricate and changing complexity of social life as a whole appears beyond our grasp. Thus the positivistic psychologist studies not people but personality traits or elements of the environment. The positivistic sociologist studies neither people nor cultures, but regularities of social life such as social class or rates of crime. There is an implicit belief that we can abstract features of the person and/or situation, study them in isolation and then add together the results to provide an explanation or at least a prediction of what is going on. (This was evident in the research studies we examined in the previous chapter.) Some, however, have rejected this attempt as futile, arguing that the whole can be studied only as a whole.

Further, reductionist research posits qualities of persons or situations which are in some sense constant – traits such as intelligence which are constant across situations, or aspects such as class which are constant across the social field and the life of the person. There is no necessary reason, however, why human social life should be conceptualized in this manner. The problem becomes yet more complex if we accept that we live in an essentially *symbolized* world. An important thing to grasp about the social world, both for research and for the participants themselves, is what things *mean* to people. A further complexity is that such meaning is not necessarily fixed but may vary from situation to situation, according to some form of local negotiation. This is broadly the position of *symbolic interactionism* and of *ethnographic* researchers – that the world has to be *read* as a series of negotiations about meaning. Broader constructionist positions would give more weight to the effects of history, and less to 'local' negotiation, but are still concerned mainly with how the world is seen and understood. Both are often described as 'appreciative' and 'interpretative': they seek to *make sense* of what is said and done. Both imply holistic research – the study of situations and locations as a whole.

The symbolic interactionist position and its holistic stance also makes naturalism an important target for the researcher. The experiment or the survey is a social situation: an unusual one, but one with rules which can be discovered or negotiated, which subjects/respondents will attempt to follow or to subvert. The behaviour of the subjects/respondents in the research situation will be essentially rule-determined. However, the rules according to which their behaviour is determined will not necessarily be those of their ordinary lives. Symbolic interactionists have sometimes argued that this *procedural reactivity* – the propensity of people to conform to what is required in a situation – is totally destructive of positivistic research, which has spent a hundred years discovering the rules of experiments and surveys but has come little closer to understanding the rules of the rest of life.

In this chapter we examine three ways in which research has been carried out from a qualitative perspective. In section 2 we look at observation and participation – that is, understanding a situation by being part of it. Section 3 is about asking questions and talking to people about how they understand their situations. Section 4 explores the critical analysis of texts and other verbal material for 'buried understandings': implicit models of the world taken for granted in the text. (A fourth style, the use of history to cast light on the present, is not discussed here but is covered elsewhere in this course – see **Book 1, Chapter 3; Book 2, Chapters 1 and 4.**)

As in Chapter 3, self-assessment and practice is provided by Activities in which you are invited to assess pieces of research. You are strongly advised to carry out these Activities at the point at which they occur in the text, *before* reading the comments which follow each Activity.

2   Seeing what goes on

A research method typical of the interactionist approach is *participant observation*, which involves the collection of information by participating in the social world that is under study. It places emphasis on:

- studying groups in their natural surroundings, with the minimum of disturbance;

- empathy and understanding;

- the direct observation of interactions and in particular on the meanings they have for participants; and

- descriptions in terms of the everyday understandings of actors in a situation.

Glossary of some useful terms in qualitative research

actor	one playing a part in a social setting which is being studied.
case	qualitative research usually involves studying one or a small number of cases in depth – people (prisoners, for example) or settings (prisons, for example) or locations within a setting (prison wings) or events (disciplinary adjudications, for example).
critical analysis	analysis of text or interviews or natural conversations to uncover underlying presuppositions – generally ideologies or discourses, but conceptual models of the social world, the person or the penal process are also valid targets. This is also called *critique*, a word not to be confused with *criticism*. 'Criticism', nowadays, means an attack on a text or else a discussion of its structure and effectiveness. 'Critique' means going beneath the surface of the text to explore what is taken for granted about the social and political world in its arguments and its forms of expression.
data	interview transcripts (or tapes or notes), field notes, books and documents – whatever is to be analysed in the research.
discourse	a term that has been used to mean everything from actual conversations to the conceptual framework through which the social world is classified and understood. In this chapter it is used in the latter sense to mean what Foucault calls 'regularities in symbolic practice' – shared, historically developed ways of categorizing and acting within and upon the social world (see also section 2 of Chapter 1).
field notes	records of what is observed – actions, what is said – and also the researcher's own impressions, feelings and tentative models.
'going native'	a term borrowed from cultural anthropology to signify the process of becoming assimilated to the situation under study, to the point where research ceases in favour of full participation.

In full participant observation, the researcher identifies an area worthy of study and enters the field without much preconception about what is to be found. The classic participant observer conceals his or her identity as researcher from the actors in the field, by *joining* or *passing*. In research into the social life of the factory, for example, researchers join the work-force as labourers or machinists (if they have the skills) and try to live the same life as the other employees for the duration of the research. They will take note of the social structures around them – who interacts with whom, and on what power basis – and of what is said and what is done. They may be able to ask questions to clarify the meaning of what is said or done, by posing as the new arrival – intelligent and amiable but uninformed, who needs things explained – but the scope for this is obviously limited by the need to maintain their cover. Little by little, the original vague feeling for what is interesting in the situation becomes focused into a more precise model of its important features (and perhaps some ideas about why it is as it is). This *focusing* is qualitative research's equivalent of statistical manipulation; it is its

holism	trying to understand a person or situation as a whole (as opposed to *reductionism*, breaking it down into component parts for analysis).
ideology	a term that has been used to mean everything from political conspiracies which misrepresent features of the situation as in the interests of the governed, to the conceptual frameworks through which the social world is classified and understood. In this chapter it tends to mean a reasonably coherent set of propositions which define a situation in the interests of the powerful but present it, probably falsely, as in the interests of the powerless – but without any necessary imputation of conspiracy or even conscious knowledge on the part of the powerful.
informant	one who is interviewed.
interview	collecting data by talking to people, in a relatively unstructured and conversational way.
marginality	remaining to a degree uninvolved in the situation, so that outside perspectives can be brought to bear on it.
naturalism	disturbing the natural situation as little as possible.
observation	one major form of qualitative analysis. Observation may be *covert* or *overt*, depending on whether the actors know that the research is taking place, and *participant* or *non-participant*, depending on whether the researcher takes a natural role in the situation.
reactivity	behaviour produced by the research, not the natural setting.
reflexivity	being aware of oneself as researcher, of the research process and of how each plays a part in shaping the data that are produced.
triangulation	obtaining information on the same topic by more than one method or from more than one source.

main form of data analysis. It continues side by side with, and as a part of, the data collection; fieldwork and analysis are not rigidly separate stages in this kind of research.

Since the 1960s, participant observation has been used to study, on the one hand, deviant sub-cultures: for example, Young's study of drug-users (Young, 1971), Patrick's observation of teenage gangs in Glasgow (Patrick, 1973) or Parker's work on car thieves and on heroin users (Parker, 1974; Parker *et al.*, 1988). On the other hand, it has also been used to get inside the workings of 'the system', as in Holdaway's *Inside the British Police* (Holdaway, 1984) or Punch's studies of the Amsterdam police (Punch, 1979) and of police corruption (Punch, 1985). Studies of prisons, which are a more difficult environment to penetrate, have been carried out mainly by existing members of staff (for example, Clemmer, 1940) or by people visiting prisons for a non-research reason (for example, Cohen and Taylor, 1972); or they have appeared in the autobiographies of prisoners (as, for example, in Boyle, 1977). Other researchers have gone in quite openly, making no attempt to conceal their role (such as Sykes, 1958). Some, like Irwin (see Irwin and Cressey, 1962; Irwin, 1980), have played both roles, being first a prisoner and later becoming a social scientist. The only true classic covert observation project I have encountered is that of Fleisher (1989), a social anthropologist who joined the prison under study by taking the qualificatory course and becoming a member of the custodial staff.

There are no formal rules for the conduct of qualitative research. However, as the model of the situation begins to emerge, the researcher will probably begin to test and extend it by sampling within and outside the immediate context, to sharpen it up and delineate its range of application (a process called *theoretical sampling*). Does the tentative model of, say, life in the psychiatric hospital hold up for all types of patients, or can it be modified to cover a greater range of patients? To what extent does it hold up for other kinds of participant, or for other types of institution? (In Goffman's *Asylums*, many of the institutional experiences of mental patients and their tactics for surviving were also shown to be shared by the staff of the institutions; see Goffman, 1961.) A later stage of theoretical sampling may seek to explore the precise boundaries of applicability in some detail by looking at people or situations selected to differ in some significant respect but otherwise to be as like each other as possible. The researcher might look at male and female patients who are otherwise similar, for example, or wards with different 'treatment philosophies' that cater for similar kinds of patient and have similar kinds of staff. Finally, the researcher might search systematically for cases that do not appear to fit the model, to see how it might be elaborated to make sense of them.

The interpretative researcher has two main strategies for establishing the validity of his or her conclusions. The first is *triangulation*, which brings more than one source to bear on the model to see if different sources complement or contradict each other. There might be more than one participant observer, working independently; or what is observed might be compared with documentary sources (diaries, letters, files); or the researcher might at some stage 'break cover' and become visible as a researcher, to be free to interview participants more formally and systematically.

The second, and more important, check on validity is the process of *reflexivity*. Interpretative researchers have to remain as aware as possible of their own impact on the situation and of its impact on them. They must document the social roles to which they appear to have been assigned and how these change over the course of the research – how the other participants in the situation make sense of the researchers (and, if it is not concealed, of the fact of being researched). Researchers must also document the changes their actions have brought about in the people in whose lives they have been participating. They must identify the aspects of the situation which participants take for granted and yet remain sufficiently alien to the situation to know when a 'taken-for-granted' is in need of explanation. (For this reason it is generally reckoned to be very difficult to research your own locality or workplace, because you already have a location within the field and share the preconceptions of other participants.) Finally, the researcher has to be as aware as possible of his or her own preconceptions – pre-formed ideas, theoretical and political positions, likes and dislikes – and must take them into account when analysing the data. Much of this should appear in the final written report, so that the reader can make his or her own judgement of validity.

Participant observation is very costly in researcher time and puts a great strain on the researcher. Few projects manage all the stages I have described; most stop short with a competent description and a tentative model of what is going on. Further, it is often not possible to 'pass' or 'join', and the researcher cannot or does not want to conceal the fact that research is going on. In this case his or her role is that of 'social researcher' and the situation changes to accommodate such a role. The researcher still tries to 'go round with' the people he or she is observing and to share their experience as far as possible, but the interchange is necessarily a trifle forced.

It is an idealization of the situation to pretend that researchers go into the field without any preconception or pre-theorization. As Maurice Punch rightly points out at the beginning of his observational study of police corruption:

> Underlying my selection of data and my interpretation of material for this study is a theoretical perspective that also colours my view of control, deviance and organisational reality. Working within the symbolic interactionist paradigm my approach particularly builds upon and extends those who adopt an interactionist perspective on the police. People working within this paradigm emphasise the extent to which social life is fragile, negotiated and in a constant process of construction in interaction with others.

> (Punch, 1985, pp.1–2)

Such theoretical perspectives do not provide clearly articulated hypotheses for testing, but they are the guiding concepts within which the work is conducted – the framework within which the researcher makes sense – and they point the observer to some aspects of the situation rather than others. Reflexivity is needed on the part of the researcher to bring the perspectives to awareness and to so shape the research that they do not close off avenues of enquiry or analysis.

A final point is that this style of research is also undertaken by people who would *not* share the stance of the symbolic interactionists or ethnographers. Very competent and compelling qualitative observation research has been carried out by people whose first aim is *not* to express participants' own understandings of their situations, but to locate their actions and experiences within a pre-theorized framework – for example, within a critical or feminist criminological framework (Appendix 4.1, an extract from Jefferson, 1990, is an example of this). What all these stances share, however, is that:

- they reject reductionism, at least at the level of data collection, in favour of a holistic approach;

- they insist on a naturalistic situation to avoid procedural reactivity; and

- they see the meaning of situations as a key datum in the understanding of people's lives.

2.1 Example 1: Mind games

Three researchers carried out fieldwork in five male prisons: a local prison, an open prison, a Category C training prison, a Category B training prison and a Category B dispersal prison. They carried out approximately 300 days of observation in total; they encouraged prisoners and staff to talk about how they experienced and dealt with prison life, and were present at everything:

from cell searches to slopping out, from reception to discharge, from adjudications to lifer review boards, from management meetings to wing applications. We were there at weekends, at high days and holidays as well as week days. Much of the time we just 'hung out' – with staff in the security office, in the detail, the mess or the wing office; with prisoners during association periods, by the canteen, or the cooker, or the kitchens, in the workshops and, for one of us [the male researcher], in their cells. On occasion we worked out with staff in the gym or played table tennis, darts and dominoes with prisoners; and we watched TV with both.

(McDermott and King, 1988, p.357–8)

Their role was as overt researchers – there was no way they could pass for either staff or prisoners, nor would they have wanted to do so – but they were there for long enough to become part of the conceptual and social furniture of the prison:

it would be foolish to assume that we saw the prison system as it really is. Of course, staff tempered their language (a bit), their demeanour and their behaviour to the presence of research workers. Of course, prisoners came to us because they hoped for some advantage, or because of the rare opportunity to talk to a sympathetic outsider ... It took time to build up relationships and confidence, but in the end we got to know prisoners from all categories of security and at all stages of sentence ... As the research progressed, while we were still obviously neither staff nor prisoners, it became more and more assumed that we were persons before whom the 'normal roles' could be acted out. Never quite completely, perhaps, ... But fully enough, often enough and long enough for us to be able to record reasonably authentically something of what life is actually like in prison.

(McDermott and King, 1988, p.358)

The researchers report that on the landings – 'where the action is' in a sense which is not true of labour, education, the gym or visits – much of the action takes the form of 'games', a substantial part of which takes place within the mind. They distinguish among a variety of such games, all of which are ways of surviving the experience of imprisonment and the conditions of prison life. They point out, however, that prison is a part of society, not something cut off from society, and that what goes on in prison is, in some sense, *willed* to go on in this way:

[Prison is] an extension of ... society and deeply embedded in its power structure. Who goes to prison, for how long, and how they are treated while they are there, reflects a particular balance of power. By the same token what staff and prisoners actually experience in prison, plainly, is not a game. Many of the incidents we witnessed were despairing or desperate attempts by people, who felt dehumanised and powerless, to maintain some conception of themselves as active, controlling agents in some small sphere of their lives.

(McDermott and King, 1988, p.375)

ACTIVITY 4.1

From the description given above, write a brief assessment of this project and the likelihood of its producing logically convincing evidence.

You should not spend more than about 20 minutes on this Activity.

The 'mind games' project was not strictly *participant* observation, of course, in that the researchers did not take on an existing role in the field but went in as researchers, importing a role from outside. However, they probably spent long enough in the field for them to become an accepted part of it, so that staff and prisoners would have regarded them as *their* researchers. There are difficulties in establishing and maintaining rapport and trust with the participants, particularly where there are two groups of people – prisoners and prison officers – who live either in conflict or at least in mutual distrust. However, the research appears to have been well conducted and to have overcome these problems, to a large extent. The availability of data was undoubtedly determined in part by the sense which prisoners and staff made of the researchers and the fact of research, but the researchers demonstrate that they are well aware of such problems.

We should note that observation does not produce 'facts', but *interpreted meanings*. The 'mind games' are not, strictly, what the researchers *observed*, but *the sense they made* of what they observed, their *account* of what they observed. Whether we are to take the conclusions at face value must be a question of trust to a large extent, as we are unable to go back and look at the data as they were being collected. (This is also often true of quantitative research, but the presentation of data as numbers conceals the fact.)

Generally, observational research is inevitably micro-research; that is, it focuses on interactions within small groups and in local contexts. As the researchers in this example themselves suggest, such studies need to be located in a wider context and should seek explanation of the interactional patterns and subjective processes, to some extent at least, in terms of wider social structural factors. Interactionist researchers and theorists have to remember that the broad structures of the social world are neither created by negotiations between immediately present participants nor, often, to much extent open to change by them.

2.2 Example 2: Policing disturbances

The second example in this section is a short extract from Tony Jefferson's book *The Case Against Paramilitary Policing* (1990) which describes a very small part of the evidence he adduces in the book. The topic area is the policing of riots and public disturbances (Jefferson's work is also cited in **Book 2, Chapter 2**.) The data come from a project carried out by Jefferson and Grimshaw into the organization and control of policework 'using a broadly ethnographic approach, inside a big, largely urban police force' (Jefferson, 1990, p.xiii). No further details of the research methods are given in this book. (The interested reader may find them in Grimshaw and Jefferson, 1987, and Jefferson, 1988.)

ACTIVITY 4.2

Read Appendix 4.1, an extract from *The Case Against Paramilitary Policing* by Tony Jefferson. Compare and contrast this research with the study by McDermott and King (1988) in Example 1. What strengths do they have in common, how do they differ, and how well is the argument put forward for trusting the evidence provided?

This Activity should take about 2 hours.

This piece of research is a curious mix between overt and covert participant observation. Jefferson was openly present as a researcher and standing with the police supervisors. His presence will not have been obvious to the officers carrying out the arrest; he was not participating in the street policing as such, but simply observing it. His privileged status as researcher gave him access to police accounts, however, which he could not otherwise have reached.

This account has enormous immediacy. It is told by someone who was actually there, some of it in words written down at the time, while the incident was still fresh in the mind. Jefferson's presence as observer enables us to see aspects of the situation that could not have emerged from the police accounts, almost as if we were watching a video of the incident – the man being picked up by his scarf, for instance. At the same time, Jefferson is able to supply what a video could not – what the situation *meant* to the police officers. It is this aspect that distinguishes *participant* observation from plain *observation*.

The more overt and potentially obtrusive prison research, however, was able to do what open research can do best – to 'move around the field'. In McDermott and King's paper we get accounts both from prison officers and from prisoners, along with the researchers' own observations. In Jefferson's work, we get his observation of the incident, in the form of field notes, plus his transcript of the police account, but nothing from the arrested fan.

Whether the material is sound as evidence, can be trusted and therefore could form a convincing basis for conclusions is more difficult to decide. A strong point of McDermott and King's paper was its careful and empathic reflexivity – its concern to explain how the data were collected, to consider the strengths and pitfalls and the extent to which the researchers' interpretation is sound or open to question. (Some examples of this are evident even in the brief extracts presented above.) There is none of this in Jefferson's book, which makes it difficult for us to form a judgement. Jefferson is a respected researcher with a history of good research, and thus we are inclined to take what he reports at face value. It would be easier to do so, however, if he showed more awareness, in the extract reproduced as Appendix 4.1, of research as an attempt to construct meaning rather than just a reportage of facts. (The sentence in the extract about different ways of seeing incidents is unconvincing. Jefferson clearly regards his own notes as a more accurate description of what went on than the police account – otherwise there would be no merit in his quoting them.) I suspect that a hostile reader might not be convinced of the quality of the evidence.

3 Asking questions

The other method much influenced by the same kind of thinking is the 'open' or 'ethnographic' *interview*. A common way of coming to understand a situation is to go and talk to the people who are in it, not with a formal pre-set questionnaire but in a fairly non-directive way, allowing the participants to describe their experiences and feelings at their own pace and in their own words. In this way the chance of learning something *new* about the situation is maximized, something that would not have been anticipated, rather than simply the answers to preconceived questions generated by the researcher from his or her own knowledge of the situation.

In a quite different spirit from the survey interviewer, the ethnographic interviewer tries to build a relationship of naturalism and trust with the informant, despite the fact that the underlying relationship is a research one; to a large extent, the aim is to let the informant determine the pace and range of the conversation. The situation is not as unnatural as it might seem. People quite like 'telling their story', and a good interviewer can get the informant talking in an unforced way and coming up with surprisingly personal and even discreditable information, with minimal prompting. There is, of course, both personal and procedural reactivity, in that the informant forms a picture of what the task is about and what the interviewer is interested in hearing, and speaks in accordance with that picture. In ordinary life, we all shape our conversations to suit our interlocutors: the topics we discuss with parents of our children's school friends are different from those raised when we talk to colleagues at work. The same occurs in research interviews. However, if the interviewer is reflexively aware of this, he or she can allow for it when interpreting the data. It may even be possible to steer the conversation outside its self-imposed bounds during the interview itself.

The clearest example of such interviewing is the *life-history interview*, where an informant is selected and interviewed repeatedly and at length, often over a period of months, until he or she has 'told the story' in sufficient detail that the researcher is sure he or she can make coherent and complete sense of it. A classic example of such work is Tony Parker's biography of 'the unknown citizen', a petty persistent criminal (Parker, 1966). Other useful and more recent examples include Raphael Samuel's extensive interviewing of Arthur Harding, who was the last man alive to have been brought up in the 'Jago', the most infamous criminal area of late Victorian London (Samuel, 1981); Pat Carlen's *Criminal Women* (Carlen, 1985), which is a series of interview accounts of the lives of women who have been in trouble with the law; and her book *Women, Crime and Poverty*, which is based around interviews with 39 women, concentrating on their law breaking and the official response to it (Carlen, 1988).

The same kind of collaboration with the informants and the same style and approach are also typical of studies which aim to cover more people in less detail and to explore a particular topic. Often, contrasting groups of people are chosen, to illuminate some key difference. While still trying to leave the apparent direction of the conversation broadly in the hands of the informant, the researcher will have a topic in mind and perhaps even a series of areas of enquiry which will have to be covered by all informants if the comparative aspect of the research is to work.

The logic of comparison and the logic of representation, which we explored in Chapter 3, are also important here. The person giving a life-history must be typical of something, or interestingly extreme in some special way, and the selection must be justified in the research report. We do not read life-histories to find out about people's personal histories, but to find out about the group or setting or historical position which they hold and represent. In wider projects, involving interviews with 10 or 20 people, or more, there will still not be enough 'cases' to permit a full and representative random sample, but the researcher still goes to some pains to obtain informants who are in some way typical or 'cover the field'. The researcher tries to sample across a range of possible positions in the field; within such 'strata' one often samples randomly where a sampling frame is available and where it is not too unnatural a social situation to select one informant and not others from within the same social location.

An interview is necessarily not as natural a situation as full participation – though ethnographic interviewing is nearer to a natural situation than standardized survey work – and the researcher is a very conspicuous and active part of the research situation. Interviewing is therefore at risk of greater personal and procedural reactivity than participant observation. Of the two varieties of study, the life-history interview is probably less reactive, in that people like talking about themselves and telling their story and they can understand it as a task, whereas they often have to cast around for a plausible explanation of what is going on in the shorter and more directive interview.

At the stage of reporting, as with participant observation, the researcher's conclusions have to be taken at least in part on trust: it is not usual to reproduce the entire text of all the interviews (with an hour's interview typically running to up to 20 pages of transcript!), nor would it be useful for the reader if we did so. A report consists of what people said, the researcher's attempt to reconstruct how *they* make sense of it overall, and the researcher's own (theory-guided) account of it (which may not be the same thing at all). At each level of this process, the account travels further and further from what the informant said and becomes more and more the researcher's. As crucial to this kind of research as to participant observation, therefore, is a 'reflexive account', giving us some idea of the data-collection phase and of the researcher who is conducting it. We need to form our own judgement of the extent to which the way the data were collected or the beliefs of the person collecting it may have coloured the accounts.

The weaknesses of open interviewing, then, are the risk of reactivity and the extent to which the researcher is the medium through which the data are read, already interpreted. The strength of the method is that people really *can* express their views and talk about their feelings and experiences in a way that makes sense to *them*, not just to the interviewer. Open interviewing is less holistic as a method than participant observation in that it is confined to words, and those are produced in a formal interview situation. It is *more* holistic, however, in that it allows us to roam across the whole life of the informant (as it is understood and remembered at present time and in the present situation) and to go beyond the immediate situation into areas where the observer could not follow – domestic privacy, for example – and into hypothetical consideration of what people might do or might have done had things been otherwise.

3.1 Example 3: Prison Boards of Visitors

For the first example in this section, we shall look at a short paper reporting on an interview study carried out in one prison on prisoners' awareness of the role and duties of Boards of Visitors and the extent to which they were seen as effective.

ACTIVITY 4.3

Read Appendix 4.2, 'Prisoners' views of Boards of Visitors: a question of credibility', by Carol Martin and David Godfrey. Outline the main conclusions and the methods used to collect evidence to bear on them, and assess the extent to which the evidence is sufficient to sustain the conclusions.

You should spend about 1 hour on this Activity.

The main conclusions of Martin and Godfrey's paper are that prisoners regard Boards of Visitors as 'invisible, irrelevant, aligned with prison management, and ineffective'; in other words, they have little or no confidence in them either as watchdogs over prison management or as a channel for prisoners' grievances. The source of evidence for these propositions is a series of semi-structured interviews carried out with 140 male inmates in one Category C prison. Seven of the sample appear not even to have heard of the Boards, but these were all men serving their first custodial sentence, and two of them were foreign nationals with poor English. A few thought that the Boards had been abolished altogether at the time when their role in disciplinary proceedings was removed, and a few confused Boards with prison visitors. Most of the information about the Boards appeared to be picked up by word of mouth from staff or, more often, from other prisoners, and it was not always factually accurate. Only 55 per cent of the sample correctly listed the functions of Boards, and 30 per cent wrongly attributed a continuing disciplinary function to them. Among those who did identify the 'watchdog' and 'grievance' functions of the Boards, a fair amount of cynicism was expressed about their effectiveness and/or their independence of the governor. Only a quarter of the sample reported ever having personal dealings with a Board member, and only two men thought the Board's intervention had solved their problems.

The method of research was the interview, which started with three fixed questions but then developed into a more general conversation. We are not told much about the interviews – how long they lasted, to what extent prisoners relaxed and talked normally, and above all what they saw as the purpose of the research and the role and status of the interviewer. From the number of interviews conducted, however, we may presume they were generally brief. We would therefore probably be best advised to treat this as a relatively unstructured attitude survey, rather than as a typical 'qualitative' interviewing project. It lacks some of the strengths of more extended qualitative work; because the report lacks reflexivity, we cannot tell the extent to which the informants expressed 'what they would say *to themselves*' – that is, if they responded naturally – rather than what they would say to an outsider with, they might presume, some kind of official standing. The quality of the responses, as illustrated by the copious quotations, suggests that a relaxed and informative relationship was developed in a significant proportion of cases. Overall, we have no reason to doubt the authenticity of the responses, but the report does not give us strong grounds for asserting that the evidence is valid.

The methods used in the study straddle both qualitative and survey approaches, in that the sample of informants is quite large for qualitative work. The sampling is not random (being collected by a mixture of 'happenstance' and 'snowball' recommendations) and is taken in a single prison (and no prison is particularly typical of any other). We may therefore legitimately question the extent to which the results generalize beyond the immediate circumstances of the research. On the other hand, as the authors say, 'we see no reason to suppose that a representative sample would have expressed substantially different views', and the sheer size of the sample overcomes many of the problems associated with more detailed qualitative studies. It might be unwise to generalize from the proportion holding a particular belief in the sample to the probable proportion in the population, and it might turn out that Boards were better or worse known, liked or trusted in another kind of prison. However, the study does establish beyond reasonable doubt that the change of function of Boards of Visitors has done little to enhance their image with prisoners in at least one prison.

3.2   Example 4: Gay police

ACTIVITY 4.4

Read Appendix 4.3, 'Homosexuality as deviance: the case of the gay police officer', by Marc Burke. Outline and assess the methods and conclusions. Compare this paper with Appendix 4.2, by Martin and Godfrey (which you read for Activity 4.3), in terms of the effects of the subject matter and the style of interviewing on the data produced.

This Activity should take about 2 hours.

Burke interviewed 36 serving or retired police officers whose sexual orientation was not conventionally heterosexual. (This information is in the abstract of the paper; there is nothing whatsoever on methods in the body of the paper.) He looks at the 'macho' police culture, its significance for women and particularly lesbian officers, the ambivalent position of homosexuality in the law, the consequent ambivalence of the police towards it (similar to but more complicated than the ambivalence of the 'general public'), and the kinds of double lives that gay and bisexual police officers have to lead to reconcile their private lives and self-image with the needs of the job and police sub-cultural values. His conclusion is that gay officers are often able neither to commit themselves entirely to the job nor to form satisfying personal relationships outside it.

A great weakness in the paper is that it is almost totally unreflexive and tells us nothing about the nature of the interviews, how introductions were effected, how the interviewer presented himself and what kinds of relationships were made. (For the interested reader, Burke has written this up elsewhere: see Burke, 1993a, 1993b.) It is also a short paper, which means that if the author wishes to give reasonable space to the 'literature' of past cognate research, then there cannot be much in the way of quoted data offered as evidence. This is always the way with qualitative interview research: the reports offer data as illustration rather than, strictly, as evidence, because what is put forward is always a small selection of everything that could be said, selected by the author to make a point. This is particularly the case in this report. The consequence, for judging the results, is that we are very dependent on our trust in Burke as a competent, sensitive and honest researcher – the more so because he does not tell us much about the circumstances of the interviews in this report.

We can nonetheless use our imaginations to make some comparison with Martin and Godfrey's paper (Appendix 4.2) by thinking about the subject matter and its consequences for the interview situation. Any kind of 'attitude survey' approach would clearly be of little value here. The subject matter is 'delicate': possibly embarrassing for the informants, and possibly harmful to them, if the fact of being interviewed labelled them as homosexual among their working colleagues. To obtain the kind of data which Burke presents, it will have been necessary to form a more personal and 'confiding' relationship with informants than was necessary for the Martin and Godfrey paper. The interviews will have had to be personal conversations of the kind which one might have with a counsellor, a close friend or (in this case) another gay person. Any suggestion of sensation-seeking or prying would have distorted the interviews to the point where the data were worthless; or, indeed, it would have made it impossible to interview at all. In comparison with the Martin and Godfrey paper, we are therefore more sharply aware of the *constructed* nature of research data. Burke does not report what people think or feel in a straightforward way, but rather uses his ability to form relationships with the informants to get them to 'tell their story' – stories which will be partly dependent on the circumstances in which they are told. From these stories, Burke then extracts his own story of what, in general, it is like to be a gay officer. The data are thus doubly constructed, and we are very aware of this fact.

Nonetheless, we do have to take a fair amount on trust in this paper. I find myself the more inclined to do so because the conclusions are what I would have expected from anything I know about the British police – or, putting it another way, because the paper tells us nothing new (see **Book 2, Chapter 2**). If the conclusions had been surprising – if it had turned out that homosexuality was a positive advantage in policework, or there was no form of perceived discrimination, or being in the police had no effect on the private lives of gay people – then we might have required better evidence before being prepared to accept the conclusions. As a result, like most people, I tend to feel that surprising results need justification, while the obvious and well known 'stands to reason'.

3.3   Example 5: Small business crime

ACTIVITY 4.5

Read Appendix 4.4, 'From fiddle factors to networks of collusion: charting the waters of small business crime', by Hugh Barlow. Make brief notes on the overall argument of the paper, but concentrate mainly on summarizing and assessing the value of evidence of the case study that is presented.

This Activity should take about 2 hours.

Barlow asserts the importance to criminology of the study of small business crime – 'white-collar' crime carried out not by large corporations nor by employees, but by small traders and manufacturers. He locates such crime as part of a 'hidden' or 'shadow' economy, which amounts to a large-scale, loosely knit criminal conspiracy among people usually seen as honest and as 'the backbone of the community'. In doing so, he extends the point that lies at the centre of labelling theory (see **Reader Guide 1, section 5.1**): that the boundary between legitimate and illegitimate activities is not a clear one and that much (most?) normal activity can readily straddle it. He also points out the continuity between politics, business and white-collar crime. A fair amount of evidence from the research literature is cited in support of his arguments. (See also **Book 1, Chapter 6.**)

The main case study is based on interviews and conversations with a small businessman who describes himself as having participated in a criminal network of this sort for five years. The problem of such evidence, as Barlow points out, is the extent to which one can place confidence in it – what Barlow calls 'the issue of trust'. Narrating one's life is necessarily 'telling a story', and the story is not the same thing as the reality that it describes and reconstructs. If the informant is entirely honest, he nonetheless has the task of making sense of his own life in a reasonably concise and coherent way – and of doing so in particular circumstances, for particular reasons, to a particular researcher whose interests are perceived in a particular way. Thus the confusion and flow of ordinary events will be constructed into a pattern with the benefit of hindsight and the help of the researcher's comments and encouragement. Barlow discusses the motivation of his informant at some length. He does *not* tell us how he met the informant, how the research was set up, what was said about it, how and where the interviews were conducted and how the relationship progressed over repeated meetings – all very useful information for the reader when a judgement of validity is to be made. From the discussion that *is* there, however, we can see that Barlow has carried out the research reflexively and that he has a strong awareness of questions of reactivity.

The story begins with the informant joining the network, partly through 'fiddles' inherited with existing contracts when he took over the firm, and partly as a result of discovering that contracts were not to be had without the payment of bribes. He quite quickly graduates from being a fringe operator to a 'fully paid-up' member of the network, benefiting from the opportunity to 'kick back' for favourable contracts, making commission on the illegal activity of others and even going into the money-lending business. Finally, the informant describes the collapse of the network and his own role as an informer. The research findings are quite correctly described as 'illustrative' rather than as establishing firm knowledge about criminal networks. There is no specific implication that any other network would function in quite the same way, and the author does not draw out general principles from the case study. Nonetheless the material gives us a feeling of insight into how such networks *can* function. Further research, as the author notes, is needed to construct a general model of small-business crime: interviews with other people or the active participation of a researcher in a network (though this would be a risky, expensive and potentially illegal kind of research!). We should need to explore the question of generalizability: whether what is said in this paper 'rings true' for other regions, in other kinds of business. In the process, the analysis of many such accounts would make it possible to look for those factors which are general to criminal networks, to distinguish them from factors specific to particular instances of networks, and thereby to form a better idea of what makes such networks possible and how they function at each stage of their existence.

4   Looking at the sub-text

We looked in Chapter 3 at quantitative analysis, which *can* be applied to the analysis of text, and in this chapter so far we have looked at qualitative or interpretative analysis, where what is interpreted is *generally* text, whether field notes, interview transcripts or letters, diaries and other documents. In this final substantive section of the chapter we look at a third approach, which is also relevant for the analysis of interview data but is at its most distinctive and obvious when it has been applied to the critique of government and other documents. This is often called 'critical analysis'.

Quantitative analysis places data in categories constructed by the researcher (and generally constructed before the data collection starts). Interpretative analysis looks at the content of interviews to give a voice to those who have been interviewed and then to see what patterns can be made by the researcher. Critical analysis applies the researcher's perspective to the informant's words and is concerned not so much with the content itself as with what the content *betrays*. It takes what is said in the document or interview as symptomatic of underlying models of the person and the world, and it looks for forms of expression which betray the writer's conscious or, more often, taken-for-granted political, theoretical and ideological stances. The critical analyst may be looking for positivist or classicist ideas buried in what is said, for example; or the adoption of or resistance to a Marxist or feminist stance may be detected. The analysis may uncover specific ideological clusters of ideas assumed and half-expressed in passages which appear to have the exact opposite meaning – and sometimes these would be acknowledged as inappropriate even by the authors of the document. There may be elements of several different ideologies or discourses in the same text, as few of us are totally consistent in our theoretical positions and our reasoning is often influenced by the 'sediment' of several positions held in the past. The search is for what is taken for granted in the text – what is at its most persuasive precisely because it is never explicitly argued but is just assumed as true by writers and, often, readers alike (see Chapter 1).

4.1 Example 6: Women in prison

Because this kind of research is best understood from an example, let us look, by way of illustration, at a passage from Carlen (1990) on women in prison.

ACTIVITY 4.6

Read Appendix 4.5, an extract from *Alternatives to Women's Imprisonment* by Pat Carlen. Make notes on what *kind* of analysis she is using on the text and what kind of results she can obtain using it.

You should not spend more than 1 hour on this Activity.

What Carlen is doing in this passage is two-fold. First, she comments explicitly on a text which has policy implications, to uncover the assumptions which its authors are taking for granted which have theoretical/political impact on the message. In this case, a model of prisons derived from experience of *men's* prisons – what she terms a 'masculinist' model – is identified in the text and in the broad 'field of ideas' out of which the text is written, and is subjected to some critique from a feminist standpoint. A second and less obvious device, however, is the *selection* of passages from the text to discuss. By bringing together passages from different paragraphs of the Report, Carlen is able to show not only how the common discourse of womanhood (different from men, weak, dependent, naturally caring, needing relationships) is assumed more or less uncritically by the authors of the Report, but also how this conflicts with some of the analysis and renders the conclusions contradictory and the recommendations possibly unworkable.

Reflexivity is as important in this kind of work as in the kinds of qualitative research discussed above. We have to take the author's selection on trust as fair, and this means we need to know the perspective from which the author is operating – though, indeed, this will *necessarily* be explicit in the discussion – and even then we have to take a great deal on trust. (The difference, in this and many other cases of this kind of research writing, is that the analysis is carried out on a text which is public and available, so we could check back if we wanted to do so and see whether we ourselves would have made a different selection and/or come to different conclusions.)

If this were a 'stand-alone' report, rather than a short extract from a longer work, it would also be relevant to raise the question of generalizability, as with any kind of 'case study' research. This is an analysis of a single document, and it is relevant to ask how typical it is of others that might have been analysed; in other words, how widespread among those who are responsible for penological policy are the discourse and the confusions which Carlen uncovers? Carlen suggests that they are indeed widespread – that this document is a particularly clear case of them and is by no means untypical – but we should have to take this, again, on trust. Alternatively, however, we can see this kind of research as demonstrating the utility of an analytical tool. Having demonstrated that the perspective that she adopts makes a useful contribution to our understanding of this particular document, Carlen is implicitly inviting us to try it out for ourselves, on other documents with which we might come into contact. Critical analysis establishes perspectives which will be judged by how useful we find them when we try to use them ourselves.

Although this kind of analysis has been combined with 'qualitative' interviewing and observation in this chapter because some of the same questions have to be asked about all of them, the Carlen extract is different from other research we have examined so far. However, it represents an equally valid way of extending our understanding. It is not 'research' in the sense that it collects and presents new data to illuminate a problem or evaluate a treatment (any more than the analysis of quantitative secondary sources such as *Criminal Statistics* involves collecting new data). Rather, it is a critique of a published document, examining the discourse which informs it and the ideological presuppositions which it embodies. In some ways it resembles some of the historical analysis in Books 1 and 2 of the course, and certainly it is underpinned by a similarly critical theoretical stance. Unlike straightforward uses of history, however, it takes a particular text as its focus. Carlen looks to see what is taken for granted as 'natural' or 'normal' by the authors, what values the report expresses and the policy consequences towards which it leans. In so doing, she lays bare the 'agenda' of the writers and the implicit weaknesses of their perspective and provides space within which the Report can be challenged.

4.2   Example 7: Police restructuring

The Carlen paper uses critical analysis to unpack the presuppositions and ideological basis of a single document; that is the clearest use of the method. Other work might also be classified under the same type, however, which ranges more widely and covers critical issues in a rather different way. The two examples around which the final Activities of this chapter are based exemplify different uses of critical analysis. The first is a short 'discussion note' on police reform by McLaughlin and Murji (1993) (made shorter still by the omission of a section on the then forthcoming Sheehy Report).

ACTIVITY 4.7

Read Appendix 4.6, 'Controlling the Bill: restructuring the police in the 1990s', by Eugene McLaughlin and Karim Murji. Make brief notes on the use of critical analysis to organize ideas and quoted material into illuminative 'themes'.

This Activity should not take more than 20 minutes.

Though basically a 'discussion paper' rather than the analysis of a particular document, this paper still exemplifies critical analysis. McLaughlin and Murji identify a problem in the acceptance by the police of a politically inspired managerial and cost-sensitive view of their own work, which is one factor in their loss of public confidence since the 1980s. The authors analyse what they see as police attitudes to their own malpractices, under the guise of forecasting their response to a then forthcoming Royal Commission. Three possible responses are identified:

1   First, the police may 'spread the blame', assigning any shortcomings to which they might admit to the general inadequacy of the system as a whole. This response is illustrated from statements made during 1992 by two senior police officers and the chief inspector of police.

2   The second response is to ask for 'understanding' – to suggest the public should sympathize with the police, who are doing a difficult and sensitive job under very difficult circumstances. This is exemplified mainly in the words of the Chief Inspector of Police, Sir John Woodcock.

3   The third response, which arises out of the other two, is to suggest that any malpractice is due to actions taken by people of good will in a system and a culture which all too easily allows and even encourages malpractice. The proposed solution is a code of ethics, and again this is illustrated by the words of Sir John Woodcock.

The paper exemplifies critical analysis in that it explicitly puts forward the arguments of its authors through an analysis of what people are saying and doing. What the authors do is to construct an analysis of how the police *might* respond to criticism and to illustrate it from what some senior police officers *have* said on some occasion. To a degree there is an empirical claim in the paper – that this is how the police do feel about questions of malpractice – and to this extent one may query the accuracy and generalizability of the claims made: How many (senior) police officers do or would say these things? And to what extent are they a true reflection of their attitudes rather than a public rhetoric? At another level, however, the empirical claims are not the core of the analysis. McLaughlin and Murji put forward a view of policing and the police which they have found useful and illuminating, and they invite us to try it out.

4.3   Example 8: Problem pages and public crime

ACTIVITY 4.8

Read Appendix 4.7, 'Personal power and public control: sex crimes and problem pages', by Moira Peelo and Keith Soothill. Outline the main argument of the paper and assess the evidence which is offered in its support.

This Activity should take about 2 hours.

The focus of this paper is the way in which the 'problem pages' of magazines (and their equivalent on radio and television) contribute to the transformation of a personal problem into a social one and determine or declare 'society's' moral stance on problematic issues. As the authors say, 'By examining problem pages, we learn more about how society defines the borderlines between private problems and public, criminal matters'. Problem pages tread a particularly interesting borderline in that, according to their function, they must deal with the personal in personal terms and at the same time be of interest to the general reader. The data for the study are drawn from a year's editions of the *Sun, Daily Mirror, People, Sunday Mirror* and *News of the World*.

The paper deals with the two 'crimes' of rape of males and sex involving persons under the legal age of consent. (The former is not a crime as such, though it could be dealt with under such charges as 'assault', and the latter is a legal offence but one which is not universally recognized as a moral offence, in the sense that the age of consent varies from society to society and from one historical period to another.) The paper explores the moral stance taken by the advisers who write the answers, the influences on them of, for example, feminist discourse and the boundaries they draw between crimes, misdemeanours, transgressions, mistakes and understandable or justifiable actions. The discussion also looks at the (slight) role of the law and the police in the advice given. The problem of giving advice on action to individuals who are often dependent and structurally 'trapped', and so not in a position to initiate action, is also explored, as is the emphasis on *personal* control at the expense of sometimes 'dodging' issues of *public* control. The main conclusion is that the problem pages help us understand how society defines the acceptable at the borderlines of sexual crime, but that the message from them is not always clear. The authors indicate that the matter they are studying shows some lack of structural analysis of the underlying problems, but they do not 'write it off' simply as unthinking reflection of popular clichés; rather, they present it as a serious attempt to wrestle with problems which society itself continues to find problematic.

This paper is not a 'critical analysis' in quite the same sense as the two preceding examples; it does not take a pre-theorized perspective and explicitly use it to analyse a conceptual area. Rather, it takes the broad clash of perspectives that characterize criminology and tries to illuminate them by reference to a particular subject matter. Thus we have, before all, the contrast between the structural and the personal which is a key preoccupation of criminological thinking. Beyond this, we have the range of conceptual categories from 'immoral' to 'understandable' and their overlap with 'legal' and 'illegal' (and the rather more difficult contrast of 'legitimate' and 'illegitimate'). What the paper sets out to establish, and to my mind succeeds in establishing, is that there is no simple way of mapping these categories on to the particular problems of specific individuals.

As research, the paper escapes some of the criticisms and caveats often levelled at critical analysis. For example, it is based on a properly drawn and quite substantial sample of problem pages and therefore escapes the usual criticism that conclusions are based on small numbers of cases. (It pays for this the typical price of 'large sample' qualitative research: that it is very inexplicit about methods of analysis and so leaves a great deal to be taken on trust by the reader.) However, the problem with this kind of analysis is the question of how typical even a large sample of newspaper articles (and a particular kind of article, at that) can ever be as a representation of 'the views of society'. (This was the problem faced also by John Clarke in analysing the discursive content of detective stories in **Book 1, Chapter 2**. To what extent do they *reflect* the thinking of an age? To what extent are they intended to *create* it?) When analysing text – and this point holds for the analysis of single government documents as much as for the more broadly based analysis of newspapers or fiction or indeed interview transcripts – the production of the text as an action in response to the demands of a particular situation must always be borne in mind. We seldom simply reflect our milieu in *anything* which we produce; rather, we work with it and around it, we act on it and within it, and sometimes we change it.

So one way of thinking about critical analysis is to see it as laying bare the presuppositions, models, discourses and ideologies, for example, which inform the thinking (and presumably the actions) of the writers or speakers. Another useful perspective is to see it as being about the role of knowledge as power: 'the relationship between those who claim to know "the truth" and those about whom they claim to know it' (Worrall, 1990, p.6):

> The relationship between power and knowledge is vital to such analyses. Worrall's viewpoint is that knowledge does not of itself give power. Rather, those who have power have the authority to know ... the exercise of power is not the naked oppression of one group by another but the production and subtle application of coherent 'knowledge' about other individuals which has consequences for what happens to these individuals.
>
> (Jupp, 1993, p.119)

This is very clearly the function of the Carlen extract which we examined first in this section. The two other papers display other facets of the same process. The McLaughlin and Murji discussion illustrates the mobilization of resistance to the reform process: the preliminary gathering up of discursive resources by the police, in preparation for an expected redefinition of their work and practices by those who have the power to do so. The final piece, by Peelo and Soothill, does not appear to be about power at all, but it *displays* power: the power of professionals and the media to apply an authoritative definition to a set of ambiguous circumstances and to have this *accepted* as authoritative. Much critical analysis is of this kind, disclosing the values which underlie apparently neutral and scientific or professional pronouncements about situations and actions.

Uncovering as it does the buried traces of power relations within often apparently descriptive texts, critical analysis does not generally aspire to neutrality. This does not mean that it deliberately misleads; on the contrary, it generally avoids deception by making its own standpoint very clear, and it is as careful to avoid deliberate or unthinking bias as any other kind of good research. Nonetheless, it is undertaken with the intent of exposing the tricks and elisions of the output of those who are (often) in an official or a powerful position. As one of its exponents, Colin Fletcher, puts it: 'In the process the author comes to realisation, if his critique is any good, if it has fired his own imagination, that he has produced a manifesto. He has determined upon a programme of personal commitment' (Fletcher, 1974, p.191).

5 Conclusion

In Chapters 3 and 4 we have looked at three kinds of research: the 'quantitative' or 'scientific'; the 'qualitative' or 'ethnographic'; and the 'critical'. (We have found the distinction between them difficult to maintain at times.) All have the same basic aim: to produce evidence, in support of an argument, which may reasonably be believed and which is strong enough to carry out the role which the argument requires of it.

All three are susceptible to the same kinds of challenges. We may reasonably ask of the evidence which is presented:

- whether the right evidence has been collected (the relevance of the setting, the text or the measures to what it is claimed they mean);

- how the evidence has been collected (whether the collection methods could lead to differences or connections or patterns which were a product of the methods themselves, or of the researcher's presuppositions, rather than descriptive of what is 'actually' there); and

- how far the results can be generalized (the extent to which they are not specific to the time, place and setting researched but can act as the basis for a more general kind of conclusion).

This chapter has criticized pieces of research, but it has not been our aim to denigrate any particular study. Rather, the attitude of the reader of research, like that of the researcher, must be one of constant questioning. Does that conclusion follow from the evidence and argument which has been offered? What are the particular strengths of the method? What are its weaknesses, and how have they been guarded against? Given that few arguments about the social world lead to absolute certainty, precisely what degree of confidence can we place in the conclusions, given the argument, the cited theory and past research, the evidence and the way in which the evidence was collected? What further information might we need to increase our confidence? It is a rare research study that can be accepted entirely at face value, but it is a rare research study from which we can learn nothing. Given the logical principles of research discussed in this chapter and the body of knowledge and theoretical frameworks outlined in the rest of the course, your task, like mine or anyone's who reads research, is to place the new knowledge gained from each report, however tentatively, within your overall map or picture of the social world and the system of criminal justice.

Finally, if a research report is an argument from a problem to a solution, then it is both *set within* theory and *contributes to* theory. A report runs from a problem to a solution, or from an area to be explored to conclusions about it. The argument which leads from the start to the conclusions is based partly on theory, partly on past research and partly on the research which is actually reported. Within the research report itself, theories about methods come to bear. Social research is not simple fact-finding, but a process of inference *from* evidence and *about* evidence, which tries to provide the logically necessary evidence to sustain the argument and to conclude from it what it is logically possible to conclude. What is to be concluded, however, will depend not on the evidence itself, but on the theory which informed the collection of the evidence. It is to theory and its place in research arguments that we turn in the next chapter.

Further reading

Davidson and Layder (1994) and Jupp (1989) look broadly at methods of research used in criminology. Burgess (1984) provides a useful introduction to field research. Hammersley and Atkinson (1995) is also an important text on ethnography. For specific methods, refer to McCracken (1988) on interviewing and Sapsford and Jupp (1996) on data collection and analysis. For a critique of both qualitative and quantitative methods, and an advocacy of critique, see Fletcher (1974).

Research methods considered in Chapter 4

observation looking at what is going on – which involves not just taking notes of observable behaviours, but listening to and initiating conversations, reading relevant documents, and, ideally, taking some part in the action oneself. Qualitative observation may vary along two dimensions: the researcher may be more of a participant or more of an observer (the latter preserving marginality, while the former gives the greater chance of being able to share the meaning of events and statements); and more or less covert or overt depending on the degree to which the researcher conceals the fact that he or she *is* a researcher. The least disruption to the natural situation occurs where the research is covert – the researcher conceals his or her identity as a researcher – and the greatest degree of sharing of concepts occurs where the researcher can legitimately join the situation or at least pass for a member of it. This is not always possible, however – as in the McDermott and King (1988) research described in section 2 – and the ethics of covert research are much open to question.

interviewing the qualitative interview is not structured in the way that a survey interview would be, but more closely resembles a natural conversation and accords a greater degree of control to the informant. While clearly more reactive than covert participant observation, in that the informant will be well aware at all times that the conversation is for research purposes, a fair degree of naturalism can be achieved.

critical analysis critical analysis of printed texts, interview transcripts and the like, seeks to lay bare the ideological or discursive categories which are used by the authors/informants. It seeks to display not the views of informants but the substructure which constrains what they say and/or the power relations implicit in how the text is put together.

References

Barlow, H. (1993) 'From fiddle factors to networks of collusion: charting the waters of small business crime', *Crime, Law and Social Change*, vol.20, pp.313–37.

Boyle, J. (1977) *A Sense of Freedom*, London, Pan Books.

Burgess, R. (1984) *In the Field: An Introduction to Field Research*, London, Unwin Hyman.

Burke, M. (1993a) *Homosexuality in the British Police*, PhD Thesis, University of Essex.

Burke, M. (1993b) *Coming Out of the Blue: British Police Officers Talk About Their Lives in 'The Job' as Gays, Lesbians and Bisexuals*, London, Cassell.

Burke, M. (1994) 'Homosexuality as deviance: the case of the gay police officer', *British Journal of Criminology*, vol.34, no.2, pp.192–203.

Carlen, P. (ed.) (1985) *Criminal Women: Autobiographical Accounts*, Oxford, Polity.

Carlen, P. (1988) *Women, Crime and Poverty*, Milton Keynes, Open University Press.

Carlen, P. (1990) *Alternatives to Women's Imprisonment*, Buckingham, Open University Press.

Clemmer, D. (1940) *The Prison Community*, New York, Holt, Rinehart and Winston.

Cohen, S. and Taylor, L. (1972) *Psychological Survival: The Experience of Long-Term Imprisonment*, Harmondsworth, Penguin.

Davidson, J.D. and Layder, D. (1994) *Methods, Sex and Madness*, London, Routledge.

Fleisher, M.S. (1989) *Warehousing Violence*, London, Sage.

Fletcher, C. (1974) *Beneath the Surface: An Account of Three Styles of Sociological Research*, London, Routledge and Kegan Paul.

Goffman, E. (1961) *Asylums: Essays on the Social Situation of Mental Patients and other Inmates*, New York, Doubleday. (Also available in Penguin Books, 1968.)

Grimshaw, R. and Jefferson, T. (1987) *Interpreting Policework: Policy and Practice in Forms of Beat Policing*, London, Unwin Hyman.

Hammersley, M.I. and Atkinson, P. (1995) *Ethnography: Principles in Practice* (2nd edn), London, Routledge.

Holdaway, S. (1984) *Inside the British Police*, Oxford, Blackwell.

Irwin, J. (1980) *Prisons in Turmoil*, Chicago, IL, Little, Brown.

Irwin, J. and Cressey, D. (1962) 'Thieves, convicts and the inmate culture', *Social Problems*, vol.10, no.1, pp.152–5.

Jefferson, T. (1988) 'Race, crime and policing: empirical, theoretical and methodological issues', *International Journal of the Sociology of Law,* vol.16, pp.521–39.

Jefferson, T. (1990) *The Case Against Paramilitary Policing,* Buckingham, Open University Press.

Jupp, V. (1989) *Methods of Criminological Investigation*, London, Allen and Unwin.

Jupp, V. (1993) 'Unit 21: Critical analysis of text', in The Open University DEH313 *Principles of Social and Educational Research*, Block 4, *Data Analysis*, Milton Keynes, The Open University.

Martin, C. and Godfrey, D. (1994) 'Prisoners' views of Boards of Visitors: a question of credibility', *British Journal of Criminology*, vol.34, no.3, pp.358–65.

McCracken, G. (1988) *The Long Interview*, Beverley Hills, CA, Sage.

McDermott, K. and King, R.D. (1988) 'Mind games: where the action is in prison', *British Journal of Criminology*, vol.28, no.3, pp.357–77.

McLaughlin, E. and Murji, K. (1993) 'Controlling the Bill: restructuring the police in the 1990s', *Critical Social Policy*, no.37, pp.95–103.

Parker, H. (1974) *View from the Boys: A Sociology of Down-Town Adolescents*, London, David and Charles.

Parker H., Bakx, K. and Newcombe, R. (1988) *Living with Heroin: The Impact of a Drugs Epidemic on an English Community*, Milton Keynes, Open University Press.

Parker, T. (1966) *The Unknown Citizen*, Harmondsworth, Penguin.

Patrick, J. (1973) *A Glasgow Gang Observed*, London, Methuen.

Peelo, M. and Soothill, K. (1994) 'Personal power and public control: sex crimes and problem pages', *The Howard Journal*, vol.33, no.1, pp.10–24.

Punch, M. (1979) *Policing the Inner City: A Study of Amsterdam's Warmoesstraat*, London, Macmillan.

Punch, M. (1985) *Conduct Unbecoming*, London, Macmillan.

Samuel, R. (1981) *East End Underworld: Chapters in the Life of Arthur Harding*, London, Routledge

Sapsford, R.J. and Jupp, V. (eds) (1996) *Data Collection and Analysis*, London, Sage.

Sykes, G. (1958) *The Society of Captives*, Princeton, NJ, Princeton University Press.

Worrall, A. (1990) *Offending Women: Female Lawbreakers and the Criminal Justice System*, London, Routledge.

Young, J. (1971) *The Drug-Takers*, London, MacGibbon and Kee.

Appendix 4.1

Jefferson: Extract from
The Case Against Paramilitary Policing

Supervision can be either direct, as occurs when a sergeant accompanies his or her officers on patrol in order to oversee their activities, or indirect, as happens when senior officers monitor the paperwork traces of prior police activity – arrest figures, complaint statistics, completed crime files, pocket book entries, and so on. My intention in what follows is to show that, despite closer supervision and greater opportunities for it, the concrete reality of the SPG's [Special Patrol Group] 'bread and butter' work – public order operations in which discretionary legal duties are uppermost – renders both kinds of supervision effectively redundant.

Direct supervision

The importance of close direct supervision of SPG work, because of the difficulties of controlling the activities of not one but a group of officers, was recognized from the outset, as the following quotation from an ACC [Assistant Chief Constable] reveals:

> When we set up the present Special Patrol Group ... my advice was that you want close supervision, and so we agreed on one and eight and it was agreed a sergeant to eight ... I think that was right for those times because a lot of their work was ... flooding an area on observations ... and dealing with crime ... the sergeant would have a fairly wide spread ... [of] men deployed you see, and I think about eight was about right. And similarly, if they are dealing with any public order situation ... I was always conscious of the fact that if you get a group of people, you can call them a group but if there's something happens and they all go their own way, they get strength from each other and they soon become a mob, and it was for that reason again I wanted very close control so that they were more disciplined, acted as individuals, thought as individuals but acted as a group, and this was the all important thing.

This view was by no means confined to the ACC. The Chief Constable, speaking of a later time (hence the reference to ten not eight men), makes substantially the same point:

> They've got to keep together in order that they can be properly supervised, because we have one sergeant to ten men, and if those ten men keep together as a group under the sergeant, if he's doing his job properly they will not get themselves into trouble, either as victims or as aggressors, 'cause he's there to see that it doesn't happen.

But, in addition to the sergeant, who was always with his unit on public order occasions, the inspector responsible for several units would also often be on hand, as would the chief inspector in charge of the whole Group. Asked when he would decide to go out with the units, the Chief Inspector said:

> I try and be with 'em all the time, purely and simply because I have always believed it's no good talking about it. One can theorize about dignity of man and all the rest of it. From sitting in a seat we're not being confronted with the violence, so I make a point of going to all of them, and in the early days, every situation that was on, regardless of whether it meant me working 12 hours a day or 16 hours a day, I was there ... There's a question of leading by example more than anything else. Once they see that I'm about, I know that things are going to run smoothly.

Moreover, public order occasions will usually have a complement of subdivisional supervisory officers, including sometimes the divisional commander, which adds a further supervisory layer. The presence of subdivisional supervisors is not, incidentally, simply additive. Because SPG supervisors will want 'their' officers to perform creditably in front of 'outside' supervisors, and subdivisional supervisors are concerned that 'outside' departments do not mess up on 'their' turf, this introduces a level of sensitivity into the situation which effectively further enhances the already high degree of supervision. Beyond that, there is the fact that the deployment of the SPG is always to the spots where 'trouble' is expected – and to which primary operational attention, supervisory and otherwise, is necessarily directed. Finally, such spots tend to be those where 'incidents' will arise, and these inevitably attract supervisory notice. SPG public order work is thus highly supervised.

Unlike ordinary policing, it is also highly visible work, not only to the various supervisors around, but also to the public, and sometimes the media. Once again, this is particularly true of the 'trouble spots', and when 'incidents' arise. SPG public order work is thus extraordinarily exposed to the gaze of supervisors, the public and the media.

Now ... in situations where the instruction is to 'hold formation', this close supervision can be absolute and highly effective. But when specific incidents occur which require officers to break formation and go into action, and offences are spotted or suspected, the rank structure is in practice effectively neutralized. At this point, supervisory powers become secondary to constabulary powers, and, given the discretionary nature of public order powers, the occupational dimension, not the organizational dimension, 'takes command'. Though an ACC did not put it this way, his remarks at least recognize the important distinction:

> In the structured ... public order situation I think the ... supervision is pretty tight and can be kept tight ... Now unless [the] ... sergeant is in full control of his unit then they are out of my control, they are out of the structured control of that public order event. So in those circumstances I make it very clear that the sergeant has got to exercise strict control, and it is there that I think that the problems might arise, where they go out to deal with any number of incidents ... In 1968 ... we had a very big exercise ... we had the political spectrum from the extremists of extreme left to [those of the] extreme right and in some situations we had Colin Jordan and his band there and we had the lefties there with just three policemen standing in between them and there was close supervision. We could see everything that was going on because they were all in —— Square and we kept tight control of it and when it all broke up they moved away and it was when everybody was breaking up and the supervision of the people moving away that ... we ... lost one area. There was trouble in one area, but it wasn't as tightly controlled, there wasn't a superintendent in charge in that area at that time. They splintered out into such small groups that ... there wasn't the tight control. I'm sure that the officers acted properly because they'd got a bit of a punch-up situation that ... it wasn't as tight then. I think I'm just trying to make the point that when it breaks out this is where the structure might break down.

Another way of illustrating what the ACC calls situations 'where the structure might break down', and what I call those (structured) situations where the occupational dimension (necessarily) takes command, is to look at a number of arrests that I (along with various supervisors) observed at first hand. No supervisors queried any of these arrests, nor the subsequent police accounts.

Indeed, supervisors were sometimes involved in the arrests. Yet my observations clearly differed. Here, then, we can hardly talk of a 'breakdown' in the structure. Rather, we are forced to recognize the 'normality' of the occupational dimension being 'in command' in such situations, and the organization's subordinate status.

The following four incidents are drawn from my field notes made during my time spent with two SPG units. They are drawn from a much larger body of similar notes encompassing a vast number of police–public interactions resulting variously in arrests, ejections, 'warnings' and the like. They have been chosen not simply because in these particular cases I was able to compare my own notes directly with the official police accounts, but also because they demonstrate, each in a slightly different way, the particularly 'tough' interpretation of their highly subjective powers routinely made by SPG officers working in public order contexts peopled by a relatively powerless public. They are thus a graphic way of illustrating the concrete meaning of the occupational dimension being 'in command'.

The incidents all took place on fine days at heavily policed football matches where there was strong 'away' team support, a police expectation of 'trouble', and many ejections and arrests. All four resulted in POA [Public Order Act] Section 5 arrests for using abusive language 'liable to lead to a breach of the peace', three before the match, one after. My notes appear just as I made them at the time; the police accounts are substantially verbatim transcripts. In both cases, only names and other forms of identification have been altered or removed.

The first example occurred before the match and is an illustration of abusive language being construed as 'behaviour liable' in a situation in which only police were present. The police account is as follows:

> Walking with 200 [same side] supporters chanting 'We're all pissed up and we're going to Wembley'. Approached, told to be quiet. Shouted, 'I'm a press officer and know the fucking law'. Again told to be quiet. Warned about language. Quietened down. Walked ten yards, turned, shouted: 'I'll fix the fucking bastards'. Arrested 'for using abusive language likely to cause a breach of the peace'. Caution, reply: 'Can I see the match. I want to phone my fucking paper'.

Here are my field notes:

> Attempt to close gap between fans. Hurrying them. Using horses. Horseman holds fan by ear/hair. [SPG] van driver apparently arrests same fan after shoving him. Two fans: one protesting at treatment of fans and/or at being hurried. Mate trying to calm. Horseman shooing him. Most of [one SPG] unit and division concentrated on him. Horseman on pavement (provocatively). Rumours of 'press card'. Separated from mate. Taken up alley by SPG man. Horseman blocked entrance. Inspectors walk up road. PCs take no notice. Journalist reappears with press card aloft. Allowed to proceed. All seems reasonably amicable. Horseman mouthing off about him ('more like a member of football hooligan's union'). Speculation as to which (radical) paper he worked for. Attempts to buy pie with others. Hurried up by divisional man. Objected (told later he said 'fuck off'). Arrested by [SPG officer] (picked up by scarf) thrown in van, driven off, squatting on floor though seats vacant. Later [arresting officer] said he'd arrested for 'mouthing off' – telling divisional man to 'fuck off' after three warnings.

The second example is an arrest before a local first division 'derby' match and exemplified the use of Section 5 for refusing to comply with police pushing and shoving by running off. We begin with the police account:

> At front of 50 [home team] supporters. Ran down a road towards larger group of [opposing team] fans awaiting buses. Seen by officers shaking his fists and

beckoning to fans. Calling companions on. No other PCs between groups. [Offender] arrested. Companions ran away. Caution reply: 'I didn't think I'd get arrested: we was only baiting them.'

My field notes are as follows:

> Group of [away team] fans being escorted onto buses. Group of [home team] fans, unescorted, nearby – singing, waving, provoking, etc. [SPG sergeant] spotted. He and [another SPG officer] broke into a run, booted them off (those that hadn't shot off fast enough), pushed and cuffed. One didn't 'shoo'. Arrested by [the other SPG officer]. Being cautioned as I arrived. (Wore glasses, white trousers, braces, skinhead.) Seemed quiet. Shoved in van. Not fast enough, apparently, since hit round the head (offering no resistance).

The third example took place after the same match as the second example and illustrates police 'embellishment' of the facts. Here is the police account:

> Seen after match walking towards [railway] station. Heard shouting 'have a fucking go you cunts' at group of youths just in front. [SPG officer] said: 'be quiet, where are you going ?' [Offender] replied: 'to the fucking station you cunt now fuck off and leave me.' He pushed [SPG officer] aside and went to continue. From [offender's] actions breach of peace feared if he reached other group. His words heard by women shoppers and children. Arrested.

And here, by way of comparison, are my field notes:

> [Away team] fans being escorted. [SPG sergeant and SPG officer] seemed to pick one out as having done something provocative. SPG sergeant smiled. Raced up steps. Seemed to be too late. Watched fans pass. Meanwhile, mention that [SPG officer] had arrested. [SPG sergeant] went over to see prisoner being loaded into van. Prisoner squatting in van, though seat available. Allowed to sit. Asked various questions including last time locked up. Asked 'what for?' Asked whether at football (yes). [SPG sergeant] in front: 'I don't know what it's all coming to, I really don't'.

The final example took place before an FA Cup semi-final between two 'big name' teams, and shows the use of Section 5 in an exemplary way. This is the police view:

> Seen walking along [road] with [one set of] supporters. On opposite side of road large crowd of [opposition] fans. [Offender] seen by officer calling over to them with his hand and was shouting: 'come and have a fucking go you cunts' whilst beckoning with his arms. If he had continued, fight feared.

My field notes record:

> [SPG officer] driving arrestees. Shouting between rival fans across road. [Team] fan shouted. [SPG driver] said 'that's mine'. [Another SPG officer] popped out and arrested on [driver's] behalf. [Driver] continued. Later found his [the fan's] foot to be in plaster (not known at time).

These contrasting accounts, and others like them, collectively constitute two very different ways of 'seeing' incidents. I referred earlier to the SPG's interpretation of Section 5 as 'tough'. In Chapter 6 I shall address how they come to see incidents in this particular way, how they acquire this particular 'working norm'. For the moment, it remains only for me to summarize the essential differences between these police accounts and my own (see Table 1), to remind readers that these police accounts are the concrete manifestations of the dominance of the occupational dimension in such situations, and to reiterate the essential conditions for this – weak legal and democratic structures, and an organizational dimension of the work structure which cannot, as we have just seen, either through policy or supervision, effectively control it.

Table 1 SPG arrests at football matches

SPG accounts emphasize	My observations emphasize
Noisiness, drink	Concrete context (few or no people around to object; fun/'symbolic' nature of chanting, etc.)
Police warning(s) reasonably delivered	Police role in precipitating aggression (where applicable)
Aggressiveness of fans	Police use of violence/'street justice'
Abusiveness of fans	Police abusiveness
Caution given	Meaningless delivery of caution/no caution given
Clear identification of persons, actions, words	Difficulty of identifying persons, actions, words
Clear motives	Ambiguity of motives
Unambiguous nature of general situation	Arbitrariness of arrest in terms of person and alleged offence
Breach of peace imminent	Breach of peace impossible in many situations

(Source: Jefferson, 1990, pp.71–6)

Appendix 4.2

Martin and Godfrey: 'Prisoners' views of Boards of Visitors: a question of credibility'

Until 1992 Boards of Visitors of penal institutions acted as quasi-judicial bodies dealing with serious offences against prison discipline, as well as being public 'watchdogs' to guard against abuses by the prison authorities, and independent channels for inmates' requests and complaints. The withdrawal of their disciplinary powers was intended to enhance Boards' credibility in their other roles by stressing their independence from the prison authorities, and was expected to reduce the long-standing scepticism of inmates about the value of Boards.

This research explored awareness of Boards of Visitors – their roles and duties, composition, independence, and effectiveness – among a sample of 140 adult male prisoners. It shows that despite the withdrawal of Boards' disciplinary powers they were still regarded by most inmates as largely invisible, irrelevant, aligned with the prison management, and ineffective. Inmates had little confidence in Boards of Visitors.

Reservations have repeatedly been expressed over the past 20 years about the effectiveness of Boards of Visitors in their roles as 'watchdogs' on behalf of the public and an independent channel for prisoners' complaints, requests, and grievances (Martin, 1975; JUSTICE, 1983; Maguire and Vagg, 1984; Ditchfield and Austin, 1986; Home Office, 1987). Despite having wide powers of access to prisons, prisoners, staff and records, a brief to satisfy themselves about the administration of the establishment and the treatment of inmates, and the right to report their concerns to the Home Secretary, it appears that Boards have failed to inspire much confidence among inmates.

The Jellicoe Committee (Martin, 1975, p.30) reported that 'Most inmates have little or no confidence in Boards, and the majority have nothing to do with them'. No improvement was evident ten years later: 'Unfortunately, virtually all the evidence available about the work of Boards of Visitors suggests that they have consistently failed to fulfil their potential. They have been shown to enjoy little confidence among prisoners' (Maguire, 1985, p.143). Ditchfield and Austin (1986, pp.38–9) asked a sample of inmates who had recently submitted or withdrawn petitions to the Home Secretary whether they had previously seen the Board of Visitors about their request or complaint. Only five of the 26 inmates in local prisons had made use of the Board, 19 out of 66 men in training prisons, and 12 out of 80 men in dispersal prisons.

One reason for the low credibility of Boards may be that prisoners are not confident about their independence from the prison management. The Jellicoe Committee recommended as a principle that Boards should be 'conspicuously independent', but there seem to be intractable problems about convincing prisoners of the reality of this independence, even if it can be achieved. Maguire and Vagg (1984, p.4) found that '… many prisoners are highly sceptical about the independence of Boards'. Sixty-six per cent of their sample of prisoners viewed the Board as part of the management of the prison, and only 23 per cent saw them as independent. About one-third thought they were manipulated by the system – 'the governor's puppets' (p.153). Woolf and Tumim (1991, p.309) found that this difficulty persisted 15 years after the Jellicoe Committee:

> We are conscious, however, that their endeavours on behalf of prisoners are inhibited by the fact that a substantial part of the prison population does not recognise the Board's members as being as impartial as they in fact are.

Doubt about the independence of Boards of Visitors from the Home Office and prison governors is not limited to inmates. Martin (1980, p.98) concluded,

> From attending quite a number of Boards I have no doubt whatever as to the members' sense of responsibility. Unfortunately, however, it is all too easy for them to interpret that responsibility as being to the Home Office; as one Chairman put it in my presence 'We are the representatives of the Secretary of State'.

Ditchfield and Austin (1986, p.35) found that

> Members' own views about their independence revealed a certain amount of ambiguity. While a clear majority (67 per cent) said they felt reasonably independent of the Governor in dealing with applications, a majority also felt that they had to support him in general – partly because of his responsibility for the discipline and security of the prison, and partly because of the need to maintain confidence in each other … Just under a quarter of their suggestions concerned ways of improving inmates' perceptions of their independence.

Some possible obstacles to credible independence have subsequently been removed, but it remains to be seen whether this will enable Boards to inspire confidence among inmates. The study reported here aimed to discover how Boards are now viewed by prisoners, whether recent changes might have changed prisoners' perceptions, and how Boards might develop greater credibility.

Sample and method

Adult male prisoners were individually interviewed on a voluntary basis at a Category C training prison during six weeks of the summer of 1992. The interviews took place in the prison library at various times of day, on both weekdays and weekends. The sample was initially opportunistic, but as awareness of the study spread by word of mouth through the inmate community 'snowball sampling' developed, until 140 of the prison's average population of about 190 had been interviewed. Six inmates declined to participate. All the prisoners had been in at least one other prison during the current sentence, and nearly all had served previous custodial sentences. The sample included inmates with previous experience ranging from junior detention centres to dispersal prisons. The prisoners' comments on Boards of Visitors reflected their experiences during both previous and current sentences. Although the sample was not selected to represent the adult male prisoner population in general, we see no reason to suppose that a representative sample would have expressed substantially different views. Each interview opened with three core questions:

Have you heard of Boards of Visitors?

If so, how did you first hear of them?

What do Boards of Visitors do?

Subsequent questions followed up issues of which the respondent claimed some knowledge or experience, or about which he expressed an interest. The general tone was informal and conversational. The interviews were tape recorded, except in nine cases where subjects objected to tape recording but agreed to written notes.

Awareness of Boards of Visitors

One hundred and thirty-three (95 per cent) of the inmates had heard of Boards of Visitors. The seven who had not were all serving their first custodial sentence, and two were foreign nationals with poor English, who apparently found much of their prison experience bewildering. A few prisoners thought that Boards of Visitors had been abolished with the recent withdrawal of their disciplinary role, and a few confused Boards of Visitors with Prison Visitors.

'Everyone's heard of them. We all know they exist.'

'Everyone knows about them. They're there, and that's it. They're there like the grass is there.'

All the prisoners were asked how they first became aware of Boards of Visitors (in most cases during a previous sentence):

- 69 (49 per cent) had heard from other inmates, 'on the grapevine';
- 12 (9 per cent) by being brought before a Board for adjudication on a disciplinary charge;
- 8 (6 per cent) from the Prisoners' Information Pack;
- 8 (6 per cent) from staff;
- 7 (5 per cent) by seeing Board members visiting an establishment;
- 5 (4 per cent) from sources outside the establishment;
- and the remaining 31 (22 per cent) either could not remember or did not specify.

In effect, it seems that Boards of Visitors were depending largely upon casual information-sharing among inmates to create awareness of their existence.

Roles and duties of Boards of Visitors

Although knowledge of the existence of Boards of Visitors was almost universal, most information about them was acquired anecdotally, and might have been inaccurate. Complaints from respondents about a lack of information were not limited to information about Boards of Visitors.

> 'You find out through the grapevine really, through the prison grapevine. Nobody ever told me anything about prisons. What I know is what I've learned.'

> 'You're never told anything here. You don't get told anything, and if you learn the wrong way you could be doing extra time.'

Many prisoners said that the shortage of full and accurate information was a major source of resentment.

Since most of the prisoners had received no official information about Boards during any of their sentences, their knowledge of Boards' duties and powers was often sketchy. When all 140 prisoners were asked what they thought Boards of Visitors do:

- 56 (40 per cent) correctly identified inspection of the prison, attention to prisoners' welfare and dealing with grievances;

- 21 (15 per cent) wrongly added adjudications (disciplinary hearings) to the list, although that task had recently been removed from Boards;

- 23 (16 per cent) thought, wrongly, that Boards conducted adjudications and/or made parole recommendations, but did nothing else;

- 4 (3 per cent) said Boards did nothing;

- 10 (7 per cent) did not answer the question;

- and 26 (19 per cent) said they did not know.

Although 55 per cent of the prisoners knew that the Boards' tasks included inspection, attention to inmates' welfare and dealing with grievances, many doubted that these were accomplished, even if they were attempted. It seems possible that the anecdotal material about Boards of Visitors passed by word of mouth among inmates contributed to the generally cynical views expressed.

> '[They do] nothing. They walk about … I suppose they have got to fill in a bit of paper somewhere to say that they've been in, that they're personally satisfied with what they've seen, but that is it.'

> '[They] come in, have a wee gander at the place, see nothing, and go back out and think everything's perfect.'

> 'They come and have tea with the Governor, and basically that's it. That is it in a nutshell. They come and have tea with the Governor, and cakes, and go home.'

> 'Well I suppose they're brought in … See, I've done a lot of prison … The Board of Visitors to me was a party that was brought in just for disciplinary action, so I don't really know the other part of what they do.'

Composition of Boards of Visitors

Forty-seven men said nothing about the composition of Boards, and 33 said they did not know anything about Board membership. Of the 60 men who commented on the composition of Boards, 58 knew that they were local members of the public or magistrates. They criticized the composition of Boards as being too old, too middle class, and generally unrepresentative of the community. Descriptions included 'shop-keepers', 'a cross between magistrates and social workers', 'the wrong people', 'upper class', 'ex-colonels', and 'successful self-made businessmen … professional people who have time … middle-aged … financially in a position to do it'.

Of the 21 black prisoners who expressed an opinion, 16 thought that there should be black Board members, but only one prisoner remembered seeing any. Opinion was evenly divided on whether black prisoners would find a black Board member more approachable. About half thought that it was largely a matter of social class, and they did not believe that the difficulty could be overcome simply by appointing black members. They were vehemently opposed to tokenism.

> 'I don't think it makes any sort of difference. If someone can't explain themselves properly then it doesn't matter what colour you are. In the end, the person that you are speaking to, if you cannot make them understand what you mean, it doesn't make no difference, you know, whether they're black or white. If they don't understand what you're saying that's it, you're finished.'

Most prisoners said that they found Board members unapproachable. Many of them had seen Board members making visits to institutions, but they were usually escorted by staff, which was considered a hindrance to inmate approaches.

> 'They are aloof, and they should go out of their way to make a point of talking to prisoners. They are always escorted.'

When 83 men were asked whether the Board of Visitors should have a permanent office in the prison, where they could be approached in confidence, 72 (87 per cent) thought this was a good idea.

> 'If they had an office where we knew where to go, that would be more logical. If there was a set time and day for them to come in … somewhere where you could aim, and get to see them. That's the ideal.'

Independence

Whilst prisoners were almost unanimous about the need for an independent body to inspect prisons and hear complaints, Boards of Visitors were not universally recognized as being independent.

Of the 106 prisoners who were asked about the independence of Boards, 47 (44 per cent) thought they were not independent, 32 (30 per cent) thought they were, and 27 (26 per cent) did not know. It was widely believed that, as Home Office appointees, members would inevitably feel loyalty to the Establishment, become friendly with the prison's management, and therefore fail properly to represent prisoners' concerns.

> 'Once they become too friendly with the Governor things become personalized … they become very informal. Therefore how can they take an independent view? Then they've got to take the prisoner's side against the Governor and his staff, [but] that's never going to happen. You need something totally independent, who doesn't really have an informal contact with the prison authorities.'

'If they're appointed by the Home Office they can't possibly be independent.'

'They seem to be intimidated by the staff. They are coerced into certain things by the staff whether they like it or not – browbeaten, whatever. Certain areas that you aren't going to see, certain things you aren't going to do.'

Among the minority who thought the Board was independent of the management there was greater confidence.

'You know you can go to them, and if you wanted to say anything to them you could … you know, I mean literally anything. So that's a good thing, I suppose.'

Effectiveness

Many prisoners doubted whether Boards of Visitors had sufficient power to be effective in dealing with requests, complaints, and grievances. Only 35 of them (25 per cent) reported ever having had personal dealings with a Board member. Of these, 27 (19 per cent) had at sometime made an application to see a Board member, but only two of these thought the Board's intervention had solved their problem.

- 8 had received replies which they considered unsatisfactory;
- 5 had never seen a Board member in response to the application, and knew of no reason for this;
- 4 received no reply;
- 3 had been transferred out of the prison (in their view as a result of asking to see a Board member);
- 1 prisoner's problem was resolved in the meantime without Board intervention;
- 1 application was never processed, despite being repeated;
- 1 inmate was told by an officer to withdraw his request to see the Board (which he did);
- and the remaining two could not remember what the outcome had been.

Of 89 men who were asked whether they would in any circumstances apply to see a Board member, 59 (66 per cent) said they would not apply to see the Board, or would do so only in very serious circumstances. One reason was that they thought the Board's lack of power made applications pointless. Of 73 men who were asked whether Boards have any power, 33 (45 per cent) thought they had none and ten (14 per cent) thought their power was limited.

'[They] don't carry no clout whatsoever.'

'No real power. They've got the power to suggest.'

'They've got powers, but they're not really in control of their powers, and they're more influenced by governors.'

'They don't have power over the Governor.'

'They've got the power to report.'

Another disincentive to Board of Visitors' applications was the belief that there might be adverse consequences. Of 80 men who were asked about possible reprisals by staff against prisoners who applied to the Board, 63 (79 per cent) believed that reprisals would be likely in some or all cases.

'You'd be straight out – ghosted [transferred to another prison]. That's how they treat people who complain.'

'Most people just want to do their prison sentence quietly, and just get on with it, and so they don't bother kicking up a fuss about things that really should be brought up. They have too much to lose.'

Asked whether Boards of Visitors made any difference to the running of the prison, about one-third of inmates thought they made no difference; one-third thought they made some difference; and one-third thought the effect was limited to periods when Board members were in the prison. It was generally believed that Board members lacked enough time and interest to find out how prisons operate.

'There'd have to be a resident Board there to know the running of the prison.'

Although some prisoners acknowledged that Board members' visits were supposed to be unannounced, it was widely believed that staff knew when Board members were going to visit.

'Staff know when they're coming in. They're always forewarned. I don't know how they know, but they know.'

Many prisoners gave as evidence for staff foreknowledge of Board visits that the meals were better on those days, and referred to the practice of staff at the gate telephoning the 'sensitive' areas of the prison, such as the segregation unit, hospital, and kitchen, to warn colleagues of an impending Board inspection.

Especially among those who had a lot of prison experience, there was little confidence in the effectiveness of the Boards against serious abuses. Several prisoners told of being advised by staff not to approach Board members with allegations of mistreatment.

'If you get beat up by the screws in the punishment block in [a particular prison] they can just make you disappear. You just get wiped off the map.'

'If you get chucked down the block, beat up by an officer, nobody comes. It still goes on. You get violence. It still goes on. You never see that.'

In major incidents, it was felt that the presence of Board members was useful to prevent abuses by staff, but many prisoners believed that staff retaliation would then merely be deferred until after the Board members had left.

Discussion

The Jellicoe Report (Martin, 1975) was not at first well received, but 'an initially sceptical reception has given way to partial acceptance at an operational level, as a result of which Boards should locally be doing a better job' (Martin, 1980, p.100). More of Jellicoe's recommendations have subsequently been implemented, including:

- Boards' role in the inmate disciplinary machinery has been ended (a key proposal of Jellicoe which was not accepted until 1991);

- An independent national association of Board members (AMBoV) has been formed, as has an official co-ordinating committee to liaise with Prison Service HQ;

- Some Boards' meetings now include sessions when the Governor is absent;

- Many Boards publish an annual report;
- Training courses for members and chairpersons have been extended;
- Many Boards make reciprocal visits to other penal institutions;
- The role of Boards in serious incidents has been clarified, and contingency plans have been made to ensure their attendance during and after major disturbances;
- Boards have been encouraged to communicate more freely with their local communities about the institution and its work.

Some further developments were not foreshadowed by Jellicoe:

- Boards are no longer involved in the restoration of lost remission;
- Boards' contribution to the parole process is ending as parole is phased out;
- A revised procedure for request and complaints includes confidential written access for inmates to the Board of Visitors Chair.

Taken together, these changes suggest that Boards should be better placed to undertake a pastoral role – 'both more than inspection and less than management' (Martin, 1980, p.98). The evidence of this study indicates that Boards have yet to convince inmates of their ability to act as perceptive but independent outsiders: in short, most prisoners found that the Boards were largely invisible and ineffective, and few had much confidence in them.

References

Ditchfield, J., and Austin, C. (1986) *Grievance Procedures in Prison,* Home Office Research Study No.91, London, HMSO.

Home Office (1987) *A Review of Prisoners' Complaints,* Report by HM Chief Inspector of Prisons, London, HMSO.

JUSTICE (1983), *Justice in Prison,* London, JUSTICE.

Maguire, M. (1985) 'Prisoners' grievances', in Maguire, M., Vagg, J. and Morgan, R. (eds) *Accountability and Prisons: Opening Up a Closed World,* London, Tavistock.

Maguire, M. and Vagg, J. (1984) *The 'Watchdog' Role of Boards of Visitors,* London, HMSO.

Martin, J.P. (1975) *Boards of Visitors of Penal Institutions* (The Jellicoe Report), London, Barry Rose.

Martin, J.P. (1980) 'Jellicoe and after – Boards of Visitors into the eighties', *The Howard Journal,* vol.19, pp.85–101.

Woolf, L.J. and Tumim, J. (1991) *Prison Disturbances, April 1990. Report of an Inquiry,* London, HMSO.

Carol Martin is a researcher and David Godfrey is a prison governor.

This research originated as part of an Open University course and was not sponsored by the Prison Department.

(Source: Martin and Godfrey, 1994, pp.358–65)

Appendix 4.3

Burke: 'Homosexuality as deviance: the case of the gay police officer'

Using interview data transcribed from original interviews with 36 gay, lesbian, or bisexual currently serving and retired police officers, this article considers the deviance value of a non-heterosexual orientation status within the police organization and attempts a preliminary assessment of its impact on individual police officers.

It is suggested that the discrepant status of homosexuality in law, the machismo sub-culture of the police and the role of the police as regulators of deviance all make it difficult for the police to adopt or accept a non-conformist orientation. The status of lesbianism is also examined in relation to police culture and it is further suggested that the experiences of women as 'deviant' in this regard may not be analogous to those of their male colleagues.

Illustrations of how officers often live 'double' as opposed to 'integrated' lives as a result of their predicament are offered, and it is proposed that the stress caused by leading two discrete existences may be detrimental to mental health and significant in the ability of officers to perform effectively at work, or form stable or satisfying personal relationships.

Increased research over the past three decades has meant that both the police leviathan and its fascinating sub-culture have become better understood than formerly. Much has been articulated regarding the police theoretically (Skolnick, 1966; Banton, 1964; Holdaway, 1979; Reiner, 1985; Chesshyre, 1989) and the attention of the media is unremitting. Media coverage of alternative sexualities has also expanded in recent years with a number of popular television soaps producing gay characters. In addition, the wake of post-gay liberation and more recently, the emergence of 'lesbian and gay studies', has resulted in an ever increasing flow of academic documentation pertaining to sexual orientation (e.g. McIntosh, 1968; Humphreys, 1970; Plummer, 1975; Foucault, 1980; Weeks, 1985; Altman, 1989). However, whilst knowledge and awareness about what it *means* to be gay, lesbian, or bisexual in terms of sexual orientation has increased considerably, there remains a deep-seated ignorance on a number of planes. Scientific knowledge about why sexual orientations differ is still scanty despite the biological, sociological, psychological, and psychoanalytical theories of the past century, and in a society that can still be overtly hostile towards 'deviant' sexual relationships there is still much to learn about the way being attracted to one's own sex, particularly in conjunction with various other co-factors such as occupation, can affect self-esteem, the development of personal identity, and general cognitive function.

The lack of harmony between the police and the gay community comes as no surprise. Indeed, their conflicting values and ideologies might predict such friction (Derbyshire, 1990). This disharmony has not gone unnoticed and recent times have seen a good measure of commentary as well as a sprinkling of (mostly US) studies regarding the relationships between these two antagonistic communities (Bayley, 1974; Swerling, 1978). However, whilst the subject of homosexuality *and* the police has been probed, albeit sketchily, almost nothing has been articulated on the direct combination of the two: homosexuality *in* the police. In this paper, I want to consider the notion of the homosexual police officer. In particular, I want to consider the deviance value of such a status within the police organization and assess its impact on the individual.

The policeman's lot

If the policeman's lot 'is not a happy one', then the plight of the gay or lesbian police officer is far worse. Although homosexuality is not prohibited *per se* by the Sexual Offences Act of 1967 as it is in the armed forces and Merchant Navy,[1] that does not seem to make it any more socially or professionally acceptable. Police officers are expected to use a range of role behaviour 'appropriate' to their role category and the normative role behaviour of the police officer is contingent upon, and a direct corollary of, both the expectations of society and those of the police organization. As a result, the police service has come to represent a highly regulated order of stability and conformity with a myriad of regulations and restrictions. Homosexuals, it seems, have no place in that order. In Swerling's (1978) study, 20 per cent of Californian police officer interviewees indicated their intention to quit the force if it started hiring overt homosexuals. This finding supports work by Niederhoffer (1967) and Jacobs (1966), whose surveys demonstrated that homosexuals were ranked by police amongst the most disliked categories of people on both coasts of the USA. The current research does little to repudiate those findings:

> The police represent the conservative elements in society. Homosexuality is not seen by them as representing conservative ideals. I doubt very much if I'd have been selected if the selection committee had known that I was gay.

> (R22, Burke 1993a)

From a police point of view then, homosexuality would appear to represent part of the societal disorder that the police officer has dedicated his or her life to eradicating. Tolerating non-heterosexual[2] officers therefore (let alone condoning their recruitment) would represent the most serious kind of contamination and the worst possible threat to the integrity of the Service. The aversion for an association between the words 'police' and 'homosexuality' is illustrated by Sergeant Michael Bennett, Chair of the Metropolitan Police Federation, who wrote in an article to *Police Review* magazine in response to news of the newly formed Lesbian and Gay Police Association (LAGPA) in 1990:

> Why the police service? We do not have a homosexual milkmen's association, or one for homosexual bank clerks. Surely police officers who are homosexual can meet each other in clubs and bars, and even advertise in the homosexual press. Why use the word 'police' in their title? … Or will we get a police bondage association, or a deviant sexual practices society?

> (Bennett, 1991, pp.164–5)

As Brooks put it:

> Cops are conventional people … All a cop can swing in a milieu of marijuana smokers, inter-racial dates, and homosexuals is the night stick.

> (Brooks, 1965, cited in Skolnick, 1966)

There may be several reasons for the status of homosexuality as distinctively deviant within police organizations. I would now like to consider some of these.

Machismo

The machismo aspect of police culture has been well documented. Gambling, sexism, and alcohol are an important part of popular canteen culture (Policy Studies Institute, 1983; Reiner, 1985; Graef, 1989). 'Beer, sport and women – preferably all at once' was the way one of Adlam's (1981, p.157) respondents put it, and it has been suggested that this core characteristic within police culture inhibits the acceptance of homosexuality:

> The whole social conditioning for masculinity in our society can be seen as a kind of aversion therapy against homosexuality ... a 'real' man is the one who is the least open to the charge of homosexuality.

(Hoch, 1979)

Loss of masculinity may be an issue here. Males perhaps, feel that in the acknowledgement of their desire, they will automatically forfeit their masculinity, ceasing to be themselves, and simultaneously undergo a rapid transformation into some grotesque, handbag carrying ambisexual. This link between machismo and the almost pathological aversion to homosexuality has not gone unnoticed by police officers. Homosexuality strikes at the very heart of the police status, and the popular homosexual stereotype that the majority of the police readily accede to is the antithesis of the machismo that is so strongly embraced within the force. The notion requires little expansion:

> It's such a macho job: you've got to be seen to be manly. It doesn't do for a policeman to be weak and effeminate, and homosexuality is wrongly perceived as that.

(O'Neill, 1990)

The former Chief Constable of Devon and Cornwall, John Alderton, commented:

> I think that there is a macho self-image about the police. I often wonder whether the police macho doesn't somehow feel itself threatened by homosexuality.

(Galloway, 1983, p.103)

In his MA dissertation, Chief Inspector Robert Anthony of the Metropolitan Police (1991) acknowledges the threat that homosexuality poses to the male police officer's notion of 'a man', but he challenges the notion that high levels of masculinity are a prerequisite for police work. 'Male homosexuality' he says, 'threatens to expose the fact that masculinity, as it is understood within the canteen culture, is not, after all, a necessary part of the equipment of a successful police officer' (p.18). The tendency to favour the contrary view is not a purely domestic law-enforcement disposition but would appear to be a common judgement within policing circles regardless of their nationality. Gay police officer Brian Aguiar of the Canadian police in Toronto asserts:

> From what I've seen and experienced, it's still not acceptable for anyone in the police force to be homosexual. There's a very macho image. Being gay is a no-no.

(Wheeler, 1990)

Such evidence leads Adlam (1981) to conclude that: 'the police do have something of a masculinity complex' and he suggests that this might be 'the conceptual key which unlocks the door to their personality dynamics' (p.161).

Lesbianism

The question of whether or not lesbianism is conceived of as more or less deviant than male homosexuality in the police is an interesting one and one, it seems, upon which police women are themselves divided. Certainly, the stigma attached to the quasi-criminal legal status of male homosexuality is absent with respect to lesbianism and it has been suggested that the machismo aspect of the collective police personality is also inapplicable to the female police officer. It has therefore been proposed that female police officers are less likely to encounter difficulties regarding their orientation:

> I think the men get it much harder than the women in the police if they're gay ...

> (R27)

However, the suggestion that masculinity is not required in women police officers is contentious. R27 made the following observation with respect to the 'machismo' syndrome:

> ... stereotype of the male gay is effeminacy, which the police doesn't want, whereas the stereotype of the dyke is masculinity and the police need women who aren't afraid to get stuck in there and do the job.

There would appear to be a suggestion here, (a) that the machismo syndrome *is* relevant to women, and (b) that unlike gay men, gay women are perceived as more, not less likely to live up to that expectation. Anthony (1991) has noted the existence of a double-edged sword which on the one hand demands from women the masculine virility which male officers often bring to the problems of policing, whilst at the same time trapping those female officers who display equal prowess 'safely in the pigeon hole of lesbianism' (p.4), thus denying them their femininity. Some of the women among the sample felt so strongly about the issue of police lesbianism that they declined to be interviewed for fear of 'rocking the boat'. The principal concern amongst these officers would appear to be the perceived threat to the existence of a well developed but informal police lesbian network which has no male equivalent. This network is very protective of its affiliates, most of whom seem quite content with an effective yet largely invisible arrangement and are concerned that an analysis of homosexual issues within the police service will only draw attention to their existence. Others, however, dislike this unassertive tendency, preferring a more independent stance where they can mix comfortably with gay male colleagues when they find them. It is the differing perceptions of the status of female homosexuality in the police which has caused the divergent stances of women on this issue, and of the following pieces, the first deals with the network referred to above, whilst the latter serve to illustrate differences of opinion:

> I believe that lesbian police officers feel less of a need to form or belong to such an association [The Lesbian and Gay Police Association] because informal networks already exist for them in a safe environment, that is, through sporting activities. As far as Force sport is concerned, the main sport is hockey and I know of lesbian officers who have formed relationships with each other or

civilians through meeting in this way. I have also known of civilians who have been connected with hockey and have subsequently joined the police because they have met and become aware of the number of lesbians that there are in the service. I believe that the fact that lesbian officers are associated with Force hockey is an 'open secret'. When I was quite young in service I was asked if I played hockey, but I was unaware of the implications of the question at the time ... From speaking to officers involved it appears that the lesbians eventually 'suss' each other out – although their sexuality is never discussed with the heterosexual members of the team and a 'straight' front is put on in public. This sort of behaviour does not appeal to me, but I feel that many lesbian officers are happy with the situation and could find the LAGPA threatening ...

(R13)

I feel that there is a greater acceptance of lesbians than gay men in the Job[3] because traditionally the police has, as have all uniform services, attracted lesbians.[4] However, the image of police women has changed and become more glamorous over the past few years through TV and films, and I would imagine that the number of lesbians joining the Job now as a percentage of women recruited is probably declining – whereas a few years ago the Job was seen as a job unsuitable for 'real' women and the percentage of lesbians was therefore higher. Even so, I would guess that proportionally, there are far more lesbians than gay men in the police.

(R14)

... the main thing about gay women is that they are petrified about coming out because they feel that they won't get promotion. It's difficult enough for a woman to prove her worth as a police officer without the additional stigma of homosexuality to cope with ... And if you're lucky enough to be respected for being a good police officer then the knowledge of your homosexuality could neutralise or detract from that. Women feel that they will be looked upon unfavourably if their orientation is known about, and since they are more likely to do the full thirty years and make a career of it, it is particularly important to them that there are no impediments to promotion.

(R07)[5]

It is clear then, that despite some disagreement over the status of lesbianism in the police, the concerns which are seen to govern women's sentiments are often distinct from those in the male arena where there is no gender stigma, and it seems likely that there may be a significant experiential difference which separates gay men and lesbians within the police structure. A more detailed analysis must, however, await future research.

Impact of the criminal law

In the case of the male homosexual, negative legislation lends support to a 'criminality hypothesis'. The Sexual Offences Act of 1967 provides that homosexual acts (between males) still constitute offences, unless certain conditions are observed.[6] More recently, section 28 of the Local Government Act 1988 has prevented the 'promotion' of homosexuality, and clause 25 (now section 31) of the Criminal Justice Act 1991 threatened to impose harsher prison sentences for those convicted of 'serious sexual offences', consensual or otherwise. Consequently, homosexuality is still synonymous with criminality in the minds of many police officers, with the result that the homosexual community is seen as a legitimate target for suspicion, particularly in the minds of officers who may have been policing before the 1967 amendment came into being. As John Alderton reflects:

> There was criminal legislation, which even in my time as a young recruit was drilled into us. It was regarded as a very serious crime, and a lot of time was spent prosecuting in this field.

> (Galloway, 1983, p.111)

I have contended elsewhere (Burke, 1992) that an officer's personal values and ideologies may, with time, become increasingly conservative as they become entwined with those values that the law attempts to uphold. Non-heterosexual officers are therefore attempting to reconcile their sexual orientation with knowledge of the way the gay communities are regarded by their peers, often empathizing with such judgements and (mis)understandings as a result of their own conditioning and police experience; both able and unable in the same moment to believe themselves deserving of such adjudication.

Ambivalence

That the stigmatized will sometimes feel uncertain about the validity of their difference due to the fact that they are in constant violation of the codes that they unconsciously accept, is inevitable. Berzon (1979) notes:

> In our formative years we were all exposed to the same antigay jokes as our nongay counterparts, the same stereotypes of lesbians and gay men, the same misinformation from our peers. For we gay people who have swallowed all this toxic material, it works against us from the inside while society's homophobes … work against us from the outside.

> (Berzon, 1979, p.3)

And Goffman (1963) points out:

> … a stigmatized person is first of all like anyone else, trained first of all in others' views of persons like himself [sic]. (p.160)

> … the standards he has incorporated from the wider society equip him to be intimately alive to what others see as his failing, inevitably causing him, if only for moments to agree that he does indeed fall short of what he really ought to be. (p.18)

Able to see themselves from a heterosexual viewpoint, they may experience a 'double consciousness'. Du Bois describes this in the context of black consciousness (although I believe that the analogy holds here) as 'always looking at oneself through the eyes of others, by measuring one's soul by the tape of a world that looks on in amused contempt and pity'. The awareness of inferiority in the eyes of others means that unless a robust counter-identity is in place to reply, insecurity can lead to peer stratification.

Goffman (1963) notes that 'deviants' exhibit a tendency similar to 'normals' to stratify their compatriots in terms of the extent to which their deviance is visible. This practice allows individuals the opportunity to embrace the negative feelings that they have been taught to have towards homosexuality in the same way that 'normals' express their repulsion:

> ... the stigmatized individual may exhibit identity ambivalence when he obtains a close sight of his own kind behaving in a stereotyped way, flamboyantly or pitifully acting out the negative attribute imputed to them. The sight may repel him, since after all he supports the norms of the wider society, but his social and psychological identification with these offenders holds him to what repels him, transforming repulsion into shame ...

> (p.131)

In this way, the anti-Semitic Jew, the racist black, and the homophobic homosexual will all suffer debilitating crises of identity since they are unable to embrace their society, yet nor are they ever completely able to reject it.[7]

With specific regard to homosexuality, identity ambivalence can be observed when lesbians or gay men deprecate those other lesbians or gays whose ways of being are perceived to lead to public alienation, either by their mannerisms or by their activities. Strong identity ambivalence can lead to attempts at *in-group purification* in an endeavour to 'normify' behaviour and gain acceptance. It is doubtful, however, that this strategy is open to all. Only those whose stigma is 'less than averagely visible' may reasonably adopt such a strategy since for those whose deviance is 'more than averagely visible', there will be fewer individuals with whom they may favourably compare themselves than with whom such a comparison would serve only to reinforce their sense of inferiority. Such a strategy is however probably open to most police officers, who, it is suggested, tend to display higher than average levels of masculinity. Respondents in the current research were found to display varying degrees of ambivalence:

> My nightmare is going to one of our gay pubs and being recognised. Like having some screaming queen come running up to me and putting her arms around me and telling me how wonderful I look in my smart uniform.

> (R10)

R10 had the following to say on the active recruitment of lesbians and gay men into the police:

> The police could encourage gays and lesbians to join the Job. The question is, would you attract the right sort of people? I see myself as being just like everyone else but once you open the floodgates how will you control what you get? How can you segregate? You can't really, and you might encourage those homosexuals who are clearly unsuitable to join and make fools of themselves and the Job.

R33 makes a point about the kinds of activities which may lead to the arrest of other homosexuals:

> They don't tell you for example what they [homosexuals] were doing to deserve the treatment they got – that they were standing there taking the piss and blowing kisses at the police and making a nuisance of themselves. Then they make out it was all for nothing and that they just got picked on for no reason.

Double-lives

The invisibility of an individual's sexual orientation makes it inevitable that many officers will choose to 'pass' as heterosexual rather than display their deviance, and even those whose sexuality is common knowledge will often 'cover' (both terms after Goffman, 1963). By covering, an individual attempts to *contain* another's knowledge of his or her deviance by 'playing it down'. R16 has been open about his sexual orientation at work for about four years, yet he still takes care not to draw attention to himself:

> I still do [disguise sexual orientation] in as much as I don't say, 'Wow, look at him!' when we're in a police car – which I would normally do. I never push it.

R20 explains that when it comes to anti-gay jokes, rather than make a fuss and highlight her deviance, she laughs. 'It's difficult,' she says, 'because I don't want to be seen to be an activist.'

The current research suggests that inception of the 'double-life syndrome' is an unusually common corollary in the gay police career. The most notable such example in recent times was the case of the Queen's Police Officer, Commander Trestrail, whose resignation as head of Royalty Protection was accepted after his public exposure in 1982. Lord Bridge, who was subsequently tasked with the investigation of Trestrail's original appointment, noted that: 'until the disclosure made in July last, no one … entertained the slightest suspicion of Commander Trestrail's homosexual inclinations, let alone of the secret double life he was leading' (1982, p.11).

Fifty-three per cent (n = 19) of those officers interviewed were living double-lives. Living a double-life involves exercising two roles – owning two identities one of which is always 'spoiled' or 'discreditable' (and therefore always camouflaged) depending on the company one is in. There develops one life at work where an officer's organizing identity is that of 'police officer' and their sexual orientation remains undisclosed and disengaged, and another 'off-duty' life, where their identity is either 'gay', 'lesbian', 'bisexual' (or simply 'confused') but where their occupation is a closely guarded secret. Others may be 'out' in one sphere but not in the other. Thus, there are varying degrees to which police officers may, or may not, entertain the notion of a double-life[8] and these are distinguished as follows. Some officers live *double* double-lives. They are those men and women whose identities are constantly camouflaged; who are 'heterosexual' at work, and who are 'bank clerks' in the evening. Others live single double-lives: they are those men and women whose identities are partially camouflaged – who are gay, lesbian, or bisexual at work, but who are 'bank clerks' in the evening, and those who are full-time police officers but who are ostensibly heterosexual at work. The distinction is an important one. I refer to the former as a *paired double-life,* whilst the latter instance is referred to as an *exclusive double-life.*[9]

The effects of such a lifestyle are various and the tension generated by constantly having to negotiate one's way through a complex maze of lies cannot be underestimated. As Richard Wells, Chief Constable of the South Yorkshire Constabulary observed: 'Police work is difficult enough already without extra pressures of that sort' *(Police Review,* 1991). The effects of this pressure can be both disruptive and destabilizing and the Weinberg and Williams study (1974) found a strong association between 'psychological problems' and the worry caused by the fear of exposure or discrimination (p.186). The data also suggest that, as might be predicted, those who live paired double-lives are generally subject to more stress than those who live exclusive double-lives. In some cases, the stress caused by an artificially constructed and enforced double-identity may be extreme and lead to a violent disruption of mental life. Evidence in support of such a claim, from mild anxiety, to psychological breakdown, was discovered within the interview sample:

Leading a double-life is a constant conflict within myself and it affects me quite badly sometimes. I don't really know what I want at the moment and it's begun to affect my health. I drink and smoke to excess and sometimes I can't sleep at night. I don't know who I can talk to about it, so I'm seeing a psychiatrist next month.

(R23)

Thirty-six per cent (n = 13) of respondents felt that the effort required in the maintenance of their heterosexual facade affected their efficiency at work:

Well, I had a nervous breakdown so I suppose it probably has put a lot of stress on me, although clearly I haven't always realised it and that may have affected my judgements from time to time.

(R32)

Thirty-nine per cent (n = 14) of respondents who had experienced 'steady' relationships felt that their situation affected either: the prospect of a long-term relationship,

The longest I managed a relationship for was six months and it was a lot of pressure because it snowballs. One lie leads to another and before you know it you're out of your depth.

(R37)

their partners,

My partner hates the police now for what it's done to me.

(R06)

or the quality of relationship with their partner,

I can't let them answer the phone if they're at my house (where we keep the curtains drawn) and if we're about to be seen together by a colleague then we have to quickly part company ...

(R27)

Conclusions

Of the two major roles/identities pertaining to the non-heterosexual police officer, either in isolation may or may not prove burdensome on its own merits. In combination, however, some degree of conflict is predicted. Both roles are stigmatized: as police officers individuals court rejection by the community at large, and particularly by some sections of the lesbian and gay communities as '(fascist) pigs', whilst in their lives at work they may be (at minimum) ridiculed by their colleagues as 'queers' or 'lezzies' where their sexual orientation is known or suspected. As such, it may be difficult to find stability in life and there are numerous instances of officers suffering breakdowns and having to leave the Service as a result.[10] That homosexuality is denigrated within the police structure is germane to the gay or lesbian police officer. As Atchley (1982) has pointed out, self-esteem is lowered and anxiety is raised, when disparity exists between a person's 'ideal self' – what they would like to be, and their 'real self' – what they know themselves to be (self-concept).[11]

In conclusion, I have tried to suggest that 'becoming deviant' is, in any form, a particularly difficult problem for police officers. As such, it is not necessary that the individual be classified as truly 'deviant' in order to attract attention. Plummer (1975, p.8) records his preference for the terms 'differentiation' or 'variation' over 'deviant', and these are useful in the current context to convey the notion that simply failing to conform is often sufficient to cause irritation. This 'conceptual conservatism' in police officers has been well documented. McInnes asserts:

> The true copper's characteristic, if the truth be known, is ... an ingrained conservatism, and almost desperate love of the conventional. It is untidiness, disorder, the unusual, that a copper disapproves of most of all: Hence his profound dislike of people ... doing anything that cannot be safely predicted.

(McInnes, 1962, p.74, reported in Skolnick, 1966)

It has been alleged that declining membership of the station's 'tea-club' or refusing to attend post-duty drinking sessions are good examples of behaviour likely to lead to disapproval (R32). More specifically, however, I have attempted to highlight some of the factors that go towards ensuring that ownership of a non-heterosexual identity within the police structure is both complex and demanding. The first of those factors is connected with the notion that membership of any highly regulated organization which has, as part of its own remit, the control of 'sexual deviance' is likely to result in the defamation of atypical sexualities at an organizational and thus, by extension, at a personal level. In addition, whilst crises of 'ambivalent identity' are suffered by many non-heterosexuals who are learning to accept their variation, proscriptions against their orientation are often subtle, implied, and indirect, whereas the explicitness of the collective police judgement on homosexuality, the machismo sub-culture, and the manifest discrepant status of homosexual activity in British law (with its related police activity) means that in trying to come to terms with a non-heterosexual orientation, many gay, lesbian, and bisexual police officers are liable to find themselves conducting multiple existences and many suffer profound psychological crises as a result. The interview data demonstrate that the passing of non-heterosexually identified officers in either life-sphere is liable to present substantial risks to: (a) their mental health, (b) their ability to function comfortably within the police environment and give maximum consideration to their duties, and (c) their ability to form or maintain satisfying personal relationships:

> I just could no longer combine the two variables of 'police' and 'gay'; I could no longer live as that schizoid entity ... I suffered some kind of a mental breakdown and in the end got retired on the grounds of ill health. It was a refusal to be a gay policeman which got me. I could be one or the other but not both. I suppose it was a poor career move really.

(R12)

Notes

1   As a result of recommendations by the Select Committee on the Armed Forces, the Conservative Government announced in June 1992 that homosexual activity of a kind that is legal in civilian law will cease to constitute an offence under Service law (Bill to follow). The provisions of the Sexual Offences Act of 1967 had not previously been extended to the above bodies. The Merchant Navy will require separate legislation.

2   I have introduced and made some use of the term 'non-heterosexual' in this paper in addition to: (a) the term 'homosexual' which excludes the bisexual (and is often perceived as excluding the female), and (b) the rather cumbersome 'lesbian, gay and bisexual'. The term 'non-heterosexual' is also intended to be more specific in referring primarily to sexual *orientation,* thus avoiding connotations with issues *of identity* inherent in terms like 'gay' and 'lesbian'. The aforementioned terms are still employed, however, in keeping with current practice. In addition, the word 'gay' is intended (unless clearly inapplicable) to encompass women in keeping with the terminology used by the female respondents in this study, although the word 'lesbian' is also used with some frequency.

3   The expression 'the Job' enjoys almost universal usage as a synonym for 'the police organization' hence, throughout this paper the word 'job', where it refers to 'the police service', has been typeset with a capital 'J'.

4   The figure of 12.5 per cent represents the total proportion of female officers in London's (28,500) Metropolitan Police (figures for 31 March 1991). The six women who took part in the research represent 16.5 per cent of the sample. When one adds to this number the lesbian officers who were known to the author but who were not interviewed, the effect is to lend weight to the observations of R14 regarding the disproportionate number of lesbians in the police.

5   Nearly 78 per cent (n = 28) of respondents in this research believed that an 'out' homosexual officer would not have the same career prospects as a heterosexual officer.

6   In the case of males, [at time of original publication] sexual activity must take place between no more than two consenting adults who have both attained the age of 21 years, in private, and neither participant may be a member of the armed forces or merchant navy. There is no legislation in this country dealing specifically with female homosexuality.

7   See the work of Lewin, 1948, Thomas, 1971, and Nobles, 1973 for the development of self-hate with regard to the Jewish and black communities.

8   It is conceivable that in the case of the gay police officer, more than one double-life might be entertained. It is clear that an officer who is married but not 'out' to his/her spouse will be adding a further dimension to their difficulties. Although no such instance was encountered in this research, in Humphreys' (1970) sample, 54 per cent of men were found to be married.

9   Increasing numbers of officers are now 'out' in both spheres (i.e., known to be a police officer on the gay scene and known to be gay/lesbian at work) either by choice or otherwise, thereby negating the need to live separate lives. The lack of an equal opportunities statement in most forces with regard to sexual orientation however, ensures that most officers remain extremely cautious about revealing their sexual orientation.

10 Further illustrations of officers suffering from discrimination, prejudice, psychological strain, and breakdown are described in Burke (1993b).

11 In reporting on the appointment of the Queen's Police Officer, Commander Michael Trestrail subsequent to his tabloid exposure in 1982, Lord Bridge commented: 'I think there is an undoubted conflict in his character between the image of himself which he has succeeded so well in projecting in his public and professional life and *which he would like to live up to* and his taste for casual and promiscuous homosexual encounters *which he himself recognised as* sordid and degrading' (Bridge, 1982, p.12; *emphasis added*).

References

Adlam, R.C.A. (1981) 'The police personality', in Pope D.W. and Weiner, D.L. (eds) *Modern Policing*, London, Croom Helm.

Altman, D. (ed.) (1989) *Which Homosexuality*, London, GMP.

Anthony, R., Chief Inspector, Metropolitan Police (1991) *Homosexuality in the Police: An Investigation of the Requirement for the Metropolitan Police Service to Include the Words 'Sexual Orientation' in its Statement of Equal Opportunities Policy*, MA thesis, Faculty of Social (Police) Studies, University of Exeter.

Atchley, R.C. (1982) 'The aging self', *Psychotherapy: Theory, Research, and Practice*, vol.19, no.4, pp.388–96.

Banton, M. (1964) *The Policeman in the Community*, London, Tavistock.

Bayley, B.H. (1974) 'The policeman and the homosexual: encounters and attitudes', *New Sociology*, vol.1, no.4, pp.18–52.

Bennett, M. (1991) 'Divided loyalties', *Police Review*, pp.164–5.

Berzon, B. (ed.) (1979) 'Developing a positive gay identity', in *Positively Gay*, Millbrae, CA, Celestial Arts.

Bridge, N.C., Baron of Harwich (1982) *Report of an Inquiry by the Right Honourable Lord Bridge of Harwich into the Appointment as The Queen's Police Officer, and the Activities, of Commander Trestrail : to Determine whether Security was Breached or Put at Risk, and Advise whether in Consequence any Change in Security Arrangements is Necessary or Desirable*, London, HMSO.

Brooks, T.R. (1965) 'New York's finest', *Commentary*, August, vol.40, pp.29–30.

Burke, M. (1992) 'Cop culture and homosexuality', *Police Journal*, vol.65, no.1, pp.30–9.

Burke, M. (1993a) 'Homosexuality in the British police', PhD thesis, Department of Sociology, University of Essex.

Burke, M. (1993b) *Coming Out of the Blue: British Police Officers Talk about their Lives in 'The Job' as Gays, Lesbians and Bisexuals*, London, Cassell.

Chesshyre, R. (1989) *The Force: Inside the Police*, London, Pan.

Derbyshire, P. (1990) 'Gays and the police', *Police Review*, pp.1144–50.

Foucault, M. (1980) *The History of Sexuality. Volume 1: An Introduction*, New York, Vintage.

Galloway, B. (ed.) (1983) *Prejudice and Pride,* London, Routledge and Kegan Paul.

Goffman, E. (1963) *Stigma: Notes on the Management of Spoiled Identity,* Harmondsworth, Penguin.

Graef, R. (1989) *Talking Blues,* London, Fontana.

Hoch, P. (1979) 'Masculinity as the avoidance of homosexuality', in Hoch, P. (ed.) *White Hero Black Beast: Racism, Sexism and the Mask of Masculinity,* London, Pluto Press.

Holdaway, S. (1979) *The British Police,* London, Edward Arnold.

Humphreys, L. (1970) *Tearoom Trade,* London, Duckworth.

Jacobs, P. (1966) *Prelude to Riot,* New York, Vintage.

Lewin, K. (1948) *Resolving Social Conflicts,* New York, Harper.

McInnes, C. (1962) *Mr Love and Justice,* London, New English Library.

McIntosh, M. (1968) 'The homosexual role', *Social Problems,* vol.16, pp.182–92.

Niederhoffer, A. (1967) *Behind the Shield,* New York, Doubleday.

Nobles, W.W. (1973) 'Psychological research and the black self-concept: a critical review', *Journal of Social Issues,* vol.29, pp.11–31.

O'Neill, S. (1990) 'Are the police looking the other way?', *The Independent,* 18 December.

Plummer, K. (1975) *Sexual Stigma,* London, Routledge and Kegan Paul.

Police Review (1991) 'Gay officer's association set up to fight discrimination', *Police Review,* January, pp.104–5.

Policy Studies Institute (PSI) (1983) *Police and People in London,* vols i–iv, London, PSI.

Reiner, R. (1985) *The Politics of the Police,* Sussex, Wheatsheaf.

Skolnick, J. (1966) *Justice Without Trial,* New York, Wiley.

Swerling, J.B. (1978), 'A study of police officers' values and their attitudes towards homosexual officers', dissertation, California School of Professional Psychology, Los Angeles.

Thomas, C.W. (1971) *Boys No More,* Beverly Hills, CA, Glencoe Press.

Weeks, J. (1985) *Sexuality and its Discontents: Meaning, Myths and Modern Sexualities,* London, Routledge.

Weinberg, M.S. and Williams, C.J. (1974) *Male Homosexuals: Their Problems and Adaptations,* New York, Penguin.

Wheeler, G. (1990) 'Officers form group to reach out to gay police', *Now* (Toronto), vol.10, no.14, pp.6–12 and 17.

(Source: Burke, 1994, pp.192–203)

Appendix 4.4

Barlow: 'From fiddle factors to networks of collusion: charting the waters of small business crime'

Abstract. Small business crime has been largely ignored in American criminology: studies of 'non-traditional' crime have focused mainly on corporate crime or on the misdeeds of employees pursuing personal gain. This paper calls for criminologists to redirect their efforts toward the systematic study of small business crime. In particular, it advocates in-depth qualitative studies that explore small business culture and opportunity structures, and that examine the networks of collusion that subvert the legitimate economy. The paper concludes with illustrations from an 'own story' currently being shared with the author by a small businessman who participated for five years in an urban crime network that infiltrated the redistributive economy.

A search of the 'white collar' crime literature shows that criminologists on both sides of the Atlantic have largely ignored small business crime, favouring instead the study of corporate crime or the misdeeds of employees pursuing personal gain. As a result, there is no coherent approach to the subject, nor does there appear to be any systematic attempt to develop one. Yet there are at least four good reasons for criminologists to engage in serious investigation of small business crime:

1   *The cost of small business crime.* One of the few things that criminologists seem to agree on is that the costs of white collar crime in terms of money, health and damage to social institutions are far in excess of those linked to so-called 'ordinary' crimes (see Barlow, 1993, pp.224–27). Although unknown, the portion of this societal burden attributable to small business crime is unlikely to be trivial.

2   *Exploration of the 'hidden' or 'shadow' economy.* Intertwined with the legitimate and taxed economy is a hidden economy, comprised of a vast array of enterprises and exchange activities that escape official documentation and taxation. The role of small businesses in the formation, growth, and persistence of the hidden economy, and the interplay between legitimate and devious economic activity, are poorly documented and not well understood. Another intriguing problem concerns the process by which ostensibly law-abiding, responsible, working adults are attracted to the borderline of crime, and the reasons why some step over and others do not.

3   *Exploration of the boundaries and commonalities between legitimate and illegitimate enterprise.* For years, open-minded criminologists have regarded the distinction between 'underworld' and 'upperworld' as more fictive than real, yet exploration of the overlap and identification of common tracks has been fitful and rather cursory. Some of the best work has been done in the realm of organized crime, but there is still much to do. One obvious place to start is with entrepreneurial activity that straddles the boundary between legitimate and illegitimate enterprise and that draws participants into networks of collusion linking underworld and upperworld.

4   *The paucity of small business research in criminology.* This is all the more unfortunate because it is one obvious direction to go in assessing general theories of crime – theories purporting to explain a broad range of facts and that are not restricted to any one time or place. Gottfredson and Hirschi's (1990) recent contribution comes to mind, but other recent ventures in general theory also call for systematic research beyond the realm of common crimes (e.g., Braithwaite, 1989; Cohen and Machalek, 1988; and Machalek and Cohen, 1991).

Gottfredson and Hirschi's (1990; also 1987) work stands out because key elements of their general theory can be adequately assessed only through examination of crime in entrepreneurial settings. Among their arguments are these: that crime is more prevalent among those outside the occupational structure than among those in it; that the social and cultural milieux of organizations do not generate criminality among members who are not predisposed to it; that crimes are interchangeable among themselves as well as with analogous acts (e.g. eating between meals, accidents, smoking and drinking) that do not involve the use of force or fraud; that white-collar crimes are essentially the same as ordinary crimes – they are simple and easy to commit and provide direct and immediate gratification. It follows, Gottfredson and Hirschi argue, that white-collar offenders do not differ from ordinary criminals.

In short, if progress is to be made in explaining the many faces of crime, it is time that criminologists study the devious side of small business enterprise. My aim in this paper is to promote in-depth qualitative studies that build on research undertaken by Henry (1978), Klockars (1974), Steffensmeier (1986), Mars (1982), Tracy and Fox (1989) and Jesilow, Pontell and Geis (1993). These studies focus on small business culture and opportunity structures and they draw attention to *networks of collusion*, where I believe much is still to be learned.

Before turning to these features of the small business terrain, however, let me pose a working definition of small business crime. This will be followed by a brief discussion of some structural conditions that facilitate small business crime, after which I shall turn to the study of its more proximate causes and the qualitative research this necessitates.

Definitions. Interestingly, there appears to be no generally accepted definition of small business, let alone of small business crime. Rather than propose any permanent solution to the thorny issue of definition, I use the following as my working definition of small business:

> a small business is any company, firm, business, or economic enterprise owned and operated by sole proprietors or working partners (including family members) who directly supervise business activities and who personally authorize all transactions.

The most significant point in this definition is that ownership and operational control of a small business are in the hands of a single individual or working partnership. All transactions, legal or otherwise, that are undertaken in the name of the company or firm, or otherwise routinely by employees in the course of doing their jobs, are the result of decisions made by individuals with a proprietary interest in their consequences. To the extent that those consequences are beneficial to the business, they directly benefit the proprietor(s) and often (but not inevitably) the employees as well.

Consistent with this conceptualization, small business crime is defined as follows:

> Any illegal activity carried out by a small business or on behalf of one by its owners, agents or employees, for which penal sanctions exist and may be applied to the company, its owner(s), and/or its employees.

Embezzlement of company funds and various forms of employee pilfering for personal gain would not qualify as small business crime, but a host of other transgressions do, from consumer fraud, insider trading, tax evasion, and extortion to malpractice, bribery, and racketeering. 'Fronting' for ongoing criminal enterprises (e.g., fencing stolen property, drug trafficking, illegal gambling, money laundering) also qualify. This definition clearly anticipates some overlap with the traditionally-defined domain of organized crime.

Criminogenic factors affecting small business activity

In his PhD dissertation on the hidden economy in England, Stuart Henry (1978) concentrated on the amateur trade in cheap, often stolen goods, where things are bought and sold usually for little more than a beer or a promise of favors returned. Many participants in Henry's study were employed in small businesses, to be sure, and some were owners (Henry, 1978, p.24). On the whole, however, the picture Henry paints is of small businesses providing 'cover' or otherwise facilitating illegal trading by employees who are acting on their own behalf. The benefits, if any, to the businesses are left obscure.

Anthropologist Gerald Mars (1982) refocused Henry's analysis in two ways: first, by examining how different occupational structures facilitate or inhibit particular types of workplace crime, and second, by demonstrating that the attitudes and inclinations of workers support and encourage routinization of those illegal activities facilitated by the occupational structure in which they work.

Mars's work is especially interesting because he singles out small businesses and small businessmen as illustrative of a distinct type of occupation/worker: the 'Hawk'. Hawk *jobs,* Mars (1982) tells us, stress initiative, autonomy, competition, and control. Hawk *people* are described as follows:

> Hawks, like their feathered counterparts, are individualists ... Their aim is 'to make it' ... Hawks ... are independent; swooping to their opportunities. energetic, adaptable, and resourceful ... [E]veryone is free to make his *own* way ... In this type of job entrepreneurial frontier principles make fellow travellers of small businessmen and big fixers, of the more independent professionals and the most successful managers and executives. All share certain attitudes: the most common are a resistance to external constraints and a high value placed on independence. Our small businessman is, therefore, typically and almost by definition a hawk.

> (Mars, 1982, pp.42–3)

Small business crimes stem from and reinforce the autonomy and entrepreneurialism central to hawk occupations. Tax fiddles are the archetypal offense. One of Mars's informants describes a simple, seemingly trivial form of small business tax evasion:

> We fiddle part of our workers' wages. All the very small businesses that I know have to be in on this kind of fiddle. If you employ someone and he earns below the amount that allows him to get the maximum supplement as a low wage-earner – then you make sure he gets the supplement. You pay him just enough to qualify for the maximum and you make the rest of his wages up in cash. This is possible because we've got a lot coming through the till.
>
> (Mars, 1982, p.40)

Cash is the key here, as it is in other common tax fiddles such as avoidance of sales tax. Cash transactions by-pass bookkeeping and therefore are difficult to monitor and trace.

In conjunction with by-passing the checks and controls of the official economy, small businessmen may become involved in networks of collusion. Besides supporting the shadow economy, these networks bridge the worlds of compliance and crime while providing opportunities and incentives for a wide range of illegal activities. I shall have more to say on networks of collusion in the next section.

Mars's anthropology of workplace crime identified an extensive list of routine crimes located throughout the occupational structure, from shortchanging customers to tax avoidance to kickback schemes. In addition, Mars uncovered 'fiddle-prone' factors, things that 'so structure economic activity as to facilitate the regular payment of a significant part of people's total reward in the form of fiddles ...' According to Mars (p.138), 'these factors depend on the underlying structural differences of knowledge, control, power, and ability held by some groups over others.'

Consider, for instance, businesses in high traffic areas catering primarily to the tourist and convention trade. Such contexts are fiddle-prone because they involve 'passing trade': the parties to a transaction typically meet only once. Furthermore, because business customers are usually strangers in the community, possibly also of different class, race, gender or ethnicity than 'regulars', the conventional morality governing exchange is suspended or modified, thus increasing the likelihood of fraudulent behavior.

Another fiddle factor favoring small business crime in the retail and service economy results from the widespread ignorance of customers regarding what they need and don't need, how to satisfy a need, and what to pay. This imbalance in knowledge is often exacerbated by an imbalance in power, exemplified when the customer cannot for one reason or another go elsewhere. Automobile repair and maintenance are prime settings for fraud (see Tracy and Fox, 1989) though the fraudulent opportunities represented by these fiddle factors are not lost on doctors, lawyers, dentists, and a host of other professionals (see Jesilow, Pontell and Geis, 1993; Vaughan, 1983).

Passing trade and the imbalance in knowledge and power probably tip the market economy toward crime independently of the supply and demand for goods and services. Yet supply and demand, and the levels of business competition associated with them, are also potential fiddle factors. When demand for products and services is low or erratic, or when supply is excessive, competition grows and rates of business failure increase. Under these conditions, the gatekeepers who control the flow of business opportunities as well as a firm's access to them, and the entrepreneurs who need the business, are encouraged to form collusive relationships through which industrial espionage, bribery, kickbacks, and other corrupt practices are facilitated. It is interesting to note in this connection that during the

Reagan years, the rate of business failures skyrocketed, from 42 per 10,000 businesses in 1980 to 120 in 1986 [US Bureau of the Census, 1990, p.530]; unfortunately, appropriate data do not exist to show whether there was a corresponding jump in business crime, but the foregoing suggests what the hypothesis would be.

If gatekeepers facilitate crime in a competitive market economy, this role is probably even more prominent in the *redistributive economy* which deals with the collection and disbursement of taxes. In the United States, federal contracts with small businesses are worth over $25 billion annually, and this is only part of the story; contracts from state and local governments, outright grants of various sorts, and certification, licensing, and other work regulation should also be added in. In relations with small businesses, the gatekeepers of the annual torrent of public funds hold a powerful hand which is made even more powerful, of course, during hard times when many businesses are struggling.

If the incentives for racketeering and corruption are greater during hard times, the risks are less. There are at least three reasons for this: (1) economic decline results in reduced enforcement resources; (2) consequently, the enforcers themselves feel increasingly vulnerable, and are more susceptible to temptation; and (3) economic declines affect decisions about where to direct enforcement efforts.

The third point is documented in a recent American survey of district attorneys. Apparently, these officials made greater efforts to control business crime when the economy improved. Even though the research in question focused on the prosecution of corporate crime, the following observation surely applies equally well to small business crime: '[w]hen general economic conditions are good communities may perceive less threat from street crime and be able to afford greater control of corporate crime' (Benson, Cullen, and Maakestad, 1990, p.21).

Of course, corruption does not disappear just because there is plenty of business to be had. Consider the case of Baltimore County, Maryland, during the 1960s. The county population was growing rapidly; huge amounts of public money were being spent on schools, sewers, and streets; zoning decisions and construction permits were being issued at a growing pace. Contractors, architects, engineers and other firms routinely kicked back five percent to county officials in exchange for lucrative contracts and other favorable decisions (Simon and Eitzen, 1993, p.215). Regardless of the state of an economy, concentrations of economic resources provide lucrative criminal opportunities for those with access to them, and it is often difficult, if not simply bad for business, for entrepreneurs to resist them (for more on this, see Braithwaite, 1990; Cohen and Machalek, 1988).

Finally, there is (in America, at least) the criminogenic impact of machine politics. Referring once again to the Baltimore County experience, Simon and Eitzen (1993, p.215) observe that '[t]he practice of kickbacks was not new. In fact, it was a time-honored Maryland custom.' As in many other jurisdictions across America, local politics had long been dominated by the party machine. The resulting symbiotic relationship between corrupt urban politicians, organized crime, and the business community has been documented quite extensively (see, e.g., Hailer, 1990; Chambliss, 1988; and Tarr, 1967).

Historian Joel Tarr (1967) elaborates on the entrepreneurial aspects of urban machine politics with this characterization of the political boss:

> The typical urban boss was a man who regarded politics as a business and who used his power for personal and party gain. He was a businessman whose chief stock in trade was the goods of the political world – influence, laws, government grants, and franchises – which he utilized to make a private profit. In short, he was a 'political entrepreneur.'

(p.55)

And on Chicago bosses in particular:

> They sympathized with the values of the business community; they admired and emulated the big businessman. Their relationship with the business community, while it resulted in mutual profit, was symbiotic in values as well as economics.

(p.57)

Tarr suggests that while the entrepreneurial spirit was born of humble origins – most machine bosses rose from poor and immigrant backgrounds – it was exploited best during boom years when 'honest graft' could flourish. In Chicago, during the period 1890 to 1910, for example, city and county bosses had a proprietary interest in construction companies holding millions of dollars in public works contracts (Tarr, 1967, pp.62–3). These businesses were a lucrative side-line to their official duties. Equally important, business ownership helped blur the distinction between the interests of the public and those of the business community, and it cemented profitable alliances between individual businessmen and the political machine.

Daniel Bell (1960, p.147) has argued, furthermore, that organized crime often functions as a stabilizing influence during periods of economic uncertainty. This is particularly true in highly competitive local products markets, which have been dominated by small businesses, with 'no single force other than the industrial racketeer ... strong enough to stabilize the industry.'

To summarize the main points of the preceding discussion, the 'fiddle factors' I have touched on – opportunity, the organization of work, unstable economic conditions, imbalance of power, ability, and control, favorable enforcement strategies, and the symbiotic relationship between business, politics and organized crime – are structural conditions that facilitate small business crime. In the redistributive economy, particularly, opportunities for criminal deception, bureaucratic structures, inadequate enforcement, and the culture and organization of local politics create a powerful criminogenic environment.

Crime networks

One important feature of the criminogenic environment of small business touched on earlier consists of networks of collusion that organize and promote criminal enterprise. While it is true that a small business may be actively engaged in crime without hooking up with others for that purpose – tax evasion can be accomplished in private, for example, and short-changing customers does not require confederates outside the business – many business crimes do require collusion and collusion itself promotes crime in various ways: for example, providing normative support, offering protection, disseminating information, and forging connections between participants.

The enumeration of these aspects of collusive networks points up a rather obvious fact: crime networks are largely indistinguishable from networks of legitimate exchange, and that makes them all the more insidious and difficult to investigate. Indeed, as I emphasize below, crime networks and networks of legitimate exchange are superimposed, each feeding off the other as well. As opportunity theory predicts, noncriminal opportunities create opportunities for crime, and vice versa.

With few exceptions (e.g., Henry, 1978; Chambliss, 1988; Steffensmeier, 1986), crime networks are largely unstudied by criminologists. Chambliss's (1988) analysis of the rackets in Seattle documents an extensive network of collusion, involving perhaps as many as 1,000 individuals. The network was financed by jewelers, attorneys, realtors, businessmen, industrialists, contractors, and bankers; it was organized and largely controlled by an assortment of businessmen, politicians, and law-enforcement officials; and working the street were hundreds of gamblers, pimps, drug dealers, loansharks, bookmakers, and prostitutes.

As described by Steffensmeier (1986), fence 'Sam Goodwin' maintained an extensive network of contacts in and outside 'American City'. His connections included other fences; good burglars and small-time thieves, bikers and truck hijackers; employee thieves and citizen pilferers; out-of-town merchants, syndicate businessmen, auction houses and second-hand dealers, and walk-in customers at his store; and also legal officials, from bondsmen to police to magistrates.

These studies provide striking evidence of the extensiveness of urban crime networks and, equally, of the overlapping of compliance and crime. In addition, they clearly refute the idea that there are two separate worlds of compliance and crime. Both worlds are so intricately bound together that one cannot be understood apart from the other. Quantitative criminology, especially that focusing on common crimes and on criminal careers, has reified a false distinction. Furthermore, while a person or event may perhaps be described as essentially compliant with the law or essentially criminal, the networks of which they are one part are both compliant *and* criminal. The tendency to separate criminal exchange from legitimate exchange leaves the overlap, and thus the complete network, unexamined.

It is precisely because networks of collusion (e.g., on-the-side trading, bid-rigging conspiracies, drug trafficking) and of compliance (e.g., legitimate trading) are superimposed one on the other that stories from the inside are indispensable to understanding small business crime (and white-collar crime generally – see Jackall, 1988; Reichman, 1990; Simpson, 1990; Vaughan, 1983, 1990). Furthermore, the social and moral order of exchange relations among network participants – concerning power and control, distributive justice, rights, understandings, and obligations, and membership itself – are *ongoing* matters of discovery and negotiation, not conveniently frozen in time and space and readily observable from the outside. There is no reason to believe that collusive networks are any different in this regard.

Yet these observations and those of the preceding section tell us little about how individual small businesses find their way into criminal activities, nor about the dynamics of collusive networks – how they emerge, prosper, and spread; how they support, influence, and control the actions of members, and how they collapse. Nor do they address the 'sensual dynamics of crime' (Katz, 1988, p.5), the seductions and compulsions that help us understand what small businessmen are trying to do when they commit crime. If we are to understand small business crime we need answers to these questions as well. To find them, criminologists must turn to the proximate causes of illegal behavior, that is, the causes closest to the decisions of people actually committing small business crime. One promising strategy is the use of autobiographical accounts by small business employers and employees who have participated in crime networks.

Needed: autobiographical accounts

As Bennett (1981) reminds readers, oral histories helped establish sociology, and prominent among them were the 'own stories' of delinquents compiled by Clifford Shaw at the University of Chicago. These human documents took Shaw inside deviant subcultures and detailed the everyday experience of being an urban delinquent. Over the ensuing years, oral histories and in-depth, loosely-guided, interview versions have been used to document the doing of crime and delinquency and its socially constructed reality as only insiders can know it.

If autobiographical accounts have been a prominent feature of delinquency research since the early days, the same cannot be said of their role in criminological research generally, and certainly not when it comes to business crime. Katz (1988, p.313) argues that with 'isolated exceptions' traditional research into white-collar crime has taken the form of muckraking from the outside, and in consequence little is known of the 'internal feel' of offending. 'This absence of naturalistic, autobiographical, participant-observational data,' Katz (1988, p.319) goes on, 'is itself an important clue to the distinctive emotional quality of white-collar crime … [White-collar criminals] rarely publicly confess; when they do confess, they virtually never confess with the sustained attention to detail that characterizes, for example, almost any mugging related by an ordinary, semiliterate hustler …'

In autobiographical research, of course, the issue of trust as a methodological problem is bound to surface, and this deserves a comment. Trust is mostly about the quality of the relationship between informant and audience. It boils down to this: can those witnessing an event or hearing a story unfold believe it as presented? Aside from the fact that the telling itself is part of the event or story, and cannot therefore be separated from it, the researcher must achieve a confident level of trust that the facts are essentially as presented. No researcher can ever be sure and that uncertainty dogs all attempts to uncover the lived experience of crime. The corroboration of other participants is a welcome commodity, but one that is often unavailable, and in any case cannot remove all uncertainty. Documentary evidence such as police reports may corroborate the telling of a past event, as a set of facts, but they are certainly not independent of the event's after-the-fact reconstruction by participants, so the problem of uncertainty remains. In their research with corporate executives, Clinard and Yeager (1979) took elaborate steps to establish trust, as did Jackall (1988) in outstanding research reported in *Moral Mazes*.

The informants used by Henry (1978) and by Mars (1982) consisted of their friends, fellow workers, neighbors, relatives, university colleagues and, in Henry's case, the local hairdresser. Neither author dwells on the issue of trust (though Mars tried to corroborate information) and the inference is that neither author thought it particularly problematic. In the end, in all these works, uncertainty remains, if not for the author then for the reader.

The salience of trust as a methodological issue is likely to increase the greater the seriousness of misdeeds and the higher the occupational status of informants. Furthermore, when the small business crook on the fringes of the underworld tells about bribery, kickbacks, racketeering, and other corruption the story is about collusion in the commission of crimes carrying potentially lengthy sentences. At the least, there are risks for the teller from co-conspirators who cannot be left out of the story but who do not want to be exposed.

An informant's motive for telling confounds the issue of trust. Revenge may be involved, or self-preservation, or a desire to 'set the record straight,' or to simply get it off one's chest. There may be a mixture of motives, as in the case of a small business informant this author is currently working with. His identity had already been exposed in the newspaper and during various trials, so he was not afraid of being identified. He had already survived three botched attempts on his life since going public, and that had made him all the more eager to tell his story and to name names.

Indeed, revenge had played an important role in his decision to become a police informant (before I met him), but it was not the only motive. Self preservation was also a factor. A series of newspaper articles on corruption and racketeering had made things hot for the authorities, and they felt pressed to do something. As was the case with the Seattle crime network described by Chambliss (1988), aggressive newspaper reporting had cracked the cement binding network participants. My informant went to some of his network partners seeking help and was brushed aside; he concluded he was being sacrificed and began immediately to make clandestine tapes of conversations with other principals. If he was going down he was taking others with him. But in the end he decided to make the first move as the only sure way to protect himself – he contacted federal authorities who then helped him bug conversations over a period of nine months. These tapes became the key evidence at future trials, and they provide verbatim corroboration of the informant's account of many events and relationships.

My small businessman informant was also angered over his treatment by federal authorities, especially the Internal Revenue Service, which confiscated much of his property and fined him thousands of dollars despite his cooperation with the FBI and the US Marshals' Service in what he thought was an agreement protecting him from federal prosecution. I have no doubt that he viewed his own story as a way of showing the world that, in the end, he was as much a victim as a criminal.

Autobiographical accounts of involvement in crime networks by participating small business personnel will shed important light on this neglected area of criminological research. The ideal strategy for studying networks of collusion includes in-depth interviews with present and past members as well as participant observation of network transactions as they occur. Needless to say, a single autobiographical account, even by a network principal, draws on experiences and constructs images from only one point of view. It is nevertheless a step in the right direction and the details will be rich. Furthermore, such accounts raise issues for future research. In the remaining section, I present a few illustrations from the autobiographical account of a small businessman with whom I am currently working.

Joining the network

Networks of collusion emerge tentatively and awkwardly. They may also take years to evolve into anything like a persistent arrangement. For this reason it is probably rare that members of an established network know how it first got started. There may well be more fortuity than design in its origins, of course, and this characterization apparently describes how many small businessmen get involved in collusion in the first place. Chambliss (1988, p.85) provides the following illustration from one of his Seattle informants:

> I met Jay (P) at the Rainier Club. We liked each other. We both played sports in college and had a lot in common. We also liked to drink and horse around. Then one day he called and told me he knew of a possibility for turning a nice profit if I had some unused cash lying around. It was a perfectly natural thing. Businessmen are always doing things like that.

The informant invested money, doubled it in two months, later discovered that he had helped finance a heroin shipment, and recounts: 'naturally, I didn't want to ask too many questions with that kind of profit' (Chambliss, 1988, p.85).

Things were different for my informant; call him John Black. In the first place locals knew corruption was widespread at City Hall, and had been for decades. The moral environment was conducive to criminal conspiracies because that was the way things had always been run. Second, he had some contact with graft in his early business dealings. When he bought his business the purchase included existing contracts; on one job he found he was expected to send men over to remodel the mayor's garage and basement. Third, his decision to get involved was deliberate and planned:

> I got involved in the kickback system primarily because of survival I guess; but on the same token I was dealing with people who my uncles had been dealing with for a number of years, so I thought that was the system. I guess that's the way it works; in order to survive you deal. My uncles had always worked around the fringe, only the little jobs. They were not a part of the political system.

My small businessman-informant might be called a beleaguered victim of marginality (see Croall, 1989). After buying out his uncles' interest in the company, he discovered that construction contracts were unavailable to those who did not participate in the kickback scheme. Work of any sort was hard to come by in a city dominated by a small number of companies with ties to city hall. Furthermore, he found that he had to compete with one of the gatekeeper's relatives:

> I bid every job that came across ... I put together in a nine month period about fifty packages of bids and didn't get anything from anyone. Bids ran from $5,000 to $200,000 depending on the job ... Anyway, I was getting nowhere and I had bought some new equipment and had payments to make, so I was getting desperate.

> Since I knew from my earlier work and the activities of my uncles something of how the system worked, and I knew [the County Board Chairman] was holding the purse strings on the hospital job that was coming up, I went to [him] but since his brother-in-law ['W'] was [a competing bidder], he said he had to give the work to him, but if things picked up he would remember me 'cause he knew my family.'

The County Board Chairman was as good as his word, for John Black got a phone call a week or two later inviting him and his wife to an ice-hockey game. The call was from a local architect whom he had earlier met while picking up blueprints for a job he wanted to bid on. John recalled the evening:

> I was slightly suspicious, but prepared to have a good night out with the architect. We went to his house and then drove together to the game. It was all very nice idle chit-chat before the game. We met his daughters, were shown around the house and all the usual things. At the game I met ['MC'] a man I didn't know. At intermission we all chatted and after the game was wound up at Trader Vics [an expensive restaurant].

John recalls that he tried to pay but the others insisted on paying for everything, saying he was their guest. A second night that same week John and his wife were invited to another game. John says he can't afford it and doesn't feel good being a freeloader but his protestations are swept aside, and he and his wife go along. This time specifics about the hospital are brought up. John learns more about the 'system' and is invited into the network.

> It turned out they were experiencing difficulties with various things. ['W'] was not playing the game … not kicking back ten percent to the mayor, who was head of the hospital board and heir apparent to [the County Board chairman]. ['W'] said 'to hell with them, I've never kicked back, and I'm not going to now.'

> I was very excited; I can see I'm about to approach the inner circles of the organization. That evening we wined and dined. Later we went for coffee to MC's home; very nice. We all got very chummy, getting sloshed, and MC again relates that ['W'] is not kicking back.

John finds out that his new acquaintances want him to be the bagman handling the kickback money from a large electrical contractor in another state 'that did not want to get involved in the nitty gritty and were looking to find a way to launder money from the company back to the mayor in cash.' The company 'owed' $4,500 and their agent arranged that John would be paid for work he did not do and then he would pass the money on to the architect for delivery to the mayor. John knew it was all illegal, but he was promised work on future projects, and agreed to take on the job 'since there was no way to get work in [the] county without participating in kickback schemes.'

Joining the inner circle

John returned from the second hockey game feeling he had scored in a big way and was 'on my way' even though he made no money out of the deal. When he took the $4,500 kickback money to the architect as instructed he was invited to meet the mayor. The two went over to the mayor's house.

> The mayor takes the money, counts it, and the mayor's secretary is right there. She doesn't bat an eyelid. He then says 'Do you think John can help us stop these guys fucking with our money?'

> I found out that ['B.B.'] was supposed to be the bagman; ['A.D.'] was supposed to pay and didn't; ['A.F.J.'] was supposed to be paying, and wasn't. ['B.B.'] was in between, the bagman. The others contended they were paying and that ['B.B.'] was not delivering it where it was supposed to go. It got to be a pissing contest between ['B.B.'] and these subcontractors.

We go out to the mayor's car and he pulls out a Thompson submachine gun and says 'This is what I've got to stop people from fucking with our money.'

John decides he's getting in deep. 'I couldn't believe that these people were going to kill anyone, but I didn't know. The mayor also said that if people didn't take him seriously there were others on the Teamster's [union] payroll who will do the work if necessary.'

John is impressed; he believes they all mean business, and he decides to take B.B.'s place as the bagman. 'I knew I was now in the rackets.' Other companies now give John envelopes with money to deliver around town. Within a few days his company also gets work at the hospital site.

I asked John why he thought he was chosen for the trusted role of bagman, which brought him into direct criminal contact with both gatekeepers and businesses. He put it down to a number [of] things: his reputation as 'steady;' he could keep his mouth shut; he didn't drink and others did; and the network was desperately in need of someone. It turned out that John got nothing from the contracts and he was expected to kick back his own ten percent from any work he got in the future. The gatekeepers had a good thing going.

Escalation

Word quickly got around that John was the new bagman. He kept track of all his transactions in a little notebook; he estimates that in the period of one month he paid the mayor around $25,000 in connection with the hospital job.

But his own fortunes turned on the development of his relationship with the architect who had invited him to the hockey games. He gradually became involved in all projects the architect was working on. Federal construction money was pouring into the area, and John's company began to prosper. He also joined other members of the network in forming corporations specifically for the purpose of rigging bids on projects. Most of them were hidden partners. Since the same people owned the companies bidding on the same contracts, they were assured of winning. To get money through the Model Cities program they installed a local Black man as a front, and John's own company qualified for minority contracts because it was in his wife's name.

Within six months of joining the network John's companies are doing jobs for the hospital board, which always included a kickback, divided equally among the five board members. He also did city hall construction work in two communities, built a public swimming pool and a skating rink, and became heavily involved in work on school district projects. For these he kicked back directly to the school board president.

By now John's job as a bagman is producing its own profits: five to ten percent of all the money he handled. He becomes a small-time moneylender as well, further broadening his role in the network and, he thought, increasing his status in the eyes of the inner circle. A lot of partying goes on, and John walks around with $2,000 in his pocket at all times.

Network regulars

John believes that ten people formed the inner circle of the network: the county board chairman, the mayors of two cities, the president of the levee district, a township supervisor and school board member, the school board president, two plumbing contractors, a supplier, and the architect who had invited him to the hockey games. Yet John insists there was no kingpin. 'Everyone who handled a piece of paper got a kickback so it would flow.'

From this inner circle the network spread out across state lines, and even reached New York City, 1,200 miles away. Within the immediate area, John had personal criminal dealings with, or knew the network association of, 63 individuals – including a nun on the school board. (John likes to point out 'If you can corrupt a nun you can corrupt anybody'.) And more network members were identified through court testimony and subsequent federal and state investigations. Thirty-two local companies, most of them small businesses, were subpoenaed to testify.

Collapse of the network

As I mentioned earlier, aggressive reporting by a local newspaper was instrumental in bringing about the federal investigation that eventually broke up the network. The reporter who pursued the story was contacted by 'W', the brother-in-law of the county board chairman. Though nepotism had worked well for him, 'W' swore that he had never participated in kickbacks or bidrigging. John used to work for him and confirms that claim.

According to John, 'W' came to the office of 'RAP', one of the companies in which John was a hidden partner, seeking specifications for a job he planned to bid on. The secretary told him she would have to check with John before giving them out. This was not the correct procedure. 'I'm not supposed to have anything to do with RAP. That's collusion,' John points out. 'W' tipped off the local reporter who then began asking questions around town, and the local State's Attorney – himself a member of the network according to John – had no choice but to begin his own 'investigation.'

Tipped off to the State's Attorney's investigation by a mutual friend and network member, who told him it would cost $25,000 to get the official investigation dropped, John went to the inner circle and asked them to contribute $5,000 each. They refused. John then 'wired' his office and telephone.

> So when [the mutual friend] came back I recorded him; made about three recordings of him. I called [the state] organized crime strike force and they took it to the US Attorney. I went along with them. The FBI was brought in. Their sole purpose at that time was to catch [the State's Attorney] in the act of collecting $25,000 from me.

John made the mistake of telling his own attorney that he was making tapes and word got out, so the state's attorney did not take the pay-off. After the state's attorney bowed out of the payoff, the FBI asked if John was interested in recording for them. According to John, they promised him that his material would be used without anyone ever knowing its source. John agreed and recorded conversations between himself and other inner circle participants for eleven months. Finally, the case got too hot:

> I got shot at and then 'M' wanted me to have 'CJ' killed. That's what brought the whole case to a climax; it had to end there, as far as the undercover work.

Three years later, seventeen people had been indicted for crimes ranging from bribery, extortion, bid-rigging, and a variety of other corrupt practices. Fourteen were convicted, eleven spent time in prison, including the nun. John escaped conviction, but the IRS took his assets and his business collapsed. The architect who first brought John into the network was never indicted.

Summary

In this paper I have argued that relatively little criminological research has been undertaken on small business crime. That is surprising given the extent of small business activity and the many opportunities there are for unlawful behavior. When one looks at serious offending such as bid-rigging, bribery, extortion, and other activities that subvert the economic, political, and legal processes, the picture is even worse.

I believe that we need in-depth qualitative studies of small business crime to provide direction for a research agenda that would uncover the process by which small businesses are drawn into networks of collusion and describe in detail what happens thereafter. Through in-depth interviews and autobiographical accounts we can learn much about small business crime and the contexts in which it flourishes. I believe it is also essential that research on entrepreneurial crime be brought to bear on the postulates of the general theories now being advanced in the field of criminology.

I am also convinced that joint research ventures bringing academic criminologists and law enforcement experts together in the study of small business crime is another promising way to advance our knowledge and understanding of the problem. Network analysis is vital to effective prosecution of much business fraud, yet data on collusion compiled by police is rarely explored by researchers outside law enforcement, and this is a missed opportunity for criminology. Working together, academic criminologists and experts in the detection and prosecution of business crime can share theories, research methodologies, and data in the development of models and explanations that address both macro- and micro-level issues pertaining to small business crime. In this way, explanation and praxis are united in a constructive manner, each informing the other.

My own efforts in this direction are incomplete, but in this paper I have shared some of the images and experiences of a businessman with whom I have had many illuminating conversations. Much more is to be done. I hope this whets the appetites of my colleagues and draws more of us into explorations of this largely uncharted territory.

References

Barlow, H.D. (1991) 'Explaining crimes and analogous acts, or the unrestrained will grab at pleasure whenever they can', *Journal of Criminal Law and Criminology*, vol.82, pp.229–42.

Barlow, H.D. (1993) *Introduction to Criminology* (6th edn), New York, Harper Collins.

Bell, D. (1960) *The End of Ideology*, New York, Free Press.

Bennett, J. (1981) *Oral History and Delinquency*, Chicago, IL, University of Chicago Press.

Benson, M.L., Cullen, T.C. and Maakestad, W.J. (1990) 'Community context and the prosecution of corporate crime', Paper presented at the *Edwin H. Sutherland Conference on White-Collar Crime: 50 Years of Research and Beyond*, May 12–15, Indiana University.

Braithwaite, J. (1989) *Crime, Shame and Reintegration*, Cambridge, Cambridge University Press.

Braithwaite, J. (1990) 'Poverty, power and white-collar crime: Sutherland and three paradoxes of criminological theory', Paper presented at the *Edwin H. Sutherland Conference on White Collar Crime: 50 Years of Research and Beyond,* May 12–15, Indiana University.

Bureau of Justice Statistics (1992) *Sourcebook of Criminal Justice Statistics 1991,* Washington, DC, US Department of Justice.

Campbell, A. (1991) *The Girls in the Gang* (2nd edn), Oxford, Basil Blackwell.

Chambliss, W.J. (1988) *On the Take: From Petty Crooks to Presidents.* Bloomington, IN, Indiana University Press.

Clinard, M. B., Yeager, P.C., Brissette, J., Petrashek, D. and Harries, E. (1979) *Illegal Corporate Behavior,* Washington, DC, US Department of Justice.

Cohen, L.E. and Machalek, R. (1988) 'A general theory of expropriative crime: an evolutionary ecological approach', *American Journal of Sociology,* vol.94, pp.465–501.

Croall, H. (1989) 'Who is the white-collar criminal?', *British Journal of Criminology,* vol.29, pp.157–74.

Gottfredson, M.R. and Hirschi, T. (1990) *A General Theory of Crime,* Palo Alto, CA, Stanford University Press.

Haller, M.H. (1990) 'Policy gambling, entertainment, and the emergence of black politics: Chicago from 1900 to 1940', unpublished paper.

Henry, S. (1978) *The Hidden Economy: The Context and Control of Borderline Crime,* Oxford, Martin Robertson.

Jackall, R. (1988) *Moral Mazes: The World of Corporate Managers,* New York, Oxford University Press.

Jesilow, P., Pontell, H.N. and Geis, G. (1993) *Prescription for Profit,* Los Angeles, CA, University of California Press.

Katz, J. (1988) *Seductions of Crime: Moral and Sensual Attractions in Doing Evil,* New York, Basic Books.

Klockars, C.B. (1974) *The Professional Fence,* New York, Free Press.

Leonard, W.N. and Weber, M.G. (1970) 'Automakers and dealers: a study of crimogenic market forces', *Law and Society Review,* vol.4, pp.408–22.

Machalek, R. and Cohen, L.E. (1991) 'The nature of crime: is cheating necessary for competition?', *Human Nature,* vol.2, pp.215–33.

Mars, G. (1982) *Cheats at Work: An Anthropology of Workplace Crime,* London, Unwin Paperbacks.

Quinney, R. (1963) 'Occupational structure and criminal behavior: prescription violations by retail pharmacists', *Social Problems,* vol.11, pp.179–83.

Reichman, N. (1990) 'Moving backstage: uncovering the role of compliance in regulating securities trading', Paper presented at the *Edwin H. Sutherland Conference on White-Collar Crime: 50 years of Research and Beyond,* May 12–15, Indiana University.

Simon, D.R. and Eitzen, S.D. (1993) *Elite Deviance* (4th edn), Boston, Allyn and Bacon.

Simpson, S.S. (1990) 'Corporate crime deterrence and corporate control policies: views from the inside', Paper presented at the *Edwin H. Sutherland Conference on White-Collar Crime: 50 years of Research and Beyond,* May 12–15, Indiana University.

Steffensmeier, D.J. (1986) *The Fence: In the Shadow of Two Worlds,* Totowa, NJ, Rowman and Littlefield.

Tarr, J. (1967) 'The urban politician as entrepreneur', *Mid-American Historical Review,* vol.49, pp.55–67.

Tracy, P.E. and Fox, J.A. (1989) 'A field experiment on insurance fraud in auto body repair', *Criminology,* vol.27, pp.589–603.

US Bureau of the Census (1990) *Statistical Abstract of the United States,* Washington, DC, US Government Printing Office.

Vaughan, D. (1983) *Controlling Unlawful Organizational Behavior: Social Structures and Corporate Misconduct,* Chicago, IL, University of Chicago Press.

Vaughan, D. (1990) 'The macro-micro connection in "white-collar crime" theory', Paper presented at the *Edwin H. Sutherland Conference on White-Collar Crime: 50 Years of Research and Beyond,* May 12–15, Indiana University.

[Hugh Barlow is a member of the Department of Sociology, Southern Illinois University at Edwardsville, IL 62026, USA]

(Source: Barlow, 1993, pp.319–37)

Appendix 4.5

Carlen: Extract from *Alternatives to Women's Imprisonment*

On 21 April 1989 the Chief Inspector of Prisons' Report on HM Prison and Young Offenders Institution Drake Hall was published (Home Office, 1989). It is a sensitive and interesting report with comprehensive coverage of all aspects of prison life and makes over 100 recommendations to the Governor. My concern here, however, will be with just one of its revelations – the difficulty which prison administrators appear to have in conceptualizing women prisoners and women's prisons. The significance of this is at least threefold. First, it becomes apparent that masculinist culture is seen to be an essential element of a *real* prison. Second, bereft of the masculinist yardstick, the inspectors have no consistent criteria for assessing the regime's relevance to the women's needs. Third, once they have accepted that women prisoners' needs may be different to those of men, the Report's authors find it difficult to 'make sense' of either Drake Hall or its inmates; they both raise the question as to whether the majority of women there need to be in prison at all, *and* remind the Governor that, none the less, Drake Hall 'remains a prison and should be managed as such' (p.33).

To begin with, the population of Drake Hall (an open prison) is seen to be contingent upon contemporary penal politics:

> There were women convicted of very minor offences including failure to pay fines who, in a slightly different sentencing atmosphere, might well expect not to be sent to prison. There were also a number of women from abroad who were convicted of drug related offences and faced deportation towards the end of their sentence. It may well be that in the future deportation will come earlier.

> (HM Inspectorate of Prisons, Information Release, 21 April 1989)

How had the women been allocated to an open prison? The inspectors 'concluded that the allocation of women to open conditions still owes much to immediate expediency and little to any reasoned system' (p.32). But a 'reasoned system' for allocation can hardly be expected of a prison system which has no consistent criteria for assessing either law-breaking women or the regimes to which they are subject. Certainly at the time of inspection (autumn 1988) the Governor did not see Drake Hall as a prison. Instead he preferred to conceive of it as an extended family. (With himself as Patriarch?) Or a boarding school. (With himself as Head-master?) The inspectors were critical of this blatantly patriarchal attitude and the passages in which they discuss it are worth quoting because they illustrate the difficulties attendant upon the concept of a 'caring (non-masculinist) prison'.

> 3.6. In his Annual Report for 1987/88 the Governor said: 'My role as Governor of this female establishment has been more akin to that of the head of a large extended family. This has demanded an intensely personal style of management.' In briefing us at the beginning of our inspection he suggested that Drake Hall was more like a girls' boarding school than a prison. Some of this was borne out by what we saw. Our view, however, is that whilst it is very commendable to develop and maintain in a prison the best of the caring relationships of an extended family and ethos of a good boarding school, it remains a prison and should be managed as such. There are also negative features of the extended family and it is by no means always an efficient form of organization. It was clear too that the majority of prisoners at Drake Hall did not want to be treated as if they were in a boarding school. That having been said, it was a small establishment with a strong network of pleasant informal relationships. Over the years it had developed a very caring ethos … .

> 3.7. The difficult task facing the Governor will be to create a more accountable and efficient organization without, at the same time, losing the warmth and informality which characterizes the establishment.

(pp.33–4)

It is interesting that 'accountability' and 'efficiency' are seen as being antithetical to 'warmth' and 'caring' and to note that no male establishment is cited as being able to combine these supposedly opposed qualities. Indeed, apart from suggesting that inmate committees be formed (as in male prisons), the inspectors again and again admit their inability to explain some of the already well-known features of women's imprisonment. For example, why in a supposedly 'caring' environment are there such disproportionately high rates of reported offences against discipline (pp.36-7)? Why is 'throughcare' more honoured in the breach than the observance (p.47)? Are women prisoners really more 'dependent' than their male counterparts? Or is this apparent 'dependency' a product of the closer supervision on the 'house-family' units (pp.86–7)? It is difficult to see how the Governor (or anyone else) could develop a consistent administrative policy on the basis of the contradictory answers given in response to these different questions. On reported offences against discipline, the Report has this to say:

> 3.17. It seemed that the higher rates of reported offences probably related to the higher staff-to-inmate ratios in open prisons for women. Drake Hall had between two and three times as many officers per inmate as we would expect to find in an open prison for men and, in 1986, there were nearly three times as many reported offences against discipline as in open prisons for men. We saw nothing to suggest the women inmates behaved more badly in open prison

than their male counterparts. On the contrary, they seemed if anything more willing to conform. We concluded, therefore, that the relatively high staff to inmate ratios not only increased the opportunities for women inmates to commit offences of disobedience or disrespect but also increased the likelihood of their being reported ...

[However, in para. 3.18] Given the atmosphere of Drake Hall as we found it we were not surprised to find any report [*sic*] for disrespect or abusive behaviour in the sample of 50 [studied]. This was, we thought, one of the most reliable indicators of the generally courteous relationships between staff and inmates.

(p.37)

On 'throughcare':

3.46. There was no evidence of a cohesive, structured throughcare plan which challenged inmates about the nature of their offending and gave them an opportunity to work out with staff how they might use the resources available at Drake Hall to restructure their life style if they chose to do so ... We felt that this reflected management's uncertainty about what it was trying to achieve during a woman's sentence ...

3.56 ... We thought that in view of the constraints laid upon the Governor and the ACPO to produce a structured programme for the throughcare of young offenders under the terms of the new unified sentence, now might be an appropriate time to form new guidelines for the throughcare of all offenders at Drake Hall.

(pp.47, 51)

And, most tellingly, on 'dependency' and 'house-family' units:

3.155 ... Inmates' needs and willingness to express their problems were much greater than we would expect to find in male establishments. The staff (particularly but not exclusively on the houses) responded patiently and constructively. The inmates also seemed to care for and support each other to a considerable extent. We speculated that women in prison have a marked need for a network of supportive relationships of a *familiar* kind and that women officers respond *naturally* to this. We thought that the emphasis on developing a 'house family' atmosphere in the three houses was very commendable. However, as we said above, the extended family is not necessarily an efficient form of organization; it can also foster dependency rather than interdependence. [And later]

3.159 ... Whilst we applaud the idea of developing the 'house family' atmosphere we detected an element of over-supervision here, too. There seemed to us to be considerable scope for ... using inmate committees as a means of extending programmes.

(pp.83–4, emphasis added)

The inspectors considered the

possibility that women officers felt a stronger need for closer supervision of their charges than their male counterparts. It could be argued too that their charges actually need more support and supervision. However, we felt that the inmates at Drake Hall might respond well to rather less supervision and more involvement in decisions about their day-to-day lives ...

[para. 4.5]

4.7. We appreciated that, for various reasons, women adapt far less readily to imprisonment than men tend to do. They may or may not have more problems and anxieties than their male counterparts but they expressed them much more readily than men would in similar circumstances. If Prison Officers are to take a primary role in supporting inmates and helping them to deal with their problems, including their offending (and we believe that they should) then the ratio of higher [*sic*] officers to inmates is justifiable. One corollary of this would be that imprisonment, as a sentence for women, must be a considerably more expensive option than imprisonment for men and the Courts should know this.

(pp.86–7)

My purpose in quoting from the Report at length was not to critique it. Indeed the Chief Inspector takes a commendable deconstructionist stance in several passages, calling into question: current sentencing policy which imprisons so many minor female offenders; the 'house-family' organization of living quarters; and the over-supervision that appears to be one unacceptable face of 'caring' in prison. Similarly commendable are the recommendations concerning the formation of various inmate committees which might lead to the more democratic control of, for instance, catering, leisure and some rule changes. Yet, at the end of it all, one is still left with the stereotypes of 'women' who 'naturally' care and who have a greater 'need' than men for 'familiar' relationships, more support and *therefore* a higher staff to prisoner ratio than their male counterparts! And maybe 'over-supervision' could be turned into more positive support – *but not in a prison*. For the conclusions to the Report commence with a reassertion that although the Inspectorate

> were impressed, for the most part, by the caring and considerate way in which inmates were treated. … Drake Hall is bound by the same policies and rules as the rest of the Prison Service. We found too many areas in which regulations and policies relating to inmates and staff had been ignored or set aside.

(p.85: para. 4.1)

So much for the possibility of developing a women-wise institution! And *that* is why I quote from the Report at length: throughout, its authors did seem to be attempting to theorize the 'as-yet-untheorized' – the implications for penal policy of the recognition that women's experiences are different to men's. This Report more than any other official penal discourse in recent times demonstrates the need for the development of a feminist jurisprudence *and* a women-wise penology. As far as imprisonment is concerned, such perspectives would call into question not only women's imprisonment but also men's (e.g. why shouldn't men's gaols be run on 'caring' lines? If petty female offenders should not be gaoled, why not empty both men's and women's prisons of minor offenders?) …

Reference

Home Office (1989) *Report of HM Chief Inspector of Prisons on HM Prison and Young Offenders Institution Drake Hall,* London, Home Office.

(Source: Carlen, 1990, pp.105–13)

Appendix 4.6

McLaughlin and Murji: 'Controlling the Bill: restructuring the police in the 1990s'

Of all the public services the police were the least affected by the Thatcher revolution.

(Howard Davies, former head of the Audit Commission, 1992)

Introduction

These are worrying times for Britain's police officers. As one crisis follows another they seem to have lost the un-critical support of the government while facing searching questions as to what structure and responsibilities are appropriate to a police force at the end of the century. As Sir John Woodcock, Her Majesty's Chief Inspector of Constabulary has conceded in his annual report, 1991 'was the most difficult year in recent police history'. Here we look at the ways in which the police are responding to demands for change, in particular to the proposals which are likely to emanate from the Royal Commission on Criminal Justice and the separate Home Office Inquiry into Police Responsibilities and Rewards. The heavily leaked proposals of the Inquiry are likely to be incorporated in a Police Bill to be introduced later this year, along with measures favoured by the Home Secretary to transform the financing and control of the police.

After the election of the first Thatcher government the police were the recipient of record pay rises and substantial increases in personnel. In the period from 1979 to 1992 a constable's pay increased by 41 per cent in real terms. The number of officers increased by 23 per cent and the number of civilian employees by 15 per cent. As the recession bit and the government made cuts in public expenditure, the police enjoyed a favoured status, seemingly immune from the government's approach to the rest of the public sector. As Mrs Thatcher stated, 'never, ever, have you heard me say we will economize on law and order' *(The Times,* 10 August 1985). It is little wonder then that other public sector workers began to view the police as the Conservative party in uniform. In return the police have handsomely repaid the government through their pivotal role in defeat of the miners in the coal dispute of 1984–85. The 'thin blue line' also held when other trade unions challenged employers, most notably at Wapping.

However, it seems that this cosy relationship is unlikely to survive into the 1990s. The police – long used to seeing the Conservatives as their natural allies on 'law and order' – have now found that they too are being subjected to government scrutiny. The 'party of law and order' has been embarrassed to find that it has presided over record increases in crime rates. The latest figures show that recorded crime rose by 11 per cent to 5.5 million offences in the 12 months to July 1992 *(The Times,* 29 October 1992). And as the latest British Crime Survey confirms, these figures are just the tip of the iceberg. The survey suggests that the 'real' crime rate is three times the total recorded by the police. Moreover, all of this has been compounded by falling detection rates.

The crime rate has doubled since 1979, whilst the clear-up rate has declined from more than 40 per cent to a little over 30 per cent (*Social Trends*, 1992).

To add to the government's discomfort there has been public disquiet about virtually every aspect of policing from the exposure of corrupt investigating practices to accusations of brutality towards suspects – both elements uncovered in the infamous miscarriages of justice. Then, of course, there are ongoing complaints about general incivility and scandals relating to allegations of racism, sexism and homophobia by officers and within the police force. Opinion polls show that there has been a dramatic drop in public confidence in the police. A recent survey reported that nearly half of the population has lost faith in the police as a result of the Guildford Four and Birmingham Six cases (*Solicitor's Journal*, 23 November 1992). What is worrying for the government is that surveys like this one suggest that the largely taken-for-granted middle class bedrock of support for the police has been undermined. This is something which seems to be clearly understood by the senior ranks of the police. As Elizabeth Neville, one of the most senior women police officers in the country has said recently,

> 'Quite ordinary people simply assume that police officers don't tell the truth. Middle-class people who vote conservative think the police are not corrupt in the sense of taking money but not trustworthy.'

> (*The Guardian*, 27 November 1992, section two, p.13)

No longer are critics of the police confined to the usual targets of police attention and a few 'alienated' sections of society. The middle classes may have been happy to support the police while they were keeping the lid on the inner cities and on recalcitrant trade unionists, but once these 'enemies within' were vanquished, expectations that the police would do something about burglary, car crime and personal safety have been continually disappointed. In this context, it is significant that Home Secretary Kenneth Clarke told Britain's chief officers at their annual conference in 1992 that reform would be necessary to win back the confidence of 'middle England' (*The Guardian*, 11 June 1992).

The government appears to have two vehicles for reforming the police. In an attempt to restore public confidence after the miscarriages of justice, it announced the setting-up of a Royal Commission on Criminal Justice. Secondly the government has decided that the police need to provide more value for money.[1] This involves a wholesale investigation into the role and responsibilities of the police. The inquiry, chaired by Sir Patrick Sheehy, is examining police structure, pay and conditions. Together these signal the Conservative government's intention to modernize British policing. The precise form which this will take will not become entirely clear until both committees produce their reports. But the police are not waiting around for the verdict. Indeed observing the police response to the two committees can be seen as an indication of where they think each inquiry is headed. It also reveals some interesting ways in which the police seek to be the agents of their own re-making.

The Royal Commission on Criminal Justice

The Royal Commission, headed by Lord Runciman, has a wide ranging remit. Its official terms of reference are:

> To examine the effectiveness of the criminal justice system in England and Wales in securing the conviction of those guilty of criminal offences and the acquittals of those who are innocent, having regard to the efficient use of resources.

The Commission will concentrate on the conduct of police investigations, the nature of the criminal justice system all the way through to relevant arrangements for considering and investigating allegations of miscarriages of justice when appeal rights have been exhausted (News section, *The Howard Journal of Criminal Justice,* 1991, pp.339–40).

The Commission still has some way to go in its timetable; however, already there are signs of the police moving to respond well before the Commission reports. Such manoeuvres serve at least three purposes: First they show the police playing an active role in setting the agenda. This generates media coverage which is usually positive. More importantly though it is linked to the second purpose, in that it shows the police acting to put 'their own house in order', well before any change is forced upon them. Thirdly, there is the attempt to deflect criticism away from the police so that the spotlight (or blame) for miscarriages of justice does not fall solely upon the police.[2]

Bearing this in mind, there are three strands in the police's response to the Royal Commission which can be delineated at this stage. The first is to spread the blame; the second is to rationalize the incidence of police rule bending through the appeal to an understanding of the difficult environment the police occupy; and the third, and the one which perhaps most directly aims to pre-empt the inquiry, is to work towards a code of ethics which would govern police conduct.

The blame-spreading strategy has two elements within it. The first is to imply that the police are merely the 'fall guys' for an inefficient system. The criminal justice system uses an adversarial approach; the police are not charged with nor do they see themselves as dispassionate seekers of the truth, concerned with laying out the evidence from which the jury and the courts can reach a decision. Rather, the onus on the police is seen to be as making the case against the accused. So, it is held to be the system itself and the procedures which the police are forced to work to and within which produces the scope for rule-bending and corruption. This theme is exemplified by Sir Peter Imbert's remarks at the Association of Chief Police Officers (ACPO) 1992 summer conference. The Metropolitan police commissioner said that the police should not behave as if it was their role to 'prop up an inefficient legal system' *(Police Review,* 19 June 1992, p.1136).

The same theme is taken up and developed by other chief police officers. For example, speaking at the Bar conference in September, John Evans the Chief Constable of Devon and Cornwall police (who headed the inquiry into the convictions of the Birmingham Six) is reported to have remarked that 'an outmoded and "arrogant" criminal justice system was as much to blame for miscarriages of justice as the police' *(The Times,* 28 September 1992, p.4). And this links directly to the second element of the blame-spreading strategy. Here police deviance is attributed to the rest of the criminal justice system itself. The police bend the rules because they perceive the odds as being stacked against them. The courts and the judiciary simply do not seem to be on the same side as the police: concerned with proving the guilt of the accused. According to Sir John Woodcock, the chief inspector of police, 'among police officers there is a widespread mistrust of the mechanisms of the judicial system which are seen as unnecessarily favouring the accused at the expense of the rights of victims.' *(The Guardian,* 14 October 1992, p.20).[3]

The second observable strand is an appeal to 'understanding', here the police are presented as doing a difficult job for which society is rarely sufficiently grateful. But the police are not asking for gratitude, only understanding. Such a view appears to be being most forcefully articulated by Sir John Woodcock, for example in his speech to an International Police Conference in October (Woodcock, 1992; see also *The Guardian,* 14 October 1992, pp.18–20). The nature of the job sometimes makes 'cutting corners' necessary, indeed it is inevitable. As Sir John points out, quoting a detective in Chandler's *The Long Goodbye,* 'Listen, buddy, there ain't a police force in the world that works within the law book.' The reason for that is simply to be attributed to the milieu which the police occupy:

> I believe that an everyday proximity to the effects of violence and an everyday experience of competing moral imperatives have a corrosive effect on police culture, which tends to make officers uninterested in the finer details of procedure.

> (Woodcock, 1992, p.1930)

The public have little understanding of the reality of police work; because of this they tend to have unrealistic expectations about how the police operate. 'Dirty realism' could be said to characterize the morally grimy world the police occupy, a world in which 'experience' of reality is seen as counting for far more than the 'knowledge' of judges and lawyers.

> The result is malpractice, not out of malice or desire for personal gain, but which begins out of good intention. It is a slippery slope with plenty of handrails to help the descent.

> (ibid.)

For the chief inspector, this is a 'structural or cultural' failure in the system, not one which can be attributed conveniently to a few bad apples. His response to this systemic failure is to argue for a Code of Ethics for the Police Service, and this is the third aspect of the police response to the Royal Commission. Floated back in August 1992 as the 'ten commandments' or 'hippocratic oath' of policing *(The Guardian,* 14 August, p.1), the code is intended as a guide to ethical police behaviour. In its draft form the code covers reporting incidents honestly, acting justly, avoiding the use of force where ever possible, and respecting the rights of suspects *(The Guardian,* 14 August 1991, p.1; *The Times,* 14 October 1992, p.5). Its proponents argue that – unlike the disciplinary code which only covers how to avoid being a bad officer – the ethical code will act as a guide to becoming a better officer *(The Times,* 14 October 1992, p.5).

There is as yet little public information available as to how the code would actually work in practice. But the underlying intent seems clear enough: it is meant to affirm that the police can act professionally and aspire to the highest standards. Symbolically as well as practically the code appears to have a dual purpose. It demonstrates to the public, the government and the Royal Commission that senior police officers are taking steps to put their own house into order. And, perhaps, it will also act as a stick with which to discipline and ultimately dismiss officers who breach the code of ethics. The latter purpose usefully combines the interests of the government who want more financial efficiency from the police, of chief police officers who want to be seen to be in managerial control of their organizations and also, presumably, it serves the public interest in having responsible public servants. This process leading to this end is already under way and it will probably not have to await the deliberations of the Royal Commission, because approaching the same conclusion from a different angle is the separate inquiry into police responsibilities.

The Home Office inquiry into police responsibilities and rewards

At the Police Federation conference in May 1992, the Home Secretary, Kenneth Clarke, announced the setting up of an inquiry into how to modernize the police. It was not the Royal Commission on policing that the Police Federation had been pressing for. Instead, Sir Patrick Sheehy, head of the inquiry, was given a much more specific remit: to examine the rank structures, pay arrangements, working patterns and responsibilities of the police. The Home Secretary also hoped that it would consider ways of 'injecting modern techniques of personnel management' into the force.

There has been much speculation as to what the final report, due to be published in May 1993, will look like. There have been various leaks to the media suggesting that the inquiry is examining every aspect of the organizational structure of policing and is considering a radical shake-up where necessary. *The Observer* (15 November 1992), for example, reported that one of the key questions the Sheehy inquiry is concentrating on is what the core functions of the police should be. Should the police be responsible for traffic control? The guarding of premises and people? 24 hours 'last resort' social services? The inquiry is also assessing the viability of present force boundaries and the present division of labour between uniformed and detective policework. It is also said to be highly critical of antiquated managerial structures and the existing structures for making the police accountable.

Police chiefs are, however, not sitting back and waiting for Sheehy to deliver his verdict because they realize that the status quo is not an option. In many respects they have been able to pre-empt the inquiry's findings by drawing upon recent Audit Commission reports into every aspect of policing in order to implement their own reform agenda. Enlightened senior officers have begun to publicly acknowledge the deficiencies associated with the traditional hierarchical model of policing and view the inquiry as an opportunity to transform the institution so that it can meet the challenges of the 21st century. There is a realization that structural change is desirable and that the real challenge is to manage that change as effectively as possible.

Hence, there have been moves to introduce more flexible, localized and efficient shift systems, working practices and management structures. At the moment, for example, six forces are participating in a part-time work experiment, where officers have the opportunity to opt for working only half of the normal 40 hour week. It is hoped that such a scheme will be of considerable help in retaining female police officers, who have difficulty in fitting in with the dominant masculine work ethic (see *Police Review,* 3 July 1992). At the same time, as policies are being put in place to retain the services of good officers, there are renewed efforts to get rid of the 'bad apples' (for example see *The Guardian,* 2 October 1992, p.4). There is also a commitment to reconceptualizing the police as a service rather than as a force and to look on the public as customers who have equal rights irrespective of race, class and gender. Thus, forces are adopting their own citizen's charters and local police divisions are actively seeking customers comments by producing their own questionnaires. Performance indicators are being put in place to measure the efficiency of forces and of individual officers and to prioritize community needs as opposed to organizational needs. This involves a renewed commitment to working with other social services and local government departments to tackle local crime and social problems. The multi-agency approach is an explicit acknowledgement that the police cannot solve crime problems on their own.

Senior officers realize that the Sheehy inquiry provides them with the opportunity to 'deepen' the changes which they have been implementing with the aim of obtaining more effective managerial control over the work force. For example, in its submission to the inquiry ACPO has proposed, among other things, an end to open ended sick pay, a rationalization of overtime arrangements and a more flexible approach to the pay structure, promotion and recruitment. Certain chief constables would also welcome proposals to rationally reorganize the map of policing whether through nationalization or regionalization, or indeed the privatization of certain functions.[4] The separation of national and local policing functions has been furthered by the establishment of the National Criminal Intelligence Service (NCIS), which came into operation during 1992. Alongside there continues to be 'in house' support for the creation of a national crime squad, a view recently re-stated by Sir Hugh Annesley, the Chief Constable of the Royal Ulster Constabulary in the annual Police Foundation lecture (21 July 1992). At the other extreme, there is a process of localization through sectoral policing, with responsibility for local policing matters and strategies being devolved from police headquarters to the divisional level.

Conclusion

It is clear that senior police officers are committed to the implementation of more cost effective managerial programmes and to the rationalization of duties and responsibilities. There is every indication that they will welcome many of the recommendations which seem likely to emerge from the Royal Commission and the Sheehy inquiry. However, what is not so clear is whether this agenda of reform will serve to enhance the legitimacy of the police. The 'sacred' social contract between the police and the community was finally broken during the events of the 1980s and it should not be forgotten that both of the current probes into policing are primarily geared towards overcoming public disenchantment and disillusionment with the police.

But, it is easier to construct new managerial systems and working practices (and indeed to establish market oriented contractual relationships with the police's customers) than it is to re-establish the social contract. Sir John Woodcock recognized this when he said that, 'In this doubting age, the service may never again return to the post-war position of being a national institution' (*The Guardian,* 18 June 1992). The police are now having to face the consequences of eagerly accepting the government's patronage in the 1980s. We can only wait to see what the impact of this postmodern 'loss of faith' will have on police–community relations in the rest of the 1990s.

Notes

1 This process has been in train for some time and is perhaps best observed through the various reports issued by the Audit Commission.

2 All of this is not meant to suggest that it is the police who are solely responsible for the miscarriages of justice. Indeed there are important questions to be asked of the other elements of the criminal justice system which seem to have wholly failed to question the police's presentation of the evidence, or the means by which it was gathered. It should also be recognized that it was police officers themselves who ultimately uncovered the evidence which led to the freeing of the Guildford Four and the Birmingham Six. There is a linked debate about the independence and autonomy of different elements of the criminal justice system. The bland proposal for an integrated Justice Ministry – which is espoused by the Labour party, for example – simply fails to consider the need for some separation between different arms of the system to enable a level of external scrutiny.

3 The idea that it is the police who represent the interest of victims is, of course, by no means as straightforward as this implies. Victims, just as much as the police, are not necessarily a homogenous group with common or singular interests.

4 However, ACPO reacted very badly to the announcement in early 1993 that the Home Secretary was undertaking his own review of police structure, funding and control, without consulting police representatives. This has fuelled police suspicions that the government is determined to achieve *radical* economies of scale; through regionalization/amalgamation of the existing 43 forces and the centralization of funding – ideas first mooted publicly by Sir John Wheeler and the House of Commons Home Affairs Committee during 1989–90. Within the new map of policing it has been made clear that the government envisages an enhanced role for private sector expertise and representation in the management of the police and a correspondingly diminished role for elected police authorities.

Reference

Woodcock, J. (1992) 'Why we need a revolution', *Police Review,* 16 October, pp.1929–32.

Eugene McLaughlin is a lecturer in the Faculty of Social Sciences, Open University, and Karim Murji is a lecturer in the Department of Sociology and Social Administration, Roehampton Institute.

(Source: McLaughlin and Murji, 1993, pp.100–2)

Appendix 4.7

Peelo and Soothill: 'Personal power and public control: sex crimes and problem pages'

Abstract: In this paper we examine the process whereby problem pages contribute to turning what some would perceive to be 'private troubles' into 'public issues', while offering public acknowledgement of crimes committed as well as solace and advice to victims of sex crimes. The two examples used, 'male rape' and 'underage sex' illustrate the complex role of moral arbiter, whereby agony aunts and uncles act as social barometers, reflecting the confusion surrounding definitions of sex crimes. By examining problem pages we learn more about how society defines the borderlines between private problems and public, criminal, matters.

Problem pages act as social barometers indicating what is acceptable to say publicly about personal troubles. Agony aunts, and occasional uncles, step through a social minefield, reflecting changes in behaviour and the confusion which surrounds shifting social values. In fact, problem pages provide a fascinating laboratory in examining the transformation of 'personal troubles' into 'public issues' (Mills, 1959). Focussing on the topic of sex crime highlights some crucial themes relating to personal power and public control, for these pages provide the researcher with a rich seam of data about attitudes to sex crimes, although the letters themselves may be treated as relationship problems only.

In Britain problem pages are traditionally associated with women's magazines, although the data used here is drawn from more recent agony columns of popular tabloids, 1992 editions of *The Sun, Daily Mirror, The People, Sunday Mirror* and the *News of the World*. The first problem pages started in the early years of the 17th century when men tackled intellectual questions about Creation, slave-trading and perpetual motion (Kent, 1979) and were more like the current 'Notes and Queries' column in *The Guardian* (and television equivalent with Clive Anderson). It was the end of the 17th century that women took over answering problem page letters (Kent, 1979, p.13). Shevelow (1989) argues that the rise of the periodical coincided with the rise of the philosophy which enforced women's role as home-based, in the private sphere. While the extension of print culture encouraged women as writers, its practices and content were helping to enclose women within the private sphere. This capacity for problem pages to reflect wider social trends is highlighted around wartime, in particular, when magazines have shown a certainty about women's role which may well have been influential. Beauman (1983) argues that the publication of hints on how to run a servantless home, after World War One, reflected the drive to expel women from the workplace, stressing that 'it would have been morally reprehensible for them to emerge from the confines of their home' (p.109). White (1977) shows how the same economic processes recurred after World War Two, with the 1950s seeing mass circulations of women's magazines underpinned by a conservative image of cosy home life seemingly untroubled by rape, incest or domestic violence.

White (1977) argues that by the 1970s the newly-diversified magazines were becoming more confident in dealing with advertisers, and hence freer in what they printed. What we now accept as commonplace for problem pages to publish was probably highly self-censored before the 1970s. So *Jackie,* for example, the once popular magazine for 11–19 year olds would only answer letters about drug-taking or sexual problems privately as their rule was that the magazine should be able to be taken into any home (White, 1977). Winship (1987), in addition, points out that house styles extend to the content of letters: with *Honey* publishing letters about incest while *Woman's Own* would only answer such letters privately.

The rise of tabloid journalism and mass circulation newspapers gave fresh outlets for problem pages at the same time as sales of women's magazines were beginning to fall. During the 1970s and 1980s a core of agony aunts and uncles were moving between magazines and newspapers, then to radio and, more recently, including television and phone-ins amongst their repertoires. Traditionally they are journalists by training, offering common-sense advice and disclaiming expert knowledge. Unlike other professional groups, agony columnists have no direct power over their readers' lives, and their responses reflect this unusual and valuable means of help which leaves autonomy with correspondents. Their styles broadly reflect this respect for individual autonomy by offering readers the means to address their own problems, through information, addresses and telephone numbers as well as advice and support.

Individual writers and publications vary in their implementation of this general approach. White (1977) comments on Anna Raeburn's employment by *Woman:* describing Raeburn as 'the most astringent of all agony column writers', White says that she was taken on to offset *Woman's* former cosy image (p.52). This 'can do' approach to answering readers' problems is of fundamental importance, for it readily makes assumptions about levels of personal control over life which letter writers clearly do not experience. *Cosmopolitan* magazine is described by Winship (1987) as displaying this philosophy throughout its contents, carrying reflective and analytic articles which always finish with strategies for action. It is this assumption of equal power between correspondent and the world which has particularly been criticized by feminist writers, where women face structural inequalities which may preclude or make it difficult to follow the courses of action suggested. Underpinning these magazines, as Winship stresses, is an assumption of heterosexuality as the norm. This assumption, together with that of personal control over life, has particular poignancy in considering sex crime.

During the same period there were strong and effective challenges to definitions of sex crimes committed against women in particular (see, for example, Hanmer and Saunders, 1984; Kelly, 1988) and by challenging acceptance of 'domestic' violence by setting up refuges for women battered by violent men (Dobash and Dobash, 1992). While sex crimes are also committed against men, the extent of victimization through rape or assault and the unequal treatment of women by the justice system was highlighted during the 1970s and 1980s (see, for example, Smart, 1976; Edwards, 1981, 1984; Eaton, 1986). In fact, this all adds to a challenge to the assumption that 'women's contexts are too private and personal to be subject to criminal sanction' which had left women without protection and therefore in danger of violence and abuse (McIntosh, 1982, p.306).

The underlying notion of separate private and public spheres was a 19th century one which has exerted a strong pull during the past century, and the notion that 'a man's home is his castle' is one which has ensured many women and their children have not been given the same protection from crime as they might have had if the same acts had been committed on them by strangers outside the home. Heidensohn (1989) argues that the doctrine of separation of spheres became a crucial part of that system which 'contains and confines women' (p.188); in effect, enforcement of certain laws is dependent on whether or not they are seen to be of public relevance (or even as public order matters), or private, domestic ones. Walby (1990) maintains that feminist campaigns have ensured that husbands 'are no longer the sole arbiter of the acceptable level of violence, which is now regulated by the state', but goes on to say that this is not the elimination of violence, merely 'a shift in the locus of control' (p.149). Smart (1989), however, warns feminists to be cautious of how and whether they resort to the use of law (p.2), as she argues that the law is, of itself, a discourse which by its nature and power disqualifies the interests of women. Smart (1989) asks if the quest to establish a feminist jurisprudence does not, in actuality, replace one hierarchy of knowledge with another (pp.66–89).

The likelihood of women and children being in greater danger of sex crimes and violence in their homes via the family or their friends (Stanko, 1990), rather than from strangers on the streets, produces the sense of betrayal, helplessness and fearfulness in personal relations that provides the meat of problem pages, which are much taken up with the apparently private sphere of personal relationships. Agony aunts and uncles tread a curious line of responding to the personal, while remaining of general interest to their readers, acting as social commentators while not attacking social structures. A useful distinction has been drawn by C. Wright Mills (1959) between *personal troubles* and *public issues*. He distinguishes between troubles and issues as follows:

> *Troubles* occur within the character of the individual and within the range of his immediate relations with others; they have to do with his self and with those limited areas of social life of which he is directly and personally aware ... A trouble is a private matter; values cherished by an individual are felt by him to be threatened ... *Issues* have to do with matters that transcend these local environments of the individual and the range of his inner life. They have to do with the ... institutions of an historical society as a whole, with the ways various milieux overlap and interpenetrate to form the larger structure of social and historical life. An issue is a public matter; some value cherished by publics is felt to be threatened.

(p.8, italics in original)

The interesting aspect for our purposes is what Pfuhl (1980), for example, notes as the enlargement of the private trouble to the point that it comes to be defined as a public issue. Pfuhl maintains that 'enlargement consists principally of moral entrepreneurs seeking to raise levels of consciousness and win adherents to their perspective, a tactic well institutionalized among advocates of women's liberation' (p.133). While part of the enlargement process, agony aunts do not display a commitment to a world view in the way one would associate with moral entrepreneurs such as the women's movement. Rather they act as arbiters, deciding which private troubles are public issues of legality, as well as arbitraments of public interest, curiosity and applicability to larger audiences beyond the one asking for help.

The two examples used in this paper to explore these themes are what is called 'male rape' and 'underage sex'. We have chosen these two examples of sex crime because of the high levels of ambivalence which surround them. Male rape has been popularly recognized for some time as a crime, which causes much concern, yet according to legal definitions does not officially exist as a crime. Conversely, underage sex is apparently straightforwardly illegal; however, while there is much public disapproval of underage sex, there is an understandable reluctance to involve the legal system in policing relationships deemed to be consensual but precocious. We include all letters in the sample year which we could identify as focussing on the two themes. In both cases, while agony aunts are trying to offer help and solace to victims of crime, they also respond to the wider social confusion which surrounds public notions of what is accepted as sex crime, and arbitrate on the legality of actions plus the utility of involving formal public agendas.

Tackling the private sphere in public

A part of the process of making sex crimes and domestic violence a matter of public concern is what Kelly (1988) describes as the feminist movement taking the power to name what women experience without which 'the extent and even existence of forms of sexual violence cannot be acknowledged' (p.139). Kinsey, Lea and Young (1986) reflect this concept when they argue that the underestimation of the prevalence of some crimes is in direct relationship to the social power of the perpetrators and the vulnerability of the victims (p.65). This social power includes the capacity to define innocence and consent, two essential elements in our assumptions as to what constitutes most sex crimes. As Walklate (1989) has written, victims' innocence is seen to lie in the whole of their life, not just in the behaviour which touches upon the crime committed against them. If their innocence can be publicly undermined then their claims to have withheld consent can be more easily set aside.

In 'naming' women's experiences of sex crimes, the feminist movement challenged the minimization of the effects of sex crime on victims. Once the step is taken of recognizing the profound harm done to adult women who have been subjected to crime, then it becomes harder to deny the damage also done to other groups of victims including children and male victims of rape or assault, whatever definitions the law might offer for such episodes. Problem pages are valuable in that they, too, can provide the vocabulary by which many people can make sense of their history and admit harm done to them, by providing a public acknowledgement of the wrongs experienced by individuals. This process can be seen to be operating with 'male rape' and letters to problem pages refer to the impact of past events: two correspondents stated clearly that they now felt able to recount their experiences because of the publicity surrounding recent cases. Three of the four correspondents about male rape show emotional signs of having been raped: depression, shame, fearfulness, loss of confidence, a sense of helplessness, doubts about safety when away from home, and a sense of being lesser people – plus an additional fear of homosexuality. Rape is about degradation and humiliation of its victims rather than about 'normal' sex which has gone wrong. Paradoxically, this is easier for people to see about males raping males once the step has been made to accepting rape as causing real emotional damage to victims (see Kelly, 1988, especially for discussion of 'Rape Trauma Syndrome', p.49 and p.188).

Male rape

One of these letters, featured in *The Sun* under the title 'FIVE-YEAR HELL OF MALE RAPE', was from a 24 year old who recounts how five years earlier he was 'raped at knife-point … and until now I've bottled up the pain', but has an obsessional need to have AIDS tests. Recent headlines had brought back scary memories for him and he wants to warn men who travel alone. Deidre Sanders comments that 'Male rape is more common than is generally thought, although it is only just beginning to be discussed openly'. She asks the writer to make a statement to the police, to help them piece together information. She concludes by suggesting that he contacts *Survivors*, a self-help group for victims of male rape (*The Sun,* 15 June 1992).

At a pragmatic level problem pages provide people with information, such as addresses, telephone numbers, or the names of organizations, thereby encouraging an autonomy in their correspondents' quests for help. As with male rape, many of the organizations suggested are in the voluntary sector and, as we shall see with 'underage sex', the police are rarely mentioned as a helpful option. The information offered is only partly directed at the letter writer, for it is also available to the wider readership who find problem pages such compulsive reading. Newspaper journalists need an awareness of what is acceptable yet gripping material, and editors require a flair for assessing when to go a little bit further, as with male rape, in making public those problems previously considered too offensive to print.

A letter headed 'Victim's story of male rape', to 'Dear Barbara, Britain's best-loved agony aunt', opened: 'Seeing newspaper reports about men being raped has made me feel at last I can tell someone this happened to me although I won't give an address because I couldn't bear to be contacted'. He feels his sex life is over as: 'since that time I have not felt any wish even to go out with a woman, let alone sleep with one'. However, his present action will be therapeutic: 'I just hope that writing it down will help me forget the events of that dreadful evening because so far I can't get them out of my thoughts'. He concludes that: 'I felt just like I imagine women who've been raped must feel, powerless and violated. I am less of a man now'. Barbara lets the letter speak for itself, commenting that little is known about male rape as men have been too embarrassed to speak out and that being 'a victim of this kind can change the way a man perceives himself'. She, too, offers a contact number for *Survivors,* the group for male victims of sexual attacks *(The People,* 22 November 1992).

Stanko (1990) would agree that violence against men is rarely articulated and does make men feel differently about themselves and the world. The subtext to feeling 'less of a man' is confusion about male rape and homosexuality. Stanko's research suggests that men, by defining themselves as heterosexual, consider themselves to be safe from sexual crime, which is, instead, directed to women; by separating themselves from homosexuality men imagine themselves to be free from sexual danger. However, work with men who abuse boys and studies of rape in men's prisons shows that the rapists define themselves as heterosexual (pp.114, 124). The intention of these heterosexual rapists is 'to dehumanise and degrade fellow inmates' by turning them into women (p.124). Such actions display not only a contempt for women, but an expectation that sexual intercourse is primarily an aggressive act enacted by the powerful on the helpless.

Outside prisons, though, there is a worse fate than being perceived to be female, and that is being seen as homosexual: a letter to the *Sunday Mirror* (3 May 1992) makes explicit the fear underlying our two previous male rape cases. Under the heading 'Has Uncle turned me gay?' a correspondent wonders whether the experience of being raped by an uncle has made him gay. Virginia Ironside assures him that this is not possible, and echoes Sanders and 'Dear Barbara' by saying this kind of crime is more common than one imagines, partly because men do not speak about it and partly because there is no such crime as 'male rape' in law; she concludes by recommending *Survivors* 'for the help you so desperately need'.

In our final male rape case the correspondent expressed no sense of grievance, apart from anxiety about his physical health, and presented his experience as a definitional query he wanted the agony uncle to answer. He wished to know if he had been raped by four girls with whom, initially, he had been involved in horseplay on a beach in Italy: 'each had sex with me while the others held me down. I didn't want it to happen at first, but afterwards I enjoyed it. Have I been raped? And what are the chances of catching AIDS?' *(News of the World,* 6 September 1992). Philip Hodson attempts definitions of male rape in his answer when he says that 'homosexual rape of men is not unknown, but the victims have usually been beaten up'. As we have already seen, rape of men by men does (like all sex crimes and rapes of women) include the exercise of power but does not necessarily require beating up; and the use of the word 'homosexual' is ambiguous here, as in popular usage and tabloid newspapers this is usually taken to mean the opposite of heterosexuality amongst men rather than its proper meaning of 'same sex' and, hence, can imply male rape is a minority problem for male homosexuals only.

Hodson states quite clearly that: 'Rape is a violation of someone's body without their consent', which is exactly the situation the letter describes. In actuality, rape is a violation of a woman's body by a man, and Hodson is exploring, on behalf of all readers, what are the outer limits of our acceptance of 'male rape'. The subtext of this arbitrament is that violation of men by men is accepted as rape, but social expectations of male and female behaviour coupled with related interpretations of 'consent' result in the phrase not stretching to incorporate the possibility of rape of men by women. In following Hodson's reasoning when coming to a judgment about the described incident there are echoes of exactly those problems which would arise if 'male rape' was legally accepted as a crime. Unlike assault against or between men, the crime of rape against women has traditionally given rise to expectations of evidence of consent, and proving consent can include attempting to show whether or not the subject of rape enjoyed the act. In deciding whether or not this incident constitutes rape, Hodson considers consent and does not find the method by which the correspondent describes being forced into sex to be sufficiently innocent and so doubts claims of non-consent: 'I think we should keep the word for people who weren't excited into co-operation like you'. Finally, the agony uncle assures the writer that the 'chances of your getting the HIV virus are probably low, but you could talk it through with an AIDS counsellor' *(News of the World,* 6 September 1992). Although it is not clear on what basis he makes this assessment of risk, it has echoes of the popular assumption that the HIV virus is a threat only to avowedly homosexual men.

Part of the difficulty in answering this letter lies in the assumption that men are always strong enough to overcome women; indeed one titillating element lies in the tacit inversion of usual power relations, to the extent that the letter seems fictitious. Indeed, the letter wrote of a situation which, had it appeared elsewhere in a tabloid newspaper, would usually be material of a male fantasy. As well as experiencing a common feeling of confusion when trying to define what constitutes consent, Hodson is also omitting from his definition of rape the notion that it occurs only when there is penetration of the victim by a male. The letter delimits the outer boundaries of what, currently, is taken seriously as male rape; on this occasion the man receives little sympathy and he is told he should not be disturbed about his own physical health.

Newspapers in general assume social rules and standards especially if individuals do not stick to them, as public exposure can only happen where rules are known and can be shown to have been transgressed. Ericson *et al.* (1991, ch.1) have made this point when describing newspapers and news-gathering as involved in a process of 'moral evaluation' whereby decisions are made about what acts are out of place, hence newsworthy. Agony aunts in particular act as moral arbiters in this sense, that they are conversing with an underlying social commentary as well as responding to individual needs. Defining, through supportive advice, what are moral boundaries to acceptable behaviour, agony writers indicate those aspects of legislation which we do not necessarily, as a society, really wish to invoke. Legalistically, in this next example, underage sex is an uncomplicated matter. But in this example, agony columnists reflect a common desire to use law as a means to substantiate a moral imperative where many of us, in practice, would not wish to see agents of the law publicly enforcing the matter.

Underage sex

The crime of underage sex is one which puts particular pressure on agony aunts as moral arbiters who, at one and the same time, are trying to be pragmatic rather than judgmental about a problem they clearly know to be commonplace. At first sight, it seems one of the easiest sex crimes to pass comment on, combining as it does society's ideas of morals with clearly and publicly defined rules about sexual activity; and, unlike rape, it makes redundant the complicating factor of consent, which is an irrelevant concept in legal definitions of underage sex. Yet legal definitions are, perhaps, the only straightforward aspects of this crime. While it is seen as a potentially harmful activity, so too is recourse to the law, which is not seen as a useful or helpful option for agony columnists to call on in sorting out the problems which can be associated with underage sex. The agony aunts' role is to respond pragmatically to the correspondents' concerns, and the appeal to criminality is invoked, in the main, as a means of expressing anger at the writers' mistreatment by others.

Agony aunts are always writing for two readerships: those who write or require specific help, and those who are reading problem pages out of interest. Those presenting private troubles are read by those who potentially see the public issues at stake. This wider readership plays a part in laying down what is acceptable to publish, and what advice is appropriate to give, and will write to the publication to lay down what these standards are. So the

'Dear Barbara' column in *The People* became embroiled in the debate surrounding underage sex and what advice should be offered. A 15 year old correspondent suggests that Barbara's earlier advice to a 13 year old girl under pressure to have sex with her 16 year old boyfriend ought to have been 'to tell the boy to get lost'. Barbara's reply to this second letter underlines the difficulty of giving complex advice to a mass audience. Barbara maintains that her earlier advice had been misinterpreted. She had suggested that the girl should confide in her mother 'so she could better understand the inadvisability of embarking on a full sex life too soon'. On the other hand, she also noted that 'surveys show more young people are apparently becoming sexually active earlier than in the past' while emphasizing the rule that 'individuals should not feel that they have to join in' *(The People,* 4 October 1992).

The dilemma agony columnists face is this: 'Dear Barbara', and every other agony writer, knows that underage sex is both illegal and commonplace. Charlotte Owen *(The Time The Place,* ITV, 19 January 1993 on helping underage girls who are pregnant) argued that an agony aunt must offer a pragmatic rather than judgmental approach to do their job – it's happened, so you've got to make decisions. In this instance 'Dear Barbara' is trying, amongst other issues, to address the correspondent's problem of coping with pressure to have an active sex life. Yet to write helpfully for those engaged in illegal and underage sex will result in the accusation, from other readers, that agony aunts are encouraging sexual activity. Only recently a local television news magazine programme ran an item on just this issue, posing the question: do advice columns lead youngsters astray *(Granada Tonight,* 21 June 1993)? This dilemma is played out daily in families and institutions throughout the country: what is at issue is what constitutes age-appropriate behaviour, and ignorance has always appeared to some readers to be the best route by which inappropriate behaviour is avoided. This is an old problem for agony aunts whose role has traditionally been to help the troubled individual in a highly public way, and one which Leonora Eyles tackled in *Woman's Own* during World War Two. To mothers who wrote complaining that she had sent information to unmarried girls concerning the 'facts of life' (one mother had burnt the material, the other felt post-marriage was the time for girls to discover 'the dreadful lot of women') Eyles wrote back that young people needed to know because the world was such a dangerous place for them, and that: 'Ignorance is not innocence; innocence is knowledge protected by a good code of behaviour' (1943, reprinted, Waller and Vaughan-Rees, 1987).

Not to face these difficult topics alienates younger readers, as 'Dear Barbara' found when she was attacked by two 16 year old girls who wrote complaining of her attitude to a 15 year old girl who had unprotected sex with a man of 23 who had asked her to marry him. They argue as if underage sex has no legal implications and accept Eyles' 'good code of behaviour' as underpinning innocence. They said that 'having sex underage doesn't matter as she must have felt ready and if marriage was mentioned, obviously they're in love. The idea isn't ridiculous, as you think, because in a year or so they could marry and if she does turn out to be pregnant and they love each other it would be quite sensible'. They finished by suggesting Barbara 'take a refresher course and get an update on what teenagers go through today' *(The People,* 25 October 1992).

The claim that the couple love each other invokes a common method of endowing sex with innocence, by using romantic love as a justification. The childhood innocence lost, in adult eyes, through inappropriately young sexual activity is replaced rather than lost in the eyes of the two 16 year old correspondents. To retain the image of innocence, girls in particular must avoid the accusation that they are promiscuous or enjoy sex for its own sake. Hence a young man of 18 writes to Deidre Sanders of *The Sun*, concerned about a 14 year old female friend who seems addicted to sex, and Sanders offers the post-feminist thought that: 'It isn't unusual for people to have one rule for boys and another for girls', although she also sends a leaflet on 'Learning About Love and Sex' (*The Sun, 17* November 1992). The post-feminism lies, as Winship (1987) has pointed out (p.149), in Sanders' accepting as commonplace what used to be a minority view, hence what was once seen as a challenging viewpoint has become absorbed into the mainstream of publishing.

Underage sex is not solely about consenting, albeit precocious, adolescents. As other letters to problem pages show, where there is an age-gap between sexual partners this often represents a power- and status-gap, making it hard to define what constitutes consent or personal choice. Marjorie Proops shows most emotion in such cases and 'criminality' is a concept used to define the degree of her anger, but not as a basis for suggesting involvement of the police or other authoritative agencies, such as schools. So, for example, one 14 year old girl made pregnant by a gym teacher claims: 'I realize it is all my fault' to which Proops gives the robust reply: 'You say you realize it was your fault. Rubbish' (*Daily Mirror*, 2 June 1992). The teacher gets the full force of her venom and Proops indicates awareness of the problems of defining 'consent' beyond the girl's agreement to particular occasions of sexual intercourse: 'For a man – particularly a teacher with a special responsibility towards his pupils – to take a kid of your age into his car, take her clothes off and take away her youth and sexual innocence is gross and criminal'.

Where there is an age imbalance in the partnership, the male partner is usually older. However, the illegality of underage sex is stressed where both parties are young, but relational matters are examined rather than the option of invoking official action. Likewise, the private, emotional dangers of underage sex are presented rather than the possible public sanctions. So 'Dear Barbara' chose as 'Letter of the Week' one from two 14 year olds indicating that they were planning to have sex. Barbara asked quite simply in the first instance: 'What's the rush?' and then made some clear and uncomplicated assertions: pointing first to the normality of sexual feelings at their age, the legal constraints and that 'making love without a long-term relationship and commitment can lead to getting hurt'; while also recommending a Family Planning Association booklet for young adults. Barbara also suggested that they should talk to their parents 'who could understand more than you think' (*The People*, 17 May 1992).

The myriad psychological dangers of underage sex are also presented retrospectively, through the subsequent problems of older people: broken marriages, destroyed lives, and even extortion. So, a 21 year old woman wrote of her problems in having married the teacher who made love to her when she was 15 (*Daily Mirror*, 9 September 1992): Proops' analysis of the situation was that the husband had been 'turned on because you were only

15 (and) having sex with you was illegal'. Unlike the two girls who took 'Dear Barbara' to task for not taking the marriage plans of adolescents seriously, Proops is suggesting parting unless the 'cold fish' of a husband makes it explicit he wishes to try to continue with the marriage. In another letter, a 24 year old woman indicates how she was constantly reminded of being made pregnant, having an abortion and being deserted by her lover ten years earlier. While Proops states the act to have been criminal, and the man to be unforgivable, she draws back from endorsing any public course of action which might cause hurt to innocent bystanders, such as pushing a note through the man's door *(Daily Mirror,* 12 May 1992).

For men there are also dire warnings about the dangers in underage sex: for the 55 year old correspondent who had been blackmailed for 30 years by a girl, following sexual intercourse, Proops has nothing but sympathy *(Daily Mirror,* 27 October 1992). He admits to having committed a criminal and stupid act and Proops, stating a detestation for blackmailers, suggests that 'it's difficult to believe that a wife you've loved for 30 years would sling you out because you strayed briefly so long ago'. Deidre Sanders, however, in *The Sun* (19 March 1992), is less sympathetic to the 26 year old man who felt his life was wrecked as his girlfriend's parents had reported him to the police. Sanders answers: 'it's time you realized that actions have consequences you will have to be responsible for', although she goes on to offer the hope that proceedings may be dropped when the family calms down.

On the only other occasion in which the police were discussed in relation to underage sex, Deidre Sanders pointed out to the parent the pitfalls of taking this route, albeit their entitlement. A parent (it is not stated whether this is the mother or father) wrote to Sanders that s/he had been considering reporting their 19 year old son's boyfriend (aged 54) to the police, as the age of consent for male homosexuals is 21 [at time of original publication]. Sanders reminds that: 'if you threaten this man your son would find out and your relationship with him might never recover' so the advice is to: 'talk with your son first trying hard not to get angry or condemn him' (*The Sun,* 21 January 1992). In this instance not only is the notion of informing the authorities of secondary consideration to the importance of maintaining the bonds with the son, but is seen to be positively harmful to future relations. Smart (1989) has used the word 'juridogenic' to describe this process as 'the harm that law may generate as a consequence of its operations' (p.12); and, as with Proops, invocation of legal definitions expresses and legitimizes anger, but any actual implementation is seen as contrary to the purposes of finding personal, private adjustments and resolutions. The oddness of the higher age of consent in this case perhaps contributes to this tacit reminder that increased age lessens parents' power to control their offspring's sexual activity. Awareness of the underlying tension concerning homosexuality is reflected in the letter's publication on the same day as *The Sun* ran a telephone helpline on 'Gay Worries'.

Conclusion

Problem pages and their radio and television equivalents are becoming increasingly pervasive but curiously neglected in the academic literature. This latter point reflects the ambivalence with which agony aunts and uncles have been seen by feminist writers, whose concern has, rightly, been located around the assumptions which columnists appear to hold about the levels of personal control which correspondents have over their lives. In brief, most women face structural inequalities which may preclude or make it difficult to follow the courses of action suggested by those giving the advice. Giddens (1992) has made a similar point when discussing 'reflexive self-talk' as a technique used to escape from co-dependent and addictive relationships: reflexive self-talk is reprogramming away from the view that one had no choices whatsoever, yet the words 'I can't' might be a realistic appraisal of the situation. Giddens comments on the reflexivity as a 'necessary condition' for such an escape, but 'not a sufficient one' (pp.91–2).

These columns and advice programmes provide a forum for problems which have often remained hidden from view, both in personal and public terms, and they are aired before an audience which is almost unimaginably large in size. This transformation of *personal troubles* into *public issues* in the problem pages of newspapers highlights some dilemmas which few other contexts so poignantly demonstrate. The advice of a social worker could, similarly, be challenged for not attacking social structures, but is rarely open to such public scrutiny. The searching press or television documentary which exposes structural issues is unlikely to have an individual client or customer to advise. In contrast, the importance of the agony columnist is that these usually distinct spheres are brought together. One witnesses the enlargement of a private trouble to the point that it comes to be defined as a public issue. What we have examined is the way that this transition, of tackling the private sphere in public, is managed or negotiated with the use of two examples in the area of sex crime.

The two examples of 'male rape' and 'underage sex' have some crucial differences but also some important similarities. The main similarity focusses on how they both reflect the confusion surrounding definitions of sexual activity in general and sex crime in particular. However, the differences are revealing. Agony columns have provided public acknowledgement of 'crimes' committed and so, to that extent, are both moulders of opinion and social barometers, indicating which problems exist in the world. In contrast to 'male rape', 'underage sex' can be clearly defined as a crime. It is generally discouraged as a relationship decision between adolescents of similar age; and suggested as positively harmful (psychologically as well as the physical consequences of pregnancy or abortion) where there is an age/status gap between a man and a girl. Here, however, unlike 'male rape', neither the illegality of the act nor the frequency of the act is in doubt. Nevertheless, while there is often a public acknowledgement in the response of the agony columnist that a crime has been committed, this does not imply recourse to the law as a means of managing an individual's sense of grievance. Most particularly, where the sex act itself is assumed to be consensual, relationship matters are paramount even though, technically, consent is irrelevant to definitions of this crime.

Certainly agony aunts do not seem to find definitions of legality useful when offering help to troubled readers, except in so far as they reinforce estimations of harm done to letter writers. They go beyond simply offering solace to individuals and the issue of 'underage sex' especially exemplifies the complex role of moral arbiter. The agony columnists do have different emphases with some, such as Proops of the *Daily Mirror,* showing more emotion while others, such as Barbara of *The People,* seem more willing to contest the issues publicly with their young readers. However, they all move together in trying to extend young people's notions and understanding of the subtleties of personal power while they dodge the issues of public control. This has echoes of Braithwaite's (1989) 'modalities of shame', in that agony aunts are part of that process of publicizing what we accept as moral and immoral behaviour, linking the micro and the macro (p.80). But agony columns operate in an essentially anonymous sphere, unlike the other pages in tabloid newspapers, hence cannot be part of Braithwaite's 'shaming' (p.83) as individual offenders, families, friends and victims all remain unknown. Reverting to Mills's (1959) terminology (p.8), as moral arbiters agony columnists are able to publicize private troubles and use legal definitions to delimit public issues, so serving the essential, comforting, purpose of publicly 'naming' the hurt done and sanctioning, therefore, correspondents' right to feel aggrieved. This process falls short of Pfuhl's (1980) interpretation of Mills's moral entrepreneur (p.133), whose commitment to a world view is the basis for campaigning and proselytizing, for while agony columns may or may not encourage a wider social awareness in readers of the need for structural reforms, the advice usually returns problems to the individual, private sphere.

Examining problem pages is instructive in many ways. Certainly we learn more about how society defines the borderlines between private and public, criminal, matters. Agony columnists act as social barometers of what can be uttered in the public sphere and on occasions they embrace a role of moral arbiter. Yet the nature of that contribution is not always clear and our two examples of 'male rape' and 'underage sex' suggest that agony columnists' contribution may vary considerably. Ericson *et al.* (1991) have argued that as newspapers establish the legitimacy of acts, so they offer stability and order in the specific sense 'of ensuring an adaptive capacity to cope with strains or changes in the environment' (p.7). With 'male rape', it is fair to say that their work may be helping to provide a wider public acknowledgement of what were formerly unacknowledged private troubles for some males, while with 'underage sex' they may assist in helping us to recognize ways in which the relationship between personal power and public control needs more than a legal intervention. Problem pages usually do lack a serious structural analysis of the issues underlying letter writers' problems, but it would be misleading to suggest that these pages simply act as indicators of popular views about the boundaries between crime and harm. The extent to which they do more than this requires further analysis which considers how their views can and do shift over time.

Note

Acknowledgements: This material is derived from a study on sex crime in newspapers, supported by the Nuffield Foundation.

References

Beauman, N. (1983) *A Very Great Profession: The Woman's Novel 1914–39*, London, Virago.

Braithwaite, J. (1989) *Crime, Shame and Reintegration*, Cambridge, Cambridge University Press.

Dobash, R.E. and Dobash, R.P. (1992) *Women, Violence and Social Change*, London, Routledge.

Eaton, M. (1986) *Justice for Women? Family, Court and Social Control*, Milton Keynes, Open University Press.

Edwards, S. (1981) *Female Sexuality and the Law*, Oxford, Martin Robertson.

Edwards, S. (1984) *Women on Trial*, Manchester, Manchester University Press.

Ericson, R.V., Baranek, P.M. and Chan, J.B.L. (1991) *Representing Order: Crime, Law and Justice in the News Media*, Buckingham, Open University Press.

Giddens, A. (1992) *The Transformation of Intimacy: Sexuality, Love and Eroticism in Modern Societies*, Cambridge, Polity Press.

Hanmer, J. and Saunders, S. (1984) *Well-Founded Fear: A Community Study of Violence to Women*, London, Hutchinson.

Heidensohn, F. (1989) *Women and Crime*, London, Macmillan.

Kelly, L. (1988) *Surviving Sexual Violence*, Cambridge, Polity Press.

Kent, R. (1979) *Aunt Agony Advises: Problem Pages Through the Ages*, London, W.H. Allen.

Kinsey, R., Lea, J. and Young, J. (1986) *Losing The Fight Against Crime*, Oxford, Basil Blackwell.

McIntosh, M. (1982) 'The state and oppression of women', in Evans, M. (ed.) *The Woman Question: Readings on the Subordination of Women*, London, Fontana.

Mills, C. Wright (1959) *The Sociological Imagination*, New York, Oxford University Press.

Pfuhl, E. (1980) *The Deviance Process*, New York, D. Van Nostrand Co.

Shevelow, K. (1989) *Women and Print Culture: The Construction of Femininity in the Early Periodical*, London, Routledge.

Smart, C. (1976) W*omen, Crime and Criminology: A Feminist Critique*, London, Routledge and Kegan Paul.

Smart, C. (1989) *Feminism and the Power of the Law*, London, Routledge.

Stanko, E. (1990) *Everyday Violence: How Men and Women Experience Sexual and Physical Danger*, London, Pandora.

Walby, S. (1990) *Theorizing Patriarchy*, Oxford, Blackwell.

Walklate, S. (1989) *Victimology: The Victim and the Criminal Justice Process*, London, Unwin Hyman.

Waller, J. and Vaughan-Rees, M. (1987) *Women in Wartime: The Role of Women's Magazines, 1939–1945*, London, Macdonald Optima.

White, C. (1977) *Royal Commission on the Press, The Women's Periodical Press in Britain 1946–76* (Working Paper 4), London, HMSO.

Winship, J. (1987) *Inside Women's Magazines*, London, Pandora.

Moira Peelo is Honorary Research Associate and Keith Soothill is Professor of Social Research, Department of Applied Social Science, University of Lancaster

(Source: Peelo and Soothill, 1994, pp.10–24)

Chapter 5
Theory, Argument and Evidence

by Roger Sapsford

Contents

1 Introduction

*I*n this final chapter of Book 3 we look at the assessment of research arguments and the theories which underlie them, bringing together ideas explored in this book and elsewhere in the course. We have not talked much about 'theory' in the last two chapters, but it is of course central to the assessment of any research. So what *is* the place of theory in research? The answer has to be that theory *precedes* research, it *constitutes* it and it *emerges from* it; research is a stage in the building of theory. Research is always informed by, and is part of, theory – even when the researcher thinks the contrary – and research is where theory and policy come together. The research used to evaluate a treatment or policy is based on and takes for granted (explicitly or often implicitly) a model of crime and society. A policy of *punishment*, based on individual deterrence, is likely to be grounded in a *classicist* understanding of the social order, whereas a policy of *treatment* is more likely to be grounded in a *positivist* understanding of the social order (see **Reader Guide 2**). Even pieces of apparently neutral and atheoretical description will almost certainly contain theory-laden assumptions and work from some (possibly unacknowledged) 'model of the world'. This constrains the imagination by making it 'natural' to look for solutions (and even to define problems) at one particular level of analysis and in one particular way. For example, the Banks and Fairhead research which you considered in Chapter 3 (Example 3) is clearly rooted in a view of the world in which social circumstances damage people to the point where the problem is one of *handling* them rather than treating them or deterring them. This makes it 'natural' to try to identify these people and find a way of diverting them from the prison system, rather than tackling their circumstances or aiming for treatment or deterrence.

Further, the research itself will fall within theoretical paradigms or traditions which will shape the kind of product it is to be. For example, it will be psychological or sociological or from a social policy stance. It will be concerned with problems of 'race', class, gender or disability, or it will overlook these factors and tend to assume that all 'normal' people are white, male, middle-class, able-bodied and in full possession of their physical senses. Within specifically criminological traditions, a paper may be grounded in biological or psychological criminology (and may or may not be described as 'positivistic' as a result), or in one of the lines of criminological theory derived from functionalist or interactionist sociology, or in a Marxist or feminist critical perspective, or in conservative or 'left' realism, and so on (see **Reader Guide 1**). The research may have its roots in administrative criminology and (in the UK) be sponsored directly or indirectly by the Home Office, or it may be an academic and/or political reaction to this tradition (see Chapter 1). Each of these broad approaches has implications for what is viewed as the nature of crime and what are put forward as explanations for it. Each also has its own notion of what is problematic about the criminal justice system and therefore of what kind of research is required.

As we have seen in the last two chapters, a research report consists of an argument developed from a question or problem to an answer or solution via, among other things, the evidence of the research. This evidence itself consists of a series of arguments about what the data mean – why they should be accepted as playing the part in the overall argument which the writer wishes them to play. The report does not stand alone, however. Both argument and evidence are embedded in the writer's 'conceptual map' of human nature and the nature of social relations. Further, they assume the writer's epistemology – the writer's position on the nature of 'truth', what constitutes acceptable proof of a proposition (or, less grandly, what makes us inclined to believe it), and what counts as a 'factual' proposition (about how the world *is*) or a 'moral' one (about how it *ought* to be) and how the two kinds of proposition should be related. It is part of the reader's task to discern where what the writer has taken for granted is not in accord with the reader's own epistemology and conceptual map of humankind and the social world, and then to determine what consequences this has for the conclusions drawn.

In this chapter we look briefly at how we judge arguments and in a little more detail at how we judge theories. In the light of this discussion we revisit the relationship between the argument of a research paper and the evidence which sustains it. The final sections of the chapter aim to pull the main threads of the whole of Book 3 together, by discussing the *assessment* and *planning* of research and helping you to develop a 'checklist' of questions to assist you with these tasks.

2   The argument

If a research paper is an argument, from a question to an answer, how do we judge the argument? First, questions must be about the logical process of the argument itself. Is it coherent? Do its conclusions follow from its premises? Does the chain of sub-arguments which lead from the first question, through the paper in stages, to the conclusion hold together as a chain, or is one of the links weak or even broken? These are the questions we must ask not only of a research paper but of *any* scholarly or professional production.

ACTIVITY 5.1

Look again at the paper by Norris *et al.* (Chapter 3, Appendix 3.1). Outline the major 'blocks' of the argument – the questions and the conclusions (with the evidence for them) – and see if they follow one from another.

This Activity should take about an hour.

Here is my outline of the major 'blocks of argument'.

The questions
1   Are black people stopped more often than white people?
2   Are they arrested more often?
3   If either is the case, is it because of:
    (a) police prejudice,
    (b) the behaviour of the black people, or
    (c) their greater offending rate?

Note that the questions are not laid out neatly in a list, but have to be looked for throughout the introduction. This is usually the case: the broad area of questioning may be announced early in the paper, but one function of the first section (or sometimes of more than one section) is to refine this broad area into specific researchable questions.

The conclusions

1   Yes, they are stopped more often. This result was already expected, from previous research. It is not new information, therefore, but corroboration in another circumstance. It is a necessary stage of the argument, however; the authors cannot explain why *these* police patrols stop black people more often than white people unless they have shown that they *do* stop them more often.

2   More formal action is taken against them, but there is not necessarily a higher arrest rate – though the authors are at pains to point out that their results are not *in*compatible with a higher arrest rate. In other words, there is a great deal of research evidence to show that black people are arrested more often than white people, but the authors are unable to demonstrate it from this particular study, though the results do not rule it out. You may find this part of the argument a little weak.

3   (a) There is some suggestion (not emphasized by the authors) of prejudice as the reason for stopping more black people; they may be questioned a little more intrusively, and they *may* be arrested more often and *are* subject to more formal procedures, which might be interpreted as an element of prejudice. (This is *my* argument – the answer is not framed in these terms by the authors.) However, the police are not more hostile or less polite to black people than white people – indeed, the converse may be true. However, these conclusions hold only to the extent that the evidence is trustworthy. I should have liked more statistical testing of differences, to assure me that they were not just random fluctuations. More importantly, the reader needs to consider whether the behaviour of the patrols when accompanied by a researcher is likely to be quite the same as when not so accompanied.

(b) Black people do not behave in a more hostile or aggressive way than white people to the police.

(c) This question is not considered at all by the research (nor could it be), and it drops out of the discussion once it has been raised. The authors do not even bring the results of other research to bear on it in their review of literature. They cite a dispute about the topic between 'radical realists' and 'writers associated with the Institute of Race Relations', but they themselves do not take a position on whether the black crime rate actually *is* higher.

Thus, in summary, the argument of the paper is mostly logical and coherent, and therefore plausible to the extent that the evidence cited is adequate. Three of the questions outlined are clearly answered in whole or part – black people *are* stopped disproportionately often, they are subject to more formal 'exit procedures' (and *may* be arrested more often), and this is not because of their own behaviour. On the other hand, one of the questions the authors outline and assign a section in the literature review – the question of differential offending – drops out of all further discussion; and the answers to the other element (our Question 3) – the question of police prejudice – is a bit confused as expressed. Material is clearly there to *begin* an answer to this question, as we can see above, but the authors tend to lose sight of it.

    The first 'line of questioning' to be applied when assessing a research report, then, concerns the logic of the argument(s) which it embodies. One of the purposes of this chapter is to help you build up a 'checklist' of questions to ask about a report. The first questions for the list might be:

1   Is the argument of the paper internally consistent – do the conclusions follow logically from the arguments?
2   Are the questions originally posed by the authors plausibly answered?
3   If not, *can* they be plausibly answered from the material which is offered?

ACTIVITY 5.2

Begin to develop your own checklist, including these three questions (and others that occur to you, if you think I have missed out anything important at this stage). You will be asked to build on it as we progress through the chapter.

A further line of enquiry will concern the *relevance* or *utility* of the work. As is pointed out in Chapter 2, section 4, influential writers on criminology have tended to reject the notion that it is the task of the academic researcher to 'advise, consult, recommend or make decisions'. As an academic paper, Appendix 3.1 (Norris *et al.*) is clearly of interest. It provides a logical analysis of the question of why black people are disproportionately present in the courts and in prison, looking at the first crucial stage of why they are stopped by the police and how they are handled. Its results, to the extent that we can accept them, dispel some ideas on this subject and offer support for others.

However, the research also has potential for more immediate and practical (that is, 'practitioner') relevance. It deals with an important practical and political issue – the extent and implications of racial prejudice in the police – and to that extent it could have an important place in political argument. Police apologists could use it as a partial demonstration that 'patrol policing' is not discriminatory at the level of behaviour towards black people. Black critics of the police could use it to argue that it *is* discriminatory at the level of decisions taken on who to stop, and possibly also in the outcome of these 'stop decisions'. It could even have practical implications, for example, in police training: if 'equal treatment' is a goal of policing, then any demonstration of respects in which treatment tends not to be equal can set up a target for the improvement of training procedures. (The research also suggests, negatively, that there may not be much point in setting up programmes to train patrol police to deal with hostile black behaviour. To the extent that the evidence is acceptable, the research tends to show that black people are *not* more hostile to the police than white people, when stopped and questioned.)

The question of a research report's utility leads naturally into questions about its political commitment: in whose interests is it conceived, and for whose interests may it be used? The main clue to this is the type of problem investigated. Research which takes the established system for granted looks for more effective ways of achieving unchallenged goals. Research which adopts a perspective of the powerful may uncover discreditable practices or attitudes, but on the whole it seeks to explain and excuse them as a product of context. The same is true of research which seeks to appreciate the point of view of the deviant; it attempts to make the position understandable, but from an outside perspective, which at one level reinforces the deviant as *different*. Research which is indubitably conceived 'from below' looks for unjust systems and for malpractice within them (see Chapter 1).

I suggest that the Norris *et al.* paper lies between these positions. It is inspired by a critical stance to social institutions – the area picked for examination is the racism of the police in practice, and the research is clearly designed to show up such racism. However, the research is honest in the sense that its conclusions are not predetermined by the design, nor forced on it by the preferences of the authors. Where there is no evidence of racist practice the authors say so; where there is, they indicate it. This makes the report useful to both the police and their critics. The question of stance and of the interests that are served is important because it suggests what may have been *omitted* from the report – what the stance of the researchers may have led them to overlook.

ACTIVITY 5.3

1 Add to your checklist of questions, if any of the above seems to you relevant for 'dissecting' a research report.
2 As you read on, take note of other questions which might be added to your list.

3 The theory

The argument of a research report is unlikely to stand by itself: it will be set within a theory which informs it and gives it purpose and direction. The word 'theory' is a confusing one, because we use it for systems of ideas at very different levels of generality. Narrowly, a theory is a set of tested or unproven hypotheses which purport to explain a phenomenon: thus labelling theory can be used to explain how a young man comes to conceive of himself as deviant, or 'learned helplessness' theory can be used to explain why people seem to give up hope of changing their circumstances. Narrow theories are set within what we might call 'middle-range' theories, more general views of how the social or personal world functions: labelling theory emerges from the broader area of symbolic interactionism and learned helplessness theory from the broader area of learning theory. In turn, these middle-range theories are located within broad 'grand theories' or 'perspectives' or 'discourses', which are maps or pictures of what the social world is like and how it may validly be described. It is in this third sense that the word 'theory' will mostly be used in this chapter. Broadly, we can identify four perspectives into which criminological and social research can usefully be divided for purposes of this analysis, presented as 'ideal types' below.

The positivist perspective
This embraces a wide variety of middle-range theorizations which might be seen as in competition with each other but which share certain kinds of assumption and ask certain kinds of question. From this perspective, crime is a socially deviant activity which needs explanation. The world-view is fundamentally one of cultures or societies which share norms and values and which are in need of protection from those who offend against them, if they are to continue to function in everyone's interests. (The kind of explanation may differ, and we can usefully distinguish between biological, psychological and sociological varieties of positivism – see **Reader Guide 1, sections 3 and 4** for an extended discussion.) More important even than explanation is prediction, cure and/or control. The task of the scientist is to produce ways of protecting society from crime, by changing the criminal or by identifying those who need to be segregated or controlled or, in some of the most recent approaches, by designing the environment to make crime impossible or very

costly to the offender. The scientist aims to use the tried and trusted methods of sciences such as physics and chemistry, modified as necessary to suit the different subject-matter. His or her task is to be neutral and to describe what the phenomenon is like rather than to determine what it *should* be like, or to produce fair evaluation of 'experimental' treatments. However, scientists are expected to be 'neutral for good' – to direct their research to the good of society (which means in this case the prevention of crime).

The classicist perspective

The *classicist* position is superficially similar, but it differs in one important respect. Positivists see crime as a kind of disease or ailment – of the person or of the form of social organization – and seek to find scientific cures for it. Broadly, classicists see the social order as a compromise between the inimical interests of all, who would naturally be in competition but have agreed or been induced to subordinate their own interests to those of the general good. Crimes are seen as the outcome of a rational decision to follow one's own interests rather than those of society in general. The cure for crime, therefore, is to inhibit people from taking such decisions. A classicist theorist, working to prevent crime, would appeal to people's reason and explain the benefits for all of obeying the laws (see **Reader Guide 1, section 2**). A classicist scientist would be looking for the most effective deterrent measures.

Interactionist and constructionist perspectives

Both positivist and classicist theoretical positions tend to take the nature of the social world and the 'rightness' of the laws for granted. Strong doubt has been cast on many of these assumptions, however (see **Reader Guide 1, section 5.1** for a discussion), and competing theoretical perspectives have been advanced. For example, the *interactionist* perspective sees norms and values not as the products of an unproblematic consensus but as locally negotiated and maintained through the interaction of people and groups. More recent *constructionist* perspectives would go further, pointing to the importance not just of local negotiation but of historically developed social structures and the discourses – ways of characterizing the social world or some part of it – which inform and maintain them (Burr, 1995). Thus interactionists would not assume a consensus of values but look to see what values *were* in fact shared, by whom, under what conditions, and how they were transmitted and maintained. (Notions of sub-cultural values are particularly typical of an interactionist approach.) Constructionists would do the same, but they would probably also be concerned with how consistent value-sets grew and changed in particular groups or over time in a culture in general, how social institutions were created in accordance with them and how these institutions helped to maintain the dominance of particular ways of seeing social life. Both tend to be particularly concerned with questions of power, but in different ways: interactionism is attracted naturally to the study of unequal negotiations, between the powerful and the powerless, and constructionism to questions of what Foucault (1988) would call 'verisdiction' – the power to determine what shall be taken for granted as true beyond argument (see the discussion of discourses and research agendas in Chapter 1).

There is diversity within each of these four theories or perspectives, but they share a way of viewing and acting on the social world; in a sense, there is a single 'moral order' within a theory. However, we should be wary of labelling a particular writer as belonging to one of the four perspectives and then assuming that we therefore know everything about his or her assumptions. The perspectives are only an heuristic device for examining theories, not a set of mutually exclusive categories, and it is possible for an author to exhibit features of more than one of them. It is also not safe to map the great 'isms' on to the perspectives in such a way that a particular 'ism' falls entirely within a particular perspective. Marxism, for example, has covered and continues to cover more than one of the perspectives. There have been classicist and positivist Marxists, concerned with the best way to create the just (classless) society, in which the consensus values will be those which promote equality and the social institutions will be designed to this end. Modern Marxists are more likely to be broadly constructionist, looking at how the current social order is maintained by its history and how the apparent consensus of values is reproduced in favour of a particular class and a particular form of socio-economic organization. Similarly, one may identify interactionist and constructionist feminists, and indeed some feminist writing exhibits elements of a classicist perspective.

Within a perspective, we look for its strengths. Positivism, for example, should give a clear account of the causes of the phenomenon under study (though it may locate these causes in social organization, or socialization, or personality and/or learning, or even biology, depending on its disciplinary roots). Constructionist critical analysis should give a clear account of the buried and implicit meanings of a text or point of view – what models of the person and the social order, what political and moral presuppositions, what kind of 'common sense' even, are taken for granted as true by the writer or proponent of the position – and will often be trying to illuminate these meanings by considering their historical origins and institutional bases (see Chapter 1), as well as their immediate service to one set of interests over another. To the extent that a paper or book clearly espouses one of these perspectives, we have a right to expect that the appropriate activity will be competently carried out. As is pointed out in **Reader Guide 1, section 1**, each perspective takes a distinctive position or range of positions on the nature of crime, the extent to which people's behaviour is voluntary or determined, and the extent to which the social order is a product of consensus or an imposition by or in the interests of a minority. We may judge a report on the extent to which it expresses and uses these presuppositions coherently and consistently.

We use *other* perspectives to criticize these presuppositions. For example, we may question the moral stance typical of a perspective and exemplified in a particular paper. To ask 'in whose interests the research is conceived' is a criticism of, for example, positivistic research from an interactionist or constructionist perspective. To ask the question is to point out that 'the control of crime' is *not* in fact the natural and inevitable goal of all criminological research; that the system shall deal justly with the disadvantaged is an equally valid goal. More often, we use other perspectives to criticize the way the research question has been formulated or even the initial choice of the question. Each of the perspectives can act as a natural critic of the others in this respect. Historically, positivism arose in response to weaknesses of classicism and attempted to change the agenda from: How do we deter crime? to: How do we treat criminals?, moving from a notion of deterring rational agents to a notion of *creating* agents who are fully rational. In later years, aspects of classicism have returned as a critical response to positivism, asserting human rights against the potentially unlimited power of the therapeutic stance (see **Reader Guide 1, section 6.1.1** and **Reader Guide 2, section 6**). The interactionist perspective questions both by changing the question from: How do we stop crime? to: Who defines an action as criminal?, a change of focus from the criminal to powerful or influential actors or groups whose definitions determine the criminal's position. Constructionists in their turn react against interactionism and change the focus from the actions of powerful individuals or groups to the system of institutions and, more important, the system of meanings within which their actions are taken. Thus, we may use an 'outside' perspective to question whether the focus of the research is competent, or whether important questions are missed because they are not naturally accessed or easily expressed within the author's perspective.

Often the 'theory' of a paper is not explicitly stated but is implicit in the questions it asks and in what it takes for granted as 'common sense'. As discussed in **Reader Guide 1**, 'common sense' is not atheoretical, but is simply unaware of the theories which inform it:

> Many of our common-sense and gut reactions to crime are grounded ... in some biological, psychological or sociological theory of crime. Similarly, our preferred solutions to crime do not arise in some theoretical vacuum, but (if they are to be consistent) will reflect our prior position on how we consider crime to be caused.

> **(Reader Guide 1, p.4)**

And, as we saw in **Reader Guide 2**, most criminal justice policies are justified by and grounded in particular theoretical formulations. Particular theories will also be reflected in our understanding of what crime *is*, in the first place, and of the nature of individuals and the social order.

There is, to steal a phrase, 'nothing so practical as a good theory'. Theoretical perspectives transform a mass of data into understanding, explanations and recipes for action. However, we should not overrate the practicality of theory (at least in the sense in which positivism would define practicality, as 'leading to practical solutions'). It is clear that many of our most treasured penal policies are based on no clear theory, are often maintained even when the research evidence runs overwhelmingly against them, and seem to continue to be acceptable even when shown to be inefficient at achieving their own declared aims (see **Book 2, Chapter 5**). It is also worth pointing out that even if criminology could devise a perfectly efficient solution to the occurrence of crime, it is not clear that we should be politically or morally free to adopt it (see **Reader Guide 2, section 2**).

In another sense, however, good research is always practical, because it is always political. We saw that the study carried out by Norris *et al.* (Appendix 3.1) had immediate practicality – it could be used in argument both by the police and by their critics. Part of assessing a research report is spying out its uses, and part of writing one properly is assessing how it might be used – and, if need be, exploring some aspects of the research more thoroughly to ensure that misunderstandings do not present an undeserved weapon to one side in a debate. (See Chapter 2 regarding the uses of research to legitimate views and actions.) In the eyes of the reader, a researcher must be held responsible for the misuses of his or her research as well as for its valid use.

ACTIVITY 5.4

Now look again at the Norris *et al.* paper (Chapter 3, Appendix 3.1), and also at the Jefferson extract (Chapter 4, Appendix 4.1). Make notes on the perspectives which are expressed or implicit in them and the ways in which the reports are shaped by these.

This Activity should take about an hour.

In both papers the alignment to 'perspectives' or practical theoretical positions is a complex one. The Norris *et al.* paper could be described as positivistic in its methodological alignment. It seeks to measure 'what is going on' by counting the frequency of observed behaviours – a methodological approach typical of positivistic stances. However, its 'model of the social world' is one of conflict, which is not typical of most positivist social theorists (unless perhaps some Marxists). It identifies groups which might be regarded as 'inimical' to each other – black people and the police – and 'expects' to find evidence of either discriminatory or inflammatory behaviour; it predicts conflict between black people and police and looks, among other things, to see whether this is due to the behaviour of the police or the behaviour of the black people. In fact, a main finding is that neither discriminatory nor inflammatory behaviour is there to be measured, once the 'incident' has been started by the police stopping somebody on the street. The greater incidence of 'stops' for black people than white people, however, suggests an *institutionalized* conflict – a propensity for one side of the potential dispute to select out the other for attention to a disproportionate extent because, presumably, of stereotyped perceptions. The 'model of the person' is almost classicist in this work – it is assumed without question that both sides make rational decisions in response to the situation – but the suggestion of structural pressures towards racist behaviour detracts from this a little. On the other hand, the conclusion suggests that it would be rational for black people to react against the police because of the differential 'stop' rate. The mixture of classical, positivist and conflict perspectives is not untypical of 'middle-of-the-road' research which shows the influence of Marxist criminology of the 1970s and 1980s but is not centrally a part of it.

In the Jefferson extract, by contrast, what is taken for granted is not just an explicit conflict between groups but a failure to understand – in other words, a conflict of interests as expressed in the differential interpretation and definition of events. Jefferson offers, in essence, alternative accounts of observed events – his own, taken from his field notes, and those of the police. In principle, he does not prioritize one account over another, presenting them as equally valid but different. This, I suggest, would be reminiscent of a fundamentally interactionist perspective, with 'truth' a product of negotiation between participants, so that the police could validly have a different 'truth' about a given incident than was held by outsiders. In practice, however, a more radical strand emerges in that it is quite clear which of the variant accounts appears to Jefferson to be 'the truth' (his own) and which is in need of explanation (the one presented by the officers concerned). He does not suggest deliberate conspiracy, however, but the influence of structural factors on both behaviour and accounts of behaviour. In other words, he is most conveniently located in a constructionist paradigm, looking for structural and historical reasons for why the world is perceived in the way that it is by a given class of informants.

ACTIVITY 5.5

On the basis of your reading and this discussion, add to your checklist anything you think might help further in analysing research reports.

4 Argument and evidence

In the progress from research question to conclusions, a key role will be played by the 'review of literature'; this is the discussion of what other writers have had to say on the topic, which is generally contained in introductory sections or chapters but is sometimes scattered throughout the paper or book. One of its functions is to contextualize the argument: for example, to establish the size of the problem by quoting statistical evidence or its perceived importance by quoting scholars or politicians. Another function, however, is to begin the argument: to offer what evidence is available, and in the process to refine the question into something answerable but as yet unanswered, in the light of previous results and previous analyses. The beginning sections of the Norris *et al.* paper, for example, outline what is known about the interaction between police and black people and also, in the process, suggest ways of formulating questions about it that can be answered. Accordingly, the review of literature is an important part of the argument of the paper or book in two respects: it helps to formulate the question with some precision, and it begins to answer it.

Beyond this, what distinguishes a research paper from a scholarly essay is that it does not attempt to answer the question from existing evidence alone, nor by logical analysis alone. Both of these will be involved in the answer, but the key element of a research paper is the provision of *new* evidence. This may involve as little as fresh analysis (say, from a new perspective) of an existing text such as a government report. Or what may be required is figures about something on which figures are already available – in government statistics, for example. Most likely, however, the collection of new data will be required – counts of behaviours, responses to a 'treatment', views and attitudes collected by structured or less structured means, secondary analysis of documents such as diaries or novels, or whatever is appropriate for the task at hand. In assessing a research report, having sorted out what the 'question' is and the extent to which it is already answered by previous research, we need to ask ourselves what kind of fresh information would be needed to provide a satisfactory answer to the question. This gives us a basis for assessing the research which has been conducted, in terms of its appropriateness for the argument presented. (In the Norris *et al.* paper, for example, we noted that one of the questions it posed – about black criminality – *could not* be answered from the kind of information collected.)

Our ideas about what would count as appropriate evidence for any conclusions can then be compared with the evidence which is actually put forward, in the light of what is *required* of evidence for the conclusions. Where, as in most cases, the evidence must convince us that all or most of a class of 'objects of study' are of a certain kind or hold a certain belief, for example, we shall require evidence that the sampling procedures lead to generalizable results or at least some argument that the particular case(s) chosen for study are typical in some way or stand in a particularly interesting relation to the topic area. Where measurements are taken, we shall require evidence that they do indeed measure, consistently, what they purport to measure. This requirement holds also for 'appreciative' research, where we need to be convinced that what was observed or what emerged in interview bears some relationship to what might have emerged in a 'non-research' situation – a reflexive account to assure us that the data are not a product of the procedures used or of the particular relationship between researcher and informant. (This is equally required in quantitative research, and seldom delivered: for example, there is not much discussion in the Norris *et al.* paper about how the police might have behaved to black suspects if there had *not* been a researcher present.)

We should remember that research is informed by theory, and that there are traditional ways of working within a theoretical perspective which will tend to be taken for granted as valid, just as there are traditional ways of formulating problems which will be taken for granted as useful. A part of assessment lies in trying to judge the research as part of the argument of the particular paper or book without being seduced by these traditions. It is often the outsider who can see most clearly where a connection is made between evidence and conclusion which does not quite stand up to scrutiny, or where the evidence brought to bear on a question does not quite cover what the question meant, because the outsider can bring more than one perspective to bear on the report.

We should note also that it is necessary to judge not only the theory and the research evidence, but also the researcher. Such a judgement is present in all evaluations of evidence, even though it remains implicit and is seldom talked about. We trust the researcher's honesty. We also trust his or her sensitivity and insight (a) to have conducted the research in such a way that the results are in some sense 'true of the world', not just an artefact of the procedures used; (b) to have 'seen through' to the most useful formulation of a given problem; and (c) to have considered the interests of those involved. The report of procedures will give us some idea about the first of these three but, however fully methodological details are reported, the account will necessarily still be incomplete. The article or book may also give us some idea about the second item of faith, the researcher's sensitivity and insight, but the reader inevitably brings other criteria to bear, such as a knowledge of the researcher's previous work. Institutional affiliation also gives a useful clue to likely 'blind spots' in problem formulation.

The final item of faith, that all relevant interests have been considered, is a different kind of assessment tool. In strict logic, ethics do not alter facts; the conclusions of a piece of research are not falsified by our ethical objections to how it was conducted. We may condemn the methods without disbelieving the conclusions. However, grossly unethical behaviour on the part of researchers might cast doubt on their 'sensitivity and insight': to the extent that they are prepared to ride rough-shod over the lives of others, can we trust them to have any real insight into those lives?

ACTIVITY 5.6

The basic question of this section has been: Does the evidence support the conclusions?, but it is capable of considerable elaboration in the light of what was discussed in the last two chapters. Consider what might constitute valid evidence for different kinds of conclusion and add to your checklist.

5 Assessing research

It is time to pull things together. In this chapter and Chapters 3 and 4 we have explored the identification of methods and the assessment of research; however, 'assess' is an ambivalent term which can carry a range of different meanings. It is also to a large extent a *personal* process, so there will be more 'I' in the next two sections than in the previous ones. I assess research in a variety of ways as part of my professional activities:

- I judge its quality when marking research projects or acting as an examiner for theses. Here, I am looking to certify that the work has been done competently, perhaps imaginatively; that it is written up in a comprehensible and professional way which makes it clear what questions it is trying to answer and what the answers *are*; that it shows a knowledge of the research and other literature and uses it competently and relevantly to extend and contextualize the argument; and so on. At the higher levels I would be seeking some originality and depth of analysis in the work and looking to say that it makes a genuine contribution to its subject area.

- I am also asked to make judgements on papers submitted to journals, to advise whether they are publishable. Here I would again be looking for competence, interest, originality, familiarity with the relevant literature, and so on. I do not have to be as judgemental as when marking or examining, however: it is not my place to assign a mark, but only to determine that the paper would be of interest to the journal's readers and that the research is not so badly done that it would bring the journal into disrepute.

- Apart from these formal 'judgement situations', I assess research routinely as part of my job as an academic. That is, I read research reports to see what the authors have discovered, whether the reports tell me anything new, the extent to which the conclusions follow from the evidence as presented (or, sometimes, what conclusions *I* can draw from the data, coming at them from a different angle), and in general how I can use them in my own writing or teaching.

It is at this last sense of 'assessment' that these three chapters have been directed. In operational terms, I have tried to help you develop tools for summarizing research papers and books succinctly, evaluating their arguments and evaluating the evidence by which the arguments are supported. The aim has not been to assign 'good/bad' labels to work, but to 'gut' it for what we can learn from it, *because* of its strengths and *despite* its weaknesses.

Allied with this 'assessment', however, is the more academic activity of 'critique':

> A critique is not a matter of saying that things are not right as they are. It is a matter of pointing out on what kinds of assumptions, what kinds of familiar, unchallenged, unconsidered modes of thought the practices we accept rest ... to show that things are not as self-evident as one believed, to see that what is accepted as self-evident will no longer be accepted as such.

> (Foucault, 1988, p.154)

An important part of coming to grips with the argument of a paper – and the political practices which underlie it and/or to which it will contribute – is identifying the discourses or models implicit in the author's way of thinking (or the clash of discourses, because we often express conflicting models in our thought) and their implications for policy and practice.

ACTIVITY 5.7

Review your checklist to see if anything needs to be added in the light of the last few paragraphs and then compare it with mine below. Add to your list anything you find useful in mine, to round it off as a tool which you can use for assessing reports of research.

I came up with a list of 14 points which I find helpful to consider when assessing research (though not all of them would be relevant to every paper or book).

A checklist of potential questions for the assessment of research

1 Is the argument of the paper internally consistent – do the conclusions follow logically from the arguments?

2 Are the questions originally posed by the authors plausibly answered?

3 If not, can they be plausibly answered from the material which is offered?

4 To what theoretical debate does the paper contribute?

5 Does it have 'applied' relevance for any group of practitioners or other 'interested parties'?

6 From whose perspective is it conceived? What are the consequences of this for how it should be interpreted?

7 By what 'theory' or 'theories' is the paper informed (remembering that more than one may contribute)?

8 What models of the person, the criminal justice system and society are taken for granted, in adopting this perspective?

9 To what extent might the initial research question or the mode of argument have been differently conceived if a different perspective had been adopted?

10 Are the differences or relationships which are reported large enough or consistent enough to be worth building conclusions on, or might they be just random fluctuations?

(Note: In reports of qualitative analysis this has largely to be taken on faith, but there should at least be illustrative quotes or descriptions of events, and these should indeed illustrate the point which they purport to make. In quantitative analysis there should generally be statistical tests, unless the differences are so large as to make testing redundant.)

11 Where statistical tests are used, are they entirely appropriate? Where they are not – for example, tests carried out on non-random samples – do they still contribute something to our understanding, and has the author looked for other sources of error in, for example, the sampling?

12 Does the argument make any claim to generality?

(a) If not, why is it of interest?

(b) If so, can the research results be generalized as far as the argument requires, and what are the consequences for the argument if they cannot be generalized?

13 Are the data which are presented what is really required for the argument? Or are they:

- something more trivial, but measurable?
- something similar, but confused by the researcher with what is really required?
- the outcome of imprecise or unreliable measurement techniques?
- a product of the procedures used rather than descriptive of what was to be investigated?

(Note: types of research have characteristic weaknesses here; quantitative research can trivialize; qualitative research can be imprecise and to an extent unreliable.)

14 To what extent are we prepared to trust the honesty, the insight and the competence of the researcher?

(Note: if this point is relevant, look for *specific* failings; general condemnation is rarely warranted.)

As you can see, I aim (a) to assess the argument of the paper in its own terms (Questions 1–3); (b) to consider its relevance (Questions 4–6); (c) to locate it in a theoretical context and apply a critique to it (Questions 7–9); and (d) to evaluate the research evidence which it presents, as part of its overall argument (Questions 10–14).

6 Planning research

Here there is less scope for excuse; the writer is not explaining what compromises had to be made in the course of research, but setting out his or her intentions for how the research shall be planned and carried out. Nonetheless, compromises still have to be made, because the overriding requirement of proposed research is that it should be feasible – that someone could, reasonably, *do* it. (If your theoretical problem would be best answered by hour-long interviews with all the inhabitants of London, or even Whitley Bay, you will have to find a different way of tackling it!) Apart from this, the same types of questions (your 'checklist') will be asked about proposals as about research reports. Some questions bulk larger when considering proposals than when reading reports, however. In particular, more consideration can realistically be given to questions of ethical and political sensitivity, because at the stage of the proposal there is time to head off or modify ethically dubious work before it is actually undertaken.

Research proposals generally fall into much the same sections as the report(s) that will finally emerge from them:

- An *introduction*, outlining the problem area and the specific questions to be answered, and explaining why the research is interesting/relevant/useful.

- A *review of literature* – which may or may not form a separate section – which gives the theoretical and practical context of the work, explains the questions and tells us what is known already (and, possibly, what methods of research are generally used and why they are inadequate).

- An *outline of methods* – what is to be done, and why.

A section which is also sometimes included is:

- A reflexive account of any *anticipated problems* – not only practical but also political and ethical considerations.

6.1 Introduction, literature review and the 'bright idea'

A short sketch would probably have only a page or so of literature and only a rough outline of how the project was to be carried out (though there should be sufficient detail to show (a) that the methods are adequate for the purpose, and (b) that the research is feasible, given finite time and resources). In a full proposal the literature review would probably cover four or five pages and the methods would be considered with great precision. Both, however, would be persuasive documents, so the introduction of even a short sketch of possible research would need to establish beyond doubt that the work was worth doing – that it had some academic and/or professional pay-off which justified the expenditure of resource and could not be obtained by easier means.

In a full-blown proposal you would be expected to make extensive use of the library: looking at relevant journals to see what has been done recently, checking out the most recent and relevant books, looking at the work to which the books and journal articles referred to see what was of relevance to your own work, using the catalogues and abstracting services to locate other relevant publications, looking at published statistics to put your problem in a numerical context, and so on. If you are only doing a short sketch, much of this would be beyond the scope of the task, but you would be expected at least to refer to relevant work which you had to hand or could easily obtain; Open University students, for example, can refer to the course texts, Reader, offprint articles, Resource File articles, and so on.

This introductory section of a proposal or sketch would start by identifying the problem or area of study, then review briefly why it is of interest and what is known about it, and lead up to a very brief description of the idea you have for the research which you propose to carry out. The idea must be of sufficient interest or practical importance to be worth the time, trouble and cost of carrying out the research.

As a running example, let us build up together a sketch of a proposal. We will do this exercise for research which I carried out in the 1970s (see Sapsford, 1983) into the experiences of life-sentence prisoners. I will start the process by constructing an introductory section explaining what is to be researched and why.

Introduction

Prison staff and others who deal with prisoners serving long sentences are convinced of the existence of a phenomenon which they call 'prisonization' or more often 'institutionalization' (see, for example, Radzinowicz Committee, 1968; Cohen and Taylor, 1972) and which is also to be found in other long-stay and penal institutions such as psychiatric hospitals (Goffman, 1961; Barton, 1959; Wing and Brown, 1970). This involves a kind of mental deterioration, a loss of the power to make decisions and a growing inability to cope with day-to-day life outside structured circumstances. However, psychological research using intelligence tests suggests that mental powers as such do not deteriorate in prison (Smith *et al.*, 1977). If there is such a deterioration, therefore, we need to look for it elsewhere than in purely cognitive ability. The work of Seligman (1975) and his colleagues suggests that both animals and humans sometimes react to being in aversive circumstances over which they have no control by settling into 'learned helplessness' – a state of apathy and an apparent belief that they have no control whatsoever over events, which in humans would be called a state of clinical depression – and this line of theory would seem to resemble quite closely what is generally meant by 'institutionalization' and to suggest a reason why it might occur. Life-sentence prisoners are an obvious group with which to explore this notion, because – in addition to the loss of personal control which all prisoners experience – the time they will serve is literally indeterminate and they do not appear to themselves to have much control over it. Research into the reactions of life-sentence prisoners to their imprisonment is therefore proposed.

This introduction to the proposal follows the stages I described above:
- It gives an indication of the phenomenon to be explored – 'institutionalization' – taking for granted that this is of practical importance.

- It says a little about what is known (using academic literature, but in fact nothing that I did not have on my bookshelves at the time).

- It makes a case for the importance of the research to theory (in this case, psychological theory).

- It ends with a single sentence outlining the research which is proposed.

The final sentence is of course inadequate even for a research sketch – it is not enough just to say that you want to look at some life-sentence prisoners. The rest of the sketch or proposal, therefore, gives brief details of how the research would be done, to show that it is adequate to the purpose, feasible and within the bounds of ethical behaviour. If we look back to the checklist for assessing research papers in the previous section of this chapter, we see that so far we have supplied material relevant to Questions 2, 4 and 7 (and implicitly Questions 5 and 8 – the relevance of the phenomenon for practitioners is taken for granted, and by failing to state a model we have implicitly adopted something akin to a positivist or 'scientific' stance, but this may be modified later).

6.2 Style of research and location

ACTIVITY 5.8

Before reading on, spend a few minutes making rough notes of how you think you might go about doing the research. Start with the question of what *kind* of research it would be appropriate to undertake – which of the methods discussed in Chapters 3 and 4 seem most appropriate for the research question. Consider the issues raised in Chapter 2 as well. Build on your notes as we work through this section.

As you will have realized whilst doing this Activity, the kind of research you are going to do, the place where you are going to do it and the number of subjects/respondents/informants you will have are all closely related – a decision about any of them determines to a large extent what the others will be. One has also to take practical constraints into account. For example, when I carried out the research into institutionalization, I was employed by the Home Office to do research on prisons, so access to prisons was not going to be an insuperable problem. However, I wanted to register the work for a PhD, so it had to be something that could be done by one person in a reasonably limited time – one or two years of fieldwork at the outside. The theoretical frame of the work – learned helplessness – suggested psychological measurement, and there are a number of widely used relevant psychological inventories and 'tests' which could be used to measure people's psychological state. Certainly some such quantitative approach seemed to be indicated.

   In principle, a self-completion survey seemed possible, by compiling the relevant inventories into a single 'battery', adding descriptive questions about age, offence, relationships with the outside world, and so on, and delivering the whole thing to all life-sentence prisoners for them to complete. This was not feasible, however. The battery would have been very long and very dull, and it is unlikely that many prisoners would have completed it. It seemed better to administer the inventories in person, and better still to split them up into batches and administer them at various points during an interview, so that people did not become bored with them and so that some kind of personal relationship could be established in the task. In addition, I did not want to rely *solely* on quantitative data. Despite the 'scientific' nature of the theorization, I was not totally happy with the model of the person as something which simply reacted to environments. People *interpret* environments, and they *do* things in them, so I also wanted just to *talk* to prisoners about what their lives in prison had been like and how they coped.

The net result was a plan for interview research in which some of the data collection was of a qualitative nature, just talking to people about their experiences, but interspersed with a fair amount of quantitative psychological data collection. This meant interviewing people one at a time, in quite a long interview. To keep the interview a bit shorter and to save asking intrusive questions about people's backgrounds, criminal histories, current offence and so on, I decided to collect these data from the men's prison files. (This also gave me the chance to collect information from the reports written regularly by prison staff.) However, one interview plus working through the files on one man was going to take the best part of a day. I decided to limit the data collection to sixty cases – in principle this meant 12 weeks' work, but in practice substantially more, as it is never possible to line up interviews neatly one after the other in your diary.

The next section in our proposal will thus be:

Methods

One interviewer will collect data from files (on the demographic and criminal characteristics of the prisoners and on staff reports) and from the prisoners themselves (psychological measures of mood, affect and capability, plus less structured information – elicited in 'open' interviewing – about the prisoners' experiences and how they cope with sentence). The methods will therefore be a mix of the quantitative and the qualitative.

This sub-section has largely covered working out what is feasible (a very important matter, obviously, in planning research), but it has also begun to answer Question 13 on the checklist, by specifying the kind of data to be collected. In a full proposal we should have to go into more detail, to demonstrate how we meant to ensure that the data were indeed relevant to the original questions, but the above will do for a sketch. We have also, at the same time, been thinking around the area of Questions 8 and 9 – the model of the person implied by the research, and how it might be otherwise. This was the reason for adopting a 'mixed' style, using both quantitative and qualitative methods.

6.3   Sampling and access

We have thus settled on long interviews (interspersed with psychological inventories) with about 60 men. We continue to think about Question 13 next and try to determine what will best answer the research question.

ACTIVITY 5.9

What sort of design would be best for the study? What comparisons are going to be needed in order to answer the research question? Add your responses to your notes.

As the question concerns change (deterioration) over time, there obviously has to be a time dimension in the research. Logically, the best thing to do would be to take a group of men and follow them over time, but this is not feasible within the scale of the project – it would take over 10 years! We shall have to settle for cross-sectional comparison, therefore, comparing men recently received into prison after sentencing with men later in their prison careers. At the time of my research, review for possible release on licence tended to involve prisoners in their seventh year of sentence. Thus, in these circumstances, the 'later in sentence' group should ideally have served about five or six years, so as not to confound anxieties about the release process with any effects of sentence. Men served on average up to 12 years at that time, so anyone who had served more than that would know he was not to be released at the average time and would probably have absolutely no idea how long he might serve; this would also be an important group to include.

To minimize the possibility of effects of different environments, the study should be confined to a single prison, if possible. At the time of my research, there were two prisons which had large 'lifer' populations of men at all stages of sentence. (Access to one of them would have to be sought from the relevant division of the Prison Department, but this was not expected to be a problem because the project would be a Home Office one.) So we should want randomly chosen men (to avoid any suggestion of selection bias) at the three stages of sentence, from the one prison. Random sampling would help to ensure that the samples were fairly typical of the lifers in the prison, and the prison was known to have a fairly average population, so the results should have some generality (Question 12).

However, reviews of release on licence is a selective process, depending on variables such as the type of offence (whether, for example, robbery or sexual assault was associated with the killing) and reported mental state. That being so, the men who had served more than 12 years, as a group, would not be much like the group of newly received men; there would, for example, probably be very many more sex offenders among them, and a greater incidence of psychiatric diagnosis.

ACTIVITY 5.10

What problems does this cause for the research, and how might you get round them? Add your responses to your notes.

Any differences between groups that were observed might be artefacts of selection; we would not know whether they were due to time served or to the different characteristics of the men in the different groups. A further set of samples is needed therefore, picking groups of newly received men and men in mid-sentence to match the characteristics of the group who had served very long terms. These samples would *not* be typical of the lifer population as a whole, but they would be comparable with each other and so help to control for alternative explanations of any results. The methods section in our proposal would thus be expanded to include this:

Random samples will be picked from the newly received men, men who have served 5–6 years (that is, just before first consideration for release on licence) and men who have served more than 12 years (that is, well beyond the average term), in a single prison. These samples should be reasonably representative of the lifer population as a whole. Because of the selective effects of offence-type and psychiatric diagnosis on the release process (Sapsford and Banks, 1979), however, a further set of matched samples will also be necessary, to control for the effects of offender characteristics. The two sets of samples will total no more than 60 men.

6.4 Further thoughts

Two more things need to be added to our sketch of a proposal. One is a technical point. Although we have settled for a cross-sectional design, comparing different men who have served different lengths of sentence, this clearly has a logical weakness; there could be 'history effects' – effects of events or changes in the outside world which have happened since the longest-serving men came into prison, but which could be confused with effects of sentence. It would be useful, therefore, to try to do *some* kind of comparison of the *same* men over time. This can be done, to some small extent, in two ways within this design:

The basic design is cross-sectional, but it will be possible to look at changes over time by analysis of contemporaneous staff reports in the prison files, and a further perspective on personal change will be provided by the 'open' interviews, in which the informants will be encouraged to give a 'history' of their time in prison.

Most of the other questions on the checklist are matters which will have to be sorted out in the conduct of the research, the analysis of data and the writing of reports. One, however, *must* be considered right from the start of the research, and that is the ethical stance implied in Question 14. A final section of the research proposal should then show that we are (as far as possible) aware of some of the difficulties that await us:

Informants will be promised absolute confidentiality; the data will not be shown to anyone outside the research team, and no account of the research will allow a particular prisoner to be identified without his consent. Conversely, the researcher will be known to informants as employed by the Home Office, and he will have to make clear to each informant that nothing said to him can affect the release process or the internal discipline of the prison in any respect.

The first of these two promises was absolutely necessary. The second was equally necessary, in order not to deceive the informants about the importance of the interviews. (It would have been a difficult promise to keep if I had uncovered evidence of, for example, any gross abuse of power by staff or planned violence by prisoners; fortunately for my peace of mind, I did not.)

Finally, what has been produced in this section is not necessarily a 'model answer' for an assignment which requires you to write a research sketch or outline. It is written to make particular points, and its structure and contents reflect its role within the chapter. Similarly, it is not a fully worked-up research proposal – a document aimed to elicit resources from a funding body or access from a 'gatekeeper'. Documents such as these would need to be longer and differently written, with detail appropriate to the recipients. However, any outline of proposed research does go through these stages in its development, and the final product is likely to resemble in some respects what has been developed here. Logically, any proposal or outline starts with an introduction which states what research is proposed, why it is interesting or useful or necessary, and preferably what is known about it. (It may also be appropriate to argue for a particular way of framing a problem or a particular methodological approach, depending on what is to be researched.) The introductory sections may also have to set the 'problem' in its context (prevalence, the nature of the setting, the administrative or legal framework) if this is not likely to be well known to the reader. This is followed by a description of what is to be done, including appropriate methods, and, finally, an outline of any problems likely to be encountered and how they might be handled. (Problems of an ethical or political nature should be discussed here if they are relevant.) There may also be some indication of the 'pay-off' – the likely outcomes and to what use the research might be put. Finally, the references should be included – a full list of the work referred to in the text.

7 Conclusion

Throughout this book we have talked about political issues as a part of the conduct of research and the writing and appraisal of research reports. We have looked at:

- Political issues as they affect the research itself (see particularly Chapter 2).

- The need to be aware when planning and conducting research that the terms and concepts we use are not neutral but the products of a historically and politically structured set of social processes, expressing relationships of power, influence and exploitation.

- The need to be aware that the act of selecting and conceptualizing a research 'problem' is itself a decision with political implications, as is each of the decisions we make in conducting the research and deciding what to report and how to report it.

We have looked at the links between theory and research (see particularly Chapter 1 and the beginning of this chapter); we have seen that theory develops as a result of research, but that the stance and tradition from which the researcher works inevitably has a strong influence on what is seen as researchable and worth researching and on how the research is carried out. We have looked also, more briefly, at the link with practice – the role of criminological research in the formation of social policy, the information of the public and the administration of the criminal justice system and the day-to-day practice of workers within it.

An awareness of the social/political context of research and of its potential uses is a part of what we need in order to make a sensible assessment of a published research report. A similar awareness shown by its authors is part of what is needed to make a piece of research plausible as evidence. Those who plan research need to think through its relationship to dominant ideologies and the extent to which its conclusions are dictated by them, and to be aware of other ways of framing problems and characterizing the purpose of investigations. Evidence that the authors are able to do this adds a great deal to our confidence in their conclusions.

The rest of what is needed to render plausible the conclusions drawn from a piece of research is a matter of due attention paid to the technicalities of design and execution (as examined in some detail in Chapters 3 and 4). Of any piece of research we shall want to ask:

- whether the measurements presented do indeed measure what is claimed (including questions of reactivity – whether any of the results are mostly a product of the situation or the researcher's personal influence);

- whether the people, settings or cases studied do indeed represent or typify or cast light on a 'population' in the way in which the authors claim; and

- that the logic of the study (the comparisons drawn) is such that the author's conclusions *can* reasonably be deduced from the evidence presented.

No piece of research will be perfect in all these respects – there are always ambiguities and, indeed, downright mistakes – and we ought not to dismiss any piece of research out of hand as useless; even flawed reports often have something to teach us. These are the technical issues which we always need to consider, however, in determining how much faith to put in the conclusions which the authors urge upon us.

References

Barton, R. (1959) *Institutional Neurosis*, Bristol, Wright.

Burr, V. (1995) *An Introduction to Social Constructionism*, London, Routledge.

Cohen, S. and Taylor, L. (1972) *Psychological Survival: The Experience of Long Term Imprisonment*, Harmondsworth, Penguin.

Foucault, M. (1988) *Politics, Philosophy, Culture: Interviews and Other Writings, 1977–1984*, London, Routledge.

Goffman, E. (1961) *Asylums: Essays on the Social Situation of Mental Patients and Other Inmates*, New York, Doubleday. (Also available in Penguin Books, 1968.)

Radzinowicz Committee (Advisory Council on the Penal System) (1968) *The Regime for Long Term Prisoners in Conditions of Maximum Security*, London, HMSO.

Sapsford, R.J. (1983) *Life-Sentence Prisoners: Reaction, Response and Change*, Milton Keynes, Open University Press.

Sapsford, R.J. and Banks, C. (1979) 'A synopsis of some Home Office research', in Smith, D.E. (ed.) *Life-Sentence Prisoners*, Home Office Research Study No.51, London, HMSO.

Seligman, M.E.P. (1975) *Helplessness*, San Francisco, CA, W.H. Freeman.

Smith, F.V., Bolton, N., Banister, P.A. and Heskin, K.J. (1977) 'Investigation of the effects of long-term imprisonment', in Council of Europe (European Committee on Crime Problems) *Treatment of Long Term Prisoners*, Strasbourg, Council of Europe.

Wing, J.R. and Brown, G.W. (1970) *Institutionalism and Schizophrenia*, Cambridge, Cambridge University Press.

Acknowledgements

We have made every attempt to obtain permission to reproduce material in this book. Copyright holders of material which has not been acknowledged should contact the Rights Department at The Open University.

Grateful acknowledgement is made to the following sources for permission to reproduce material in this volume:

Text

Chapter 1: Harper, K. (1995) 'Study links crime with the dole queue', *The Guardian*, 15 February 1995; Boseley, S. (1995) 'Genes' link to crime may be cited in court', *The Guardian*, 14 February 1995; 'Student notes taken from a lecture given by Hermann Mannheim', courtesy of Mrs G. Stanton; Extracts from *The British Journal of Delinquency*, vol.1, no.1, July 1950, and the *British Journal of Criminology*, vol.35, no.1, Winter 1995, The Institute for the Study and Treatment of Delinquency, reprinted by permission of Oxford University Press; Cohen, N. (1995) 'Crime study unit faces sell-off', *Independent on Sunday*, 8 January 1995; Jupp, V. (1989) *Methods of Criminological Research*, Routledge, © V. Jupp 1989; **Chapter 2:** Travis, A. (1994) 'Ministers suppress research. Findings contradict Howard crackdown', *The Guardian*, 4 July 1994, cartoon by Austin; Jenkins, S. (1994) 'Home Office crime', *The Times*, 28 September 1994, © Times Newspapers Limited 1994; 'Assisting with enquiries: studying a criminal justice élite', © Robert Reiner 1991. Reprinted from *Chief Constables: Bobbies, Bosses, or Bureaucrats?* by Robert Reiner (1991) by permission of Oxford University Press; Waddington, P.A.J. (1991) *The Strong Arm of the Law: Armed and Public Order Policing*, Clarendon Press, reprinted by permission of Oxford University Press; Grimshaw, R. and Jefferson, A. (1987) *Interpreting Policework. Policy and Practice in Forms of Beat Policing*, Routledge, © R. Grimshaw and A. Jefferson 1987; 'BSA statement of ethical practice', *Sociology, The Journal of the British Sociological Association*, vol.26, no.4, November 1992, The British Sociological Association; **Chapter 3:** Norris, C., Fielding, N., Kemp, C. and Fielding, J. (1992) 'Black and blue: an analysis of the influence of race on being stopped by the police', in Rock, P. (ed.) *British Journal of Sociology*, vol.43, no.2, © London School of Economics 1992, by permission of Routledge; Walker, M.A. (1994) 'Measuring concern about crime: some inter-racial comparisons', *British Journal of Criminology*, vol.34, no.3, The Institute for the Study and Treatment of Delinquency, reprinted by permission of Oxford University Press; Raynor, P. and Vanstone, M. (1994) 'Probation practice, effectiveness and the non-treatment paradigm', *British Journal of Social Work*, vol.24, © 1994 The British Association of Social Workers. All rights reserved. By permission of Oxford University Press; **Chapter 4:** Jefferson, A. (1990) *The Case Against Paramilitary Policing*, Open University Press, Copyright © Tony Jefferson 1990; Martin, C. and Godfrey, D. (1994) 'Prisoners' views of Boards of Visitors: a question of credibility', *British Journal of Criminology*, vol.34, no.3, The Institute for the Study and Treatment of Delinquency, reprinted by permission of Oxford University Press; Burke, M. (1994) 'Homosexuality as deviance: the case of the gay police officer', *British Journal of Criminology*, vol.34, no.2, The Institute for the Study and Treatment of Delinquency, reprinted by permission of Oxford University Press; Barlow, H.D. (1993) 'From fiddle factors to networks of collusion: charting the waters of small business crime', *Crime, Law and Social Change*, vol.20, no.4, November 1993, © 1993 Kluwer Academic Publishers. Reprinted by permission of Kluwer Academic Publishers; Carlen, P. (1990) *Alternatives to Women's Imprisonment*, Open University Press, Copyright © Pat Carlen 1990; McLaughlin, E. and Murji, K. (1993) 'Controlling the Bill: restructuring the police in the 1990s', *Critical Social Policy*, issue 37, vol.13, no.1, Sage; Peelo, M. and Soothill, K. (1994) 'Personal power and public control: sex crimes and problem pages', *The Howard Journal of Criminal Justice*, vol.33, no.1, Blackwell Publishers Ltd.

Figure

Figure 3.1: Campbell, D.T. (1969) 'Reforms as experiments', *American Psychologist*, vol.24, p.419, Copyright © 1969 by the American Psychological Association. Adapted with permission.

Tables

Table 3.1: adapted from Farrington, D.P. and Kidd, R.F. (1977) 'Is financial dishonesty a rational decision?', *British Journal of Social and Clinical Psychology*, vol.16, p.142, © The British Psychological Society 1977, by permission of Cambridge University Press; *Appendix 4.1, Table 1:* Jefferson, A. (1990) *The Case Against Paramilitary Policing*, Open University Press, Copyright © Tony Jefferson 1990.

Cover

Photograph by Nigel Francis. Robert Harding Picture Library.

Index